The Emergence of Social Enterprise

- What are the characteristics of social enterprises?
- What are the future prospects for social enterprises?
- What do social enterprises contribute?

Analysing social enterprises in fifteen different countries *The Emergence of Social Enterprise* seeks to answer these important questions whilst investigating the remarkable growth in the "third sector".

Presenting the results of research carried out under the auspices of the EMES European Research Network, the authors compare the different experiences of social enterprises in all EU states. They use social enterprises as cases studies, while also combining theory and practice into a compelling argument to support the concept of an "emergence" of social enterprise.

Written by leading academics, in an accessible yet informed style, this book is vital reading for all those studying and teaching non-profit organizations, social policy, social economy and civil society.

Carlo Borzaga is Professor of Economic Policy in the Faculty of Economics at the University of Trento, Italy. At the same university he has also founded and manages a research center on non-profit organizations (ISSAN). He has carried out several research projects at national and European level and is collaborating with the European Commission and the OECD on topics relating to non-profit organizations. He has published several books and papers, both in Italian and English.

Jacques Defourny is a Professor of Economics at the University of Liége, Belgium and Director of the *Centre d'Économie Sociale*. He also acts as a co-ordinator for the EMES European Research Network which gathers research centres from most EU countries. His work focuses on conceptual and quantitative approaches of the "third sector" as well as the behaviour and the performance of non-profit organizations and co-operatives. In addition to numerous articles, Professor Defourny is the author or editor of ten books among which several, first published in French, have been translated into English, Spanish, Dutch and Japanese.

Routledge Studies in the Management of Voluntary and Non-Profit Organizations

Series Editor: Stephen P. Osborne

The Emergence of Social Enterprise

Edited by Carlo Borzaga and Jacques Defourny

with the assistance of Sophie Adam and John Callaghan

Routledge
Taylor & Francis Group

LONDON AND NEW YORK

First published 2001
by Routledge
11 New Fetter Lane, London EC4P 4EE

Simultaneously published in the USA and Canada
by Routledge
29 West 35th Street, New York, NY 10001

First published in paperback in 2004

Transferred to Digital Printing 2003

Routledge is an imprint of the Taylor & Francis Group

Typeset in Baskerville by Taylor & Francis Books Ltd
Printed and bound in Great Britain by Biddles Ltd,
Guildford and King's Lynn

British Library Cataloguing in Publication Data
A catalogue record for this book is available from the British Library

Library of Congress Cataloging in Publication Data
The emergence of social enterprise/edited by Carlo Borzaga and
Jacques Defourny.
Includes bibliographical references and index.
1. Charities–European Union countries. 2. Nonprofit
organizations–European Union countries. I. Borzaga, Carlo.
II. Defourny, Jacques.

HV238 .E54   2001
361.7'6'094–dc21   00-068421

ISBN 0–415–33921–9

Contents

Illustrations

Tables

Figures

Contributors

Alberto Bacchiega is a research student at the University of York and a research fellow at the University of Trento and ISSAN. His research interests include the theory of industrial organisation, incomplete contract theory and the study of non-profit and co-operative organisations.

Eugène Becker is a teacher of economics in Luxembourg. He is involved in associations which fight social exclusion and a chairman of the co-operative *Co-labor* since 1998. His main interests are the relations between political economy and social exclusion.

Steen Bengtsson is a senior researcher at the Institute of Social Research in Copenhagen and assistant professor at Roskilde University. He has specialised in the organisation of social services and relations between citizens and system.

Carlo Borzaga is a professor of economics at the faculty of economics and president of ISSAN at the University of Trento. His main research interests are the political economy of labour market policy and the non-profit sector, with particular reference to the related questions of employment and service supply.

Nikos Bouzas is a researcher in the Institute of Social Policy at the National Centre for Social Research, Athens. His research focuses on issues related to employment and vocational training policies and measures including methods of evaluation.

Jacques Defourny is a professor of economics at the University of Liège and director of the *Centre d'Économie Sociale*. He is also the founding co-ordinator of the EMES European Network formed for the research project which gave birth to the present book. He mainly works on economic analysis of co-operatives and associations, work-integration social enterprises and conceptual approaches of the third sector in industrialised as well as in developing countries.

Paul Delaunois is the manager of the co-operative *Co-labor* in Luxembourg. He is also the co-ordinator of a European network working on the 'Mobility behaviour of the victims of social exclusion'. His main interests are integration policies and the development of the third sector.

Adalbert Evers is a political scientist. He is a full professor for comparative health and social policy at the University of Giessen and is one of the directors of the *Institut für Sozialforschung* in Frankfurt am Main. His research activities deal with the third sector, the welfare mix as well as social services; a special focus of his social policy research is on issues of civil society and democratic governance.

Lars Hulgård is an associate professor at the Department of Social Sciences, Roskilde University in Denmark. His research focuses on social change, innovative trends in social policy, social entrepreneurship and evaluation.

Maria Ketsetzopoulou is a researcher in the Institute of Social Policy at the National Centre for Social Research, Athens. Her research deals with issues related to income inequality, exclusion from the labour market and flexible employment.

Jean-Louis Laville is a sociologist, researcher at the National Centre of Scientific Research in Paris and founding president of the *Centre de Recherche et d'Information sur la Démocratie et l'Autonomie*. He is mainly interested in economic sociology in contemporary societies, directing a collection called 'economic sociology' in the publishing house Desclée de Brouwer and teaching such an approach in various universities in Paris.

Kai Leichsenring is a senior research fellow and consultant at the European Centre for Social Welfare Policy and Research in Vienna. His main research interests are personal social services, ageing and care policies. He is also working as a consultant in organisation development of public administration and non-profit organisations.

Marthe Nyssens is a professor in the Department of Economics and coordinator of a research team on social and non-profit economics at the *Centre de Recherche Interdisciplinaire sur la Solidarité et l'Innovation Sociale* at the Catholic University of Louvain. She works mainly on the third sector and evaluation of social policies.

Patricia O'Hara is research associate with the Centre for Co-operative Studies, University College Cork and, since 1999, senior policy analyst with the Western Development Commission (a new agency for regional development in Western Ireland). Her main research interests are regional and local development, social exclusion and associated issues.

Pekka Pättiniemi is a development manager and a member of the management board of the Institute for Co-operative Studies at the University of Helsinki. His research focuses on the development and management of employee-owned businesses and social enterprises.

Heloísa Perista, sociologist, is a senior researcher and the director of the *Centro de Estudos para a Intervenção Social*. She has a wide research experience in fields such as ageing and elderly people, equal opportunities, migration dynamics, local employment initiatives and social economy.

Piet H. Renooy is co-founder and managing director of Regioplan, an independent research agency. He has specialised in social security and all forms of irregular labour like black labour, voluntary labour and subsidised labour.

Alceste Santuari is a senior lecturer in non-profit (comparative) law and director of ISSAN at the University of Trento. His main research interests comprise legal, organisational and tax problems of non-profit entities and companies at large, with particular reference to international comparison.

Matthias Schulze-Böing is head of the Department for Economic Development, Employment and Statistics, City Council of Offenbach am Main.

Luca Solari is assistant professor of organisation and human resource management at the University of Trento and researcher at ISSAN (Research Institute on Non-profit Organisations) in the same university. He is involved in research projects on the evolution and change of organisational forms both at macro (population) and micro (individual) level.

Roger Spear is chair of the Co-operatives Research Unit and teaches systems in the Centre for Complexity and Change, Open University, Milton Keynes. He also chairs the International Co-operative Alliance Research Committee.

Yohanan Stryjan is a sociologist and professor of business administration at Södertörns Högskola, South Stockholm. He works mainly on organisational theory perspectives, institutional transformation and social entrepreneurship.

Isabel Vidal is a professor in the Business School and funding director of the research centre of Citizenship and Civil Society at the University of Barcelona. She is president of *Centre d'Iniciatives de l'Economia Social*. Her main research interests are labour market policy and job creation, economic theory of the third sector and related questions of delivering personal services and social audit.

Dimitris Ziomas is a researcher in the Institute of Social Policy at the National Centre for Social Research, Athens. His research covers issues related to labour market policies, human resources development, social policy and the social economy in Greece.

Acknowledgements

This book represents the results of work undertaken within the 'Targeted Socio-Economic Research' (TSER) programme of the European Commission (DG XII). Researchers from all EU countries formed the EMES Network, which worked from the summer of 1996 until the end of 1999 on 'the emergence of social enterprises in Europe'.

We want particularly to thank Enzo Pezzini from CECOP (Brussels) who provided outstanding assistance to Jacques Defourny in the co-ordination of the Network. He took charge of all the administrative and technical matters related to the project. Moreover, he organised all the joint work sessions, which were held twice yearly throughout Europe.

We are also grateful to Sophie Adam (*Centre d'Économie Sociale, Liège*) who did a heroic job as editorial assistant for the preparation of this volume. The final product owes much also to John Callaghan and Patricia O'Hara who carefully executed the final linguistic editing. Our thanks also go to Roger Spear who generously assisted in the early stage of the book's preparation.

Finally, we wish to express our thanks to all the organisations and enterprises that were visited or surveyed in each country. What they allowed us to discover and analyse made our joint research so stimulating that the EMES Network has decided to continue as a specific European scientific network and to launch other common research projects (www.emes.net).

Carlo Borzaga and Jacques Defourny

Introduction

From third sector to social enterprise

Jacques Defourny

Introduction

In almost all industrialised countries, we are witnessing today a remarkable growth in the 'third sector', i.e. in socio-economic initiatives which belong neither to the traditional private for-profit sector nor to the public sector. These initiatives generally derive their impetus from voluntary organisations, and operate under a wide variety of legal structures. In many ways they represent the new or renewed expression of civil society against a background of economic crisis, the weakening of social bonds and difficulties of the welfare state.

The importance of the third sector, which is often called the 'non-profit sector' or the 'social economy', is now such that it is broadly associated with the major economic roles of public authorities. The third sector is involved in the allocation of resources through production of quasi-public goods and services. It has a redistributive role through the provision of a wide range of (free or virtually free) services to deprived people via the voluntary contributions (in money or through voluntary work) which many associations can mobilise. This sector is also involved in the regulation of economic life when, for example, associations or social co-operatives are the partners of public authorities in the task of helping back into work poorly qualified unemployed people, who are at risk of permanent exclusion from the labour market.

The persistence of structural unemployment in many countries, the need to reduce state budget deficits and to keep them at a low level, the difficulties of traditional social policies and the need for more active integration policies have naturally raised the question of how far the third sector can help to meet these challenges and perhaps take over from public authorities in some areas. Of course there is no simple answer to this question, and the debate is still wide open. Some commentators regard associations as made-to-measure partners for new transfers of responsibility and parallel reductions in public costs. The qualities usually attributed to private enterprise (flexibility, rapidity, creativity, a willingness to take on responsibility, etc.) are expected to lead to improvements in the services provided. Others fear that the third sector will become an instrument for privatisation policies, leading to social deregulation and the gradual unravelling of acquired social rights. Yet others stress the fact that advanced industrial

societies are moving towards a redefinition of relationships between the individual, the intermediate structures of civil society and the state. In any case, we
are probably moving from a welfare state to a new welfare mix where responsibility should be shared among public authorities, for-profit providers and
third-sector organisations on the basis of strict criteria of both efficiency and
fairness.

In the crucial debate on the place and role of the third sector, the aim of
the present work is to expose and analyse a major impetus in this little-known
area of our economies, i.e. the increasing numbers of economic initiatives we
will call 'social enterprises', which bear witness to the development, throughout
Europe, of a new entrepreneurial spirit focused on social aims. But let us be
quite clear. The social enterprises we are about to discuss are new entities
which may be regarded as a subdivision of the third sector, but they also set out
a process, a new (social) enterprise spirit which takes up and refashions older
experiences. In this sense they reflect a trend, a groundswell involving the whole
of the third sector. This work hopes to offer insights, which will enrich and
even renew, at least in part, existing approaches to, and analyses of, this third
sector.

Before discussing the notion of social enterprises, we need to set out the
main approaches developed over the last quarter of a century, in order to have
a grasp of the situation in the third sector. In this perspective, we first point out
the main steps, which led the scientific community to rediscover the third sector
as a whole in the last decades (section 1). The two subsequent sections are
devoted to two major (already mentioned) conceptual frameworks which were
built on the basis of this growing interest, i.e. the notions of the social economy
(section 2) and the non-profit sector (section 3). We also try to identify clearly
the convergences and divergences of these two approaches (section 4) and the
kinds of limitations they may have, especially in capturing the dynamics
currently being witnessed within the third sector (section 5). Indeed, as we will
argue, the innovative features which can be observed may be regarded as a new
social entrepreneurship (section 6) and this leads us to propose a definition of
the social enterprise, namely the one which has been used as a working basis
for the whole joint research project which gave birth to this book (section 7).
We then show that such a conceptual basis enabled us to identify a wide variety
of social enterprises in all EU countries (section 8). Focusing on a limited
number of these initiatives, we present the main questions which have guided
the in-depth analysis undertaken by researchers in each of the fifteen countries
and which have been discussed within this European scientific network (named
the EMES Network)[1] throughout all joint sessions held during the four years of
the project (section 9). These questions may be considered as the red line of all
the country chapters that form the first major part of the book. They also
represent the point of departure of the theoretical contributions, that constitute
the other major part of the book, as explained in the final section of this
general introduction.

1   The (re)discovery of the third sector

For a long time, there have been scientists interested in economic initiatives of a 'third type' that belong neither to the for-profit private sector nor to the public sector. A rich literature has developed throughout the twentieth century about co-operatives, an enterprise type organised according to specific co-operative principles which has spread to all parts of the world.[2] In the late 1960s, workers' co-operatives and the so-called 'labour-managed firms' even entered the heart of neo-classical economics and gave birth to a widely respected theoretical and empirical corpus.[3] In other disciplines, like sociology, a lot of research on voluntary organisations has been undertaken since the middle of the century.

However, the idea of a distinct third sector, made up of most enterprises and organisations which are not primarily seeking profit, and which are not part of the public sector, really began to emerge in the mid 1970s. Such organisations were already very active in many areas and were indeed the subject of specific public policies. But the idea of bringing these bodies together and the theoretical basis on which this might be done had not really been put forward until then.[4] As problems caused by the economic crisis deepened, awareness of the limitations of the traditional public and private sectors steadily grew. Against this background, the interest in other kinds of economic organisations was strongly reactivated, somewhat like the search for a 'third way' of development between capitalism and state socialism by newly independent countries during the 1950s and 1960s, though on a different scale.

In the United States the work of the Filer Commission, and, in 1976, Yale University's *Program on Non-profit Organisations*, involving 150 researchers, marked a decisive step in defining the theoretical basis of non-profit organisations (NPOs) and the non-profit sector. Since then, a vast scientific literature on NPOs has developed, with contributions from disciplines as diverse as economics, sociology, political science, history, and law.[5]

In Europe, widely varying socio-political, cultural and economic national circumstances have not allowed such a wide-ranging and rapid awareness of the third sector to develop. However, the economic entities that gradually came to light through a third-sector approach were already important factors in most countries. They were also rooted in solid and long-standing traditions, insofar as mutual organisations and co-operatives had to some extent existed everywhere for more than a century, and association-based economic initiatives as well as self-help movements had also been increasing in numbers for some considerable time.

In fact, without denying that the general public's view is strongly characterised by the historical context of each country, it may be said that two theoretical approaches to the third sector gradually spread internationally, accompanied by statistical work aimed at quantifying its economic importance. One is the 'non-profit sector' approach already mentioned. The other, French in origin, forged the concept of the 'social economy' to bring together co-operatives, mutual societies and associations (with increasing frequency, foundations are also included).[6] Although the first view has the advantage of simplicity and the strength of a framework designed to grasp the US situation, the second approach has found an ever-greater resonance throughout Europe and has been taken up by the European Union's institutions.[7]

Other theories of the third sector have also been developed internationally. An example is the tri-polar approach which sees the economy in terms of three poles, sometimes represented by three types of agents – private enterprise, the state and households – (Evers 1995; Pestoff 1992), sometimes according to the principles and methods by which exchanges are regulated – the market, public redistribution and reciprocity – (Laville 1994) and in other cases according to the types of resources involved (commercial, non-commercial or non-monetary). In such a perspective, the third sector is viewed as an intermediate space in which the different poles can combine. Because of their flexibility such approaches can help to reconcile the notions of non-profit sector and social economy, and they occupy an important place in the theoretical chapters of the present work. But for now we shall confine ourselves to the first two lines of approach, and shall examine their particular features, their points of convergence and their differences with a view to showing to what extent they can account for the social enterprise phenomenon.

2   The concept of the social economy

Virtually all work on the social economy attempts to understand it on the basis of its legal/institutional characteristics or by emphasising the principles that its organisations have in common. As we discuss below, these approaches are usually combined nowadays.

The legal/institutional approach

In most industrialised countries, third-sector enterprises and organisations may be grouped into three major categories, viz. co-operative enterprises, mutual societies, and those organisations which might generally be described as associations, whose legal form may vary considerably from one country to another. This is an approach to the social economy which has deep historical roots. Organisations of this kind have existed for a very long time, although they have only gradually been given legal recognition for activities based on the free association of their members, which remained informal and sometimes even secret throughout most of the nineteenth century. Although this way of looking at the social economy originated in France, its relevance goes far beyond French borders, since the three main components of the social economy are to be found almost everywhere:

- *Co-operative-style enterprises*: from the middle of the nineteenth century, co-operatives have spread internationally and they are now to be found worldwide.[8] The co-operative movement is like a great tree whose branches continue to spread. There are agricultural co-operatives, saving and credit co-operatives, consumers' co-operatives, insurance co-operatives, retail co-operatives, housing co-operatives and so on. A great deal of long-standing co-operatives have developed in markets which became quite competitive; as a result, they have been pushed to behave increasingly like their profit-maximising competitors. However, most of them still keep some specific co-operative characteristics and, even more importantly, in the last decades, the co-operative movement has continuously been renewed by the emergence of initiatives like workers' co-operatives in new fields of activity or social co-operatives.

This first component of the social economy also covers various initiatives that are not explicitly called co-operatives but which adopt closely related rules and practices. This is especially true in developing countries, but also holds good for industrialised countries where some enterprises, not set up as co-operatives but having a social purpose, can also be categorised under this heading (for instance the Spanish *sociedades laborales*).

- *Mutual-type organisations*: mutual help societies have existed in most places for a very long time. In many cases, they have gradually been institutionalised and in various industrialised countries they have become major players in social security systems.[9] However, the mutual component of the third sector also includes many organisations of various types[10] which cater for the need of local communities to organise for themselves community insurance systems, for instance in countries where social security systems are at an early stage of development and only cover a small part of the population. They may mutualise a wide range of risks, including health (costs of treatment, medicines, and hospitalisation), death (material support for the family of the deceased), funerals, and bad harvests or catches.

- *Associations*: the freedom of association is formally recognised in most countries of the world but in a wide variety of legal forms and under more or less favourable circumstances. In practice, this third component includes a lot of advocacy organisations which may also be seen as providers of services to their members, to other people (as Save the Children, for example) or to the whole community (for instance Greenpeace). More generally it includes all other forms of free association of persons for the production of goods or services where making a profit is not the essential purpose. Obviously these organisations have a wide variety of names, such as: associations, non-profit organisations, voluntary organisations, non-governmental organisations, *ideell* associations, and so on. Foundations and some other country-specific organisations (such as charities in the United Kingdom) are also often considered under this heading.

Finally, let us stress that although this first line of approach to the social economy is based on identifying major institutional types, it does not impose any great degree of legal formalism. Certainly, for the purposes of assembling statistical data, the legal status of these organisations is often an essential means of identification. But depending on the point of view adopted, we can also include in these three components a number of long-standing informal initiatives. This is a most

important point, since there are large numbers of *de facto* associations in industrialised countries and even more informal activities in the countries of the South,
which appear to be of co-operative, mutual or associative type.

The normative approach

The second way of regarding the social economy consists of emphasising the
principles that its organisations have in common. In other words, it is a matter of
showing as precisely as possible why certain very different enterprises and organisations deserve the same designation, and in what common fashion they may be
distinguished from the traditional private sector and the public sector.

This normative approach is crucial and cannot be considered as an optional
complement to the first one. Doing this would convey a risk of opposing the
long-established organisations which easily fit the main categories of the institutional approach to the newer third-sector initiatives which often refer more to
specific values and practices than to legal forms.[11]

Today there is broad agreement that these common features relate to the
productive purpose and to the internal structure of these organisations. There
are several ways of defining the social economy, but the one which follows has
the advantage of combining the legal/institutional approach already described
with an affirmation of the values and principles which underpin the third sector
(the normative or ethical approach). This definition, which is used in several
countries, states that:

> The social economy includes economic activities carried out by co-operatives
> and related enterprises, mutual societies and associations whose ethical
> stance is represented by the following principles:
> - the aim of serving members or the community, rather than generating
>   profit;
> - an independent management;
> - a democratic decision making process;
> - the primacy of people and labour over capital in the distribution of
>   income.
>
> (CWES 1990: 8)[12]

With the first principle, emphasis is placed on the fact that activities carried out
in the social economy provide a service to members or to a wider community
and are not primarily a means of making a financial return on capital investment. The possible generation of a surplus may thus be an outcome of
providing the services or a way to improve them, but not the main motivation
behind the activity.

The independence of its management is a principal means of distinguishing
the social economy from public entities producing goods and services. The
economic activities carried out by the latter do not in general benefit from the

wide-ranging management independence that provides an essential impetus in voluntary initiatives.

The need for a democratic decision-making process derives from the 'one member, one vote' principle central to co-operatives. Although this may be expressed through a great variety of effective practices, the rule of 'one share, one vote' is clearly excluded and there is at least a strict limit placed on the number of votes per member in the body which holds the ultimate decision-making power.

Finally, the fourth principle – the primacy of people and labour in the distribution of income – derives directly from the others (and may thus be seen as less essential). It covers a wide range of practices within organisations in the social economy, including: limited remuneration of capital, distribution of surplus among the workforce or members/users in the form of bonuses, the creation of reserve funds for business development, and the immediate use of surpluses for social purposes. As already mentioned, the concept of social economy is increasingly used in the European Union and since the 1980s numerous studies have been carried out to further the empirical knowledge of this concept.[13]

3   The concept of the non-profit sector

As in the case of the social economy when viewed through an institutional approach, the concept of the non-profit sector is deeply rooted in history, especially in America. As stated by Salamon, one of the factors which accounted for the early growth of the American penchant for voluntary association was 'the deep-seated hostility to royal power and centralised state authority that the religious non conformists who helped populate the American colonies brought with them when they fled the Old World' (Salamon 1997: 282). But it is only in the late nineteenth century that the idea of a distinct non-profit sector really began to take shape. Non-profit organisations were then promoted not simply to supplement public action but as superior vehicles for meeting public needs. Although the expansion of the non-profit sector in the 1960s and 1970s was strongly linked to partnership with government which increasingly supported these organisations, American perception of the latter remains marked by anti-state attitudes as shown by the growing use of the term 'independent sector' to refer to these entities.

Tax-exemption as a key criterion

It is mainly through the tax laws that the non-profit sector has come to be legally defined in the United States. The federal tax code identifies some twenty-six different categories of organisations that are entitled to exemption from federal income taxation. These organisations must operate in such a way that 'no part of (their) earnings inures to the benefit of theirs officers or directors' and their founding document must stipulate this.

Although these tax-exempt organisations are of various kinds and include member serving organisations as well as primarily public serving organisations, much of the discussion on the non-profit sector in the recent American literature focuses on the second category, or more specifically on a subset of organisations that are tax-exempt and eligible to receive tax deductible gifts under Section 501 (c)(3) of the Internal Revenue Code. These organisations, which represent a very large range of public benefit activities, and include schools, colleges, universities, hospitals, museums, libraries, day-care centres, and social service agencies, are therefore thought of as the heart of the non-profit sector.

A definition for cross-national comparative purposes

Given this quite specific historical background, it is not surprising that no universally accepted definition of the non-profit sector can be found today. However, significant efforts have been made in the last decade to undertake cross-national comparative studies. Increasing reference is made to the conceptual framework established by the vast international study which has been co-ordinated by the American Johns Hopkins University since 1990.[14]

For the researchers involved in this project, the non-profit sector consists of organisations with the following characteristics:

- they are formal, i.e. they have a certain degree of institutionalisation, which generally presupposes a legal personality;
- they are private, i.e. distinct from both the state and those organisations issuing directly from the public authorities;
- they are self-governing, in the sense that they must have their own regulations and decision-making bodies;
- they cannot distribute profits to either their members, their directors or a set of 'owners'. This 'non-distribution constraint' lies at the heart of all the literature on NPOs;
- they must involve some level of voluntary contribution in time (volunteers) and/or in money (donors), and they must be founded on the free and voluntary affiliation of their members.

4   The non-profit sector and the social economy: convergences and divergences

Before examining how the non-profit sector and the social economy may encapsulate the realities on which we focus, it may be useful to briefly compare these two concepts. At first, the comparison between the above definitions reveals important similarities[15] insofar as the requirement for a formal structure in the non-profit sector echoes the legal/institutional approach of the social economy even though the latter only underlines three types of legal status.[16] The private nature of entities involved in the NPO concept is implicit in the other approach since the legal status of social economy organisations is generally much closer to that prevailing in the private for-profit sector than in the public sector, while the criterion of self-governance is close to the requirement for independent management in the social economy. Finally, the last criterion for NPOs, which is influenced by the British voluntary sector tradition, is satisfied in practice by most organisations in the social economy insofar as the legal statutes of co-operatives, mutual societies and associations generally stipulate that membership should be freely entered into, and the board members of these organisations usually act on a voluntary basis.

Moreover, it should be stressed that both the non-profit sector and the social economy are defined in terms of their basic structure and organisational rules rather than in terms of their sources of revenue. Although voluntary contributions are given an explicit role in non-profit organisations, none of the concepts imposes any requirement as to the extent of market income, state subsidies or other resources. In fact, the main points of divergence are found in three areas: the specification of goals, the control over the organisation and the use of profits.

Firstly, the social economy approach clearly indicates that the major goal of the organisation is to serve members or the community rather than to seek profit. On the contrary, the NPO approach is not explicit as to the goals of the organisation. Of course, the latter are set by the organisation's own governing bodies and a strict constraint on the use of profits normally induces goals which are quite different from those pursued by traditional private firms. However, it does not seem impossible for an NPO to actually seek maximisation of profits, or any other goal, provided that profits are not distributed to owners and managers.

Secondly, the social economy has at its heart the requirement of a democratic decision-making process which, in addition to giving weight to actual members' involvement and voice, represents a structural procedure to control the actual pursuit of the organisation's goals. In the NPO approach, such a control also comes from inside the organisation through its governing bodies but without any formal democratic requirement. As to the non-distribution constraint, it certainly represents an important limiting rule (generally imposed by law) but its accounting and administrative nature keeps it far from being a dynamic control process.[17]

Thirdly, the non-profit approach prohibits any profit distribution and thus excludes the entire co-operative component of the social economy, since co-operatives generally redistribute a part of their surplus to their members. It also excludes some mutual societies; for instance, mutual insurance companies which return part of their surplus to members in the form of reductions in future contributions.[18]

Another way of summing up these differences would be to say that the conceptual basis of the non-profit approach is the non-distribution constraint, which gives it a particular relevance for public benefit associations. The social economy concept, on the other hand, owes much to co-operative thought which of course gives more emphasis to mutual interest organisations and a central place to democratic control over the organisation's goals and functioning. Let us stress however that these differences only apply strictly from a theoretical point of view; they might be much less significant when investigated by empirical research. Especially, a democratic decision-making process should not be taken for granted in all social economy organisations, because in many entities the actual power often tends to be concentrated within a few hands, in spite of democratically held general assemblies. Moreover, foundations which are increasingly mentioned as a fourth component of the social economy, generally do not rely on the 'one member, one vote' principle in their governing bodies. The third major conceptual difference, referring to surplus distribution, should not be overestimated either, since distribution of some profits is quite frequent in co-operatives and mutuals but it is limited by internal and external regulations.[19]

5   The limitations of the two concepts

Of course, many aspects of the third sector have already been the subject of a great number of studies. But the concepts of the non-profit sector and the social economy, as such, present two major limitations for the purposes of our analysis, i.e. how to understand the emergence of social enterprises, their forms and their importance, and the impetus behind them.

Firstly, the non-profit sector and the social economy are both very general concepts covering a wide range of organisations with various roles. They attempt to cover the whole third sector at once, with a single, all-encompassing definition. In reaching this synthesis they cannot help relying on the largest common denominator to be found among all the organisations in the third sector. As a consequence, they are necessarily unable to reflect situations which only partly conform to their definitions, features that are not found throughout the sector, or characteristics which only affect some organisations. At the same time, they cannot easily describe entities that are somehow located on the boundaries rather than at the heart of the third sector.

Secondly, the very nature of these two concepts is static rather than dynamic. They produce a snapshot of the many and varied situations to be found in the third sector. But beyond this descriptive capacity, they are not very helpful in capturing the underlying dynamics of all or part of the elements concerned. For instance, none of these two notions refers explicitly to entrepreneurial behaviours or the economic risks induced by the latter. They can certainly account for some developments, for example the growth in employment or the changes of other key parameters during a given period. But these results are generally obtained by taking a snapshot of the non-profit sector or the social economy in a fairly static fashion at different times.

Of course it is true that much of the literature on the non-profit sector has been written from an explicitly or at least implicitly historical perspective, and various analyses have tried to explain the reasons for the existence of the third sector and the conditions in which it emerged.[20] But in theories regarding the non-profit sector, as in various studies about the conditions under which the social economy developed,[21] it is more often a matter of *a posteriori* analysis than of studies of developments as they happen.

Finally, as will be shown later, a lot of social enterprises seem to combine elements of co-operatives and non-profit organisations. For this reason, the traditional NPO approach is clearly not the best starting point. On the contrary, the concept of social economy is able to include social enterprises but a further element is needed as none of its three (or four) main components directly corresponds with social enterprises. None of this means that we will not draw heavily on existing literature in our efforts to improve our understanding of social enterprises. Simply, we do not want to limit ourselves to these notions of the non-profit sector and the social economy in our search for an adequate conceptual framework to approach social enterprises.

6   A new social entrepreneurship?

We will now describe more precisely the realities we want to study in this book. It should be clear that social enterprises are more than simply a new development of the non-profit sector or the social economy and that they deserve an analysis that goes beyond these two concepts. Firstly, we will try to explain why they may be seen as real enterprises and even more particularly as the expression of a new entrepreneurship. Secondly, we will see to what extent these entities and this entrepreneurial behaviour may be qualified as social.

Entrepreneurship as an innovative behaviour

Among theories concerning entrepreneurship, the classic work of Schumpeter (1934) may still be used as a starting point. In the latter's opinion, economic development is a process of 'carrying out new combinations in the production process' (Schumpeter 1934: 66) and entrepreneurs are precisely the persons whose role it is to implement these new combinations. Entrepreneurs are not necessarily the owners of a company, but they are responsible for introducing changes in at least one of the following ways: (1) the introduction of a new product or a new quality of product; (2) the introduction of a new production method; (3) the opening of a new market; (4) the acquisition of a new source of raw materials; or (5) the reorganisation of a sector of activity. Following the work carried out by Young (1983, 1986) and a survey undertaken by Badelt (1997), this typology can be adapted to the third sector and it is pertinent to examine, at all levels, to what extent a new entrepreneurship can be identified.

New products or a new quality of products

Numerous analyses of the third sector have demonstrated that enterprises have often been developed in response to needs in areas where the traditional private sector or the state were unable to provide a satisfactory solution.[22] There are countless examples of organisations that have invented new types of services to take up the challenges of their age. Nowadays, as in the past, this is the expression of entrepreneurship. But have the last two decades been different in any specific ways? We believe that it is possible to speak of a new entrepreneurship which is probably more prevalent in Europe than in the United States. The crisis of

European welfare systems (in terms of budget, effectiveness and legitimacy) has resulted in a more autonomous development of third-sector initiatives, and public authorities increasingly look to private initiatives to provide solutions that they would have implemented themselves if the economic climate had been as good as in the glorious 1945–1975 period. The shrinking of public initiative is undoubtedly the most striking in the United Kingdom, but the same trend is apparent in most member states of the European Union, albeit to differing degrees.

These new developments are particularly clear in some fields of activity. The work integration of unskilled people and personal services have seen multiple innovations in terms of new activities being set up or ensuring that services are better adapted to needs, whether in regard to vocational training, providing centres and facilities for young children, services for elderly people, or aid for certain categories of disadvantaged persons (abused children, refugees, immigrants, etc.).[23] These are areas to which we will pay special attention. This entrepreneurship seems all the more innovative as, even within the third sector, it contrasts sharply with the highly bureaucratic and only slightly innovative behaviour of certain traditional organisations (for example, the large welfare organisations in Germany).

New methods of organisation and/or production

It is common to see the third sector organise its activities along different lines from the traditional private and public sectors. But what is most striking in the current generation of social enterprises is the involvement of different, even diverse partners or categories of partners. Salaried employees, voluntary workers, users, supporting organisations and local authorities are often partners in the same project, whereas the traditional social economy organisations have generally been set up by more homogeneous social groups.[24] If this does not necessarily revolutionise the production process, it often transforms the way in which the activity is organised. In some cases, such co-operation could even be described as an alliance of interested parties, for example when service providers and users co-operate in the organisation and management of certain neighbourhood services. The setting-up of childcare centres run by parents in France or in Sweden is just one of many examples of such co-operation. In other cases, such a 'multi-stakeholder' structure may lead social enterprises to compete more effectively with for-profit enterprises in existing markets.

New production factors

One of the principal, long-standing specific characteristics of the third sector is its capacity to mobilise volunteers. In itself, the use of volunteers is not an innovation, but it is significant in numerous recent initiatives because voluntary workers make it possible to produce goods or provide services that were not previously available or which were only available with the help of paid workers (in which case it is rare that it is really the same 'product'). It is also noteworthy that volunteering has changed in nature over the last few decades. It seems to be not only much less charitable than forty or fifty years ago, but also less 'militant' than in the 1960s or the 1970s. Today's voluntary workers are fairly pragmatic and focus more on 'productive' objectives and activities that correspond to specific needs. Moreover, it is not unusual to find the entrepreneurial role, in the most commonly used sense (launching an activity), carried out by voluntary workers.

Paid work has also seen various innovations. On the one hand, many third-sector organisations have been at the forefront of experiments regarding atypical types of employment, such as absorption into employment programmes, the development of semi-voluntary formulas or part-time work (with very reduced working hours), etc.[25] On the other hand, it can be said that the traditional employee status is often 'enriched' when employees are recognised as members of the governing bodies of the social enterprise in their own right, with the resultant control and decision-making powers that the members enjoy. Finally, the mix of volunteers and paid workers may itself be seen as an innovative production factor (which requires specific human resources management skills) in activities so far carried out exclusively by one of these two categories of workers.

New market relations

In some countries, the supply of certain services had long been restricted to public providers, as in the Scandinavian countries, or to informal providers (family or neighbourhood), as in Italy, Spain, Portugal and Greece. However, there existed a demand which remained unsatisfied and third-sector initiatives began to invent market relations in these formerly restricted spheres. In a growing number of countries, the situation has changed rapidly and families increasingly externalise services they formerly provided, due to such factors as increasing female participation in the labour market and the isolation of family members. At the same time, there is a trend towards 'contracting out' and towards the development of quasi-markets for certain services which were previously carried out by the public authorities or by non-profit private bodies particularly favoured by the state. In fact, with a view to reducing costs and ensuring that the services are better adapted to user needs, public authorities are making increasing use of calls to tender, which bring different types of service providers into competition for public funding. It was the conservative government in the UK that went furthest in this direction, but this switch from 'tutelary control' to 'competitive control' is becoming more and more commonplace almost everywhere.

Such profound changes in the welfare state inevitably have major ramifications at different levels. For the purposes of this introduction, it is sufficient to emphasise the factors that tend to accentuate the entrepreneurial character of the associations, in the sense that they have an increasing number of characteristics in common with traditional companies and also, in part, in terms of the 'new combinations' referred to by Schumpeter:

- existing associations find themselves in competitive situations, sometimes with traditional companies, when tendering;
- they are consequently obliged to install or reinforce internal management structures very much modelled on those of the commercial sector;
- the ending of certain public monopolies (for example in Sweden) or of the monopolies enjoyed by large welfare organisations (for example in Germany) encourage the emergence of new private initiatives (for-profit or non-profit organisations) structured from the outset to reflect this context;
- last but not least, both for old as well as new associations, the economic risk is greater since their financing henceforward depends on their ability to win these quasi-markets and to satisfy users.[26]

Finally, it goes without saying that this is reinforced by the increased demand among private individuals with adequate financial resources for certain services that become accessible because of the continued rise in the living standards of an important part of the population. Thus for example, elderly people who receive a decent pension or who have accumulated considerable savings represent new markets, which are often very competitive.

New forms of enterprises

The recent introduction of diverse legal frameworks in the national legislation of various European states tends to confirm that we are dealing with a somewhat original kind of entrepreneurship. These legal frameworks are intended to be better suited to these types of initiatives than the traditional non-profit or co-operative structures. The Italian Parliament has been a pioneer in this regard, by introducing in 1991 a 'social co-operative' status. This new legal form has been very successful from the outset and the astonishing development of the Italian social co-operatives continues to be followed with interest by other national governments. In 1995, Belgium introduced into its legislation the concept of a 'company with a social purpose', whilst Portugal introduced the 'social solidarity co-operative' and Greece the 'social co-operatives with limited liability' respectively in 1998 and 1999. Other countries, and France in particular, are considering introducing similar legislation.

Generally speaking, these new legal frameworks are designed to encourage the entrepreneurial and commercial dynamics that are an integral part of a social project. They also provide a way of formalising the multi-stakeholder nature of numerous initiatives, by involving the interested parties (paid workers, voluntary workers, users, etc.) in the decision-making process. However, it must be emphasised that apart from Italy, the great majority of social enterprises are still using traditional third-sector legal forms, even though the latter sometimes may hide significant changes; for instance, workers' co-operatives which open their membership to users tend to become closer to public benefit enterprises.

Enterprises which may be called 'social'

If, as seems to be the case, we can identify a new entrepreneurship, it remains to explain why we should describe their enterprises as 'social'. More precisely, one may wonder if the new economic trends in their behaviour are compatible with explicit social dimensions. We have argued so far that these initiatives belong to the third sector, conceived either in the non-profit sense or as the social economy, and that these two concepts provide the necessary elements to embody the social dimensions we now want to identify. Of course the actual presence of these elements in the organisations in question is still to be confirmed, but from a theoretical point of view, the main issue here lies in the combination of the innovative economic practices just listed with social dimensions embedded in the traditional conceptualisations of the third sector as presented in the second and third sections above. In summary, we may say that the traditional conceptualisations of the third sector allow us to identify three levels on which the 'social' nature of initiatives may be detected.

The purposes of the activity

The concept of the social economy includes as a key criterion 'the aim of serving members or the community rather than generating profit', while the non-profit sector stresses the impossibility of members or managers receiving a proportion of any surplus. Although the social economy does not exclude the possibility of a limited distribution of profits to members, particularly in co-operatives, the common feature of these two approaches should be stressed here, as it is found in all social enterprises. The common feature is the requirement (absolute or in part) for the production surplus to be 'socialised', that is to be reinvested in the development of the activity or to be used for the benefit of people other than those who control the organisation.

Non-commercial resources

As just stressed, both concepts involve benefits to the community or to target groups. Such benefits very often justify the payment of subsidies to third-sector organisations. This is also true for most social enterprises that are financed both by resources deriving from the market and by non-commercial resources allocated by the public authorities in the community's name. Usually non-monetary resources are also involved, such as voluntary work and/or donations, these elements being also stressed by the non-profit approach. This broad mobilisation of resources across the society, and the goodwill on which third-sector organisations can rely due to their role in providing services, are characteristics which we will address extensively later in this book, especially when trying to assemble elements for a theory of social enterprise.

Particular organisational methods

The two concepts embody the view that a third-sector organisation should be autonomous or even independent, with its own decision-making bodies. The social economy approach also stresses that there should be a democratic decision-making process. Such features are often found in social enterprises since they are generally founded on a participatory dynamic which involves their members (paid workers, volunteers, users and/or other partners representing for instance the local community) in management and controlling bodies and since members' power is generally not proportional to any capital stake they may hold. So we clearly have here characteristics which may be classified as social.

7   Towards a definition of the social enterprise

We have argued so far that a new phenomenon can be identified within the third sector of modern economies and that it may be seen as a new social entrepreneurship whose features are partly out of the range of traditional non-profit and social economy approaches. Taking this for granted, let us now turn to the way the EMES Network organised its research to identify and analyse this phenomenon. The main steps of the research that we are presenting here reflect the structure of the whole book and are found as well within each of the 'country chapters' that form the first major part of this volume.

One of the hypotheses of the EMES project was that social enterprises as new entities and/or as a new dynamic in existing third-sector organisations are likely to be found throughout the European Union. This is why the research network was formed and the study undertaken by researchers from all fifteen EU member countries. Of course this meant a considerable diversity and heterogeneity in the work contexts.

In order to build the research on common ground, the first step of the EMES work was to define a set of common criteria which would be used to identify social enterprises in each of the fifteen member states. This set of criteria was considered from the outset as a working definition of the social enterprise that might need to be revised in the course of the project, but as it turned out, this initial framework concept proved to be fairly robust and reliable.[27] This working definition distinguishes, on the one hand, between criteria that are more economic and, on the other, indicators that are predominantly social. Let us begin with the economic and entrepreneurial dimensions for which four criteria have been put forward:

A continuous activity producing goods and/or selling services

Social enterprises, unlike the traditional non-profit organisations, are normally not engaged in advocacy activities as a major goal or in the redistribution of financial flows (as, for example, grant-giving foundations), but they are directly involved in the production of goods or the provision of services to people on a continuous basis. The provision of such goods or services represents, therefore, the reason, or one of the main reasons, for the existence of social enterprises.

A high degree of autonomy

Social enterprises are voluntarily created by a group of people and are governed by them in the framework of an autonomous project. Accordingly, they may depend on public subsidies but they are not managed, directly or indirectly, by public authorities or other organisations (federations, private firms, etc.) and they have both the right of 'voice and exit' (the right to take up their own position as well as to terminate their activity).

A significant level of economic risk

Those who establish a social enterprise assume totally or partly the risk of the initiative. Unlike most public institutions, their financial viability depends on the efforts of their members and workers to secure adequate resources.

A minimum amount of paid work

As in the case of most traditional non-profit associations, social enterprises may also combine monetary and non-monetary resources, voluntary and paid workers. However, the activity carried out in social enterprises requires a minimum level of paid workers.

To encapsulate the social dimensions of the initiative, five criteria have been proposed:

An explicit aim to benefit the community

One of the principal aims of social enterprises is to serve the community or a specific group of people. To the same end, a feature of social enterprises is their desire to promote a sense of social responsibility at local level.

An initiative launched by a group of citizens

Social enterprises are the result of collective dynamics involving people belonging to a community or to a group that shares a certain need or aim and they must maintain such a dimension in one way or another.

A decision-making power not based on capital ownership

This generally means the principle of 'one member, one vote' or at least a voting power not distributed according to capital shares on the governing body which has the ultimate decision-making rights. The owners of the capital are obviously important (although all social enterprises do not have equity capital) but the decision-making rights are shared with the other stakeholders.

A participatory nature, which involves the persons affected by the activity

Representation and participation of customers, stakeholder orientation and a democratic management style are important characteristics of social enterprises. In many cases, one of the aims of social enterprises is to further democracy at local level through economic activity.

Limited profit distribution

Social enterprises not only include organisations that are characterised by a total non-distribution constraint, but also organisations, like co-operatives in some countries, which may distribute profits only to a limited extent, thus avoiding a profit-maximising behaviour.

8   A wide spectrum of initiatives across countries

With such a working definition, it was clear from the beginning that the fulfilment of these criteria would vary greatly and that social enterprises would appear in each country more as a wide spectrum than as a clear-cut set of well-identified organisations. At the same time, it seemed quite important to link the analysis of social enterprises with the other parts of the third sector and with the whole socio-economic context of each country (in some countries even the notion of a third sector remains unclear). Against such a background, it was then feasible to identify and list those types of initiatives which, to varying degrees, may be named 'social enterprises' according to the working definition just presented. Although the term itself may not be used in some countries, several categories of organisations clearly appeared to correspond with the new social entrepreneurship in which we were interested.

In a second phase of the research, it was agreed on that one or two main types of social enterprise or fields of activity would be analysed in-depth in each country. As a result of this selective approach, all researchers focused on a particular set of social enterprises which seemed particularly interesting in one way or another, including: the process through which they were created, the mix of resources on which they rely, the kinds of services they provide, the category of users to whom they supply these services, their innovative features to fight social exclusion, and so on. The number of initiatives was seldom the major criterion in this selection although it was also taken into account.

Finally it appeared that the social enterprises chosen in most countries operate in two broad spheres of activity: firstly, the training and reintegration into employment of persons excluded from the labour market and, secondly, the rapidly developing sector of personal services. However, this sectoral classification should be seen only as a way to gain a first quick and superficial idea of the fields that are covered in the country chapters. In several cases social enterprises combine both fields or go much beyond them. More importantly, many other classifications could prove to be more relevant depending on the aspects to be recorded, such as the role of the leadership, the extent of volunteering and/or paid labour, the relations to the market, or the support of the local community and the public authorities.

In order to visualise the groups of social enterprises that are analysed in the fifteen subsequent country chapters, the following is a brief look at their main features.

In Austria, the activities of 'child-minders' – originally provided on a voluntary and unpaid basis – have witnessed a remarkable professionalisation process. Of particular interest in this field is the development of 'children's groups', which are small groups of about twelve children with two nurses or specially trained child-minders that are supported by the self-organised involvement of parents. Childcare centres involving parental participation are also quite popular in France, while other social enterprises there are developing new forms of home help services for elderly or dependent persons. More generally, as is also the case in Belgium, social enterprises in France seem to be particularly innovative in the whole sphere of what is increasingly called 'proximity services', the proximity being objective (as for services provided at the local level) or subjective (when the proximity mainly refers to the relational dimension of the services provided). Indeed they often mobilise additional resources that do not emerge from the market or from the state and they go beyond the functional logic of the latter. This also appears clearly with thousands of Italian social co-operatives that provide social services, whether residential or not, especially in support of disabled people, elderly people, drug addicts and young people with family difficulties. In the United Kingdom home care co-operatives have emerged in response to market or state failures within a particular context of fast developing quasi-markets and competitive contracting practices with the local public authorities.

The frontier between provision of welfare services and activities oriented towards reintegration in employment of persons excluded from the labour market is not at all a neat one. In several countries, social work or services for people with mental illness, functional impairments or other difficulties have evolved to more productive activities that happened to serve as a basis for the starting up of social enterprises offering temporary or even stable jobs. This hybrid nature is well illustrated by the case of Denmark where social work, community development and productive activities are mixed in various types of initiatives such as production communes, social residences and folk high schools, the latter two being known for their ability to take care of young people with social problems. Sweden has witnessed the development of social worker co-operatives for former mental patients and for handicapped people since the state embarked on a reform including the phasing out of the big mental health institutions in the 1980s. Although these co-operatives do not offer standard jobs, they show an entrepreneurial spirit supported by local co-operative development agencies. In a quite different context, Portuguese CERCIs, i.e. co-operatives for education and rehabilitation of mentally handicapped children, started as special education schools and evolved with an increasing productive and job creation orientation as their users got older.

In many cases, there is no clear-cut boundary either between social enterprises seeking work integration of people with mental or physical disabilities and those oriented towards persons who are socially excluded (e.g. drug addicts, prisoners, or early school leavers). Social enterprises of both types, sometimes mixing target groups, may be found in Italy, Luxembourg, and Greece as well as in Spain across several fields of activity, with waste collection and recycling activities particularly important in Spain.

Many social enterprises offer stable jobs for excluded persons or represent the only work prospect for some specific target groups. However, many others must be viewed as part of 'transitional labour markets', that is as a step on the way back to the regular labour market and to 'normal' employment. Various social employment initiatives in Germany, particularly those specifically named 'social enterprises' in three *Länder*, Finnish labour co-operatives which aim at employing their members by subcontracting their labour to other employers, as well as Dutch neighbourhood development schemes which try to provide services and employment opportunities to inhabitants in old and poor urban areas, must all be seen as transitional institutions with temporary support from the public authorities.

Even when they seem to have rather narrow and clearly defined objectives, for instance providing on-the-job training or work experience to help people come back to regular employment, social enterprises generally combine these aims with other dimensions and challenges. Among those that were not mentioned in the above examples, one should stress social enterprises' participation in the local development dynamics in disadvantaged areas. This is particularly true of 'ABS' organisations in the new Eastern German *Länder*, the Greek agritourist co-operatives operated by women in remote rural areas, as well as the Dutch neighbourhood development/rehabilitation schemes in urban areas. Sometimes concerns for local development come first, as in Ireland, where a wide range of initiatives in proximity services and community businesses would not have emerged without mobilisation of the local population and the building of local partnerships.

Finally, let us stress the fact that all these examples should not be considered as forming the whole landscape of social enterprises in the European Union. They are simply features to which attention will be drawn to answer the main questions of the EMES research programme.

9   Three key questions

Social enterprises in the fifteen countries have been analysed on the basis of a common grid that can in fact be summed up in three key questions.[28] These questions were addressed both at the level of each individual country and from an international comparative perspective.

Question 1: What are the actual specific characteristics of social enterprises?

In particular we have tried to ascertain the context favouring the emergence of social enterprises, the support they have received and continue to receive, how they have evolved in terms of objectives and available resources, as well as the relations with users and public authorities. The way social enterprises are structured internally, their legal form and the profile of their workers have also been examined.

Question 2: What do social enterprises contribute?

We have examined the question of whether social enterprises have particular strong points compared with other types of private or public organisations, notably as regards the mobilisation of resources that might be out of reach for others. We have also endeavoured to ascertain whether they succeed in satisfying certain needs that would not be met otherwise. Along the same lines, the results that they achieve have been assessed, notably their contribution to the fight against unemployment and social exclusion. But we also question whether or not they are handicapped by certain intrinsic weaknesses, possibly at the level of their financial resources or their organisational efficiency.

Question 3: What are the future prospects for social enterprises?

Do social enterprises provide purely temporary solutions or can they aspire to playing a medium or long-term role? What is the position regarding their long-term role if the public authorities decide to address the social problems in areas where the social enterprises are involved? On the contrary, to what extent can they interact with the public authorities? Will their development be handicapped if the increasing financial resources of the private individuals that they serve attract traditional private sector firms? Do the current prospects of steady economic growth in Europe reduce the need for social enterprises or their development opportunities? It is on the basis of such questions that we have tried to draw up a picture of the most likely scenarios and the conditions favourable to a possible future development of social enterprises in their respective sectors.

10 Towards a theory of social enterprise

These three key questions not only served as a basis for the description, analysis and comparison of social enterprises in the different countries. All information and knowledge gathered from an empirical point of view also provided the basis for conceptual constructions and theoretical proposals that were discussed at each joint work session of the research process.

Beyond the definition of social enterprise already presented, the theoretical challenges that the EMES Network encountered may be illustrated in a simple way by Figure 1. The latter shows particularly how traditional visions of the third sector may be used to somehow locate social enterprises and how it was necessary to go a step further.

The first major point of reference is provided by the co-operative world, a distinct component of the social economy, which has its own research traditions and schools of thought. In several countries, indeed, social enterprises are registered as co-operatives as is shown by examples listed above. Moreover, workers' co-ops appear closer to social enterprises than traditional (often rather large) users' co-ops as is demonstrated by the cases of Finnish labour co-ops, Greek agritourist co-ops or British home care co-ops. However, social enterprises often combine different types of stakeholders in their membership and are more oriented than classical workers' co-ops to the benefit of the whole community.

The other major reference is the world of non-profit organisations, in which production-oriented entities are certainly closer to social enterprises than are advocacy organisations and grant-making foundations. In several European countries social enterprises do actually have the legal status of a non-profit organisation or association. However, as was shown in the fourth and fifth

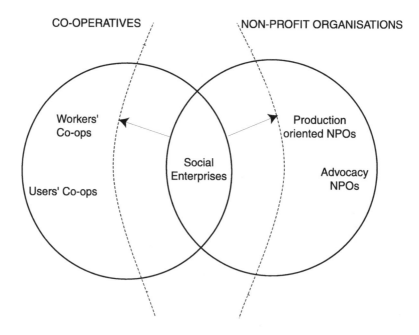

Figure 1   Social enterprises at the crossroads of co-operatives and the non-profit sector

sections of this general introduction, the NPO literature is not able to embrace the whole reality of the social enterprise. This remains true in spite of new laws that have recently been passed in Italy, Portugal, Greece and Belgium, to promote the development of firms with social aims.

The growing intersection of the circles in the figure represents precisely those trends that drive each circle closer to the other as the nature of social enterprises somehow relies on the combination of characteristics from both types of organisation. But it should not be interpreted in a static way, as only some social enterprises are simultaneously real co-operatives and pure non-profits organisations. Incidentally, the dotted lines also suggest another perspective which corresponds to what has been explained from the beginning, i.e. that part of the phenomenon of social enterprises is clearly made up of newly created organisations but it also represents a dynamic process which is transforming existing third-sector organisations.

The attempts made to build a specific theory of social enterprise are presented in the second major part of this volume. The first contribution, by Bacchiega and Borzaga, uses the tools offered by the institutional theory of organisations to highlight the innovative nature of social enterprises. The criteria forming the EMES definition of social enterprise are interpreted as shaping an original incentive system within these organisations. That incentive structure is based, on the one hand, on a mix of monetary and non-monetary elements where the latter tend to assume more importance than the former and, on the other hand, on the necessity to combine the possibly conflicting objectives of different categories of stakeholders. The authors also examine to what extent these specificities may contribute to explaining the plurality of social enterprises in the European context as well as their main strengths and weaknesses.

In the second theoretical chapter, Evers proposes a more socio-political analysis of the multiple goal and resource structure of social enterprises. He shows that such a structure may be better understood by bringing in the notion of 'social capital', although this concept is widely used today with quite diverse meanings. The author focuses on what might also be called 'civic capital' in order to encompass those non-market and non-state resources which are of considerable importance for social enterprises, like the readiness for dialogue, co-operation and civic commitment. He also argues that taking into account social capital-building as one of the goals of third-sector organisations helps to give more visibility to a number of their civic concerns and effects, which correspond to a broad notion of the public good, including democratic dimensions. In this perspective, social capital-building can become an explicit purpose of organisations like social enterprises. Finally, links between social capital and public policies are highlighted and it is stressed that policy-making and programmes should probably acknowledge as well as reward the mobilisation and reproduction of social capital by social enterprises, instead of taking it for granted.

The third contribution, by Laville and Nyssens, is the broadest one as it attempts to combine economic, social and political dimensions within a single tentative integrated theory of an 'ideal-type' social enterprise. It first examines relations between the specific aims of social enterprises and their ownership structure. The purpose of serving the community is defined as the explicit enhancement of collective externalities, i.e. collective benefits associated with the main production activity. Such a goal, however, does not seem to require any single model of ownership structure. The authors also extend the analysis of the specific features of social capital in social enterprise, showing that such a key resource may reduce transaction costs and production costs as well as generate socio-political effects. Then, after focusing on internal relations, they turn to the types of economic exchanges between social enterprises and their environment. Building on Polanyi's distinction between the economic principles of market exchange, redistribution and reciprocity, they show how the social enterprise mixes these modes of exchange in different socio-political contexts. From this point of view, the emergence of such enterprises can be understood as a reciprocal impulse and the consolidation process reveals a tension between institutional isomorphism and hybridisation of different economic principles.

The second major part of the book ends with a contribution from C. Borzaga and L. Solari in which they explore the main challenges confronting managers and members of social enterprises. While examining the more critical issues, they suggest strategies and areas of intervention for managers. Managers may in fact play a major role in overcoming the internal weaknesses and the external barriers highlighted in the preceding chapters. The authors emphasise particularly the role of managers in establishing legitimacy for social enterprises with respect both to external actors (such as society, public decision-makers and customers) and internal actors (including workers and volunteers). While some regulative legitimacy has been established in particular EU countries through legislation, they underline the role of managers in identifying different governance forms, organisation design and human resources practices which can promote the effectiveness of social enterprises in comparison to other organisational forms operating in the third sector.

Finally, in the concluding chapter of the book, we try to summarise the main empirical and theoretical results of the entire joint research project. We first synthesise the reasons for the emergence of social enterprises in all EU countries as well as the great diversity of these initiatives. It is argued that country variations may be explained by referring to the level of economic and social development, the characteristics of the welfare systems, the role of the traditional third sector and the existence of specific legal frameworks. We also survey the main contributions of social enterprises to the transformation of existing welfare systems, employment creation, local development, building of social capital and social cohesion and new dynamics within the third sector. These contributions however cannot hide internal weaknesses of this very special type of organisation that may prove to be quite fragile in some contexts. Moreover, external barriers often hinder their development and that is why this book ends by looking at policies which might better acknowledge their specificities and their potential in the context of strengthening the fundamental pluralism of European economic systems.

Notes

1 EMES refers to the title of the research project as submitted in French to the European Commission: *L'Émergence des Enterprises Sociales en Europe*.

2 Among the oldest and still existing scientific journals fully or partly dedicated to co-operatives, we should mention the *Revue des Études Coopératives* (founded in 1921 by Ch. Gide) lately renamed *RECMA* (see note 6), and the *Annals of Public and Co-operative Economics* (founded in 1908).

3 The journal *Economic Analysis and Workers' Management* launched in the late 1970s effectively represented this line of research. Now published under the shorter title *Economic Analysis*, it still covers the economics of self-management and workers' co-operatives but it has enlarged its scope of interest to encompass the 'economics of participation'.

4 From the 1930s through the 1960s, Western economies had been increasingly regarded as mixed economies made up of two major sectors as state intervention and the public sector became a second major component alongside the private for-profit sector.

5 The international scientific journals *Non-profit and Voluntary Sector Quarterly* and *Voluntas* provide a valuable overview of this literature.

6 This approach is well illustrated by the evolution of an already mentioned French journal (see note 2) which became the *Revue des Études Coopératives, Mutualistes et Associatives* (*RECMA*).

7 For some considerable time there has existed a 'social economy intergroup' within the European Parliament and the Economic and Social Committee and a 'social economy unit' was set up a decade ago by DG XXIII of the European Commission; more recently the latter officially recognised a 'consultative committee on co-operatives, mutual societies, associations and foundations'. Some of these bodies are currently undergoing significant changes but, more generally, an increasing number of action programmes and decisions from the Council of Ministers refer explicitly to the social economy, as for instance the guidelines for National Action Plans all member state governments have to design.

8 A key reference point in the first wave of co-operative development is the Rochdale Society of Equitable Pioneers, which was founded in 1844 north of Manchester by a group of weavers. Its constitution is usually seen as the first expression of those 'co-operatives principles' which, in spite of several revisions, continue to inspire the co-operative movement throughout the world. Today the International Co-operative Alliance (ICA) encompasses over 750 million members of co-operatives over five continents.

9 Many of these mutual societies are members of the *Association Internationale de la Mutualité* (AIM).

10 Often arising from local culture and reflecting the values or practices of community solidarity.

11 This happened in France in the 1980s and gave birth to another notion, the '*économie solidaire*', which is intended to reflect specific features of new initiatives. Therefore, the third sector as a whole is sometimes referred to as the '*économie sociale et solidaire*'.

12 See Defourny and Monzón Campos (1992) for an international comparative analysis of the third sector based on this social economy approach.

13 See Defourny and Mertens (1999) for a brief summary of comparative statistical studies carried out across the European Union. See also CIRIEC (2000) for an recent attempt to update these figures.

14 This project, which still continues, has generated a whole series of publications. See among the first and the latest Salamon and Anheier (1994) and Salamon, Anheier and Associates (1999).

15 On these similarities, see also Archambault (1996).

16 In practice, the majority of NPOs have a status which places them with associations or mutual societies, assuming that a sufficiently broad view of the latter is taken as outlined above.

17 Reviewing Clotfelder's book *Who Benefits from the Nonprofit Sector?*, Ben-Ner (1994) argues that the US situation requires improving access to the decision-making process of NPOs by consumers, sponsors and donors and allowing them to assert more oversight on management.

18 For a more detailed analysis of the differences, see *inter alia* Mertens (1999), and Defourny, Develtere and Fonteneau (1999).

19 We can also note that the difference between mutual and public benefit organisations decreases when mutual interest organisations have an 'open door' principle for their membership.

20 Among the most traditional surveys of these theories, see for example James and Rose-Ackerman (1986).

21 See for example Defourny, Favreau and Laville (1998).

22 That is indeed one of the major themes of studies devoted to identifying the principal reasons for the existence of the third sector.

23 On the subject of work integration, see Defourny, Favreau and Laville (1998); on personal services, see Borzaga and Santuari (1998).

24 This greater homogeneity is reflected in particular in the names of the different types of co-operatives or mutual societies, e.g. workers' co-operatives, agricultural co-operatives, mutual societies for civil servants, craft workers, farm workers and so on.

25 Once again, care must be taken when interpreting this evolution. Part of this innovative behaviour comes from the organisations themselves, but it is also a question of reactions and adaptations to the impetus or constraints inherent in public policies.

26 On this trend, see Laville and Sainsaulieu (1997).

27 Among others, OECD (1999) prepared a report on social enterprises relying heavily on the EMES approach and on EMES interim reports (1997 through 1999).

28 It should be noted that most of these field studies were carried out in 1997 and 1998. This explains why many data refer to these years or are even a bit older.

Bibliography

ARCHAMBAULT, E. (1996) *Le secteur sans but lucratif. Associations et fondations en France*, Economica, Paris.

BADELT, CH. (1997) 'Entrepreneurship Theories of the Nonprofit Sector', *Voluntas*, vol. 8, 2: 162–78.

BEN-NER, A. (1994) 'Who Benefits from the Nonprofit Sector? Reforming Law and Public Policy Towards Nonprofit Organizations', *The Yale Law Journal*, vol. 104: 731–62.

BORZAGA, C. and MITTONE, L. (1997) 'The Multistakeholder versus the Nonprofit Organisation', Università degli Studi di Trento, Draft Paper no. 7.

BORZAGA, C. and SANTUARI, A. (1998) *Social Enterprises and New Employment in Europe*, Regione Autonoma Trentino-Alto Adige, Trento.

CIRIEC (2000) *The Enterprises and Organizations of the Third System*, International Center of Research and Information on the Public and Cooperative Economy, Liège.

CLOTFELDER, C.T. (1992) *Who Benefits from the Non-profit Sector?*, University of Chicago Press, Chicago.

Conseil Wallon de l'Économie Sociale (1990) *Rapport à l'Exécutif Régional Wallon sur le secteur de l'économie sociale*, Namur.

DEFOURNY, J. (ed.) (1994) *Développer l'entreprise sociale*, Fondation Roi Baudouin, Brussels.

DEFOURNY, J. and MERTENS, S. (1999) 'Le troisième secteur en Europe: un aperçu des efforts conceptuels et statistiques', in GAZIER, B., OUTIN, J.-L. and AUDIER, F. (eds) *L'économie sociale*, tome 1, L'Harmattan, Paris, 5–20.

DEFOURNY, J. and MONZÓN CAMPOS, J.-L. (eds) (1992) *Économie Sociale – The Third Sector*, De Boeck, Brussels.

DEFOURNY, J., DEVELTERE, P. and FONTENEAU, B. (eds) (1999) *L'économie sociale au Nord et au Sud*, De Boeck, Brussels.

DEFOURNY, J., FAVREAU, L. and LAVILLE, J.-L. (eds) (1998) *Insertion et nouvelle économie sociale*, Desclée de Brouwer, Paris.

EMES (1997a, 1997b, 1998a, 1998b, 1999a) *Semestrial Progress Reports*, EMES European Network, Brussels.

—— (1999b) *The Emergence of Social Enterprises in Europe. A Short Overview*, EMES European Network, Brussels.

EVERS, A. (1995) 'Part of the Welfare Mix: The Third Sector as an Intermediate Area', *Voluntas*, vol. 6, 2: 159–82.

GUI, B. (1991) 'The Economic Rationale for the Third Sector', *Annals of Public and Co-operative Economics*, vol. 62, 4: 551–72.

HANSMANN, H. (1987) 'Economic Theories of Nonprofit Organisations', in POWELL, W. (ed.) *The Nonprofit Sector. A Research Handbook*, Yale University Press, New Haven, 27–42.

JAMES, E. and ROSE-ACKERMAN, S. (1986) *The Non-profit Enterprise in Market Economies: Fondamentals of Pure and Applied Economics*, Harwood Academic Publishers, London.

LAVILLE, J.-L. (ed.) (1994) *L'économie solidaire*, Desclée de Brouwer, Paris.

LAVILLE, J.-L. and SAINSAULIEU, R. (eds) (1997) *Sociologie de l'association*, Desclée de Brouwer, Paris.

MERTENS, S. (1999) 'Nonprofit Organizations and Social Economy: Two Ways of Understanding the Third Sector', *Annals of Public and Co-operative Economics*, vol. 70, 3: 501–20.

OECD (1999) *Social Enterprises*, OECD, Paris.

PESTOFF, V.A. (1998) *Beyond Market and State. Social Enterprises and Civil Democracy in a Welfare Society*, Ashgate, Aldershot.

—— (1992) 'Third Sector and Co-operative Services. An Alternative to Privatization', *Journal of Consumer Policy*, vol. 15: 21–45.

ROSE-ACKERMAN, S. (ed.) (1986) *The Economics of Non-profit Institutions. Structure and Policy*, Oxford University Press, New York.

SALAMON, L.M. (1997) 'The United States', in SALAMON, L.M. and ANHEIER, H.K. *Defining the Nonprofit Sector: A Cross-National Analysis*, Johns Hopkins Nonprofit Sector Series, vol. 4, Manchester University Press, Manchester, 280–319.

SALAMON, L.M. and ANHEIER, H.K. (1994) *The Emerging Sector: An Overview*, The Johns Hopkins University Institute for Policy Studies, Baltimore.

SALAMON, L.M., ANHEIER, H.K. and Associates (1999) *Global Civil Society. Dimensions of the Nonprofit Sector*, The Johns Hopkins University Center for Civil Society Studies, Baltimore.

SCHUMPETER, J.A. (1934) *The Theory of Economic Development*, 3rd printing, 1963, Oxford University Press, New York.

SPEAR, R., DEFOURNEY, J., FAVREAU, L. and LAVILLE, J.-L. (eds) (2001) *Tackling Social Exclusion in Europe. The Contribution of the Social Economy*, Ashgate, Aldershot.

YOUNG, D. (1997) 'Non-profit Entrepreneurship', to be published in *International Encyclopedia of Public Administration*.

—— (1986) 'Enterpreneurship and the Behavior of Non-profit Organizations: Elements of a Theory', in ROSE-ACKERMAN, S. (ed.) *The Economics of Non-profit Institutions*, Oxford University Press, New York, 161–84.

—— (1983) *If Not for Profit, for What?*, Lexington Books, Lexington, MA.

Part I

Social enterprises in the fifteen EU countries

1 Austria

Social enterprises and new childcare services

Kai Leichsenring

Introduction

The Austrian welfare mix, i.e. the division of tasks among various actors to provide social security and to sustain social cohesion, has been shaped mainly by the following historical traditions and developments: first, the important historical influence of the Catholic church and its social welfare paradigms and, in particular, the principle of subsidiarity; second, the importance of welfare organisations affiliated to the socialist (now social democratic) movement, which favoured consumer co-operatives rather than producer co-operatives; and third, the corporatist approach to state regulation (*Sozialpartnerschaft*).[1] Another important feature of the Austrian society after 1945 has been the far-reaching 'pillarisation', which has created a universe of (welfare) organisations affiliated to political parties or religious entities.

In addition, it has to be underlined that the Austrian system of social security is characterised by an extremely high share of benefits in cash, which make up to 73 per cent of the total social security expenditures, education excluded (Badelt and Österle 1998). Social services and other in-kind benefits to combat poverty and social exclusion are generally organised and funded by the regional governments within their specific Social Welfare Acts.

With respect to active labour-market policies and/or policies against social exclusion, Austria has been, since the 1970s, one of the OECD countries with the lowest rate of unemployment. This has been due, *inter alia*, to a largely nationalised industry, which was heavily subsidised during the economic crisis of the 1970s. However, the times when Austria had been labelled an 'island of the blessed' have receded, and problems connected to unemployment and social exclusion have increased in political importance during the past ten to fifteen years.

In the beginning of the 1980s, the Austrian government, and in particular the Ministry of Labour and Social Affairs, introduced – in addition to traditional training and mobility programmes – specific instruments to support reintegration of long-term unemployed persons into the 'normal' labour market. This so-called 'experimental labour market policy' included subsidies for projects in disadvantaged rural and alpine regions, the foundation of self-governed firms, and an action programme to create, initially, 8,000 jobs for long-term unemployed by means of subsidies for training, wage subsidies and projects promoted by local governments or non-profit organisations. This latter action programme, which was commonly called '*Aktion 8,000*', has been the main instrument of the experimental labour-market policy, as it allowed public and non-profit organisations to create new and/or additional jobs in the areas of social welfare services, and cultural or environmental activities.[2] In 1996, *Aktion 8,000* was renamed Public Integration Allowance (*GEB, Gemeinnützige Eingliederungsbeihilfe*), but its main characteristic remained unchanged. During a pre-defined period of time (usually one year), it provides up to two-thirds of labour costs, as an incentive to create jobs in non-profit organisations. Since 1984, about 50,000 long-term unemployed have benefited from this scheme. *Aktion 8,000* (now *GEB*) assisted the traditional welfare associations, and in addition, the programme helped to create social-economic enterprises (*Sozialökonomische Betriebe*) in Austria.

This contribution will focus on initiatives that were introduced since the 1980s using the instruments of the experimental labour-market policies such as *Aktion 8,000/GEB*. These policies have been administered by the Ministry of Labour and Social Affairs and the Labour Market Administration (*Arbeitsmarktverwaltung*). The latter was partly privatised in 1994; it is now called the Labour Market or Employment Service (*AMS, Arbeitsmarktservice*).[3] In the first section
we will provide an overview of the newly emerging initiatives, projects and enterprises. We will focus especially on different types of work-integration projects. In the second section, the definition of social enterprises in Austria will be examined. The third section will then focus on one particular area of personal social services, namely childcare, in which social enterprises have helped to create new jobs, to promote new ways of delivering services and, at the same time, to fight social exclusion of disadvantaged groups.

1   Traditions of local co-operatives, socio-economic enterprises and social welfare associations

To analyse the emergence of social enterprises in Austria, it is necessary to distinguish different, sometimes overlapping, spheres and the development of intermediary organisations. Such bodies help to maintain the social fabric, to reintegrate special target groups into work and/or society, to cover areas in which merely market-oriented organisations are not active, and to offer complementary responses to statutory measures. Several types of initiatives can be considered as 'social enterprises' as defined for the purpose of this study. In this section, we will focus more specifically on those that can be described as work-integration enterprises.

Self-governed local employment initiatives

The first kinds of organisations can be defined as self-governed local employment initiatives. Self-governed producer co-operatives can be classified among these. Since the beginning of the 1980s, when structural unemployment started to increase, and governmental subsidies for such projects were provided, some local initiatives of this kind came into being. They were particularly influenced by OECD programmes with respect to rural development and local employment initiatives (*BMSV* 1984). For instance, several craft firms in structurally weak regions that were threatened with bankruptcy were transformed into co-operatives to secure jobs. This development was followed up by the foundation of two quasi-public consultancy organisations specialising in such initiatives, as well as in consulting services for other non-profit organisations. Initially, the emphasis of these initiatives was much more on autonomy and self-government than on employment as such (*BMSV* 1984).

These initiatives obtained rather good results in terms of employment, but a steady increase of their number and a dissemination of the values of self-governance could not be achieved. An evaluation of twenty-nine such co-operatives (crafts, tourism and culture, trade and services) which had been founded between 1981 and 1991 and supported by active labour-market policies demonstrated the following (Paulesich 1996):

- usually, the co-operatives had started as associations that held the largest part of limited liability companies, but they had evolved into conventional firms (with single owners), limited liability companies with external partners or even public limited companies;
- with respect to returns on investment, personnel costs and cash flow, all co-operatives showed positive results. Problems existed with respect to liquid assets;
- the original employment objective was achieved in twenty-two of the twenty-nine co-operatives and especially, in small industrial firms, where the labour force increased;
- interviews with the current management showed that the 'co-operative idea' that had initially guided the organisation had eroded. While nineteen firms had been founded on grounds of self-government, only nine mentioned this guiding principle at the time of the survey. This might be due to the fact that more than 50 per cent of the founding members had left.

The general climate of co-operation was reported to be satisfactory, and the instrument of self-government was characterised as an important mechanism to improve the quality of working conditions and, in particular, to facilitate the foundation of a new enterprise (Paulesich 1996).

Social-economic projects

A second category of organisations that has developed within the realm of experimental labour-market policies arose from socio-economic projects aimed at providing (temporary) employment and training for disadvantaged groups (homeless, young unemployed, women, people with disabilities). These projects have often been initiated by social workers, particularly in areas such as environmental activities, culture and social services. Even if the target groups are heavily disadvantaged on the general labour market, the main aim of these projects is to provide transitory assistance and to reintegrate their trainees or clients into the general labour market. Unemployed persons thus receive training to qualify or requalify for jobs through apprenticeships or other means leading to qualifications for trades and services.

However, many of these projects have become established enterprises – a fact which is reflected in their new identity as so-called Social Economic Enterprises (*Sozialökonomische Beschäftigungsbetriebe*). Although their commercial performance is somewhat reduced by the fact that most workers try to leave the enterprise after a limited period of time, the commercial aims of these firms are part of their basic philosophy. This is expressed, for instance, by their organisational and legal form as limited liability companies (*GesmbH*). These projects or firms are, on average, recouping about 37 per cent of their costs from their economic activities. About 48 per cent of the overall budget of about 400 millions Austrian Shillings (about 29 million Euro) is co-funded by the *AMS*, and the remaining 16 per cent is covered by provincial governments and – since 1995 – increasingly by the European Social Fund (*AMS* 1997).

In 1996, there were forty-five such enterprises offering 719 jobs to 1,606 temporarily employed persons. In addition, about 315 persons, the so-called 'key staff', were employed. The number of projects remained stable in the past six years, while the numbers of key staff and temporary staff increased (by 25 per cent and 40 per cent respectively) between 1992 and 1996. As far as the gender and age structure of staff is concerned, it has to be noted that, interestingly enough, the number of women in these enterprises is relatively low (about 30 per cent). About one-third of the transitory staff are under twenty-five, and about 21 per cent are over forty (*AMS* 1997).

With respect to the performance of these social economic enterprises, two aspects have to be considered. In the first place, figures for the employment effects, in terms of transitory staff who left the enterprises during 1996, show that on average, about one-third of the workers were transferred to the general labour market; about 8 per cent went into further training; 27 per cent left the firms as pensioners, on family leave etc; and 31 per cent left the firms but remained unemployed. The overall average, however, tells only part of the story. In reality, there are huge differences between the individual firms and between provinces. For instance, the proportion of persons who re-entered the labour market during 1996 ranges from 23 per cent in the five social enterprises in Carinthia, to 56 per cent in the three enterprises in Burgenland. The proportion of persons who had left the enterprises but had remained unemployed during this period is between 18 and 40 per cent (*AMS* 1997).

Secondly, the economic performance must be taken into account. The selected enterprises generate between 8 and 82 per cent – on average about 34 per cent – of their total budget by their own economic activities. *AMS* subsidies represent on average 8 per cent, while other subsidies (mainly provided by regional or local authorities) amount to 27 per cent (*AMS* 1997). Subsidies are needed to cover investments, social and pedagogic support, and unforeseen events. A study conducted in the early 1990s (Biffl *et al.* 1996) showed, for instance, that the more or less constant staff turnover calls for special organisational attention by key staff.

Much depends on the type of economic activity and on the type of persons joining (and leaving) the enterprise. For instance, *BAN* (in the province of Styria) is focusing on homeless persons and ex-prisoners. It provides thirty transitory and fifteen key-staff jobs in the area of environmental counselling (recycling) and clearance of refuse. This kind of work is also offered by the *ARGE Nichtsesshaftenhilfe*, in Vienna, while *Chamäleon* (also in the province of Styria) is active in general services (household, gardening etc.) and textiles (patchwork, tablecloth, rugs) and offers fifteen transitory jobs for long-term unemployed girls and women, people with disabilities and former drug addicts.

'Sheltered workshops Ltd'

In Austria, a special legal status for enterprises with a social aim has been developed only for sheltered workshops. These workshops offer regular employment to persons with disabilities (according to defined eligibility criteria) and function as special forms of limited liability companies within the framework of the Disabled Persons Employment Act. Thus, additional subsidies for these companies are guaranteed directly by the state.

Since 1979, nine sheltered workshops have been founded. They currently employ about 1,200 persons, three-quarters of whom are persons with disabilities, who are paid wages according to norms stipulated by a general collective agreement. These sheltered workshops produce goods in the areas of skilled trades (metal, wood, printing, textiles) and services (copying, laundry). The turnover is about 400 million Austrian Shillings per year (about 29 million Euro) including about 25 per cent subsidies (Blumberger and Jungwirth 1996).

Other initiatives focusing on social inclusion and support to employment

Apart from the regional labour market exchange offices run by the Employment Service (*AMS*), there are special information points, usually organised by non-profit organisations or associations, which focus on persons with specific social problems such as personal debts, illicit drug use, psychiatric problems, or on victims of discrimination or violence. Such centres offer counselling and information (on mental health and social problems, job seeking, family and life planning, etc.) as well as facilities for communication, leisure time and other activities.

In Vienna, there are about sixteen such information points, established by different provider organisations. They offer, for instance, information with respect to childcare needs, job application training or counselling for migrants and young unemployed persons. In addition, there are some initiatives that offer appropriate housing opportunities, such as 'women's houses' (*Frauenhäuser*), shelter for homeless persons, group housing for young people, people with disabilities and ex-prisoners.

Non-profit organisations providing personal and proximity services

In the area of social service provision, social welfare associations have a long-standing tradition, in particular those large voluntary organisations that are affiliated either to the political parties (*Volkshilfe*, *Hilfswerk*) or to the churches (*Caritas*, *Diakonie*). Apart from the general reimbursement and/or subsidies they receive from regional governments, these organisations have used the opportunities of the *Aktion 8,000/GEB* offered by the Employment Service (*AMS*) to co-finance additional or new kinds of services. Smaller initiatives and new associations have also been given the chance to develop innovative services by means of the *GEB*. Examples for such initiatives can be found particularly in the area of day-care for children (day-mothers, children's groups) which will be described in greater detail below.

2   Towards an understanding of social enterprises in Austria

Given the social, political and cultural background of Austria and the fact that – apart from sheltered workshops – there are no specific legal regulations with respect to organisations that are active in the sphere of social inclusion, it seems appropriate to conceive the term 'social enterprise' in a wide sense. In the Austrian situation, both self-governed employment initiatives, social economic enterprises, sheltered workshops, and associations active in the area of social services should be considered as social enterprises which address social exclusion, since they meet the following requirements:

- they have a permanent production activity of goods and/or services;
- they have a relatively high degree of autonomy;
- they are characterised by a significant level of economic risk (which tends to rise over time);
- their operation is based on paid work, although unpaid voluntary work and partly remunerated or 'paid' volunteering can sometimes be observed. For instance, associations have boards that consist of volunteers who may receive some remuneration for their expenses. Another example would be 'children's groups' in which parents collaborate in order to keep monetary contributions to an affordable level.

The legal forms of social welfare associations and/or non-profit organisations are usually based on the Association Act (*Vereinsgesetz*). This Act regulates the registration procedures, some tax exemptions and general rules on accountability, compulsory functions and basic rules. However, some traditional associations and new initiatives, particularly those with economic activities, have turned into the organisational form of a private limited liability company (*GesmbH*), as the board of an association is liable for all financial risks linked to the association's activities. Some initiatives have also turned into registered societies (*Gesellschaft Bürgerlichen Rechts*) or co-operatives (*Genossenschaft*), although the legal regulations for each of these are quite complicated in Austria.

It must be underlined that all the organisations enumerated above are important agents for the maintenance of the Austrian social fabric, i.e. they are the basis of civil society, social inclusion and social control.

The social initiatives that have been founded during the past ten to fifteen years explicitly focus on three main objectives: offering employment opportunities; promoting (re)integration by means of training; and achieving a good economic performance through a market-oriented approach. At the same time, their principles and those of other voluntary organisations are deeply rooted in associative and co-operative concepts with a long-standing history (Hautmann and Kropf 1976; Tálos 1981). Notwithstanding this history and the respective linguistic meanings, it would be useful to introduce the term 'social enterprise' into Austrian discourse (complementary to the already existing term *Sozialökonomischer Betrieb*) in order to promote a specific kind of innovative organisational form focusing on social inclusion in changing 'labour societies'.

The term social enterprise will thus be used in the following section to describe a specific form of childcare services that has developed during the past twenty years in Austria, particularly in Vienna. In order to comprehend this evolution, we will first give a short overview of childcare services in the context of more market-oriented service delivery.

3   Social enterprises in the area of childcare

Ongoing debates on reform of the welfare state offer opportunities to reconsider the reality of welfare production and to develop new ways of planning, steering, providing and controlling personal social services. On the one hand, this means acknowledging the different agencies that are producing welfare – including households, private non-profit organisations, social initiatives, statutory providers, market-regulated supply – and discussing appropriate regulations for a mixed social welfare economy (Evers and Olk 1996; OECD 1996). On the other hand, new models of public management have been introduced which seek to promote more market-oriented methods in planning, financing and providing social services. These methods include a split between clients and providers, more competition and a new notion of social services as products with defined costs and outcomes. Thus, reforms should support and strengthen the non-governmental type of service provision, for instance by means of contracting-out and compulsory competitive tendering (Naschold 1995). This development should also result in better conditions for newly emerging social initiatives if they can prove their impact and their usefulness with respect to filling the gaps between reduced statutory provisions and the market.

In Austria, these developments have been introduced in a somewhat oblique way. Of course, there is also a general trend for cost-cutting and austerity in social welfare policy, for more efficiency in public management and more market orientation. However, most emphasis is still being put on the difference between the state and the market, rather than on intermediary organisations. Nevertheless, and given the existing structure of social welfare provision in Austria, debates about 'new public management' and the 'welfare mix' are worthwhile. We would like to exemplify this by focusing our attention on the area of childcare.[4]

The Austrian welfare mix in the area of childcare

Day-care for children is only just about to be acknowledged as a statutory responsibility with corresponding rights for parents with children. Given the fact that there is still no parental right to childcare facilities, the discussion has become more contentious during the past few years, especially with changing life patterns and expectations of younger women claiming equal opportunities and the right to combine family and employment.

Up to now, the responsibility for expanding day-care facilities for children has been with the provincial governments and municipalities, who have often contracted out the provision of services to the large voluntary non-profit organi-

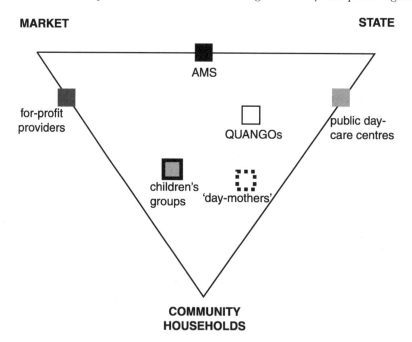

Figure 2   The welfare triangle of childcare in Austria

sations. In addition, and due to the lack of adequate facilities in terms of quantity and quality (e.g. inflexible opening hours), the number of small-scale initiatives has been mushrooming.

Figure 2 illustrates the existence of a mix of different providers that are serving different needs with various standards and rationales. However, this situation has not resulted from conscious decisions about financing and the different roles and functions of the various actors. For instance, associations have not always been considered as partners by public policy-makers but more often than not as opponents, although they helped to improve quality standards in terms of user-friendly and flexible service provision.

In this situation, the Employment Service (*AMS*) – a kind of hybrid organisation itself – has played an important intermediary role, especially in Vienna, where about 65,000 children are frequenting one or the other type of day-care centre (50 per cent public, 50 per cent voluntary organisations, as shown in Table 1.1). During the past few years the Employment Service has introduced

Table 1.1 Childcare facilities in Vienna: places, employed staff and turnover, 1997

Provider	Places	Staff	Turnover (in thousands)	Average yearly costs per child
Public childcare facilities	32,378	5,500	3,171,000 ATS (230,446 Euro)	97,958 ATS (7,119 Euro)
Private and voluntary non-profit providers	33,908	3,644	1,256,000 ATS (91,277 Euro)	
Private day-care centres in Vienna	9,000	900	339,000 ATS (24,636 Euro)	37,667 ATS (2,737 Euro)
Catholic day-care centres	11,288	844	385,000 ATS (27,979 Euro)	34,135 ATS (2,481 Euro)
Kinderfreunde	9,762	1,100	350,000 ATS (25,435 Euro)	35,853 ATS 2,606 Euro)
'Children in Vienna' (KIWI)	700	96	32,000 ATS (2,326 Euro)	46,214 ATS (3,358 Euro)
Day-mothers ('Parents for children')	165	69	15,000 ATS (1,090 Euro)	94,303 ATS (6,853 Euro)
Wiener Hilfswerk (day- mothers)	109	38	8,000 ATS (581 Euro)	73,835 ATS (5,366 Euro)
Viennese Children's Groups	480	89	30,000 ATS (2,180 Euro)	62,975 ATS (4,577 Euro)
Forum of Children's Groups	72	14	5,000 ATS (363 Euro)	65,944 ATS (4,792 Euro)
Other providers	1,300	150	55,000 ATS (3,997 Euro)	42,700 ATS (3,103 Euro)
Freelance day-mothers	1,032	344	37,000 ATS (2,689 Euro)	36,000 ATS (2,616 Euro)
Total	66,286	9,144	4,427,000 ATS (321,723 Euro)	66,825 ATS (4,856 Euro)

Source: *Gemeinde Wien* (MA 11); provider organisations, own estimates

three different instruments of active labour-market policy. These are oriented towards both parents and institutional childcare providers:

*   the Child Care Allowance (*KBH, Kinderbetreuungsbeihilfe*) is a cash transfer targeted at low-income parents so that they can afford day-care services for their children, if they need such services after having found a job;
*   the Subsidy for Child Care Providers (*KBE, Beihilfe für Kinderbetreuungsein-richtungen*) is a special scheme within the already mentioned *GEB*. It provides supportive wage subsidies (66 per cent of wages) for a period of up to three years (instead of only one year) and is geared towards childcare providers so that they can afford to employ more (formerly unemployed) nursing staff;
*   support for training of unemployed men and women as professional child-care staff (day-mother/day-father).

These instruments particularly helped to support innovative service providers, such as associations that employ and organise day-mothers (child-minders) and initiatives that organise children's groups, i.e. small groups of about twelve children with two nurses (child-minders). The initiatives are like parents' co-operatives (comparable to *Kinderläden* in Germany). Although both these approaches make up only about 2 per cent of the entire childcare market in Vienna, they are of particular interest with respect to the involvement of parents and staff.

Parents have to pay different contributions to public and private voluntary

Table 1.2   Parents' monthly contributions for forty hours of care per week, 1997

Provider/kind of care	From	To
Public childcare facilities[a]	*0 ATS (0 Euro)*	*2,870 ATS (209 Euro)*
Private and voluntary non-profit providers		
Private day-care centres Vienna[b]	2,900 ATS (211 Euro)	4,600 ATS (334 Euro)
Catholic day-care centres	1,420 ATS (103 Euro)	2,700 ATS (196 Euro)
Kinderfreunde[b]	2,290 ATS (166 Euro)	2,935 ATS (213 Euro)
'Children in Vienna' (KIWI)[b]	2,950 ATS (214 Euro)	3,800 ATS (276 Euro)
Day-mothers ('Parents for Children')[b]	2,700 ATS (196 Euro)	3,000 ATS (218 Euro)
Wiener Hilfswerk – day-mothers[b]	2,900 ATS (211 Euro)	3,000 ATS (218 Euro)
Viennese Children's Groups[c]	2,000 ATS (145 Euro)	3,000 ATS (218 Euro)
Forum of Children's Groups[c]	3,300 ATS (240 Euro)	4,000 ATS (291 Euro)

Sources: *Gemeinde Wien* (MA 11); different providers
Notes:
[a] contributions of parents depend on family income
[b] inclusive of meals
[c] without meals

Table 1.3 Shares (%) of funding with respect to the overall costs of different providers in Vienna, 1997

Provider	Municipality (%)	AMS (%)	Parents (%)	Others (%)
Public childcare facilities[a]	87.0	0.0	13.0[b]	(0.0)
Private and voluntary non-profit providers				
Private day-care centres Vienna	1.0	7.0	92.0	0.0
Catholic day-care centres	29.2	0.0	66.9	3.9
Kinderfreunde	33.0	0.1	48.0	18.9
'Children in Vienna' (KIWI)	38.0	4.0	55.0	3.0
Day-mothers ('Parents for Children')	42.0	33.0	25.0	0.0
Wiener Hilfswerk – day-mothers	50.0	14.0	34.0	2.0
Viennese Children's Groups	18.0	31.5	50.5	0.0
Forum of Children's Groups	16.0	25.0	59.0	0.0

Sources: *Gemeinde Wien* (MA 11); different providers

Notes:

[a] In 1997, the federal government also included a special budget line for the extension of childcare facilities; the municipality of Vienna received about 160 million ATS (about 11.6 million Euro), i.e. 4 per cent of the municipalities' budget for childcare, out of this federal programme

[b] Average – in reality, parents' contribution ranges from 0 to about 35 per cent

facilities (Table 1.2). Users of public services may benefit from the fact that individual contributions depend on the family income. Parents who use private voluntary providers usually pay between 2,000 and 3,000 ATS (145 to 218 Euro) per month (for forty hours of care per week, including meals). This situation is only marginally compensated by the *KBH*, an entitlement paid to low-income families as a reimbursement for childcare expenditures.

The unbalanced distribution of public finances is only marginally compensated by the *AMS* that supports, in particular, innovative facilities. Table 1.3 gives an overview of the specific mix in the economy of childcare facilities in Vienna.

Experiences of social enterprises who organise day-mothers and children's groups

The Viennese Children's Groups

The first Children's Groups in Vienna were founded at the beginning of the 1970s but it was only at the beginning of the 1980s that an umbrella organisation was created, by which time there were about forty autonomous Children's Groups. A definition of a Viennese Children's Group was agreed, i.e. it had to be 'founded and organised by parents and child-minders'. The objectives were to create facilities for the individual development of children, to offer opportunities to learn democratic and mutually supportive ways of living, and to organise childcare through co-operation between parents and child-minders by means of regular collaboration of the parents and monthly group meetings. These meetings served to take the most important decisions with respect to management and daily practice.

The umbrella organisation was founded in order to enter into negotiations with the municipality about complementary funding and relevant regulations. Until then, the individual associations were financed by parents' contributions (in kind and in cash) and by means of the *Aktion 8,000* only.

Currently, there are thirty-nine Children's Groups; they provide about 450 places for children between two and ten years. Altogether about ninety child-minders (at least two per group) are regularly employed, on average for about thirty hours per week. About 80 per cent of the child-minders are supported by the special scheme of the Employment Service (*KBE*). Most of the staff also received training provided by the umbrella organisation and financed by the Employment Service. A study showed that out of forty-nine participants in these courses, all of whom were long-term unemployed or never regularly employed before, about 50 per cent were still in regular employment three years later (Leichsenring *et al.* 1997).

The total cost of a Children's Group (about twelve children per group) is about 3,700 Euro per month. Parents pay on average about 190 Euro per month plus meals, altogether about 50 per cent of the overall costs. In addition, they provide, on average, about fifteen hours for cooking, cleaning, meetings etc. The municipality of Vienna pays a lump sum of about 70 Euro per child per month. The wage benefits of the Employment Service cover about one-third of the total costs.

The umbrella organisation has negotiated strongly with the municipality in order to achieve an agreement to secure the financing of the Children's Groups after the wage benefits of the Employment Service end (subsidies are paid for only three years per child-minder). Although a short-term subsidy has been granted, a long-term agreement still remains to be settled. Nevertheless, the umbrella organisation is currently drafting a new measure for advanced training of child-minders in Children's Groups and defining a specific job profile for a limited number of them. The social capital that is generated by this type of childcare organisation is both their main strength and their main weakness. The number of parents who are prepared to get actively involved in Children's Groups has proven to be limited, but networking on the national level is geared to promoting the particular advantages of Children's Groups insofar as they facilitate social learning both for children and for their parents.

The Day-Parents Centre in Vienna

The Day-Parents Centre is affiliated to a larger association called Parents for Children Austria that is also specialising in the area of adoption and foster care.

The starting point for this initiative was the huge demand in day-care facilities, which was articulated by foster parents. Thus, in 1989, Parents for Children approached the Employment Service to ask for financial support to develop courses for child-minders. Initially, these courses involved about 160 hours of training plus one week of practice. In addition, regular supervision and advanced training was obligatory. This form of training has been developed to the point that, in the future, more than 600 hours of training will be required in order to fulfil the specific job profile for day-mothers (see below). The evaluation by Leichsenring *et al.* (1997) showed that participants in courses for day-mothers that were financed by the Employment Service had been from among the most disadvantaged groups in the labour market. Out of eighty-three participants, only seventeen had been employed before the training, while almost two-thirds were employed one year after.

Currently, the Day-Parents Centre employs about sixty day-mothers who care for about 170 children. This means that, on average, each day-mother provides care for about three children. Children are aged between four months and seven years. Day-mothers of the Day-Parents Centre are employed regularly and remunerated according to the number of children that they care for (not more than four, including their own). For instance, for three children and forty hours per week, a day-mother earns the equivalent of the currently agreed minimum wage (about 900 Euro) plus a lump sum for meals.

The organisation is financed by means of user contributions (about 200 Euro per child per month), the municipality (40 per cent) and *KBE*-wage subsidies of the *AMS* (30 per cent). Without public subsidies, the service would be too dependent on user contributions and day-mothers could not be guaranteed regular employment – a practice that was applied at the beginning of this service. Thus, the continuity of subsidies, or a regulated market with clearly defined purchaser/provider relationships is of utmost importance to secure employment.

Given this background, the main objective of Parents for Children is to further professionalise the childcare sector by implementing the above-mentioned extended education (comprehensive curriculum) and by defining a proper job profile for day-mothers. These activities tend to develop within national and international networks. Networking on the national level (with similar organisations) and lobbying have resulted in negotiations towards a comprehensive curriculum to be regulated on the federal level or at least equally by all regions. An international project has helped to promote these objectives. The project, entitled Cinderella, is co-ordinated by Parents for Children in the framework of the EU Programme Employment NOW (New Opportunities for Women) and involves Austrian organisations with partners from Germany, Italy and the UK (Cinderella 2000). The search for common features in professional-ising this type of childcare in Europe also contributed to the fact that Cinderella and the aim to create 3,000 jobs for day-mothers in Austria are mentioned in the Austrian Action Plan for Employment.

Key challenges

With respect to social enterprises in the area of childcare, several tensions and contradictions remain to be tackled on the political and administrative levels. These include:

*   tension between central social policy tasks and the pluralism of providers: social policy objectives with respect to universal rights, guarantees for childcare facilities and quality have to be balanced with specific needs of different user groups;
*   tension between statutory responsibilities and individual rights and duties: the question is whether childcare may be defined as a 'public good', especially with respect to social and economic integration of (potential) users. If labour-market participation is the only way to prevent social exclusion, equal chances will also be promoted through the existence of decent childcare facilities;
*   tensions among different statutory and quasi-public bodies: the complexity of the federal constitution, in combination with the fact that there are several quasi-non-governmental bodies responsible for social security, increases the need for co-ordinating mechanisms, i.e. the continuous harmonisation of aims and means, if the objective is to create a balanced welfare mix in Austria. Given the lack of even informal communication among the different bodies, this seems to be of major importance;
*   tensions between democratic values, increasing user-orientation and user-involvement, respectively, and new values of choice and market-orientation: new ways of participation and partly autonomous organisation of services are challenging statutory providers as well as financing bodies. With the increasing number of private providers that are accepted or even self-organised by the users, public providers (and their specific way of organising and financing service provision) will become a reservoir for those who are not able to finance alternative facilities, unless they take on their competitors. In effect this means that public providers try to secure their privileged market position not only by means of more competitive prices but also by quality standards of service (e.g. more flexible opening hours, more user involvement etc.).

Conclusions

Undoubtedly, social services are among those areas in which additional employment opportunities are envisaged. At the same time, social services are at the forefront of the effort to combat social exclusion. Thus it seems only logical to conceive and to promote organisational forms that combine both the employment factor and concepts of social exchange, self-organisation and community orientation. Social enterprises that are guided by these fundamental values are therefore important partners for public authorities in particular, if the latter are seeking to increase their steering capacities as against their capacities for producing services.

There is a good chance for the growth of social enterprises in the area of social service delivery if both sides – social enterprises themselves and the state – agree on their mutual benefits and shortcomings. On the one hand, the evolution of a regulated 'quasi-market' equal for all actors would be necessary to reduce bureaucracy, hierarchical dependencies and financial constraints. On the other hand, a debate on social enterprises with respect to their specific status, e.g. a debate about a legal regulation for 'social enterprises', could help to develop common strategies and guidelines. The first steps have been taken in both directions but it will still take time, organisational learning and political will for social enterprises to find their identity in a well-balanced welfare triangle in Austria.

Notes

1   The system of social partnership has served as an instrument to reduce tensions between work and capital by means of mutual consultation; collective bargaining that went far beyond the regulation of wages and labour law; and tripartite political exchange between the unions, employers' organisations, and the state. An important precondition for the functioning of this regulation mechanism, which helped to secure social development and peace, was the fact that, after the Second World War and occupation, major industries were nationalised so that all actors involved had a common interest in this kind of governance.

2   For an extended analysis, see Lehner (1998); Fehr-Duda *et al.* (1995a, 1995b); *AMS* (1996).

3   One could argue that active labour-market policies in Austria have partly been privatised or, else, that the organisational framework for these policies was changed into a more 'hybrid' form, between the state and the market. Suspicions are that this kind of 'hybridisation' is avoiding investments in active labour market rather than enhancing a more pro-active strategy towards public stimulation of employment opportunities, but it is too early to demonstrate a definitive turn-around. In particular, the latest engagement in employment policies on the EU level (National Plans of Action for Employment) has given hope to some new initiatives.

4   See also Evers and Leichsenring (1996).

Bibliography

ALTHALER, K.S. and DIMMEL, N. (1993) 'Sozialpolitische Handlungsfelder der experimentellen Arbeitsmarktpolitik. Aushandlungsformen, Kooperation und Konflikt zwischen Arbeitsmarktverwaltung, Ländern und Gemeinden', *ÖZP*, vol. 22, 3: 343–60.

AMS (Arbeitsmarktservice Österreich) (various years) *Sozialökonomische Betriebe*, Jahresberichte, *AMS* Österreich, Wien.

BADELT, C. and ÖSTERLE, A. (1998) *Grundzüge der Sozialpolitik – Band 2: Sozialpolitik in Österreich*, Manz, Wien.

BIFFL, G., HOFER, H. and PICHELMANN, K. (1996) 'Sozialökonomische Beschäftigungsprojekte und soziale Kursmaßnahmen', in *AMS* (ed.) *Ergebnisse der innovativen Arbeitsmarktpolitik*, Wissenschaftsverlag, *AMS* report, no. 1, Wien, 7–25.

BLUMBERGER, W. and JUNGWIRTH, Ch. (1996) *Geschützte Werkstätten GmbH – Unternehmen mit sozialpolitischem Auftrag, Bundesministerium für Arbeit und Soziales* (Forschungsberichte aus Sozial- und Arbeitsmarktpolitik, no. 57), Wien.

Bundesministerium für Soziale Verwaltung (1984) *Lokale Beschäftigungsinitiativen in Österreich, BMSV* (Forschungsberichte aus Sozial- und Arbeitsmarktpolitik, no. 6), Wien.

CINDERELLA Network (2000) 'Edu-carer. A New Professional Role in Family Based Childcare', Vienna (mimeo).

EVERS, A. and OLK, T. (eds) (1996) *Wohlfahrtspluralismus. Vom Wohlfahrtsstaat zur Wohlfahrtsgesellschaft*, Westdeutscher Verlag, Opladen.

EVERS, A. and LEICHSENRING, K. (1996) *Reduktion oder Redefinition politischer Verantwortung? Modernisierung sozialer Dienste in Delft und Stockholm*, Europäisches Zentrum (Eurosocial Report, no. 60), Wien.

FEHR-DUDA, H., FRÜHSTÜCK, B., LECHNER, F., NEUDORFER, P., REITER, W. and RIESENFELDER, A. (1995a) *Anforderungsgerecht. Die Wirkung des Beschäftigungsprogrammes Aktion 8000*, L&R Sozialforschung/AMS Österreich, Wien.

FEHR-DUDA, H., LECHNER, F., NEUDORFER, P., REITER, W. and RIESEN-FELDER, A. (1995b) *Die Effektivität arbeitsmarktpolitischer Beschäftigungsmaßnahmen in Österreich. Ergebnis einer Wirkungsanalyse der 'Aktion 8000'*, Wissenschaftsverlag (*AMS* Studien, no. 1), Wien.

HAUTMANN, H. and KROPF, R. (1976) *Die Österreichische Arbeiterbewegung vom Vormärz bis 1945. Sozialökonomische Ursprünge ihrer Ideologie und Politik*, Europa Verlag, Wien.

Institut für Arbeitsmarktbetreuung und -forschung (eds) (1997) *Arbeitsmarktpolitische Maßnahmen in Wien*, IFA, Wien.

LEHNER, P.U. (1998) 'Autriche: Des initiatives récentes ancrées dans une forte tradition d'action publique', in DEFOURNY, J., FAVREAU, L. and LAVILLE, J.-L. (eds) *Insertion et nouvelle économie sociale. Un bilan international*, Desclée de Brouwer, Paris, 245–62.

LEICHSENRING, K., THENNER, M., FINDER, R. and PRINZ, CH. (1997) *Beschäftigungspolitische Aspekte der Kinderbetreuung in Wien. Evaluationsstudie im Auftrag des AMS*, European Centre, Wien.

NASCHOLD, F. (1995) *Ergebnissteuerung, Wettbewerb, Qualitätspolitik. Entwicklungspfade des Öffentlichen Sektors in Europa*, Sigma, Berlin.

OECD (1996) *Reconciling Economy and Society. Towards a Plural Economy*, OECD, Paris.

PAULESICH, R. (1996) 'Kooperative Unternehmensgründungen. Die Zehnjahresbilanz eines Instruments zur Arbeitsmarktförderung', in *AMS* (ed.) *Ergebnisse der innovativen Arbeitsmarktpolitik*, Wissenschaftsverlag (*AMS* report, no. 1), Wien, 47–63.

Plattform der OÖ. Sozialprojekte (ed.) (1997) *Für viele ein Neubeginn … – 110 Oberösterreichische Sozialprojekte in Selbstdarstellungen*, Plattform der OÖ. Sozialprojekte, Linz.

TÁLOS, E. (1981) *Staatliche Sozialpolitik in Österreich. Rekonstruktion und Analyse*, Verlag für Gesellschaftskritik, Wien.

2 Belgium

Social enterprises in community services

Jacques Defourny and Marthe Nyssens

Introduction

From the beginning of the 1990s, the social economy began to be gradually recognised as a third sector, made up of co-operatives, mutuals and associations. In fact, however, its roots lie far back in the workers' and peasants' associations of the last century, and they have been growing throughout the twentieth century. The co-operative movement has long been present in the agricultural sector, in credit and insurance and in pharmaceutical distribution. Since the end of the Second World War, mutual societies have been heavily involved in the organisation of the national health insurance scheme and the provision of a variety of associated services. But it is the associations that have formed far the largest part of the Belgian social economy. Fairly recent statistical studies show that they account for around 305,000 paid jobs[1] and that the volunteer work which they mobilise represents more than 100,000 full-time job equivalents. Belgium, along with Ireland and the Netherlands, is one of the countries in which the non-profit sector carries the most weight (Salamon, Anheier and Associates 1998).

Though an increasingly broad consensus exists about the concept of the social economy,[2] the idea of the social enterprise is more recent and less well defined. The term is nevertheless more and more frequently used, with a dual meaning.

On the one hand, it tends to be used to stress the entrepreneurial approach taken by an increasing number of organisations in the social economy, particularly by the many associations that are developing commercial activities. This trend is reflected, *inter alia*, in the introduction of a new legal framework. In 1995, the Belgian Parliament approved a law allowing the creation of 'companies with a social purpose'. This law concerns all kinds of commercial companies (including co-operative societies and private limited company). Since July 1996, any commercial company may be called 'company with a social purpose' (*SFS, Société à finalité sociale*) if it is 'not dedicated to the enrichment of its members' and if its articles of association respect a series of conditions.[3] So far, however, this legal status has met with only limited success since it brings with it a considerable number of requirements in addition to those associated with the traditional company.[4] This legal framework will only become attractive for players in the social economy if future measures yield financial and other advantages for *SFS* insofar as they provide services to the community and/or compensate for the specific costs which handicap them.

On the other hand, the term 'social enterprise' is also used to designate all or some of the initiatives promoted by co-operatives or associations aimed at the occupational integration of people excluded from the labour market.[5] During the last two decades there have been many innovative experiments in this field, which have gradually been recognised and are increasingly supported by the public authorities. These different kinds of organisations have already been the subject of several studies,[6] which is why they will simply be briefly listed here before moving on to examine another large area of activities, viz. that of community services, where social enterprises are emerging in ever greater numbers and showing significant potential for growth.

1   Social enterprises and work integration

The initiatives we find in the field of work integration fall into two major categories, according to whether they offer their target public training through fixed term work or more stable jobs.

Work-based training

During the 1980s, a series of small enterprises was set up, with the legal form of non-profit association, to offer people who had broken with the traditional education system an opportunity to work whilst receiving training through supervision by specialised monitors. These enterprises developed on the fringes of the law. It was not until 1987 that 'enterprises for occupational training' (*EAP, Entreprises d'Apprentissage Professionnel*) were recognised. In April 1995 the public authorities of the Walloon Region[7] adopted a new decree broadening the conditions of access for trainees and renaming the former *EAP*s and some other associations working in the field 'enterprises for training through work' (*EFT, Entreprises de Formation par le Travail*). In 1999, there were around sixty *EFT*s in French-speaking Belgium. These structures offered in total around 1,000 training places, and about 2,000 trainees passed through the system each year.

In Flanders, rather similar formulas exist under various names, e.g. 'on-the-job training enterprises' (*Leerwerkbedrijven* or *leerwerkplaatsen*) or 'work-experience projects' (*Werkervaringsprojecten*). The main distinguishing features of work-based training in Flanders are certainly the absence of strict criteria for entry, and the type of status offered to people receiving training, which is close to a work contract.

Job-creation initiatives

Sheltered workshops

Initiatives for helping the least qualified to find a lasting job were at first aimed at people with a physical or mental disability. In Belgium, in 1999, there were more than 170 sheltered workshops or 'adapted work enterprises' (*Entreprises de Travail Adapté*); they offered stable paid work to around 20,000 disabled people. Employees take part in the production of goods and services sold on the market, which ensures a relatively high degree of self-financing (on average 60 per cent) for these private enterprises. They take the legal form of non-profit association and receive public subsidies under strict rules. These subsidies are meant to enable them to finance the supervision of disabled people and to compensate for their lower productivity.

Social workshops (Sociale werkplaatsen)

In Flanders, the idea of sheltered jobs, which had hitherto been reserved for people with physical and mental disabilities, found broader application in the last two decades. Since the beginning of the 1980s, particularly disadvantaged people with serious 'socio-occupational disabilities' (i.e. people who are poorly qualified, illiterate, have a criminal record or a difficult family background etc.) have been employed in 'social workshops'. These organisations are developing some commercial activities but need a high degree of subsidy. In 1994, the Flemish Region government allowed them an experimental legal and financial framework which was stabilised in 1998. In the long term, regulations covering all sheltered employment (both sheltered workshops and social workshops) are expected.

In 1999, there were a little over eighty social workshops. These provided work for almost 900 people who had great difficulty in integration, and also provided about 150 supervisory posts.

Integration enterprises

Since the mid 1990s, a new stage has been reached with the appearance of enterprises with the same social purpose but which have a full market orientation. Though these enterprises need some public subsidies, particularly during the first years, their objective is to operate in the traditional markets and to get most of their resources there.

In Flanders, around twenty-five integration enterprises (*Invoegbedrijven*) have appeared during the course of the last few years. They aim at creating lasting jobs for long-term unemployed people with poor levels of qualification. These enterprises are founded with commercial company status. During the first three or four years, they receive significant public support to cover a decreasing proportion of the salaries of people undergoing integration.

In French-speaking Belgium, the King Baudouin Foundation has played a crucial role in supporting seven pilot projects in Wallonia and five in the Brussels Region. In 1998, these two Regions set out conditions for authorisation and subsidisation of integration enterprises. *Inter alia*, the latter must adopt *SFS* status and they receive, during the first years, a subsidy for covering the wages of the managing founder and of workers recruited from the target public. In 1999, more than thirty such integration enterprises were being supported through these measures.

In 1995, the Walloon Region also set up a public fund for the market-oriented social economy, the *SOWECSOM* (*Société Wallonne d'Économie Sociale Marchande*), to encourage enterprises of this type and indeed the whole of the social economy functioning commercially. The *SOWECSOM* is a public holding company with significant resources (around 12 million Euro), the purpose of which is to provide credit, guarantee other loans and make capital investments in enterprises.

2   Social enterprises and community services: the historical background

Though insertion through work has attracted a great deal of attention during this period of persistent high unemployment, we have chosen here to focus our analysis on another prime area for the development of social enterprises – what is more and more often referred to as 'proximity services' (*services de proximité*).

Community or proximity services are regularly evoked both as new sources of jobs to be explored urgently, and as a response to new needs which can be met neither by market forces nor by the intervention of the public authorities alone. The idea of community or proximity services is itself a rather broad one, but it has been gradually refined both as a concept and in practical terms.[8] We have therefore chosen to examine the particular role of social enterprises in such services with special reference to three specific areas which have been the subject of recent investigations, viz. social housing and the regeneration of deprived areas, home help and childcare (Gilain *et al.* 1998).

As we will see through an historical overview, each of these fields coincides, and in some cases has long coincided, with important initiatives designed to help groups on the margins of society. The similar or divergent development of these initiatives should throw light on the nature of social enterprises and the particular contribution they can make to the fight against social exclusion.

Social housing

The first initiatives

It is usual to claim that the great waves of development of the social economy correspond to the major changes in our economic systems, and a comparison is often made between the rapid industrialisation of the nineteenth century and the last twenty-five years, which have been marked by the recession which followed the oil crisis, the information technology revolution and the globalisation of the economy. Today's problems, such as deprived inner-city areas and suburbs and homelessness, can be seen in a new light if we examine the emergence of working-class housing, and then social housing, during the course of the nineteenth century.

Throughout the last century, Belgium, and especially Wallonia, which underwent industrialisation immediately after the industrial revolution in England, experienced great migrations of population within the country. At the time, no preparations were made to receive them and they were frequently housed in sub-human conditions. But to attract and keep the labour force as close as possible to enterprises which were sometimes located out of town, industrialists were also forced to take matters into their own hands. And so the first mining villages and workers' towns were built, from 1810–1820 onwards.

The first workers' dwellings thus originated in private business initiatives. Fears for the social order were also involved, as it was considered that through improved housing it might be possible to 'civilise' these poor, savage, starving and drunken labourers who were yet so necessary. However, in this climate, char-itable movements and political and social utopias also flourished, such as the '*familistères*' founded by Godin at Guise (near Lille) and also in Brussels and Liège.[9]

This mixture of social and economic motives, altruism and self-interest, can certainly be found nowadays in many initiatives for the regeneration of certain neighbourhoods and for the social reintegration of the homeless, beggars or other 'embarrassing' victims of social breakdown.[10]

The public authorities take up the challenge

The start of a genuine public policy for social housing only dates back to 1919 when the government set up a national housing fund to provide affordable housing.[11] With the creation of this fund, responsibility for building social housing was transferred from private to public initiative. However, instead of adopting a centralised approach, the public fund registered local societies throughout the country which were most often set up by local authorities.[12] During the 1950s, these societies built more than 7,000 dwellings a year, and this rate was more than doubled in the late 1970s in an attempt to stimulate the economy through major public works. So it may be said that social housing policy, which began as a measure to maintain order, was used as an instrument for smoothing the negative side-effects of the economic growth during the 1950s and 1960s and finally played a part in the fight against unemployment in the 1970s.

In the last decades, social housing has been in a very precarious situation. Firstly, many of the registered societies have experienced severe financial prob-lems, in part because rents have been hit by the falling incomes of many tenants. This led the public authorities to introduce the idea of profitability in social housing, obliging societies to attempt to balance their books and leading to a preference for tenants on average incomes. An important report on poverty published in 1994 indicates that of the 410,000 families who were then living below the poverty threshold, only 27 per cent received help from housing soci-eties. The remaining 300,000 families were forced to rent from the private sector, though at the same time the housing societies were letting 140,000 dwellings to families from outside their target group.[13] Moreover, over the years social housing has become a rich ground for vote-catching manœuvres, and this

evolution clearly shows in the many ways devised to by-pass the rules for allocation and priority.[14]

New initiatives

During the last decade, the impoverishment of many urban areas and the
housing problems experienced by increasingly marginalised groups have led to
the emergence of various innovative initiatives from the association sector.
Sometimes these have developed quite independently, but most often they have
come about in partnership with local or regional public authorities, because of
the extent of financial resources generally required in the property sector.

Broadly speaking, we can identify several types of initiatives. A first category
of organisations acts as an interface between, on the one hand, public and
private landlords, and, on the other hand, tenants who, without this mediation
and firm support, would be unable to gain the confidence of the landlords. The
first initiative of this kind dates back to 1989 and involved a partnership among
around a dozen associations.[15] The scheme was then taken up by the Walloon
Region government and is now available in every local authority area with more
than 50,000 inhabitants. These Social Estate Agencies (*AIS, Agences Immobilières
Sociales*) are now in essence quasi-local authority bodies, but depending on local
circumstances they may call more or less regularly on associations, *inter alia* to
provide social mentoring for their beneficiaries. Furthermore, as there is a real
risk that Social Estate Agencies will take on a managerial role which does not
encourage tenants to assume direct contractual responsibility *vis-à-vis* the
owners,[16] some associations have introduced a 'sliding lease' which empowers
tenants and leads them gradually towards a normal contractual relationship.

Other associations are investing in the renovation of unoccupied dwellings and
they generally depend upon public finance made available for this purpose.
Sometimes they involve the future tenants from the start through a 'self-renovation
contract'.

Associations have also been involved in setting up a number of campsites
which provide more or less long-term accommodation for people without
resources. Through organising collectively, these people try to have their rights
recognised in these somewhat unusual circumstances. Similar movements uniting
the homeless can also emerge following the occupation of abandoned buildings
('squatting').

The range of initiatives is, in fact, very wide (Prick 1994). Some associations
provide emergency accommodation for a few days, others provide short-term
accommodation, and some offer the possibility of renting a house on a long-
term basis, with perhaps even the chance to buy it.

The last few years have also seen the emergence of a growing number of
neighbourhood management schemes. Thirty or so are linked to social housing
companies and aim to provide training and rehabilitation for young people in
social estates through various kinds of work (minor repairs, maintenance of
public open space, etc.). A dozen more focus on urban regeneration, mobilising

local people to renovate depressed areas. However, although in principle these schemes are based on the French model of the *régies de quartier*, the Walloon versions tend to be the result of public authority or social housing company initiatives, which often limit their margin for manoeuvre and their entrepreneurial scope (Defourny 1998).

Childcare

The first initiatives

In a different field, but in the same socio-economic context, 1845 saw the appearance of the first crèches in Belgium. They too were private. Their origins were philanthropic or charitable, and they were organised by charitable societies and financed by individual subscriptions, by the church, by local and provincial authorities and by contributions from families towards child-minding costs. The purpose of these initiatives was to provide the children of mothers working in factories with day-care of a higher standard than that available in sordid and often clandestine nurseries (Dubois *et al.*1994).

The public authorities take up the challenge

Although there are clear differences between this field and that of social housing, the development of childcare shows the same increase in public authority intervention and, even more markedly, a parallel growth in the number of beneficiaries. Until the Second World War, crèches were among the measures set up to protect deprived children. However, during the 1960s, the attitude towards crèches gradually altered, and the laws of 1970 and 1971 profoundly changed their image, imposing standards of training and introducing a system of subsidy which no longer depended on the attendance of children from low-income families. Today, the social aspect of these services still shows in the fact that the financial contribution made by parents depends on their incomes. However, it is quite clear that this is an essential service for a large part of the population, irrespective of social class.[17] The services themselves are very varied and private bodies still represent a large proportion – sometimes even a majority – of the options available alongside public provision.[18]

New initiatives

The 1990s have seen the appearance of a large number of initiatives in this area to meet new needs thrown up by socio-economic changes. These include care for sick children, emergency childcare to enable unemployed people to attend vocational training courses or look for work, after-school schemes or 'flexible childcare' outside the normal opening hours of institutions. These initiatives originate in various ways, with the public bodies for vocational training, schools, local authorities, associations etc. The history of these schemes is often closely associated with 'social entrepreneurs' who have sought to find answers to newly emerging needs. Many initiatives began in small associations working in deprived neighbourhoods or districts to meet the needs of families in difficulty, particularly from a socio-professional point of view.

The sector has held a long and lively debate on the question of competent authorities for the regulation and financing of these initiatives. Should childcare be regarded as an aspect of family policy, and thus a regional and community responsibility in Belgium, or of social security, in view of its direct link with providing parents with access to work? Today the various competent authorities have reached an agreement on sharing this authority.[19]

Home help

The first initiatives

In the field of home-help activities, the first initiatives arose during another very difficult period. The Second World War and the years that followed brought severe hardship to many families. Voluntary initiatives sprang up to help families with needs which were not met by mutual help within the family. These initiatives were rapidly integrated into a broader movement, run mostly by women, which hoped to mark a move away from simple financial assistance (e.g. families would pay a modest sum for the services they received) and the paternalism often prevalent in social assistance (the first family assistants would receive training and a modest salary).

The public authorities take up the challenge

Home help for families too has undergone increasing public regulation, and the range of both services and beneficiaries has broadened. The first legal framework for family assistance was established in 1949. During the 1960s the target widened to include the disabled and elderly alongside the mothers of families in difficulty. Gradually the profession developed into an important link in the chain of social services. It is regulated today by the Regions and organised by voluntary associations and local authorities.

New initiatives

Given the rapid ageing of the population, changes in life-styles and family structures and the socio-economic crisis, the field of services in the home is now faced with changing and more complex demands, including long-term care for elderly people, and various needs connected with family breakdown. To respond to these needs at a time of great change, new initiatives have emerged.

Innovative forms of co-ordination among all those involved first developed informally, at the initiative of doctors, nurses, associations or public bodies. Since 1989 a decree has recognised and promoted the co-ordination of the different kinds of care and services delivered in the home to improve the overall quality of care for dependent persons. However, within the associative sector, this decree has revealed tensions between the structures close to mutual organisations – which are responsible in Belgium for the interface between the general public and the national health insurance system – and the more independent associations. These two groups take markedly different approaches to co-ordination, the first group focusing on medical needs, and the second on trying to enhance the central role of aid to families as part of the overall support of users.

Other initiatives, mostly in the association sector, have also appeared, sometimes depending on volunteers and sometimes on paid workers. The associations calling mainly on the help of volunteers are often involved in tasks in which relationships form an essential element, or offer services for which no public subsidy can be expected, including help with mobility, shopping and minor repairs. The associations which draw principally on paid employees generally seek to provide services to people on modest incomes, but given the fact that the demand for these services is not matched by the ability to pay for them, such organisations are dependent on public employment programmes for a significant proportion of their staff.[20]

3 Associations and social entrepreneurship

In the wide-ranging initiatives which we have just reviewed, is it possible to discern a real social enterprise dynamic, as defined in this work? We shall consider both the social and the economic criteria defined by the EMES Network, comparing them with the results of a survey of around a hundred initiatives in the community services sector.[21] In fact, not all the experiments observed in this survey are part of the social economy; some come from the public sector, and others are even private for-profit enterprises. We shall try to determine whether some, at least, of the associations are animated by this dual impulse, at once social and entrepreneurial.

The entrepreneurial dimension

In the Belgian debate on the social economy, only one segment of the latter, i.e. the 'market-oriented social economy', is generally recognised as having an entrepreneurial basis. The crucial distinction, in this case, is based on the importance of market income in financing the enterprise (generally, a social economy organisation is considered as market-oriented if over 50 per cent of its income derives from the market). But this is a very narrow conception of the enterprise. Economic theory, and in particular the theory of organisations, defines the enterprise as 'an independent entity capable of making contracts (in the broad sense of the term) and of taking risks' (Milgrom and Roberts 1992: 289). To some extent, the special feature of an enterprise is thus that it 'takes economic risks'. Because the organisation enters into contracts with a wide variety of players (suppliers, customers, workers etc.), the possibility of

reforming the organisation by amending these contracts, as well as the independence of management in its relations with third parties, are both
indicators of an entrepreneurial dimension which should also be taken into
account.

If we examine the situation on the ground, the survey reveals that associations
active in the provision of community services develop numerous *de facto* contractual links with their users, their paid employees, or their funders. It also shows
that on average 57 per cent of an association's budget is derived from non-
commercial sources, though this average hides a variety of scenarios. Though
this proportion of public finance is markedly lower than in initiatives run directly
by the public authorities (where it stands at 90 per cent on average),[22] does this
not mean that they have lost control of their own management? In other words,
who holds the ultimate power of decision in these associations? Who takes the
economic risks?

In practice, responsibility in associations devolves upon the management
board. It is therefore helpful to consider its composition. The survey shows that
public authority representatives sit on a little over a quarter of management
boards in the associations under consideration. However, there are widely
differing levels of public representation within this subgroup – ranging from 7 to
65 per cent. It should also be noted that the proportion of non-commercial
resources is very high in those associations where public authorities have majority
representation. To this extent it would perhaps be better to consider such associations as 'para-public organisations' or as 'secondary public organisations'.

But this is only the case for a minority of associations. Though the proportion
of non-commercial resources in the budget of associations in general is relatively
high, which implies a certain dependence on public authorities, the make-up of
most decision-making bodies indicates that for most associations, management
independence remains a reality.

These data confirm our feeling that it is too restrictive to regard the market-
oriented social economy as the only segment with a truly entrepreneurial
dimension. This is, firstly, because associations working in the field of community services combine commercial and non-commercial sources of finance in
almost equal proportions, which brings into question any distinction between the
commercial and non-commercial social economy. And, secondly, because even
though the payment of public subsidies has a significant impact on the structure
of associations, it remains true that in most cases the economic risk remains their
ultimate responsibility.

The social dimension

The social dimension of social enterprise resides mainly in the fact that they
result from the initiative of a group of citizens and depend on a participatory
approach, expressed in various ways, such as the implication of users in the
organisation's operation, the mobilisation of volunteers and donations, or the

development of local partnerships. The involvement of actors in the social enterprise comes close to the notion of 'social capital', as has been stressed elsewhere.[23]

The survey confirms the existence of two special features. Firstly, the involvement of many different partners is greater in the associative sector than in either the public sector or the private for-profit sector. This involvement is expressed in a variety of practical ways. For example, users sit on the management board, or contribute to the planning or production of a service; workers participate in management; and volunteers – absent from the public sector or private for-profit concerns – bring their own contribution. Secondly, most associations state that they would like to develop local partnerships.

In principle, the social dimension also comes from the fact that the main aim of social enterprises is not to reward capital nor the people who control the organisation, but to provide some form of service to the community.

In Belgium as in many other countries, the legal form under which associations operate forbids them to distribute profits. In the same way, since there is no provision for capital ownership by members, voting power is linked to persons and not to shareholding. What is then, in practice, the purpose of associations working in the field of community services?

Firstly, there are services which aim to fight social exclusion or, in other words, to integrate or reintegrate users into society. The associations surveyed mainly worked with people on low incomes and those on benefit, that is to say, with disadvantaged groups, particularly in services linked to neighbourhood development, whereas the public services address a wider public. Users of the private for-profit sector belong to average or higher income groups. This observation suggests that the associations are mainly seeking to respond to unsatisfied demand from a socially vulnerable public. Segmenting the public in this way induces a risk of dual provision in community services and the stigmatisation of disadvantaged users.

Associations are also engaged in the socio-professional integration of their employees through the jobs and traineeships they generate. Although 80 per cent of associations do not take the re-employment of unemployed people as their main aim, they use active employment policies for the reduction of unemployment as a source of finance for 40 per cent of all jobs. Around 20 per cent of associations in the sample do take socio-professional insertion of their workers as an explicit aim (such as enterprises for training through work, integration enterprises, neighbourhood management schemes). However, this raises the tricky question of the relationship between the objectives of public policies for the integration of low-qualified workers on the one hand, and the priorities of associations whose main purpose is to offer a high quality service to their users, on the other hand.

The provision of a service also involves the creation of collective externalities, i.e. indirect effects of the activity which benefit the whole community.[24] Community services strengthen social cohesion, through reducing the isolation of elderly people, socialising children, providing help to families etc. Their role in preventing failure at school, delinquency and social exclusion and in creating links between people who live in the same neighbourhood, contributes to the well-being not only of the people helped directly but of society as a whole. The existence of community services can also generate local externalities, i.e. benefits attached to a particular geographical area, improving the quality of life and encouraging local development. Activities which help improve the conditions of life also encourage people to remain in the neighbourhood, and attract other economic activities. Finally, in the current context of structural unemployment, the development of these services can generate externalities in the form of job creation and a reduction in unemployment.

What is striking in these associations, as the survey confirms, is that these collective benefits are not mere secondary effects caused by a main activity but an essential dimension, wholly or partly designed as an integral part of the project by its promoters. In this sense it could be said that building on these collective externalities is a major motivation for the commitment of people working to develop community services within associations.

4   The place and role of social enterprises: challenges ahead

The initiatives that are emerging in the field of community services certainly seem to represent a flourishing social economy dynamic. What place can these organisations really assume? What questions and problems are raised by their development? What is their relationship with the public authorities, which have undeniable responsibility in these sectors of activity? What special contribution can they make to public measures? We shall try to sketch some answers to these questions in the light of the historical developments discussed above.

A pioneering role taken up by public intervention

We have seen, both in the beginning and in later initiatives, that private – often voluntary – measures generally precede state intervention in responding to the needs of people in difficulty. Associations have taken a pioneering role in clearing the way for meeting emerging, but non-remunerative social demands. At a later stage the public authorities arrive to regulate their activities, *inter alia* providing financial support. The need for such public intervention is underlined by various writers who demonstrate the limits of the private non-profit sector. These limits include 'philanthropic insufficiency', i.e. the difficulty of mobilising enough voluntary resources, and 'philanthropic idiosyncrasy', i.e. the risk that some groups would be favoured to the detriment of others.[25] The involvement of the public authorities also reflects the desire to serve the general interest in these quasi-collective services. Most of the services offered are not uniquely a source of private benefit but benefit the community as a whole, which justifies public finance.

A lasting place in the provision of services

Beyond the phase of social innovation, associations still retain a role in the provision of services. Firstly, this is because the state finds it difficult to respond to differentiated, heterogeneous demands since its management approach is centralised and bureaucratic. Secondly, because in certain contexts associations have a very specific place.[26] In Belgium, the joint presence of public and voluntary dimensions in certain major sectors (education, health etc.) reflects a historical compromise between different philosophical 'pillars' (Roman Catholic and secular) which is deeply embedded in the structure of Belgian society. Finally, it should be stressed that the ability of associations to mobilise voluntary resources enables them to develop complementary services responding to more specific demands which are not met by the public authorities.[27]

A sometimes difficult relationship with public authorities

Whatever the context, the question of the partnership between the associative sector and the public authorities is often posed in an acute form (Gilain and Nyssens 1999). For example, Belgium has inherited from the French Revolution a sort of permanent tension between two perspectives. On the one hand, there are the defenders of a view of the public interest embodied almost exclusively by the state, with a minimum of interference between state and citizen. On the other hand, there are those who believe that the development of 'intermediate bodies' of the association type are essential to protect the citizen from domination by a centralising state or an exaggerated individualism. Today, as many initiatives to combat social exclusion are being taken, or taken over, at local authority level, it is precisely on this local level, depending on the majorities in place, that relations between public authorities and associations can be most difficult.

Objectives in partial conflict

It should also be noted that community services experience a growing tension between differing objectives. Given the crisis in the labour market and increasing budgetary constraints, public authorities favour the integration of poorly qualified workers within these services through active labour-market policies. However, the organisations which provide the services stress above all the benefits of these services for users, including social insertion for dependent people through services in the home and for the homeless, and socio-professional insertion for the users of childcare facilities. Nevertheless, these same organisations make use of employment policies, insofar as they become a source of finance enabling them to develop their services, despite the obvious limitations of this strategy. Apart from the insecure status and high turnover of staff, linked to the fact that state support is time-limited, these projects are also affected by the difficulty of finding people who at the same time meet the profiles demanded by employment policies and the profiles required by the nature of the activities.

Challenging institutionalisation

In the areas that have been examined, two major factors emerge from historical developments. There is a growing institutionalisation of services being provided for growing numbers of clients, while more rigorous management is required under the strains of increasing budgetary constraints.

Despite these trends, new initiatives have emerged outside these well-established organisations, in the same or closely related fields, to address new problems or problems which had not yet been tackled. Expressed otherwise, there is perhaps a sort of life-cycle for many initiatives, from the most informal to the most institutionalised, with areas constantly coming to light which call for new formulas and new combinations of players and resources to rise to the challenges of the times.

5   Conclusions and future prospects

The results of our analysis in the field of community or proximity services suggests that social enterprises do present quite specific features. Furthermore, like similar initiatives which emerged in the past century, they have an original contribution to bring, and they can play a part in shaping the contemporary socio-economic landscape. However, the importance of their future development is largely conditioned by the opportunities which will be open to them for maintaining and cultivating their own identity. The very nature of the social enterprise is such that it presupposes a certain balance between its two major elements, the economic and the associative. This balance can be encouraged or rendered almost impossible by various external factors.

Although it is not the only issue, the future financing of social enterprises is at the heart of discussions about their future. These are crucial matters for social enterprises which are heavily dependent on public finance. Everywhere, there is a trend towards the development of contractual relations between public authorities and associations for the provision of well-defined services. This contractual relationship may mean that the spending of public money is being better controlled, and that associations have increased responsibility for the services they provide, but it may also shackle their autonomy and innovative capacity. This can also happen where support for social enterprises is systematically linked to programmes for getting the unemployed back into work. In this case, there is a risk that social enterprises may simply be used by the public authorities, which could lead to their more or less deliberate stifling.

No less threatening is the prospect of regulation by market forces alone. If social enterprises are confined to providing services for which their clients can afford to pay, they will risk entering into competition with traditional commercial companies and ultimately will have to adjust their behaviour accordingly. Paradoxically, such a scenario could receive some support from public polices to promote the third sector if, as happens in Belgium, they tend to give preference to the market-oriented social economy.

Clearly the prospects for the development of social enterprises would be quite different if the synergies between the state and the market, dating back to the post-war boom years, were to be gradually replaced by a more pluralistic view of our economies. This pluralism should be particularly reflected in the recognition of a broad array of socio-economic players (partnerships among them), different kinds of entrepreneurial approaches, and combinations of market, non-market and even non-monetary resources. Belgium is not the worst country in its efforts to support social enterprises and the full recognition of the third sector, but much remains to be done to contain the pressures of public or commercial isomorphism.

At the very least, whatever the future changes in the socio-economic environment, history seems to show that there will always be new areas where the creativity of the community and the entrepreneurial abilities of citizens can come together to find new solutions.

Notes

1 Defourny, Dubois and Perrone (1997). When schools of the so-called 'free' (catholic) network are included, we arrive at a total of 470,000 jobs (Mertens *et al.*, 1999). However, these schools are usually regarded as being half-way between the social economy and the public sector.
2 The Report of the *Conseil Wallon de l'Économie Sociale* (1990) has played a crucial role in this respect, by proposing a definition which remains the standard.
3 The *SFS* articles must state that 'the members are only seeking a limited profit or no profit', that they 'do not seek as the main aim of the company to procure members any indirect profit' (where the company provides members with a direct limited profit, it may not exceed a rate of return currently set at 6 per cent). The constitution must also set out 'a policy for distribution of profits appropriate to the internal and external purposes of the company'. In case of liquidation, 'after all the liabilities have been met and the members have been repaid their capital, any surplus should be allocated to purposes as close as possible to the social purpose of the company'. The *SFS* also introduces a certain degree of democracy into the enterprise: the constitution must set out 'practical procedures whereby each member of staff may acquire membership status, one year after joining the company at the latest'. It may also be stated that 'no-one taking part in a vote at the general assembly may exercise a number of votes exceeding one tenth of the votes deriving from the shares represented; this percentage is one twentieth where one or more members are staff members engaged by the company'.
4 Most of the initiatives which are included under the heading 'social enterprises' adopt the legal form of *ASBL* (*association sans but lucratif* – non-profit association). This is a very flexible form, and less demanding than that of the commercial company. It is also often necessary in order to qualify for public subsidies for activities with a strong social dimension. Last, but by no means least, the *ASBL* can carry out an industrial or commercial activity provided that this activity is of secondary importance and subordinate to the main purpose of the association, which must be of a non-profit nature.
5 See, *inter alia*, a book published by the King Baudouin Foundation (Defourny 1994). A 'Network of Social Enterprises' has also been set up in the French-speaking part of the country.
6 Among the most recent works, see for example Lauwereys, Matheus and Nicaise (2000).
7 Belgium is divided into three regions: the Flemish Region, the Walloon Region and the Brussels Region.

8 See for instance Laville and Nyssens (2000).
9 These settlements were a highly 'developed' version of workers' housing, offering unheard of comfort for the time (apartments along passage-ways overlooking a court-yard). But the private lives, as well as the working activities, of the labourers came under the highly paternalist control of employers.
10 A significant difference, however, is made by the vastly more important role played today by the public authorities.
11 In 1956 this became the National Housing Society (Société Nationale de Logement) which was subsequently reorganised on a regional basis.
12 Many of these companies were established as tenants' co-operatives and opted for a 'garden city' type of development, characterised by a very rich social and cultural life. The few remaining tenants' co-operatives have now passed into public control (Horman 1985). The decentralised approach taken in Belgium avoided huge public housing developments of the kind seen in France and Italy.
13 *Rapport Général sur la Pauvreté* (1994).
14 In the early 1960s, Detrez and Klein (1962) noted that 'it is not uncommon for party membership to be an essential condition for obtaining a social housing tenancy'. In 1994 the *Rapport général sur la pauvreté* disclosed that only 37 per cent of Flemish social housing societies clearly followed the regulations and allocation procedures for housing.
15 Known as *Gestion Logement Namur*.
16 Since an *AIS* is financed in relation to the number of dwellings it manages, there is a strong temptation for them to aim above all at increasing this number and thus to leave the tenants in a permanent state of dependency – which also suits the landlords, since they prefer to deal with more stable parties.
17 In Belgium, almost 20 per cent of the children aged three years and under of working mothers have access to some kind of registered or subsidised childcare.
18 Having originally opposed, and subsequently supervised, private child-minders (who look after an average of three children in their own homes), the public authorities incorporated them into the system of subsidised childcare in 1975. This formula costs the authorities much less, and has shown the strongest growth over the past two decades, to the great disappointment of those who had hoped to raise the profession-alism of the sector and provide a more formal status for those working in it.
19 In 1997, the federal authorities financed almost 480 new projects for childcare in Belgium. Today the Regions and the Communities finance traditional crèches and projects for childcare after school hours. In 1998, the federal authorities financed 188 projects for the care of sick children, and 522 out-of-school and flexible projects.
20 The market is very segmented according to the income of the users. For some services, where the relational aspect is less important (shopping, meals delivered to the home, minor repairs etc.), better-off users turn either to private, profit-making companies or the black economy, whilst the associations take care of the demand from those unable to pay.
21 This survey, carried out by Gilain, Jadoul, Nyssens and Petrella (1998) aimed to study the methods of organisation used in community services across a whole range of public, private and associative initiatives over a restricted geographical area – Charleroi – in four areas of activity: home help for families and the elderly, childcare (up to six years), neighbourhood development (neighbourhood management schemes and community centres), and assistance in obtaining housing. The database which was built up covers ninety-two organisations with 1,500 employees. It should be noted that the study was limited to initiatives which were to some extent 'institutionalised', in the sense that it did not attempt to investigate the informal sector (services provided by family and friends and the black economy), because of the difficulties of collecting information in these areas.

22 In the kind of activities covered here, the traditional private sector has no access to public subsidy.
23 See the chapters by Evers and by Laville and Nyssens in the present work.
24 More exactly, externalities appear when the actions of an agent have positive or negative effects (not regulated by the price system) on the well-being of other agents. See also the contribution by Laville and Nyssens in this book.
25 See among others Salamon (1987).
26 Why does the state delegate part of its production to the associative sector and not to the private, for-profit sector? The answer may lie in theories of trust (Hansmann 1987). We are in a situation where the public authorities finance services but do not produce them. They can only control the behaviour of the providers, and thus the use of public subsidy, with difficulty. In this case, the status of the association, with its constraints on redistributing profits and its social purpose (providing a service to users), may inspire trust.
27 See Weisbrod's theory of excess demand (Weisbrod 1977). The state's manner of functioning, characterised by a political decision-making process based on the preferences of the median voter, leaves an important, heterogeneous part of demand unmet.

Bibliography

Conseil Wallon de l'Économie Sociale (1990) *Rapport à l'Exécutif régional wallon sur le secteur de l'économie sociale*, Namur.

DEFOURNY, J. (1998) 'Les régies de quartier en Wallonie: une perspective comparative', paper presented at the XIth Social Economy Morning, Solidarité des Alternatives Wallonnes and Fondation Roi Baudouin, Brussels.

—— (ed.) (1994) *Développer l'entreprise sociale*, Fondation Roi Baudouin, Brussels.

DEFOURNY, J. and DEVELTERE, P. (1999) 'Origines et contours de l'économie sociale au Nord et au Sud', in DEFOURNY, J., DEVELTERE, P. and FONTENEAU, B. (eds) *L'économie sociale au Nord et au Sud*, De Boeck, Brussels and Paris, 25–56.

DEFOURNY, J., DUBOIS, P. and PERRONE, B. (1997) *La démographie et l'emploi rémunéré des ASBL en Belgique*, Centre d'Économie Sociale, Université de Liège.

DEFOURNY, J., FAVREAU, L. and LAVILLE, J.-L. (eds) (1998) *Insertion et nouvelle économie sociale*, Desclée de Brouwer, Paris.

DEFOURNY, J., NYSSENS, M. and SIMON, M. (1998) 'De l'association sans but lucratif à la société à finalité sociale', in DEFOURNY, J., FAVREAU, L. and LAVILLE, J.-L., (eds) *Insertion et nouvelle économie sociale*, Desclée de Brouwer, Paris, 73–98.

De l'utopie au réel. 1919–1994, 75 ans de logement social en Wallonie (1994), Les Chiroux Éditions, Liège.

DETREZ, R. and KLEIN, E.C. (1962) *Pour un secteur paritaire du logement social*, Édition du Centre Paul Hymans, Brussels.

DUBOIS, A. (1996) 'Le Fonds d'équipements et de services collectifs', in *Grandir à Bruxelles*, Cahiers de l'observatoire de l'enfant, no. 2: 9–12.

DUBOIS, A., HUMBLET, P. and DEVEN, F. (1994) 'L'accueil des enfants de moins de trois ans', *Courrier hebdomadaire du CRISP*, nos 1,463–4, Brussels.

GILAIN, B. and NYSSENS, M. (1999) 'L'économie sociale dans les services de proximité: pionnière et partenaire dans un champ en développement', *Revue des Études Coopératives, Mutualistes et Associatives*, no. 273: 40–55.

GILAIN, B., JADOUL, B., NYSSENS, M. and PETRELLA, F. (1998) 'Les services de proximité, quels modes d'organisation socio-économiques pour quels enjeux?', *Les Cahiers du CERISIS*, 98/6, Charleroi.

GUI, B. (1992) 'Les fondements économiques du tiers-secteur', *Revue des Études Coopératives, Mutualistes et Associatives*, nos 44–5: 160–73.

HANSMANN, H. (1987) 'Economic Theories of Nonprofit Organizations', in POWELL, W. (ed.) *The Nonprofit Sector, A Research Handbook*, New Haven, Yale University Press, 27–42.

HORMAN, D. (1985) 'Le logement social et les comités de locataires', *Alternatives wallonnes*, no. 32: 12–15.

LAUWEREYS, L., MATHEUS, N. and NICAISE, I. (2000) *De sociale tewerkstelling in Vlaanderen: doelgroepbereik, kwaliteit en doelmatigheid*, Hoger Instituut voor de Arbeid, Leuven.

LAVILLE, J.-L. and NYSSENS, M. (2000) 'Solidarity-Based Third Sector Organizations in the "Proximity Services" Field: A European Francophone Perspective', *Voluntas*, vol. 11, 1: 67–84.

'Lutter pour un toit' (1995) Report in the journal *Traverses*, no. 101: 3–8.

MERTENS, S., ADAM, S., DEFOURNY, J., MARÉE, M., PACOLET, J. and VAN DE PUTTE, I. (1999) 'The Nonprofit Sector in Belgium', in SALAMON, L.M. *et al.*, (eds) *Global Civil Society. Dimensions of the Nonprofit Sector*, The Johns Hopkins Comparative Project, Baltimore, 43–61.

MILGROM, P. and ROBERTS, J. (1992) *Economics, Organization and Management*, Prentice Hall International, Englewood Cliffs.

NOUVELLE-CORDIER, C. (1990) 'Solutions alternatives aux problèmes du logement social wallon', *Wallonie*, no. 7: 23–30.

NYSSENS, M. (1998) 'Raisons d'être des associations et théorie économique', Discussion Paper no. 9811, IRES, Université Catholique de Louvain.

—— (1996) 'Associations et services aux personnes âgées', Contribution to the 'Associations' CIRIEC working group, Liège.

PRICK, F. (1994) *Rapport sur les nouvelles initiatives de logement social*, Les Sans Logis Asbl, Liège.

Rapport général sur la pauvreté (1994) Fondation Roi Baudouin, Brussels.

SALAMON, L.M. (1987) 'On Market Failure, Voluntary Failure, and Third Party of Government Relations in the Modern Welfare State', *Journal of Voluntary Action Research*, vol. 16, 2: 29–49.

SALAMON, L.M., ANHEIER, H.K. and Associates (1998) *The Emerging Sector Revisited*, Johns Hopkins University, Baltimore.

SPEAR, R., DEFOURNY, J., FAVREAU, L. and LAVILLE, J.-L. (eds) (2001) *Tackling Social Exclusion in Europe. The Contribution of the Social Economy*, Ashgate, Aldershot.

TRIGALET, P. (1997) 'Les exclus ont-ils droit au vert?', *Traverses*, no. 119: 3–12.

WEISBROD, B.A. (1977) 'Collective-Consumption Services of Individual Consumption Goods', *Quarterly Journal of Economics*, vol. 78: 471–7.

3 Denmark

Co-operative activity and community development

Steen Bengtsson and Lars Hulgård

Introduction

In spite of the tradition of co-operative enterprises and of citizens' engagement in fields other than the social, the concept of 'social enterprise' has not been used so far in Denmark. However, there is a huge number of projects and initiatives, which have developed during recent decades, which could be taken into consideration when talking about social enterprises. They are often financially supported by experimental pilot and action programmes. Such programmes have had a considerable influence on social work practice and probably also on the modernisation of the welfare state. After presenting the main features of Danish social policy as a background for understanding the conditions for social enterprises today, we shall give a short outline of the two forms of co-operative enterprises.

1 The Danish system of social protection

The Danish welfare system is characterised by a sizeable public service sector in the social, health and educational fields. Danish welfare is primarily financed by income taxation and VAT. Social assistance and a great deal of social insurance benefits are financed by general taxation. Employers and insured people contribute only modestly to the overall social budget. Apart from this, Denmark has primarily a system of universal coverage, in which application of social rights is related to inhabitancy rather than citizenship. The only exceptions are unemployment and pre-pension insurance which are occupational[1] but heavily state supported.

The main characteristics of the Danish welfare system are thus universal coverage and public involvement in financing as well as in producing the services. Since the 1960s, social welfare in Denmark has been dominated by public authorities – primarily municipalities – which are also the main producers of social services. The basic structures of the local welfare system were defined in a comprehensive set of reforms starting at the end of the 1960s. The reforms started with amalgamations that reduced the number of municipalities dramatically to make them big enough to handle new social tasks (Villadsen 1996). In the so-called 'second decentralisation', which took place from the 1980s, the municipalities have given their institutions freedom of action within the frameworks of finance and general policy.

This public, universal model is a rather new phenomenon. Before 1960, the Scandinavian social systems were not that different from other European models, but the conditions for developing universalism can be traced far back in history. The Protestant tradition, in which the church is part of the state, has no doubt produced a general political culture of consensus. The unusual degree of municipal freedom, which we find especially in Denmark, has links to a tradition from the 1800s of power-sharing between city and countryside. With the modern economic and social planning which was the ideology of the leading civil servants in the 1960s and 1970s, the municipalities were made the main public service producers in a decentralised political system (Knudsen 1995).

There were no confessional differences that could preserve a structure of welfare associations, and the sick-benefit associations had become formal structures in the framework of a health system which was generally considered to be public. In 1970, the sick-benefit associations were set aside and the full responsibility for paying health services taken over by the state.

Building up the welfare state has entailed a public take-over of some of the social work previously carried out by the non-profit sector. Most voluntary organisations still formally exist as private entities, but co-operate with public authorities so that most of their institutions are functioning exactly as if they were part of the public system. However, this has not meant the total disappearance of the third sector. The voluntary organisations have rather taken the role of cultivating new areas of welfare work, which thereafter have become the responsibilities of public authorities. But while innovative social works done by private voluntary organisations have earned widescale respect in society, charity work in general, and especially in areas which are already the responsibility of public authorities, is generally disliked.

2   Social enterprises

The Danish situation today is marked by social enterprise being almost non-existent as a concept in the general consciousness. But in spite of this conceptual absence, we will argue that the main ingredients of social enterprises have played a substantial role both in the historic formation of the Danish welfare state and in the more recent process of the soft modernisation of the welfare system. In the first period the workers' and farmers' co-operative movements were the most influential actors concerning social enterprises, but during the latest two decades we have seen a new type of social enterprise as an important feature in social work and the production of social services.

The traditional types of social co-operation

Traditionally there have been two distinct co-operative movements in Denmark: a farmers' movement and a workers' movement. The farmers' co-operative movement has been of central importance for the protection of the economic interests of farmers, but it has not had any goals of serving more general interests in society (apart from its consumers' retail aspect). Workers' co-operatives, however, have had a number of goals of furthering social interests. These goals have been:

- retail sale of inexpensive quality products;
- production of inexpensive quality products and of inexpensive quality housing;
- establishment of working places for persons who have difficulties in finding a job;
- development of model workplaces; and
- development of an expert knowledge base concerning enterprise and business. The Co-operative Union is working together with the so-called 'Business Council of the Workers' Movement',[2] an agency making business and economic analyses for the workers' movement.

The first consumers' co-operative for retail sale of everyday necessities for common workers was initiated by a clergyman in 1866, and later in the century production of everyday necessities such as bread and oatmeal was taken up by workers' co-operatives.

Establishment of working places for persons who had difficulties in finding a job was an important purpose of workers' co-operatives. The difficulties that these co-operatives aimed to overcome, however, were related to class struggles. In 1899 a major labour-market conflict had occurred and many workers who had been active in strikes had been blacklisted. This inspired the trade union movement to establish its own firms, particularly in the building trades. In the summer of 1899, the first limited companies were formed by bricklayers, joiners, carpenters and blacksmiths. Later on, similar companies were set up in the painting, plumbing and electrical trades. In 1918 and 1927 further labour conflicts brought about, among other things, the opening of co-operative barber and hairdresser shops in Copenhagen. The unions were the owners of these companies through foundations established for this purpose.

From the thirties, development of model workplaces became another goal of the union-owned companies. Besides providing work for the members, they acted as spearheads for the union movements' fight for better pay and working conditions. In these companies, the labour movement was able to demonstrate that their demands were realistic and could be satisfied within the framework of a reasonable economy. These frameworks, however, had to be respected if the co-operative movement was to be able to continue. 'The co-operative should not become a milk-cow', as a book from the co-operative publisher put it (Vernerlund 1972).

Development of expert knowledge and a power base on business policy is the latest goal. In 1953 the Trade Union Federation, the Social Democratic Party and the Co-operative Union established a council for business policy related to

the Co-operative Union. This council conducts analysis of economic development for the unions and the Social Democratic Party, and in the 1970s it played
a role in making proposals for a policy on economic democracy. These proposals,
and the adjustment of the co-operative enterprises to economic democracy, were
among the main points concerning the future in a book on co-operation of that
time.[3] Although the proposals for economic democracy were never realised, the
main function of the Co-operative Union and of the co-operative enterprises in
the recent period has been to act as the economic laboratory of the workers'
movement. The associated Business Council of the Workers' Movement makes
its own economic forecasts and calculates the consequences of different political
proposals, and thus plays a role in the political debate.

The development of the workers' co-operatives

The establishment of workers' co-operatives took place in waves and was partly
determined by circumstances such as labour conflicts, war difficulties and state
support. Many of the products were basic commodities – such as bread, beer,
fuel – which were demanded by workers and the people at large. A number of
other products could be produced because of the market niche created by the
co-operative retail shops.

As mass consumption developed, a general concentration took place in
production. This happened in the co-operative sector also. In most spheres
rationalisation has led to mergers. The number of co-operative companies has
been reduced in this way, but not their total volume. The enterprises of the co-
operative sector – members of the Co-operative Union – most often are
organised as limited companies, with trade unions, other co-operative societies
or other parts of the labour movement as shareholders. Bager points to the fact
that the workers' co-operative enterprises have been more and more dependent
on the unions, which has weakened the autonomy of their workers *vis-à-vis* the
enterprises (Bager 1992).

In recent decades, many of the traditional goals of the co-operatives have
become redundant. It seems that the last goal, of being a power base on business
policy, has now become the most important one. The old workers' co-operatives
can no longer be considered social enterprises. They do not have the function
anymore of providing work for persons who are unable to find employment in
the ordinary job market because of union activities.[4]

In recent times, the consumer retail co-operatives of the farmers and the
workers' co-operations have merged and renewed their social ambitions, and in
the last decade they have played a leading role in the introduction of ecological
food products.

Lately, the workers' co-operative movement has initiated activity in social
services. A co-operative housing society for young people had developed during
the 1980s, but the activities were badly managed and the society went bankrupt.
This experience discouraged, for some time, an obvious line of development in
social services. However, in the 1990s, the Co-operative Union began to investi-

gate the possibilities of entering this area.[5] In 1993 the Co-operative Idea Centre was established with the purpose of creating new co-operatives to give employment to long-term unemployed and disabled persons, and it established a translation service and a telemarketing company with related training for blind people. In recent years, the Co-operative Union has been actively investigating the possibilities of establishing – in co-operation with a number of municipalities – companies for the provision of social services to the elderly. There have been at least two reasons for this. When unemployment rates were still high, the objective was to create working places for long-term unemployed union members who were about to lose their rights to unemployment benefit. In 1998, wage subsidies to persons with reduced working abilities were introduced, and now it is planned to use these means to create new co-operatives and give employment to workers who are difficult to place. The second reason is that the use of private – instead of public – service providers has been discussed in recent years. Even if few municipalities have so far contracted out social services, the commercial firms are prepared to go into this new market, and the Co-operative Union wants to participate. The special resources of these co-operatives consist of the support that they have in the Co-operative Union, and the support network of the trade unions and the Social Democratic Party.

Voluntary social work

The co-operative movement has served a number of social functions, but the thinking has mainly been economic and political. Functions such as the employment of people with disabilities have only quite recently been taken up, and social services are, for the moment, just in the planning phase. Earlier, charities and organisations of people with disabilities were alone in these sorts of activities. In the 1960s much of this work was taken over by the public system. In many cases the organisations remained formally private, but they now work in the context of an agreement making them in reality part of the public system. In the 1980s, however, new voluntarism marked a reversal of these trends. A new commitment to grassroots social work arose, and new types of social enterprises were formed, at first outside the established co-operative tradition.

3   New types of social enterprises

Since the end of the 1960s, a variety of new social projects and initiatives have developed. These new social projects largely conform to the social enterprise model, but in different ways. Though major differences are found among the new social enterprises, it is necessary to emphasise their common background in the cultural revolution sweeping through most liberal democracies in the late 1960s. The experimentation with life-styles in the wake of the 1960s involved new ways of living, but it also nourished the idea of connecting community to production. Since the 1980s, the above-mentioned experimental orientation in social protection has entailed a number of projects which could be considered social enterprises. The experiments with life-styles have also led to major changes in the social work tradition. From the early 1970s, three types of social work initiatives have developed with links to the social enterprise tradition, viz. small social residences (*Opholdssteder*), non-residential folk high schools (*Daghøjskoler*) and production schools (*Produktionsskoler*).

In an article about the historical background of the experimental strategy within social policy and social work, Hegland (1990) stresses the link between life-style experiments and experimental social work. He emphasises the fact that some of the ideas in the life-style projects and the commune movement (*Kollektivbevægelsen*) in the late 1960s and the 1970s were channelled into the urban sector, the social sector and the educational sector. 'Alternative' was the new expression widely used. Social workers talked about 'alternative social work', educators talked about 'alternative education' and both talked about 'alternative institutions'. Hegland stresses the existence of a direct link from these bottom-up activities to the Social Development Programme (1988–1993) and to other types of experimental and developmental social work often concentrated on objectives similar to those of social enterprises (Hegland 1990).

The influence of pilot and action programmes

During the last decade, several pilot and action programmes within the field of social policy have played a crucial role in the dissemination of social enterprises. The programmes can be understood as a special Danish way of experimenting with the social enterprise model and the role of third-sector organisations in fighting social exclusion. Denmark has experienced pilot programmes and cross-sectional programmes as a way of renewing social policy in general, while developing strategies against social exclusion and urban policies with emphasis on social objectives. One important reason behind the decision to start the social innovation programmes was related to the general growth in the public sector and indeed the growth in social expenditure. A number of programmes are aimed at restructuring the social services by strengthening the role of local community, local partnerships and the participation of third-sector organisations. This type of social programme, with an emphasis on the pilot and experimental approach to social work and social service, has had two major consequences for social work.

The first consequence is that, during the last decade, professionals and citizens other than formally educated social workers, have gained influence in social work practice. A variety of professions, citizens and volunteers are mixing with frontline workers engaged in community work, partnerships at local level, and in empowerment projects fighting social exclusion.

The second consequence is that the social work profession is in transition. Many social workers, professionals and citizens engaged in social work and local community building are becoming change agents. Change agent is the classical Schumpeterian definition of entrepreneur. As an entrepreneur, the social worker becomes a crucial intermediary in a society marked by comprehensive transition.

It is our hypothesis that the above-mentioned structural changes in social work as well as the influence from pilot and action programmes are showing the importance of the social enterprise approach to social integration. These changes in social work and the production of social services have been backed up by a considerable number of pilot and action programmes. A few figures may illustrate this. The largest single initiative within the experimental orientation in social policy was the Social Development Programme (1988–93), usually referred to as the *SUM* Programme.[6] In 1988 the Parliament decided to spend 350 million DKK (about 47 million Euro) on the programme, which was set to run for a period of three years. The programme was carried out on the basis of a broad consensus in Parliament. The Social Development Programme is usually considered to be the cornerstone in the Danish pilot and action programmes with an emphasis on experimentation. The amount of money spent was large, and this programme has certainly been important. Even since the termination of the programme we have actually seen a broad variety of experimental programmes targeted at different user-groups and policy issues within the field of social policy.

Thus the amount of 350 million DKK is just a part of a much bigger sum used since the mid 1980s for pilot projects within the area of social policy and health. An estimation from 1997 showed that the Ministry of Social Affairs administered social innovation programmes with a total cost of 1,374 million DKK (about 184.8 million Euro) in the period 1994–97.

The Social Development Programme

The Social Development Programme has substantial similarities to the social enterprise strategy. The goal of the Programme was to promote the restructuring of social policy in the direction of strengthening preventive activities by enhancing the role of the local community and establishing cross-sector co-operation i.e. by reinforcing the role of third-sector engagement. The key elements of the Social Development Programme as formulated by the Social Committee in Parliament are the following:

- local communities must play a far more proactive role in social policy;
- local citizens shall be encouraged to become active and participate in decision-making concerning their own lives;
- solutions must be promoted across sector, administrative and professional lines; and
- the ability to find common solutions across the public–private barrier must be improved.

In practical terms this meant that social workers should change their functions from being primarily controllers and 'treaters', and instead become 'catalysts' in the process of helping people (clients and citizens) become active in their own lives by combating social problems as well as establishing networks and reinforcing the local communities. The programme should have contributed to the solution of social problems by reducing and overcoming sector, administrative and professional boundaries which had been confining social policy through a lack of legitimacy. The development programme attempted to increase social integration (the citizens' participation in production of social welfare) as well as system integration (i.e. better co-operation within the public sector, between state, counties and municipalities as well as between public and private organisations).

To many local activists, civic entrepreneurs and professionals in third-sector organisations, the programme served as the legal background, making it possible to develop new, more responsive social institutions.

The Social Development Programme financed approximately 1,700 pilot projects all over the country. Special priority was given to projects:

- in the areas of activation and rehabilitation i.e. activity that provides people of working age, who have no contact with the labour market, with the opportunity to return to work or begin a more active existence;
- with a focus on new approaches in local society and local administration; and
- about children/young people and their families, elderly people, and special groups such as disabled, refugees, immigrants and excluded groups.[7]

Since the days of the Social Development Programme, several other funds with an emphasis on pilot and development work have developed. At least two programmes are interesting from a social enterprise point of view: (1) the Activity Pool[8] with an annual budget of DKK 30 million (about 4 million Euro), and (2) the *PUF* Fund,[9] which finances pilot and development work for DKK 50 million per year (about 6.7 million Euro) (Hegland 1997). The *PUF* Fund, which was previously called the 'Poverty Fund', gives financial support to voluntary organisations' activities and initiatives involving socially excluded people. The local voluntary job centres are examples of projects supported by the *PUF* Fund (Hegland 1997).

The Ministry of Social Affairs has established a database showing all projects funded by pilot and action programmes. The data collection started with the 1,700 projects supported by the *SUM* Programme, and since then all projects financially supported by the various social funds have been added to the database. According to the database for projects with 'activation' as one of their keywords, 643 projects were financed by different funds from the end of the 1980s and onwards. A search with the keyword 'job-training' shows 146 projects; while twenty-seven projects are registered with 'alternative workplaces' as a keyword. Several of these projects meet the criteria of social enterprise as defined for the purpose of this study. The projects presented below as new types of social enterprises are very often subsidised by the social funds. Typically the projects show a great creativity in getting financial support, and they are often subsidised from a variety of pools, programmes and funds – public as well as private.

Two projects from the database, financed by the *PUF* Fund and the Activation Pool, serve to illustrate this dimension of social enterprises:

- The Culture Swing, which will be described in more details later on, is financially supported by the *PUF* Fund. The aim of the Culture Swing is 'to create a working place where socially marginalised people can be integrated, and where personal development is increased through responsibility and active engagement. ... The project is organised in four self-governing divisions.'[10] The four self-governing divisions are all engaged in the twin activities of social enterprises, viz. production of service and production of social capital;
- The café and shop Jasmin is financially supported by the Activation Pool, the EU Social Fund and the municipality of Fakse. According to the database description, '[the] primary goal is to create a democratic unit governed by the participants and aimed at developing the whole human being. ... The secondary goal is partly to create a multi-cultural catalyst of social networks, partly to sell products and food produced by the unemployed in job training'.[11]

Four types of new social enterprises

Four types of initiatives in particular, which can be considered as social enterprises, have experienced significant development. The four types meet the economic criteria, and although there are some differences between them, they all produce, to some extent, goods or services. As far as the social dimension is concerned, social enterprises are, in some way or another, established from the bottom-up; they originate in the self-organisation of the people involved, and they seek the enhancement of the local community and democracy.

Production communes and collective workshops (type 1)

In their 1984 study, Nørrung and Kjeldsen investigated 117 'production communes' (*Produktionskollektiver*) and 'collective workshops' (*Arbejdsfællesskaber*) in Denmark. In both kinds of initiatives, people work together and, in the 'production communes', they also live together. The authors define the term 'production commune' as a community where at least three adults are living and running an enterprise together. Ownership and collaboration are shared by all members of the community, though not always formally, due to some legal restrictions (Nørrung and Kjeldsen 1984).

In the mid 1980s, these 117 communities were producing not less than ninety-nine different kinds of goods and services. The products covered a wide range of goods, including furniture, agricultural products, stoves, pottery and movies. A popular type of production and service was communication. The communes could be involved in communication in a number of ways such as publishing firms, printing-houses, magazines and bookshops and through photography. Also, many communities were producing and selling a variety of services, such as auto-repair shops, restaurants, theatres, plumbing, radio-repair shops, groceries, or providing legal assistance.

The most famous alternative community is Freetown Christiania, which has been an intensively debated institution for almost thirty years. It was founded in 1971 by a group of squatters, who were offended by the existence of an abandoned military camp at a time when there was a serious lack of housing. In the winter of 1971, they occupied the area including a major part of the old rampart of Copenhagen and declared it to be 'Freetown Christiania'.

Several social enterprises have been established in Christiania over the years. Many have been functioning from the very beginning. In 1984 there were 850 people living in Christiania and approximately 400 self-established and self-organised jobs (Nørrung and Kjeldsen 1984). In 1997 approximately 1,000 children, young people and adults were living in Christiania. With its restaurants, bars, music-clubs, theatre companies and bands, Christiania has for decades made an important input to the cultural image of Copenhagen. Some innovative products have even been developed by Christiania's craftsmen, e.g. the Christiania bike and the Christiania oven. Christianits (the inhabitants of Christiania) proudly boast that the Christiania bike, an effective carrier cycle, has been exported to Mercedes Benz in Germany, where it is used for local transportation purposes in the factory.

Community work with production of goods or services (type 2)

This type/category is mainly an umbrella concept for social work projects with the goal of empowering the participants. Since the 1980s, Danish social policy has been marked, as already mentioned, by great experimental programmes, and in a small fraction of these projects some economic activity has taken place. The projects are generally involved with the production of a wide range of cultural, educational and social services for the local community. Two examples are presented here: *Kulturgyngen* (Culture Swing) and *Sidegaden* (Side Street).

The Culture Swing is a social and cultural project in Aarhus, the second largest city in Denmark. The project offers training and job practice in an enterprise which consists of a restaurant and a café, a music club (the 'Music Café'), a youth hostel ('City Sleep-in') and an advertising agency (*Kultursats*). The Culture Swing is aimed at activating people having difficulties in getting or keeping a regular job or training (where 'activating' is understood as providing a socially useful job which is a condition for receiving social assistance). Some lack identity and self-confidence, while others have had little or no contact with the labour market or with education/training and are uncertain about future possibilities. When the Culture Swing was founded in 1987, the idea was to form a project which incorporated social work and practice skills while offering people a social network. In the beginning, the only business was a restaurant. The production of other services was added later.

As a social enterprise, the Culture Swing offers a method where persons with different life experiences and resources collaborate in the production of services. There are ninety-six people involved in the project, made up of sixteen permanent workers who are the members of the association behind the enterprise, and eighty temporary workers. Of these temporary workers, sixty are in job-practice, ten in rehabilitation and ten are volunteers. The restaurant has a business of 237,510 Euro, the music club, 100,000 Euro and City Sleep-in, 200,000 Euro. The Culture Swing has received private and public funding, including 200,000 Euro from the EU Social Fund.

The Side Street is a community work and job training project in Copenhagen, which also combines entrepreneurial and social aspects. Johs Bertelsen, the founder of the Side Street, wanted to deal with two problems when he first had the idea of establishing the enterprise, back in 1986. The local area, a few blocks behind the central station, was distinguished by its many abandoned shops. At the same time, there were many unemployed young people in the area. By 1997 the Side Street consisted of eleven shops, run by forty young people in job-training activities. The Side Street receives public subsidies in return for job-training the young unemployed people, but the eleven professionals working in the Side Street are continuously concerned about keeping a high degree of autonomy in the enterprise. Consequently, although they receive public funding for their job-training activities, they are not managed – directly or indirectly – by public authorities. From the perspective of the Side Street, one way of maintaining and extending its autonomy has been to expand the activities and the funding. The EU Social Fund, the Ministry of Health, the Ministry of Social Affairs and several private foundations are among the main contributors to the enterprise.

There are three basic and interrelated ideas behind the Side Street. The first is that new initiatives must be developed from the bottom-up, which means that a close relation to the local community is a guiding principle for the enterprise. No experts from outside the area tell the local community what to do, and what kind of enterprise to get involved in. The second idea is that the enterprise must be based on the interpretation of the social processes in the local community and the group of participants. The third feature has been the hardest to put into practice, since it involves the process of transforming the individual empowerment of the participants into the collective or political empowerment of the local community.

Although these two projects are just examples, they illustrate an important type of social enterprise which is based upon the desire to develop jointly the local democratic culture and the autonomy of the enterprise. This type of project is continuously seeking to develop entrepreneurial (economic) activities with a social dimension, although constrained by legal restrictions specifying that it is not allowed to establish 'pure' market activities.

Social residences (type 3)

In 1997, there were approximately 300 social residences (*Opholdssteder*) in Denmark. They are rooted in the same ideological environment of the late

1960s and the 1970s as the working and living communities described above. Jørgensen stresses how 'the social residences developed as an alternative – a contrast – to the traditional residential homes for children and young people (*Døgninstitutioner*) which functioned more according to the needs of the planners, leaders and professionals than to the needs of the young people placed in the institutions' (Jørgensen 1997b: 1).

In the 1970s, many social residences were organised as communities combining production and living. Production of goods or services was integrated with social care and treatment in the social residence. According to Jørgensen, during the last decade there has been a growth in the number of social residences, but today the emphasis is more on education and treatment than on production.

The reason for including the social residences in this typology must be seen in the historical origin of the social residences and the practice of the residences in the initial period. For example, the institution 'Scorpio' was a typical social residence fifteen years ago. It was a production and residential community with pedagogical and caring functions integrated in the enterprise. In 1984 there were twenty adults living and working in Scorpio. They had a mix of resources, based partly on production in the workshops (auto-repair, plumbing, radio-repair, carpentry and bricklaying) and partly on the public funding of job-training activities in the various branches of the social enterprise (Nørrung and Kjeldsen 1984). The job training activities and the social care were aimed at maladjusted young people.

This way of running a social residence was quite common at the time. The above-mentioned evolution towards a less production-oriented functioning is linked, *inter alia*, to the fact that the youngsters placed in social residences by public authorities today are younger and in need of more care. It appears that less attention is paid today to young people above the age of sixteen or seventeen, who in the past formed the majority of people hosted by these residences, and who were only marginally maladjusted and did not need any treatment other than a simple community work experience.

Schools (type 4)

The original 'folk high schools' (*Folkehøjskoler*) aimed at giving the young generation of farmers self-confidence through educating them in agricultural as well as in cultural matters – the latter in a folk-cultural style as opposed to the bourgeois academic culture, which they called the 'black school'. Non-residential folk high schools are schools based on the tradition of the residential folk high schools, but situated in the cities. The first non-residential folk high schools were established with the advent of mass unemployment in 1974; in fact they were set up to address the needs of the unemployed. In a similar way to their predecessors these new non-residential folk high schools aimed at giving the unemployed the self-confidence they had often lost.

In 1998, eighty-five non-residential folk high schools were members of the

Association of Non-Residential Folk High Schools in Denmark. According to an estimate by the administrative leader of the association, eleven of these conform to the definition of a social enterprise. Under specific circumstances, non-residential folk high schools are allowed to undertake enterprise activity, but it must be separated from their educational activity. The association maintains that only a small number of the non-residential folk high schools are engaged in such earning activities, which are most often local assignments with a cultural or service character. For example, the non-residential folk high school of Norddjurs (in East Jutland) acts as an historic cultural centre and takes care of local archive functions and tourist services.

Some residential high schools have also been engaged in enterprise activities. In the beginning of the 1970s, a group of school teachers founded a type of folk high school in Tvind, in Western Jutland, on a more or less Maoist basis, with a foundation called *Fælleseje* (Common Ownership) as owner. All teachers were to commit themselves to transfer a substantial part of their salary – which was paid by the state – to this foundation. The foundation bought a number of buildings over the years, and the schools in the group rented these buildings with other state subsidies. Therefore the construction was in fact a way to channel considerable amounts of money from state support to the foundation 'Common Ownership'. These folk high schools soon grew into a large group of residential schools of all kinds, named the Tvind Schools (after the location of the first school of the group). Many of these schools were known for their ability to take care of young people with social problems. The Tvind Schools, however, used the legislation of folk high schools and other forms of schools in a way that was not intended by law-makers, earning several hundreds of millions for their foundation, and in 1997 they were stopped by a special law. In 1999, however, the High Court decided that this law was unconstitutional, and because of this event, many folk high schools are now more cautious about engaging in too many enterprise activities.

4 The contribution of social enterprises today – strengths and weaknesses

Many of the production communities and working collectives from the 1960s and 1970s have disappeared, but some of the big ones – such as the production community of Svanholm or Freetown Christiania, in Copenhagen – still exist. Other social enterprises with roots in the youth rebellion of 1968, which had a great impact in Denmark, and the many activities stemming from the Students' Front in Aarhus or similar milieus are providing special residential places for children and young people. The dividing line between social enterprises and other social projects, however, is not very clear and it is difficult to estimate numbers.

One of the special resources of these types of social enterprises consists in the culture of 1968, which they have been able to capitalise on in the 1980s and 1990s to the benefit of young persons who are generally distrustful and suspicious of grownups. This is a very positive development of the 1968 culture, especially when compared to other possibilities, such as creating a subculture of terrorism or a generation of disillusioned anomic persons. Other resources are the green principles that point to solutions other than high technology, and the ideology of solidarity with its ability to create enthusiasm and engagement in work. With this background, social enterprises not only create social solutions, but at the same time create meaning and a social place for marginalised groups. In this sense, it can be said that social enterprises are able to mobilise 'social capital' and turn forces, which could easily have become destructive, into constructive elements in the economy and society.

Although there are in Denmark, as we have seen, several examples of successful social enterprises, there is no common designation or public awareness of their existence. When hearing of enterprises in the social area, most Danes immediately think of commercial for-profit enterprises. If the reference is to social treatment areas, the warning lights are turned on. Besides the above mentioned social enterprises in these areas, there is a limited number of more commercial enterprises, but most often they are small and try to gloss over whether or not they earn a profit, because this is not popular with the financing authorities. Economic activities carried on by enterprises working in the field of publicly supported social services have been impeded by the trade unions, which have been afraid of unfair competition from such activities. In recent years, however, the unions seem to have become more tolerant of such activities.

In the case of social support areas, such as childcare or services for the elderly, the situation has been a little different. In these areas, an open debate has gone on for a couple of years about the advantages and drawbacks of public versus private commercial service providers. Until now, this debate has not significantly changed the overall picture of public service provision, but it has created a picture of for-profit enterprises as the only possible alternative to municipal social service, thus hiding the possibility of non-profit initiatives such as social enterprises. The unions of public social workers have been strong proponents of public sector social service, and consequently all leftist forces, including unions and the Social Democratic Party, have supported this line, and the co-operative solution has thus been without any basis of support.

The weaknesses of social enterprises are due to their lack of visibility and to the absence of a concept that describes this reality. As already underlined, the concept of 'social enterprise' is not used in Denmark, and whereas so-called 'voluntary' social work has maximum visibility and political attention in areas such as homelessness and drug and alcohol abuse, the commercial sector has concentrated on areas such as elderly care and childcare. The lack of visibility of social enterprises means that the use which is made of them and even their very existence often depend on the civil servants who happen to take the decisions. Politicians are seldom aware of their existence and potentials, and their users often do not know that they are something different from the ordinary municipal service. Social enterprises are dependent on the organisational cultures in the public authorities. The administrative culture in the municipality of Aarhus, for example, which has been much influenced by the spirit of 1968, is more open to social enterprises than the culture in most other cities, especially the municipal administration of Copenhagen, with its more 'bureaucratic' and know-all attitude.

5 Prospective considerations and conclusions

The foregoing examples of social enterprises in Denmark present much evidence of the specific potentials of the social economy. The main problem, however, is the absence of the concept of social enterprise in the social consciousness. As a result, they are not taken into consideration, their strengths are not perceived and they are given little chance of developing at present. The field of social services, however, is at a point where it is open to new developments, and a search for new possibilities is taking place. So far this has meant an interest in voluntary social work, charities and commercial solutions. But it is still possible that social enterprises will come into the picture as a possible model for future social protection activities.

This depends, to a great extent, upon the course of societal development in the coming decades. The 'Europe scenarios 2010' (1998) envisages a number of possibilities for economic and social cohesion in Europe by 2010, the more prominent ones being:

- every one for themselves or the new-right style of reform;
- the creative society or the universal right to be useful;
- the partner state.

The 'new-right' thinking, which is known from Britain in the 1980s, is still quite influential in Danish social thinking.

The 'creative society' represents green and social values, and this scenario gives place to social non-profit enterprises with the purpose of employing the 10–15 per cent of the labour force who would be difficult to employ on pure market grounds. As green and social values are beginning to gain influence, it can be contemplated that a niche for social economy will open up here.

The last-mentioned scenario imagines that the public/private dichotomy will be softened up through a radical decentralisation and a widespread use of public/private partnerships in solving problems. This is a more structured and less bottom-up alternative than the creative society, but there should nevertheless be room for social enterprises to take part in solving the problems. It seems that this scenario is the more likely one in countries with a strong tradition of public leadership, such as the Scandinavian countries, because it gives the state and municipalities a role in the partnerships. At the same time it is a scenario that could be possible for the countries in the continental European tradition.

In contemplating the prospects for social enterprises, therefore, a decisive factor is whether the new liberal style will continue to dominate the thinking of social development, or if green and social values and partnerships will become more influential themes.

This value-oriented reflection must however be reconciled with the real political situation where unions of municipal social workers are opposing any alternatives to public social services, the right-wing political forces are committed to introducing a commercial alternative to the public social services, and the only visible alternative to these is the so-called 'voluntary' or charity sector.

Notes

1 The unemployment scheme is optional for persons that have been employed for some weeks. Rights to the benefit are obtained after one year of membership of an unemployment fund with payment of contributions and a half year of employment.
2 Arbejderbevægelsens Erhvervsråd.
3 *Det Kooperative Fællesforbund* (1975).
4 Apart from this, it could be discussed whether this was social protection or protection of the right to organise.
5 Kooperativ Udvikling (1996); *Rapport* (1997).
6 Socialministerets Udviklings Midler, i.e. The Social Ministry's Development.
7 Jensen (1992)
8 Støtte til erhvervshæmmede i virksomhederne.
9 The *PUF* Fund, i.e. Puljen til udvikling af frivilligt socialt arbejde.
10 The Ministry of Social Affairs: Socialministeriets Projektdatabase.
11 The Ministry of Social Affairs: Socialministeriets Projektdatabase.

Bibliography

ALS, J., CLAUSEN, J. and OKSEN, A. (1979) *Arbejderkooperationen*, Soc., København.

BAGER, T. (1992) *Andelsorganisering*, Sydjysk Universitetsforlag.

BJØRN, C. (1986) *Andelsbevægelsen i Danmark*, Andelsudvalget, København.

Det Kooperative Fællesforbund (1975) *Kooperationen – i dag og i fremtiden*, Fremad, København.

'Europe Scenarios 2010. Partial Scenarios: Economic and Social Cohesion in Europe' (1998) (Working group no. 2), Discussion paper, Forward Studies Unit, European Commission, Brussels.

HEGLAND, T.J. (1997) 'From a Thousand Flowers to Targeted Development', Papers in Organisation, no. 24, Copenhagen Business School, Institute of Organization and Industrial Sociology, Copenhagen.

—— (1990) *SUM-programmet – en historisk sociologisk baggrundsanalyse*, SUMma Summarum, vol. 1, 1, December, København.

—— (1985) *Arbejds- og levemiljøer med socialpædagogisk sigte – en systematisk oversigt*, Aalborg Universitetscenter, ALFUFF, Aalborg.

HULGÅRD, L. (1997) *Værdiforandring i velfærdsstaten*, Forlaget Sociologi, København.

JENSEN, M.K. (1992) *Slut_sum*, Socialforskningsinstituttetrapport 92:18, København.

JØRGENSEN, G. (1997a) *Børn, unge og voksne på opholdsstederne*, Forlaget Nordkysten, Silkeborg.

—— (1997b) *Opholdsstedsbogen 1997*, Ictus, Gilleleje.

KNUDSEN, T. (1995) *Dansk statsbygning*, Jurist- og Økonomforbundet Forlag, Gentofte.

KOLSTRUP, S. (1996) *Velfærdsstatens rødder*, SFAH, København.

Kooperativ udvikling indenfor social – og sundhedsområdet, ældreområdet, det boligsociale område (1996), Dialogpapir, Det Kooperative Fællesforbund, København.

KRAG, J.O. (1945) *Kooperationen, fremtiden og planøkonomien*, Det Kooperative Fællesforbund, København.

NØRRUNG, P. and KJELDSEN, J. (1984) *Produktionskollektiver og arbejdsfællesskaber*, Aalborg Universitetscenter, ALFUFF, Aalborg.

Rapport om udlicitering og kooperationen (1997) Det Kooperative Fællesforbund, 24 November, København.

SUMma Summarum 1. årgang no. 1, December 1990, Socialstyrelsen, København.

VERNERLUND, O. (ed.) (1972) *Kooperation – en idé!*, Aof / Fremad, København.

VILLADSEN, S. (1996) 'Local Welfare Systems in Denmark in a Period of Political Reconstruction: A Scandinavian Perspective', in Bent Greve (ed.) *Comparative Welfare Systems. The Scandinavian Model in a Period of Change*, Macmillan Press, London, 133–64.

4   Finland

Labour co-operatives as an innovative response to unemployment

Pekka Pättiniemi

Introduction

In this chapter, we will focus mainly on the new co-operative social enterprises active in the field of work integration. We will thus only briefly mention the more traditional (in the Finnish context) social enterprises, such as workshops and sheltered workshops, which emerged in the country after the Second World War, in order to bring people affected by the war back to the labour market and to normal life.

Finnish society has, especially since the Second World War, concentrated its efforts on the building industries such as the wood and metal industries. At the same time, the country developed a welfare state in which public institutions played a central and overwhelming role. The municipalities, in particular, have had – and still have – a key role in providing social and welfare services. This policy has been unanimously backed by the various social associations and polit-ical parties. As a result, the third sector in general, and social enterprises in particular, have played only a minor role as employers in Finland. Local initia-tives, voluntary organisations or social economy solutions have had practically no involvement in organising welfare services, except in a few sectors such as services for war veterans and people with disabilities. Today, about 3 to 4 per cent of the total employment is organised by associations, and if we also take into account co-operatives and mutuals, the rate rises to about 6 to 8 per cent.

Full employment has been a general feature of the labour market from the 1950s. This was helped by emigration to Sweden and other more industrialised countries from the 1950s to the early 1970s. The state has traditionally been responsible for employment policies, and the Ministry of Labour has labour agencies in almost every municipality.

National regulation of the labour market and a comprehensive social policy encouraged and made possible the steady growth of the Finnish national economy. These measures were also instrumental in significantly increasing the welfare level of citizens. Labour-market policy was seen as an integral part of economic policy.

The welfare state continues to provide good educational opportunities regard-less of family wealth, free or almost free healthcare and good social security for all citizens. The welfare state has made it possible to increase the quality of the labour force and to achieve high standards of living and general education.

However, the deregulation of national economic policy changed the situation. The shift to more global markets and deregulation in the past ten years, together with mass unemployment in the early 1990s, have resulted in a shift in labour-market policy. The former policy has become ineffective; it sometimes produces results contrary to its objectives of encouraging economic growth and promoting social welfare (Koistinen 1996: 17–20).

In the early 1990s, the unemployment rate reached a peak, at about 20 per cent. Depending on the source, it was estimated that between 100,000 and 200,000 unemployed would become long-term unemployed during the late 1990s and thus no longer be eligible for the reasonably good unemployment benefits provided by the state.

Over the period 1987 to 1993, atypical employment forms, such as temporary jobs and part-time work, markedly increased. In 1993, every third new job was a part-time job. In the same year, three-quarters of new jobs were temporary, and only 20 per cent of the new jobs were traditional, permanent full-time jobs (Parjanne 1997). Mass unemployment problems in the first half of the 1990s have resulted in a rapid development of private local initiatives in employment creation.

In public discussion, co-operatives and other enterprises with democratic, equal and common ownership are not often seen as being part of the third sector or of the social economy. This view has deep roots in Finnish history, where the large agricultural and consumer co-operatives and mutual insurance companies have always been seen as private firms, rather than as a part of the social economy. Associations are traditionally seen as representatives of various citizen groups and not as active entities in the economic or social sectors.

1   Co-operative social enterprises in work integration

In this section, we will briefly describe different types of co-operative social enterprises active in the field of work integration, while in the next section, we will focus on one particular type – labour co-operatives – which we will describe in more detail.

Co-operatives and social enterprises for the disabled

The hundreds of protected (sheltered) workshops for disabled people organised by the associations for the disabled can be considered as a traditional way of trying to integrate mentally or physically disabled people into work situations or to achieve rehabilitation through work. The sheltered workshop movement has existed for decades. There are also four Fountain House clubhouses for persons with mental health disabilities offering work-like activities and/or transitional jobs.

Nowadays, various associations of persons with mental or psychiatric disabilities are establishing co-operatives or other social enterprises in the field of work

integration. New social co-operatives have been created, and some of the traditional workshops or sheltered workshops are in the process of transforming
themselves into actual businesses that are trying to finance their own functions to
a larger extent. In many cases, this is due to the fact that regulations concerning
state aid for rehabilitation have changed, so that a person can now receive state
aid for rehabilitation only for a restricted period of time. In many municipalities,
this means that the workshops can no longer receive state aid for their regular
workers who are physically or mentally disabled.

In 1997, such social enterprises were employing 153 persons who were at risk
of being excluded from normal work contracts, and 946 persons in workshops.
The projects managed by these associations and foundations employed an additional 343 persons at risk of being excluded from labour markets.

An example of these co-operatives is *Osuuskunta Järvenpään Oma Oksa* (Co-
operative Own Branch), in Järvenpää municipality, thirty kilometres north of
Helsinki, which is working as a subcontractor, assembling and packing products
in the plastic and chemical industries, and is also running a laundry. This co-
operative originated in an old sheltered workshop that was to be closed down. It
now consists of eight workers – five of whom are mentally disabled – and three
other members: the municipality, the local association for the mentally disabled
and a local worker co-operative. According to the manager, the five mentally
disabled members greatly improved their capacity to work after the sheltered
workshop was turned into a co-operative owned by the workers and other interested parties. The financial results are also improving and it is estimated that the
co-operative will be self-sufficient in the near future. There are even pressures to
have new and larger premises for its expanding activities.

Social workshops and Local Associations for the Unemployed

The number of social workshops for the young unemployed has risen from 60
to 350 in the last four years (Andersson 1997). Some of these are organised
by associations. About 300 workshops are members of the Finnish Workshop
Association. These workshops provide a half-year experience of work, in areas
such as arts and crafts, repairing cars and motorbikes, and in woodworking.

There are about 350 (of which 250 are registered) Local Associations for the
Unemployed in Finland. These are local initiatives deriving from the needs of
the unemployed for information, social connections and further education. The
Associations have established a nationwide central association, called 'VTY'.
The associations for the unemployed provide one example of the new types of
citizen action and self-help reintegration in Finland. It appears very important
for these associations to advance their members' working skills by training them
for the contemporary labour market. For example, one course offered by one of
these associations aims at the improvement of their members' language and
computer skills. Most instructors are volunteers, but some teachers and paid
employees (often a manager and a secretary) are hired with a state subsidy. This
subsidy is paid by the local employment office for people who have been unem-

ployed for more than one year. Usually, the contracts are made for a minimum of six months.

To advance and maintain the social, physical and mental condition of the unemployed, some of the associations act as a form of self-help and mutual aid. For the unemployed, the opportunity to meet and interact with other people in a similar life situation in order to share ideas, experiences and information appears to be really meaningful. Giving and receiving support also strengthens the members' self-confidence and identity. New social contacts can bring new friends or even job opportunities. In addition, many associations offer possibilities to participate in sports and handiwork. Premises are often provided free of charge by local parishes or municipalities. Low-priced meals are served by the unemployed themselves.

Some of the associations for the unemployed arrange courses on issues such as 'how to apply for a job' or 'how to start a co-operative or a private enterprise'. These courses and seminars are usually arranged free of charge or for a minimal fee to members. Most of the inputs to activities in these associations are provided by volunteers; usually, there are only one to three subsidised employees. The associations are not self-sufficient enough to employ staff without subsidies (Pättiniemi and Nylund 1997).

An example of how associations can develop different work-integration activities is illustrated here by the work of the *Hyvä Arki* Group ('Good Everyday Life'). The *Hyvä Arki* Group consists of three different enterprises: the *Hyvä Arki* Association; the *Hyvä Arki* Services Co-operative; and a biological food retail co-operative, *Hyvä Arki*. The *Hyvä Arki* Association is an association with a social purpose. It arranges activities including discussion groups, training courses, working in workshops, and preparation of cheap meals, to involve the long-term unemployed. It also arranges short-term 'training' jobs for the unemployed. The aim of the *Hyvä Arki* Services Co-operative is to sell proximity services, such as home cleaning or preparing and serving inexpensive lunches for the elderly; to hire out workers to municipalities and big companies in the region; as well as to repair apartments and houses of private citizens, using primarily the labour of the unemployed. The activities of the *Hyvä Arki* Association and Services Co-operative form pathways from unemployment and social exclusion to working life. The excluded persons can informally train in the basics skills of working life through the activities of the Association, and can then be employed for a longer period in one of the real jobs of the Co-operative.

About 3,500 persons take part annually in the activities of the Association, which employs twenty persons full-time. The Co-operative employs about forty persons on a full-time basis and it offers job opportunities to an additional 110 persons for a longer or a shorter period annually. The short experience of the *Hyvä Arki* Services Co-operative (established in spring 1997) shows that it is possible for the groups which have the most difficulties in integrating themselves in work, to find jobs. The co-operative is run professionally; it markets its services to key clients and actively arranges vocational training for its workers as well as pre-job training for the excluded persons to whom it intends to offer jobs. Its work is widely respected by Espoo City and the other municipalities that use its services.

Housing associations and estate co-operatives

Some organisations for the unemployed also address their housing problems. *Sirkkulan puisto yhteisö* (Sirkkula Park Community Association) is an experiment in associative housing and work integration for excluded groups. The community tries to integrate people with severe alcohol problems into work and into society. The people in the community have built good homes for themselves and they have various kinds of workshops where the members produce (mainly hand-made) goods for sale on the market.

In some suburbs there is a movement to form estate co-operatives. Three co-operatives of this type have already been set up and new projects are under development. These co-operatives were formed by unemployed residents, land-lords, volunteers and voluntary associations working in the estates. In some cases, municipalities and Lutheran parishes are also actively involved as members. Usually, estate co-operatives operate in the fields of housing improvement, public space development and proximity services (mainly childcare). Clients are primarily landlords and the municipality.

Village co-operatives

In the countryside, some village societies or voluntary committees (about 3,300 in number) have taken the initiative to create village co-operatives. Frequently, village co-operatives are formed by the majority of villagers, together with the associations working in the villages, to improve and develop the village in general. Some of the main goals are to secure services such as local shops, post offices, banking services, primary schools and social services (Hyyryläinen 1994). Village societies are increasingly producing social welfare and healthcare services and are proceeding to employ unemployed villagers. Information about the employment effects of these initiatives is not yet available.

2   Labour co-operatives – a self-help answer to unemployment

The emergence of the labour co-operative movement and its relation to other worker co-operatives

The first wave of worker co-operatives appeared at the beginning of the century in the transportation and construction work sectors, while the second wave came in the same sectors after the Second World War. The worker co-operatives of the third wave were a self-help solution to the mass unemployment of the early 1990s. A new feature of the 1990s development is that worker co-operatives have emerged in new sectors, especially in knowledge-intensive areas like training, consulting and planning.

About half of the 350 worker co-operatives established after 1987 can be considered as traditional co-operatives. They work in one or two industrial sectors, and their ideas are mostly related to services for businesses or private households (Pättiniemi 1998). The other half of the worker co-operatives consists of multi-sectoral worker co-operatives and labour (or work) co-operatives. These co-operatives are formed mainly by unemployed people willing to re-enter the labour market after a period of unemployment. The idea of labour co-operatives is to rent out or lease their members' labour to other companies or to households. The labour co-operatives differ from other worker co-operatives in that the members are not permanently employed by the co-operative. There are times when a member is employed by the co-operative and times when he/she is not employed and is receiving unemployment benefits from the state. Finnish multi-sectoral worker co-operatives and labour co-operatives resemble more closely social co-operatives in work integration than 'genuine' worker co-operatives.

The first labour co-operative was established in autumn 1993 in Kirkkonummi, a municipality 35 km west of Helsinki. The establishment of the *Työosuuskunta Uudenmaan Aktio* (Labour Co-operative, in Uusimaa country) was initiated by the Local Association for the Unemployed earlier in the same year.

The Local Association for the Unemployed (see section on Social workshops and Local Associations for the Unemployed above) had experimented with how they could find temporary or permanent jobs for their members. They advertised the willingness of their members to do temporary work. They also placed a notice board in their office, where the companies or private households that needed workers could put their notices. The experiment was successful. However, there were some problems insofar as the notes from private persons or enterprises offering jobs often disappeared from the notice board, and some jobs that were offered were from the black economy. The association then called a meeting of members, in order to discuss possible ways to avoid these problems. On the agenda there was also a suggestion to establish a co-operative whose aim would be to arrange temporary working opportunities for the association members. The co-operative would rent its members work time to households or companies needing temporary or permanent labour. The co-operative would also take care of the essential employer's duties, such as paying the worker's taxes, value added taxes, social security benefits and so on. The association's members decided to back up the idea. The co-operative held its founding meeting in November 1993, and it began its activities after its registration in the same year (Suominen 1995).

The establishment of *Aktio* received wide publicity and a very positive response from the media. Soon afterwards, other Local Associations for the Unemployed convened similar meetings or, alternatively, backed up the establishment of similar labour co-operatives.

Over the years 1994 to 1996, many labour co-operatives were formed on the

Table 4.1   Development of worker and labour co-operatives in Finland, 1993–1998

Year	Number of worker co-operatives	Of which labour co-operatives
1993	23	1
1994	50	17
1995	80	40
1996	163	65
1997	257	130
1998	350	190

Source: *Uusosuustoimintaprojekti* (1998)

initiative of, and with the help of the Local Associations for the Unemployed. At the beginning, labour co-operatives were concentrated in the cities, but today there are more and more of them in the small country towns and villages (Pättiniemi 1997). The number of labour co-operatives has risen from one in 1993 to about 190 in 1998 (see Table 4.1).

The social and economic goals of labour co-operatives

The explicit aim (mentioned in the statutes) of labour co-operatives is to promote the economic and social well-being of their members by offering them work opportunities. They aim at employing their members full time by hiring out their labour to other employers. However, part-time and temporary working opportunities are also welcome. In practice, part-time or temporary work increases the possibilities of getting a permanent, full-time job. It also means that the member's contact with the labour markets and his/her ability to work is maintained.

Some of the labour co-operatives have additional social goals. For example, they may select from two competent members for a particular job, the one with the greater social need for it (Pättiniemi 1995). Karjalainen found in his research that about 10 per cent of the worker co-operatives in Finland (especially the smaller ones) have this kind of additional goal (Karjalainen 1996). Many of the labour co-operatives have also arranged training opportunities for their members. Sometimes, it is even provided for in the statutes that surplus revenue should be used for the training and education of members. A couple of labour co-operatives define their goals in terms of benefits for the community in which they are operating.

All labour co-operatives agree that, while employing their members themselves is not really important, it is necessary to offer them employment opportunities and to help them enter the labour market. This aim can just as well be attained by helping them to be employed directly by other companies. It is regarded as a good result if a member is employed full-time outside the co-operative and therefore leaves the membership. In fact, a couple of the labour co-operatives have already ceased their activities because practically all the members had been employed directly by other companies.

Some labour co-operatives also consider themselves as training providers, where the members can develop their own business ideas and plans, test them and later, if the plans are viable, begin their own businesses as independent entrepreneurs (Karjalainen 1996). The Finnish authorities and employer organisations consider labour co-operatives as a good path or channel through which members can become conventional private entrepreneurs (Karjalainen *et al.* 1998).

Labour co-operatives provide their members with new relations and a functioning community where they can discuss their problems and solve them by mutual self-help. In this way, labour co-operatives help their members overcome the mental and social consequences of unemployment. A recent study concerning one labour co-operative based in Helsinki, found that the majority of the members considered that attending the co-operative meetings and doing non-paid work helped them mentally and socially while unemployed (Eloaho and Koivuniemi 1997).

Labour co-operatives are a new kind of economic self-help organisation, in which not only the economic goals but also the social aims are important. It can thus be said that a new kind of social solidarity is being formed.

In what sectors are labour co-operatives operating?

Most labour co-operatives are operating multi-sectorally. About 60 per cent of them offer their services in construction and office work – the two sectors that have been most affected by the recession. About 40 per cent also offer computer or data services, while 30 per cent offer the services of accounting, cleaning, social services, training, metal work, textile work and maintenance of premises (Karjalainen 1996).

Representatives of business in Southern Finland estimate that co-operative solutions work best in social services; in work integration; in services provided to other enterprises; in training and consulting services; in the renovation of public spaces and, on a small scale, in other construction services (Karjalainen *et al.* 1998).

Who are the founders of labour co-operatives?

Labour co-operatives are typically established by people who have been unemployed for one to two years. Two-thirds of the members are between thirty-six and forty-five years old. Generally, people of this age group have considerable experience of working life and some old contacts with the companies they have worked for in the past. These contacts can make it easier for the co-operatives to enter business. In Finland, people over forty are regarded as 'too old' to be employed as new employees and they are often excluded from the labour markets. In the management structures of the co-operatives, men and women are equally represented. In 1995, about 43 per cent of the ordinary members were women.

Immigrants have established ten co-operatives, involving about 300 members.

The establishment has sometimes been accomplished with the help of immigrants' cultural associations. Especially active have been the immigrants from the former Soviet Union while immigrants from Somalia have also created their co-operatives. But there are also multi-cultural co-operatives, with members from different ethnic backgrounds. The aim of these co-operatives is to integrate the members with Finnish business and work life. These co-operatives are active, for example, in import and export, the catering and restaurant business, retail of ethnic foods and childcare for ethnic groups.

Reasons for establishing labour co-operatives

The main reason for establishing labour co-operatives has been the unemployment of the members. According to Karjalainen members consider that labour co-operatives can produce the following benefits (Karjalainen 1996):

* opportunities for temporary employment are increased;
* entering a labour contract becomes easier;
* one can actively affect one's own job; and
* professional skills can be maintained.

The democratic and participative nature of co-operatives has also been important for the members. These features have been clearly highlighted in newspaper interviews with women who have established co-operatives (Hovi 1998).

One of the reasons for establishing labour co-operatives, especially during the deepest recession, was that official labour agencies could not produce or identify employment opportunities for the fast increasing masses of unemployed. In most of the municipalities, labour offices were accustomed to unemployment rates of 4 per cent, but within a few years, the unemployment rate increased to about 20 per cent. The few new jobs offered had either high qualification requirements or were temporary in nature. On the other hand, the recession also made private companies reluctant to enter into labour contracts for temporary work with private persons, because they feared that they might later have to form permanent labour contracts. The creation of a labour co-operative thus appeared as a new and more effective tool through which to get employment. The fact that a co-operative is a legal entity with the right to make contracts with other companies, with private persons or with the public sector, and is obliged to fulfil all the employer obligations, made it easier to fill temporary or short-term jobs. The co-operative can draw up business contracts with other companies, while its members can enter into ordinary labour contracts with their own co-operative and thus be ordinary employees. This entitles them to all the benefits that the Finnish labour market offers to an employee. The co-operative pays the wages, employer payments, taxes and other legal payments arising from the labour contract.

As a matter of fact, according to Finnish law (the unemployment benefit law concerning private entrepreneurs), if someone owns less than 15 per cent of the decision-making power of an enterprise and works in the enterprise, he/she is not regarded as an entrepreneur but as an employee. Having the status of an entrepreneur would imply a risk of losing the relatively good unemployment benefits that workers receive while unemployed.

In some cases, labour co-operatives are quite similar to multi-stakeholder enterprises (Borzaga and Mittone 1996), community enterprises or local partnerships, where various local interests are combined to fight unemployment for the benefit of the community. The members of labour co-operatives are trade union branches, municipalities, parishes and other associations as well as local banks and even other entrepreneurs. Labour co-operatives resemble local partnerships or community enterprises especially in the countryside.

In Ähtäri municipality, in Central Finland, for example, the local partnerships have taken the co-operative form. In other cases, as in St Michel, in Eastern Finland, local partnership projects have been promoting the establishment of labour co-operatives in the region.

The members of labour co-operatives consider it important to enforce collectively-bargained wage levels in the work contract with their own co-operative. Labour co-operatives are active in sectors like construction work, where labour black markets are present in Finland, where they keep up the collectively bargained wage levels and pay the taxes and insurance fees of employees. Consequently, labour co-operatives also hold back the emergence of labour black markets and the officials of state and municipalities respect this.

Another reason for the high rate of co-operative establishment might be that, from September 1996, the minimum own capital required for establishing a joint-stock company has been increased to 50,000 FIM (more than 8,400 Euro). This is an amount beyond the financial capabilities of people who have been unemployed for a long period.

Employment and economic effects of labour co-operatives

In 1995, worker co-operatives (labour co-operatives included) provided employment opportunities to about 1,500 people, while in 1996 it was estimated that worker co-operatives gave employment opportunities to over 4,500 people. Recently, the Ministry of Labour has estimated that new co-operatives give at least some earnings to about 19,000 people annually (Paasivirta 1998).

In the Kainuu region, in the Northeast of Finland, ten new co-operatives have enrolled 180 members. From January to August 1997 these co-operatives employed temporarily about 125 persons on a short-term basis. In another study of the same region (Kotisalo 1998), it was estimated that labour co-operatives have had a total impact on employment of thirty full-time equivalent jobs. An additional fifty members were employed outside the co-operatives (Nivala 1997). The wages paid in all new co-operatives in Kainuu in 1997 amounted to about 2.15 million FIM (361,000 Euro). Consequent social security and wage-related payments plus public incomes from VAT and income taxes totalled about 2.3 million FIM (385,000 Euro) (see Table 4.2). Adding savings in public spending,

Table 4.2   Public sector's income from labour co-operatives in the Kainuu
region, 1997

Income from VAT	995,000 FIM (167,347 Euro)
Turnover: 4.52 million FIM (760,200 Euro)	
Income taxes	645,000 FIM (108,481 Euro)
Wages: 2.15 million FIM (361,600 Euro)	
Social security, other work/wage related	645,000 FIM (108,481 Euro)
insurance and wage related payments	
Total public sector income	2,285,000 FIM (384,309 Euro)

Source: Kotisalo (1998: 116)

one reaches a net impact on the public budget of about 4.3 million FIM (about
716,000 Euro), as shown in Table 4.3.

The essential outcomes of the evaluation of the impact of labour co-operatives in the Kainuu region are that:

- the co-operatives employ temporarily a substantial number of the unemployed in the region (about 200 persons). These persons can maintain or
  even develop their vocational skills;
- the new enterprises, which are mainly labour co-operatives, are based on
  connecting and networking of different kinds of skills and do not need
  heavy capital investments;
- in the local economy and in society at large, these new enterprises produce
  economic, social and psychological net benefits;
- there is an opportunity to export products and services from the region and
  to add to the region's wealth.

(Kotisalo 1998)

Since autumn 1996, four labour co-operatives from the South of Finland have
been attending the 'Haviva – ADAPT' project, which aims to develop the business skills of the new co-operatives. By the end of October 1997, eighteen new
permanent jobs had been created inside these co-operatives and fifty-two
members had found permanent jobs outside the co-operatives. About 48 per
cent of the 147 members had found new permanent jobs within a year
(Kostilainen and Pättiniemi 1997).

Table 4.3   Net impact of labour co-operatives on the public budget in the Kainuu
region, 1997

Public sector incomes	2,285,000 FIM (384,309 Euro)
– Subsidies to labour co-operatives	185,000 FIM (31,115 Euro)
+ Savings in public spending	2,160,000 FIM (363,286 Euro)
(unemployment benefits and other social	
benefits)	
Net impact on the public budget	4,260,000 FIM (716,480 Euro)

Source: Kotisalo (1998: 117)

The success of labour co-operatives has even led some regional public labour agencies to take similar actions. These labour agencies have begun to lease temporary workers to private companies so that they have the status of public sector workers and the labour agency collects the fees. In some regions, state employment agencies even consider labour co-operatives as their rivals.

Since labour co-operatives are mainly working in the areas in which their members have become redundant, they do not necessarily produce new jobs; they are rather a modern private vehicle to organise post-industrial temporary employment possibilities. Labour co-operatives are part of new co-operative business solutions. In general, these new solutions do not have global importance in employing people, but the local impact of these solutions can be, and is, significant. New co-operative enterprise solutions are seen as pilot projects that can, if they are successful, increase the popularity of co-operatives and other people-centred business organisations (Karjalainen *et al.* 1998).

Organisation of the Finnish labour co-operatives

New co-operatives are in general quite small. Their size varies from 5 to 120 members. Finnish Co-operative Law provides that the ultimate decision-making in the organisation is based on a system of general meetings, held once or twice a year. In general meetings, members participate in the decision-making process according to the 'one member, one vote' principle. Members decide the strategies of future work; accept, or not, the balances; and elect the board of directors (usually formed by the members) and the auditors.[1]

The board of directors elects the managing director[2] (if required) who, together with sectoral team managers, takes care of the business on a daily basis. The managing director is paid only on a half salary basis for the management duties and has to make the other half from the actual work. In co-operatives, voluntary work can be used only in the management of the organisation and for the maintenance of the premises. The directors are usually not paid for their work on the board.

Using the Co-operative Law as a basis, labour co-operatives have developed participatory and well-functioning organisations. But the multi-sectoral nature of most labour co-operatives also creates some internal problems. Labour co-operatives tend to concentrate their activities in the sectors that prove to be most successful, thus neglecting the members that could be employed in other sectors. As a result, in some cases, members from the least successful sectors have been asked to resign from the co-operative, or they have become passive members, who do not take part in the co-operatives' activities.

Lack of competent managers is a major problem, while lack of business planning and of marketing skills are also generally seen as factors that hinder the development of labour co-operatives. In research conducted by the Institute for Co-operative Studies of the University of Helsinki, the new co-operatives were asked to define their needs for training. A total of 190 new co-operatives answered the enquiry. The resulting training needs are set out in Table 4.4.

Table 4.4   Training needs of new co-operatives

Specific training needs	% of co-ops
Marketing	86
Co-op. entrepreneurial skills (e.g. management training for members and managers)	85
Business economics	85
Business legislation	73
Computer skills	59
Product development	52

Source: *Uusosuuskuntien koulutustarpeet* (1997: 5)

These responses suggest that the problems experienced in labour co-operatives are mainly linked to business and management skills. This is hardly surprising in view of the fact that people who attempt to establish these enterprises do not have a managerial background.

Finance

Labour co-operatives have the same kind of financial problems as other small companies. Among these problems, the lack of own capital is the most important. Access to loans and other financial means is limited, as it is for other Finnish small enterprises in the service sector. Generally, the own capital of new worker and labour co-operatives is small. In 1995, it was on average 12,363 FIM (about 2,080 Euro). The amount of the membership share was on average 622 FIM (about 105 Euro) and it ranged from 100 FIM (about 17 Euro) to 1,500 FIM (about 252 Euro) (Karjalainen 1996).

Since the beginning of 1996, new co-operatives, if they were established mainly by the unemployed, have had the opportunity to apply for self-initiative support from the Ministry of Labour. This support covers 80 per cent of the costs during the establishment period. There is, theoretically, no limit to the amount of the support but, in practice, it is limited to 60,000 FIM (about 10,090 Euro). The co-operatives can use this support to cover the establishment costs; to employ managers or office staff; to buy computers or to rent a telephone or fax; and to fund items which are not directly connected to trading. Recently, a condition has been introduced which stipulates that, in order to receive the grant, the co-operative must have a viable business plan. This condition is somehow paradoxical, since one of the purposes of the support given is actually to help plan a viable business.

Municipalities, local training institutions, trade union associations, parishes, Lions Clubs and local banks rent out premises to worker and labour co-operatives at below market prices or even free of charge. Another kind of financial help received by the new co-operatives is employment training financed by the Ministry of Labour. A group of unemployed people wanting to establish a co-operative can have free-of-charge training in co-operative entrepreneurial skills, in business economics, in co-operative management, in co-operative law, in marketing, in developing service concepts and products, and in business planning.

Labour and other co-operatives have, in theory, the same opportunities to receive state support and loans as companies generally. There is only one exception, viz. the 'enterprise founder loan' which is by law confined to joint-stock companies founded by one or two persons. The problem with labour co-operatives is that they are practically all working in the service or construction sectors and, in these sectors, loans or support from the state financial institutions are not allowed. Although labour co-operatives have only a small amount of own capital and financial resources – a characteristic which is considered a major obstacle to the development of their activities – they have made little use of the subsidies for employing long-term unemployed or of other state or municipally supported employment possibilities.

3 Support structures

Support structures for new co-operatives and other forms of social enterprises have been developed only recently. Support for establishing and developing a co-operative can be obtained from the Institute for Co-operative Studies of Helsinki University and from nine regional co-operative development agencies (CDA). The Institute has been promoting new co-operative solutions for problems in the countryside as well as in cities since the late 1980s. Its role has been essential to the development of labour and worker co-operatives. It has organised (together with the Ministry of Labour, the People's Educational Association (KSL) and the *Finncoop Pellervo*) some 200 presentations on co-operative self-help solutions.

Co-operatives participate in seminars, conferences and training courses organised by the Institute and by CDAs. In the period 1997/98 *Finncoop Pellervo*, together with the Institute for Co-operative Studies and the Ministry of Labour, organised the 'New Co-operative Project', aimed at producing materials and at providing other forms of help for the establishment of new co-operatives (Piippo 1997). Besides its co-operation with other organisations, the Finnish Co-operative Central Union *Finncoop Pellervo* (an association of agribusiness and banking co-operatives) also works on its own to support the emerging new co-operatives.

A group of labour co-operatives has recently formed an association for political lobbying. In the Hämeenlinna region, 100 kilometres north of Helsinki, labour co-operatives and other new co-operatives have established a secondary co-operative to help them organise training, financing and lobbying. Another secondary co-operative has been established in Northern Finland, in autumn 1998. Other social co-operatives also receive professional support from the nationwide and/or local associations in their specific social or health sectors.

4   Co-operative social enterprises and social capital

The revitalisation and popularity of new co-operatives in Finland is a sign of the entrance of social and community matters into entrepreneurial life. There was a social need for the widening of scope of entrepreneurship from private and selfish economic pursuits to co-operation and to fulfilment of common needs and goals (Köppä 1998). As we have seen, new co-operative social enterprises have, especially in the smaller communities, a multi-stakeholder character. This is mainly the case where local associations, Lions Clubs and other societies, parishes and municipalities are members of the co-operative and/or are financially or morally backing their activities. Even if this backing is sometimes very nominal, it represents a new, unforeseen solidarity in the society. Important horizontal connections are formed to tackle the needs of the community and to develop its economic and social welfare. New social capital is formed, insofar as the horizontal solidarity among the members and the new kinds of economic and social self-help solutions represent a new form of solidarity in the modern capitalistic society.

5   The future of co-operative social enterprises in work integration

In Finland, associations in the economic or social sectors are traditionally seen as representatives of various citizen groups rather than as acting in their own right. Therefore, the idea that associations can be employers is a novelty of the mid and late 1990s. The possibility of the third sector employing people was first raised in 1997, but active measures in employment have been taken throughout the 1990s.

Measures aimed at the reintegration of people threatened with exclusion appeared simultaneously in rural villages and in major cities with high unemployment rates. The first type of organisations to appear were the Local Associations for the Unemployed, at the end of the 1980s. They provided reintegrative services for the unemployed (such as training to maintain and improve the working skills and other capacities of the unemployed) aimed at helping their members to re-enter the labour market. Both the services produced and the social life in these associations are considered to be important.

Labour co-operatives and other new co-operatives provide employment for their members either inside the co-operatives or in other enterprises after a 'training period' provided by the co-operative. Labour co-operatives and other new co-operatives can be viewed as new initiatives both in employment policy and in economic life. In economic life, they represent a new way of doing business, where people take their destiny into their own hands without depending on the public sector or on large private enterprises. Labour co-operatives can be seen as transitional enterprises with two purposes. Firstly, they are a preliminary step in developing an employee-owned business. Secondly, they can be a tool for their members in transition from unemployment to wage earner status.

On the other hand, the Finnish welfare state is still considered to have the main responsibility in the field of social welfare and of healthcare services. The public sector still has the old habit of adopting ideas for new services from the associations. It is predicted that the reintegrative actions of associations will gradually grow in importance and in number during the next few years (Pättiniemi and Nylund 1997).

The numbers of labour and other co-operatives in work integration have risen sharply during the last four years, and although the worst recession and unemployment crisis is now over, the number of co-operatives keeps rising. Originally, labour co-operatives represented a self-help solution by the unemployed themselves; but gradually, municipalities, the state and associations have become interested in them.

Labour co-operatives can be an important development force for the local and regional economy. The positive effects of labour co-operatives are especially noticeable in villages and suburbs affected by high unemployment. The co-operatives can produce a meaningful environment for their members to practise and develop their skills and to participate actively in the society. At the same time, they can also form social communities where the depressing effects of unemployment on the persons affected can be reduced and new social capital can be produced.

Labour and other co-operatives in work integration have produced – with minimal inputs from the public sector – both new job opportunities and opportunities to renew or improve vocational skills for thousands of the unemployed. With a little more support from the public sector (be this financial or other support), Finnish society would greatly benefit from the job creation and financial effects of the co-operatives in work integration.

Co-operative social enterprises other than labour co-operatives are still young, but the commitment of associations and other co-operative members, together with the relative success of these experiments, indicate that these initiatives are going to gain a permanent place in Finnish society. They represent a further step on the way from the traditional municipality or association-run sheltered workshops or work centres to a more business-oriented way of working. On the other hand, these experiments have shown that social enterprises cannot achieve full self-financing (Mannila 1996) when working with severely handicapped people.

The public interest in the positive employment effects of new co-operatives has led to a reinterpretation of the regulations regarding who is an entrepreneur and who is allowed to receive unemployment benefits as well as to a new support measure for establishing co-operatives (see the section on Finance).

Labour co-operatives can be seen as a transitional phase in a process that can evolve in three directions. First, a labour co-operative can evolve into an ordinary worker co-operative or into an employee-owned business. The co-operative then gradually develops its own products and services and employs its members or at least part of them on a full-time basis. A second possibility is that the *raison d'être* of the co-operative gradually disappears, as its active members become employed directly by other companies and the original purpose of reintegration of the members is met. In the third possible scenario, labour co-operatives develop their local connections to municipalities, other businesses and associations and gradually develop into a local partnership organisation or a community business, where other local stakeholders also take responsibility for the local unemployment problems.

Notes

1   Co-operative Law, Chapter 8: 13–17 and Chapter 9: 17.
2   Co-operative law, Chapter 9: 17–19.

Bibliography

ANDERSSON, C. (1997) *Kolmannen sektorin työllistävää vaikutusta vahvistettava*, Press Release of Minister of Culture, Helsinki.

BORZAGA, C. (1997) 'The Emes Network – The Emergence of Social Enterprises in Europe', ISSAN, Trento.

BORZAGA, C. and MITTONE L. (1996) 'The Multi-Stakeholder Versus the Non-profit Organisation', Paper presented at theVIII Riunione Scientifica della SIEP, Pavia, 4–5 October.

ELOAHO, M. and KOIVUNIEMI, V. (1997) *Tutkimus Osuuskunta Itämeren Ansion jäsenten työllistymisestä osuuskuntansa kautta ja työsuhteiden pituudesta*, Osuuskunta Itämeren Ansio, Helsinki.

Finnish Co-operative Law (1994) Finn Coop Pellervo, Finnish Consumer Co-operative Association and Finnish Co-operative Development Centre, Helsinki.

HIETALA, K. (1997) *Kolmas sektori potentiaalisena työllistäjä*, Labour Policy Studies, no. 176, Ministry of Labour, Helsinki.

HOVI, T. (1998) 'Uusosuustoiminnan julkisuuskuva viidessä suomalaisessa sanomalehdessä – 1995–1997', manuscript for pro-graduate paper, Helsinki.

HYYRYLÄINEN, T. (1994) *Toiminnan aika*, Vammala.

KANANEN, P. (1998) 'Talous, demokratia ja kolmas sektori', in KINNUNEN, P. and LAITINEN, R. *Näkymätön kolmas sektori*, Sosiaali- ja terveysturvan Keskusliitto, Helsinki, 169–88.

KARJALAINEN, J. (1996) *Työosuustoiminta työllistämisen välineenä*, Labour Policy Studies no. 154, Ministry of Labour, Helsinki.

KARJALAINEN, J., PIIPPO, T. and PIRINEN, K. (1998) *Yhteisöyrittäjyys ja uudet kysyntäalueet Uudellamaalla*, Publications 18, Institute for Co-operative Studies, Helsinki.

KOISTINEN, Pertti (1996) 'The Lessons to Be Learned. The Labour Market Policies of Finland and Sweden in 1990–1996', Paper presented at the 18th Conference on European Employment Systems and the Welfare State, July 9–14, University of Tampere, Finland.

KÖPPÄ, T. (1998) 'Yhteisöllisyys, yrittäjyys ja arvot', in KOSKINIEMI, E. *Osuustoiminnallinen yhteisyrittäminen*, KSL julkaisut, Tampere, 11–28.

KOSKINIEMI, E. (ed.) (1998) *Osuustoiminnallinen yhteisyrittäminen*, KSL kirjat, Tampere.

KOSTILAINEN, H. and PÄTTINIEMI, P. (1997) *Haviva-ADAPT projektin väliraportti 1997*, Institute for Cooperative Studies, Helsinki.

KOTISALO, Y., (1998), 'Kainuun esiyrittäjyys kokeilun vaikutuksen arviointi', in PÄÄSKYLÄ *et al.*, *Lex Kainuu. Alueellinen työllisyyskokeilu 1999–2003*, Kainuun Liitto, Vihanti, 114–19.

MANNILA, S. (1996) *Social Firms in Europe. Some Practical Aspects*, Stakes, Saarijärvi.

NIVALA, T. (1997) *Raportti Kainuun uusosuustoiminnasta*, Kainuun Uusosuustoiminannan kehittämiskeskus, Kajaani.

PAASIVIRTA, A. (1998) 'Labour Co-operatives and Employment', Paper presented at the seminar on Development days for co-operative businesses, November, Helsinki.

PÄÄSKYLÄ, E., KARPPINEN, T., MIKKONEN, E., HEIKKINEN, K., KARJALAINEN, S. and HÄRKÖNEN, A. (1998) *Lex Kainuu. Alueellinen työllisyyskokeilu 1999–2003*, Kainuun Liitto, Vihanti.

PARJANNE, M.-L. (1997) *Työmarkkinat murroksessa*, B 135 Series, ETLA, Helsinki.

PÄTTINIEMI, P. (1998) 'Worker Co-operatives and Self-managed Enterprises in Finland – Development Trends and Problems', Paper presented at the Swedish seminar of self-management, April 18, Marienhamn.

—— (1997) 'Suomalainen työosuustoiminta osana Eurooppalaista uusosuustoimintaa', in PUHAKKA, S. (ed.) *Sanastosta sanomaan – Osuustoiminnan ideologiasta ja arvoista*, Publications of the Institute for Co-operative Studies 16, Helsinki.

—— (ed.) (1995) *Sosiaalitalous ja paikallinen kehitys*, Publications of the Institute for Co-operative Studies 11, Helsinki.

PÄTTINIEMI, P. and NYLUND, M. (1997) 'Integrating Social Enterprises in the Finnish Society', Paper presented in the Nordic Seminar of Social Policy Researchers, November 13, Vaasa.

PFED-Foundation (1997) *Preliminary Study on Employment in the Sector of Mental Rehabilitation*, Helsinki.

PIIPPO, T. (1997) *Uusosuustoiminnan tukiorganisaatiot Isossa-Britaniassa, Ruotsissa ja Suomessa*, Publications of the Institute for Co-operative Studies 14, Helsinki.

SCHLUTER, R. (1996) 'Worker Co-operatives and Social Co-operatives in Europe', CECOP Seminar on Social Economy, March 3, Kokkola.

SUOMINEN, A. (1995) 'Uudenmaan työosuuskunta Aktio', in PÄTTINIEMI, P. *Sosiaalitalous ja paikallinen kehitys*, Osuustoimintainstituutti julkaisuja 11, Helsinki.

Uusosuustoimintaprojekti (1998), Institute for Co-operative Studies, Helsinki.

Uusosuuskuntien koulutustarpeet (1997), Institute for Co-operative Studies, Helsinki.

5 France

Social enterprises developing 'proximity services'

Jean-Louis Laville

Introduction

In France, the term 'social economy' refers to co-operatives, mutual societies and those associations with an economic dimension[1] which altogether represent a total of around 1.7 million jobs (Bidet 1997). The components of the social economy have underlying similarities because they come from the same original modern associationism which appeared in the first half of the nineteenth century. They were all citizenship-related and fundamentally socio-political but the various legal statuses defined during the years 1890 to 1920 led to quite distinct forms of development. Co-operatives became part of the market economy and, after a period between the wars, during which there was a division of labour between the capitalist and co-operative sectors, competition emerged in the same fields of activity. On the other hand, the mutual societies focused on less commercial activities, managing health insurance schemes and then providing supplementary cover for the same risks when social security was made widely available to the population (Manoa, Rault and Vienney 1992). Moreover associations that had become involved in the provision of services drew support from the welfare state after the Second World War, while taking on tasks associated with public responsibilities[2] (Demoustier, Hofman and Ramisse 1996).

But with the financial constraints that began to weigh on social policy during the 1970s, the idea of the 'associative enterprise' (Alix and Castro 1990) spread, demonstrating a trend towards a lesser degree of dependence on the public authorities. In France, the term 'social enterprise' did not appear until the second half of the 1990s and remains little used. However, in the context outlined above, and in terms of the general definition used in the present book, it is possible to distinguish two groups of associations that may be regarded as following the social enterprise rationale. Both of these have emerged in France over the last two decades.

Organisations belonging to the movement for labour-market insertion through economic activity (insertion enterprises, intermediate associations etc.)[3] constitute the first group. These organisations aim at creating jobs for those unemployed people who are excluded from the labour market because of their low level of qualifications. The objective is to combat negative discrimination in employment, given that paid work is an indispensable vehicle of social integration. They have mainly developed in routine activities which can be standardised in industry and services, or in some personal services in commerce or the hotel and catering business, while adapting working methods to make them more suitable for the target public. Some publications discussing this question regard enterprises for insertion through economic measures as the only social enterprises in France (Bernier and Estivill 1997).

Problems in obtaining paid work, however, are not the only sources of exclusion. The increased social inequalities that characterise contemporary society (Fitoussi and Rosanvallon 1997; Giddens 1994) produce other kinds of exclusion, such as the absence of services from which some parts of the population suffer because of inadequate income levels or because they live in disadvantaged urban or rural areas. Other organisations have, therefore, been set up to create services to fulfil unsatisfied social needs in the context of local development, and these organisations constitute the second group of social enterprises. Many of them have been set up in the field of 'proximity services',[4] that can be defined as services responding to individual or community demand, within a proximity that may be defined objectively in terms of a local area, but can also be conceived subjectively, i.e. referring to the personal dimension of the services provided (Laville 1992; Nyssens and Petrella 1996).

In fact, the geographical proximity – arising from the fact that services are either delivered to the home or provided within a short distance of it – leads to a personal dimension, since the service provider either visits a client at home or becomes involved in family or neighbourhood relationships.

Social enterprises working in the provision of 'proximity services' have tried to avoid being restricted to serving certain 'target publics'. Their work in the fight against exclusion is thus expressed through their wish to reconcile initiative and solidarity, basing their services on citizens' initiatives and ensuring that the services provided are accessible to the largest number of people possible in a local area. There are three main differences between them and private, for-profit enterprises working in the same field of activities: they are not based on the expectation of profit from capital invested; users are not merely consumers, they are stakeholders in the service; and the choice of clients according to their ability to pay is outlawed in the name of social justice.

This study focuses on an analysis of these social enterprises, and falls into three parts. The first part shows how services have developed in two typical areas of activity, viz. childcare and home help, during the period of expansion preceding today's changes, at a time when the discourse was about social services, rather than proximity services. The resources then available for redistribution made it possible to develop the public provision of childcare and an increasing professionalisation of home help services, and the associations which played a pioneering role were able to access public finance for their work. The second part focuses on the emergence of proximity services, the issues surrounding them, and the appearance of social enterprises in the areas of provision concerned. Finally, the third part examines their interactions with public policy.

1   The development of social services

For a long time personal services were provided by the household or by charities or volunteers of one sort or another. The period of economic growth that began after the Second World War changed this situation. The establishment of social protection for all – under what was to become known as the welfare state – gave the social services financial resources on an unprecedented level and, at the same time, the public authorities were empowered to issue regulations to govern the use of these resources.

Childcare

Under the French social security system, at departmental level, 115 Family Allowances Funds (*CAF, Caisses d'allocations familiales*) are directly responsible for social benefits and assistance. The *CAF*s play a key role, together with the local authorities, in providing childcare facilities for children up to the age of three. The state's concern for childcare is reflected in the development of rules governing the childcare premises, usually created by the public sector, and in the classification of the professions involved. However, the state's intervention has not ruled out the predominance of associations.

Collective childcare

Most of the collective childcare facilities are crèches and are part of the public sector. Local crèches, which provide more than 80 per cent of all places, are run by the local authorities, associations or the *CAF* and are open to local residents. These crèches offer permanent daily service for working parents. Staff crèches, providing less than 20 per cent of all places, are run by hospitals, administrations or businesses and are intended primarily for employees.

Playgroups offer a partial service, primarily for non-working mothers. These were regulated in 1962, and in the following decade their numbers grew rapidly as a result of the growing concern of parents for their children to socialise at an early age. Like crèches, playgroups are financed by the local authorities, the *CAF*s and families. The local authorities pay half the average daily cost. It is this area of childcare that absorbs most *CAF* funding.

'Multi-purpose' centres serve as both crèches and playgroups and reflect the trend towards a more flexible type of childcare, which is of shorter – but regular – duration.

'Children's nurses', employed not only in childcare but also in hospitals or in maternal and childcare agencies, have an extra year's training after they obtain their diplomas as state-registered nurses, midwives or social welfare workers. 'Paediatric auxiliary nurses' are the personnel who are present with the children in the crèche; the administrative work is carried out by children's nurses. Crèches also employ pre-school teaching staff.

Home-based childcare

In addition to collective care, there is also the possibility of home-based childcare, using a child-minder. Child-minders are not required to have any training. However, for several years now, training has been made available to them through the Departmental Directorates for Health and Social Welfare. In 1977, child-minders obtained recognition of their professional status as employees. This status, which provides them with limited old age and sickness insurance, was recognised belatedly and is still inadequate, although the public authorities are trying to improve it. Child-minders must go through an authorisation procedure that is carried out through a home visit by the appropriate health authorities' representative. They are then usually allowed to care for a maximum of three pre-school children.

Since 1971, the 'family crèche' system has enabled child-minders to form organisations, based around a director who has medical training and who supervises their work, while they continue to work at home. In the past, the focus of the childcare professions has always been on the medical and health aspects, but this approach has gradually broadened as new types of childcare have become available. None the less, the status and pay of the different professions still vary considerably and there is a real need to harmonise practices and the types of jobs available. Little attention has been paid to co-operation with families, and training systems are still underdeveloped. These professions continue to be generally under-valued, underpaid and predominantly female.

Home help

In the field of home help, just as in the area of childcare, the state's intervention, although important, has not altered the predominance of associations. For many activities, initially covered by social assistance, the sources of funding have become more diverse as policy on the elderly has developed.

The elderly have long been assimilated into the category of the poor and this gave them access to the social welfare services at a very early stage, before policy on the elderly had been formulated. The first state funding was under the social welfare umbrella and was intended to enable the elderly to have help in the home. The first specific reference to social assistance for the elderly (the monthly home help allowance) was in the Decree of 29 November 1953. In 1954, benefits in kind were introduced. Until 1962, such benefits were dependent on the medical condition of applicants. The origins of home help were thus mainly medical; this activity was considered as a means of relieving the pressure on hospitals (Nogues *et al.* 1984).

In the 1960s, policy on the elderly began to take shape and the state's role grew. In the 1970s, the home help service was organised, using the resources available. It was possible to obtain home help under the National Employees' Old Age Insurance Fund (*CNAVTS, Caisse nationale d'assurance vieillesse des travailleurs salariés*). In spite of the difficulties created, in particular by the division between medical and social assistance, the concept of home help gradually became established, although its funding came from several sources. The average structure of these resources was the following: social assistance, through local taxes, covered nearly half the cost of home help; one quarter was paid for by the *CNAVTS*; 10 per cent by other pension schemes; and approximately 15 per cent by users.

Furthermore, as the service grew and became more organised, the home helps themselves were anxious to gain professional status. In 1982, the Secretary of State for the Elderly recognised that the home help plays a social role. Similarly, the Ministerial Circular of 7 August 1982 acknowledges that the home help's work is not restricted to housework. Home helps asked for recognition, which they were given through the National Collective Agreement of 1983. In this agreement, the work of the home help is defined as complementing that of doctors, nurses and assistant-nurses' specialised tasks. The task of the home help is to provide material, moral and social support for the elderly insofar as they enable beneficiaries to continue to be independent, to remain at home and to keep in touch with the outside world. They may perform similar duties for people who are no longer able to lead an active life and whose material or social situation is such that they require external help. Their duties extend to the point at which other professional skills are needed.

At the same time, in the 1980s, public demand for support in the home as a real alternative to hospitalisation and for a better solution than unnecessary hospitalisation for dependent elderly, resulted in the establishment of home nursing services together with home carers for the seriously dependent or disabled.

In spite of the different types of funding and professional specialisation which have been superimposed over the last thirty years, the structure of the home help services has continued to be based on associations which are part of large federations. These associations can be defined as 'employment associations' because their main role has been to employ women in this field of activity. Their success has been considerable, both in the number of services provided and in the number of jobs created. These associations identified social needs not recognised by the state, and as the funds available for redistribution increased steadily, they poured money back into job creation in the sector.

The level of technical knowledge demanded by the state[5] (understanding of the organisation of funding, drafting of activity reports, qualifications of permanent staff) further increased the level of professionalism in the associations. Finally, state intervention between 1945 and 1975, the years of prosperity, meant that the initiatives of the associations became heavily dependent on the public authorities while voluntary work gradually decreased to give way to paid employment in the associations which were managing the home help services. Of course, the effects of these developments varied and some organisations were able to hold on to their original values to a large extent. Nevertheless, financing procedures have led to funding being divided among different budgets, which affects the development of projects, and the role of volunteers in the associations is often confined to co-ordination, management and representation.

2 Proximity services and social enterprises

Their integration into the welfare state provision gave the associations a pioneering role and induced a strong dependency on state support. For a long time, the public and associative service providers enjoyed a local quasi-monopoly. With no incentive to be innovative, and cocooned in a protected situation, they were affected, like any other organisation, by personal power strategies or bureaucratic behaviour, and experienced institutional isomorphism, which turned some of them into quasi-administrations (Di Maggio and Powell 1983).[6] In contrast with the situation in other European countries, associations in France have not only been engaged in advocacy and pioneering functions; they have also been a major provider of services, but many of them have experienced a process of bureaucratisation. However, the passage to a welfare pluralism (Evers 1993) provoked the appearance of innovative and collective initiatives which have tried to provide new associative solutions, different from arrangements such as individual child-minders.

Experience has proved that voluntary status in itself does not guarantee service quality and user respect. What is important is the way in which this status is used in day-to-day practice. In the long term, the legitimacy of service provision by the associations depends on their ability to ensure a dialogue with users, to mobilise diverse voluntary commitments and to find appropriate new financial balances within a new, less sheltered environment. The associations able to achieve these conditions are characterised by a more participatory and entrepreneurial approach.

In fact a number of long-standing or more recently founded associations are attempting to organise or re-organise themselves in this direction. For example, in the area of pre-school care, where public-sector supply dominated, voluntary-sector innovation has been the source of a new community childcare model, promoted by the Association of the Collectives of Children, Parents and Professionals (*ACEPP, Association des collectifs-enfants-parents-professionnels*). Although no similar new model – based on mobilising families – has been introduced in the area of home help, where delegating tasks is a more painful process for the households concerned (Croff 1994) and where there is a relatively wide variety of federations, there have been many experiments focusing on the professionalisation of jobs, the involvement of users and the quality of services. Some of these have involved innovative national networks, such as the Agency for the Development of Proximity Services (*ADSP, Agence pour le développement des services de proximité*). This expression 'proximity services' is increasingly used and tends to reflect the growing interest in the new services, which represent opportunities to improve the quality of life.

In the following section, we will focus on those 'new' associations, and those collective initiatives in the fields of childcare and home help that meet the criteria of the definition of the 'social enterprise'.

Childcare centres involving parental participation

With the steady increase, since the 1960s, in the numbers of women participating in the labour force, the question of childcare provision has become more acute. There are not enough places available in crèches and working hours frequently tie in very poorly with the restricted opening hours of traditional crèches. At the same time, many parents now regard socialisation as an important element in their child's development. This, together with their usefulness to part-time working women, explains the success of playgroups which take children for a few hours or a few days each week.

According to Leprince (1985), the measures adopted remain partial and do nothing to resolve the contradictions generated by the present development of modes of pre-school childcare: the contradiction between the desire to promote prevention and encourage equality of opportunity and the desire to develop the least costly modes of childcare for the community; the contradiction between the acknowledged wish for children to socialise at an ever earlier age and the transfer of childcare responsibility to the family environment; the contradiction between the educational role conferred on collective crèches and the relatively well off backgrounds of the parents who use them. It is against this background that parental crèches have developed.

First created in 1968, informal crèches put the emphasis on parental responsibility and on teaching children to socialise. Combining a self-management approach with a 'pedagogic' approach, they operated in a field previously characterised by a strong emphasis on public health and a non-participatory model excluding parents from the services functioning. Thus, these informal crèches remained voluntarily outside the jurisdiction of the public authorities, which distrusted them. They attempted to make childcare more of a life experience for the children. The idea was that there should be no separation between the parents and the professionals, or between the children and the parents. The parents took over the collective care of the children and gave special prominence to activities designed to promote their development and awareness of the world around them. This new approach contrasted with the partitioning and specialisation common in traditional modes of pre-school care.

From 1980, there were developments on two fronts, motivated by the social and economic crisis. The informal crèches sought to stabilise their functioning and their structure by seeking subsidies to allow them to reduce their operating and investment costs and to recruit paid employees. And the public authorities began to take an interest in the informal crèches' low costs and child-socialisation philosophy.

Finally, in February 1981, the Association of Collectives of Children and Parents (*ACEP, Association des collectifs-enfants-parents*) was created,[7] and on 21

August 1981 the informal crèches received official recognition and were to be known henceforth as 'parental crèches'. The parents pay half of the crèches' operating costs. The other half comes from:

- *CAF* allowances and subsidies, which are paid if at least 50 per cent of the parents are in receipt of *CAF* allowance. The 1989 reform of *CAF* allowances enabled the daily child allowances paid to parental crèches to be aligned with those paid to other collective structures, and this was a significant improvement;
- local authority subsidies are also needed to balance the management costs, but they leave the crèches vulnerable to interference from the local authority, which can sometimes be problematic because numerous local leaders still know nothing about this mode of organisation.

Other difficulties persist. Despite some advances, such as the 'Ministerial Fund to Support Parental Initiative Structures', which is used for equipment expenditure, the slowness of the funding procedures and the complexity of the set-ups still pose a threat to many projects. In addition, organising parental duty rosters in the crèches is by no means straightforward, since too many workers still do not benefit from reduced, reorganised working hours. It is still very difficult for some categories of workers to find the free time necessary to participate in the crèche. On average, parents are expected to give between six and eight hours of their time each week. Parents must therefore be either in part-time employment or be fairly 'heroic' to add this extra burden of hours to their already heavy workload, particularly as it is a voluntary service which they must carry out before they can reap any of the benefits that their participation might bring.

In spite of everything, these crèches, partly run and managed by the parents who participate in the general assemblies and nominate the board members, have mushroomed. A number of them have also been created by professionals and the national network became the Association of the Collectives of Children, Parents and Professionals (*ACEPP*) at the beginning of the 1990s to reflect this enlargement in the stakeholders. The number of parental crèches doubled almost every year between 1981 and 1984. There were 566 in January 1989, compared with only thirty in January 1982. Parental crèches represent 3 per cent of all available crèche places. The spread has been both geographical and social. In 1989 there were 102 parental crèches in major conurbations, 138 in rural areas and 326 in small and medium-sized conurbations, with a widening social spread of parents involved.

By January 1994,[8] there were 720 parental crèches, with space for 10,800 children. Of these structures, 477 offered 7,300 'multi-purpose' places, combining collective crèches and playgroups, and creating the equivalent of approximately 3,000 full-time jobs. More generally, childcare initiatives involving parental participation have created two-thirds of community childcare places in the last ten years.

Initiatives in the field of home help

In the field of home help, the desire to establish an *ACEPP*-type relationship between families and professionals can be found in the associations, which, despite differences in size or generation, are alike in the attention they pay to employees and users. Since it is not possible to mention them all, one particular example may serve to illustrate the process.

Etre[9] is an association whose aim is to set up home help networks in liaison with small care centres for elderly or dependent persons.[10] Why prolong life, if not to make it enjoyable to the end? It was in an attempt to answer this question that a number of persons of like minds came together. Sharing similar experiences, both in their professional and personal lives, they took a critical look at the status and place given to old age in our society by institutions and by families.

It was this, and the feeling of not being listened to in their day-to-day dealings with the medico-social world, that convinced the promoters of this project that an innovative response was needed. The setting down of a plan on paper gave substance to their thoughts. Calling the project 'Ageing and Dying in the City', they set out the objectives as follows in the association's statutes:

> To help people to continue to live at home; to offer services enabling families to envisage or continue supporting a physically or mentally dependent person at home, through the provision of educational, psychological or material assistance; and to enable families and individuals to look after dependent persons, so as to re-introduce the reality of disability, old-age and death into daily life.

They requested meetings with a wide range of people and bodies, including regional services, elected representatives of several municipalities, administrations operating in this field, associations, health professionals such as doctors, pharmacists and nurses, ministers, etc. They managed to arrange more than forty meetings, in which they found backing for their own views, got those they met interested in the 'philosophy' of the project, and established that no similar initiatives of this type were known of locally.

Etre has a director involved in developing the community project, as well as administrative staff, who play an important co-ordination role with the employees and users. The number of employees providing assistance to elderly persons has deliberately been kept down to approximately sixty persons for seventy families assisted, in order to ensure frequent direct personal contact, but creation of similar initiatives based on the pilot experiment is in progress. The promoters propose not only home help but also work for the realisation of small care centres/units for disabled persons, integrating in their formation the relations with the families concerned. The staff of a care centre comprises a full-time house-mistress or organiser, two assistants and seven other persons to cover nights and weekends. There are thirteen volunteers in the association's management bodies, and added to these are all the volunteers who provide daily support for the persons assisted.

Such organisations, which encountered many obstacles, felt the need to join forces with other groups working on similar projects. For this reason the founders of Etre became involved in the *ADSP*, whose dynamic new approaches in proximity services are well proven.

Since 1989, the *ADSP* has united a wide range of individuals such as service managers, project supporters and promoters, professional and elected members of institutions and associations, trade unionists, researchers and academics. The network they established was thus not specialised in one field of activity. It was based on a common approach to developing proximity services, distinct from other methods. Their approach can be summarised by two key points:

- Proximity services can constitute a real economic sector. Because of a large number of socio-demographic factors, there is a strong 'social demand' which can no longer be met by ad hoc arrangements which reduce this potential source of jobs to no more than a favoured area for the socio-professional insertion of the most disadvantaged people.
- However, given their particular nature, these services can only be provided by a new kind of entrepreneurial organisational form, able to interlink different kinds of financial and non-financial resources and resting on contract-based solutions at both local and sectoral level.

In contrast with public services, these proximity services (Berger and Michel 1998) try to get the users involved in planning and running the services. In contrast with the social treatment of unemployment, they aim to avoid confusing proximity services with the insertion of disadvantaged people. In contrast with measures that focus on the number of jobs created, they aim to structure employment through setting up collective groups. Finally, in contrast with the commercial services sector, they do not only target a financially secure public nor restrict the role of users to that of mere consumers, but try to involve them as citizens.

3 Public policies and social enterprises

From the mid 1980s, the public budgets dedicated to social services began to be insufficient for the growing demand in personal services. The extent of the state's influence was linked to the resources of the welfare state, in turn dependent on the economic growth rate. The slowing of the growth rate triggered a crisis in the welfare state. Steps were therefore taken to develop proximity services, as a means of both creating jobs and curbing social spending.

Strong changes in public policies

The first attempts to develop proximity services through new public policies were based on the simple fact that there are, on the one hand, a number of unsatisfied needs and, on the other, a large number of unemployed people. Consequently, it seems logical to encourage the creation of new jobs in an area that can satisfy unanswered needs. For unemployed people, access to employment has been improved by the introduction of new intermediate forms of employment, between unemployment and social assistance. This was the basis for the social measures introduced to give the unemployed access to 'bridging' jobs, firstly, through the youth employment scheme (*Travaux d'utilité collective*), and then through the so-called 'employment solidarity contracts' (*Contrats emploi-solidarité*), with the recognition of 'intermediate associations' (*Associations intermédiaires*) whose role is to provide temporary work.

These social programmes produced disappointing effects, mainly because they gave rise to confusion between new services and job integration. They led to the devaluation of the jobs created, because they were designed more for the people who were to be integrated into the labour market than for the users in a sector where a high level of social skills was required. Beneficiaries found themselves in jobs which they had not been able to choose; they were allocated simply because they happened to be available at that moment, and the tasks involved had, for the most part, little relationship with one another. Entering the personal services more by necessity than by choice, the unemployed were moreover offered only temporary jobs, with no provision for learning in the long term. This situation created particular problems in a sector where a high level of social skills was required.

The development of the services was impeded by the turnover inherent in temporary employment schemes. For this reason, various measures were taken from the end of the 1980s, to ensure that users had the resources to pay for these services, without having to resort to social unemployment measures. In the field of childcare, allowances such as the 'allowance for childcare at home' (*Allocation de garde d'enfant à domicile*) and the 'family aid to employ an approved childminder' (*Aide à la famille pour l'emploi d'une assistante maternelle agréée*) were introduced. In the field of home help, an attendance allowance and exemptions from social contributions and taxes were introduced for private individuals employing someone at home. These measures, applying only to private individuals, discriminated against the associations offering the same kind of services. As a result, the public authorities introduced a special status of 'mandatory association', making it eligible for the same concessions as private individuals because, in such an association, the private individuals keep the legal responsibility of the employer. Consequently, the workers are not employed by the association but directly by the household – the association being only an intermediary. This status, which is financially attractive, was adopted by many associations, e.g. the National Union of Associations for Rural Home Help (*Union nationale d'aide à domicile en milieu rural*) which provided 18 per cent of their working hours through mandatory associations in 1992 and 30 per cent in 1994.

All these measures aimed at encouraging households to recruit personnel, placed the emphasis on job creation as an end in itself, in contrast with the previous objective of work access for disadvantaged people. The new maxim was the creation of 'real jobs', which the 'family jobs' programme set out to achieve in 1991. The main innovation of this programme was the introduction of tax credits for all taxable households that create jobs at home.[11] Although additional measures were taken to help associations, in practice, the family jobs programme has tended to encourage the conclusion of contracts between private individuals and employees.

For some important private businesses, this system has still to be improved in order to enable supply to be organised adequately. According to the National French Employers' Council (*CNPF, Conseil national du patronat français*), which has made this one of its central themes, the time has come to 'remove the obstacles to the emergence of a family services market, for which there is a strong demand'.[12] According to the employers' council, commercial investment in this field is only feasible if accompanied by reforms concerning demand. From the demand side, enterprises want to see a bigger shift towards free-market regulation and want the advantages enjoyed by private employers to be extended to embrace employees forming part of an enterprise's workforce. The plea for a genuinely market-based system rests on criticism of the state system as practised during the period of expansion.

This line of argument reduces the diversity of existing forms of supply to a single model, that of a 'collectivised' system. Behind this attack on the existing forms of organisation of this field of activity lies the conviction that proximity services need to be made more market-based to enhance their credibility. The private sector can bring to proximity services 'its competence, its competitiveness and its capacity for organisational engineering'. According to the *CNPF*, a quality service from service enterprises will restore consumer confidence in service-providers, once freedom of choice has been given back to the consumer. Through intense lobbying, the Union of Personal-Service Enterprises (*Syndicat des entreprises de services aux personnes*) set up by the *CNPF* and incorporating some of the largest private groups in terms of workforce size, has succeeded in getting the tax exemptions allowable for 'family jobs' extended to enterprises, under the terms of a law adopted in 1996.

These changes in public policies affected the place of public services and associations. In childcare, even if the presence of the for-profit private sector remains very weak, the public service has lost its monopoly in the provision of services and it was the same for associations in the case of home help.

Negative discrimination at the national level

The move of the national public policies in proximity services to competition-based regulation translates in practical terms into discrimination against social enterprises. In the case of pre-school childcare provision, according to the *ACEPP*, whereas associations formed by parents and professionals have accounted for two-thirds of the new places created in pre-school childcare facilities over the past ten years, the measures which have been taken to mobilise resources on the demand side mainly concern non-collective forms of childcare and ignore the specific nature of these original initiatives.

The sector of pre-school childcare is marked by the separation between 'black-market' and official childcare, and between individual and collective provision. In fact, the majority of childcare is provided on an undeclared basis. In response to this situation, priority has been given in recent years to the possibility of creating or regularising jobs in the childcare sector. The new measures adopted in favour of child-minders and the measures on family jobs are evidence of the approach taken in this area, under which clear encouragement is given to employment at home. The foundations have been laid for giving recognised status to these jobs through the introduction of compulsory training for child-minders, and the policy implemented by the *CAF* in this area has tried to impose the provision of individual child-minding services.

However, the aim of creating jobs has led the state to take measures inapplicable for collective child-minding, thereby creating a situation of competition distorted by inequitable public assistance in favour of individual childcare to the detriment of collective childcare (*ACEPP* 1996). Tax deductions for family jobs can be as much as 45,000 FF (6,860 Euro) a year for the employment of a person to look after children at the employer's home, whereas families that obtain child-minding services through an association are not eligible for these tax deductions. An allowance like the *Allocation de garde d'enfant à domicile* is also unfair in its attribution criteria, because it does not take into account the differences in income and does not cover parents who use collective child-minding services.

In the face of this negative situation, the *ACEPP* proposes the following:

- the harmonisation of child-minding policy so as to give families a real choice of childcare provision for their children on the basis of quality, rather than financial criteria;
- the recognition of the role and specific character of associations responsible for managing a collective child-minding structure; the contribution of voluntary work has to be integrated in the cost price in order to adjust the amount of public finances granted to these parental initiatives, and the provision of an increased allowance when they provide childcare to families suffering social exclusion or on low incomes;
- an increase to 45,000 FF (6,860 Euro) of tax deductions for the cost of collective childcare, which are currently limited to 3,750 FF (572 Euro). The ceiling for these tax deductions would then be the same as that for family service jobs.

According to the *ACEPP*, these proposals are not designed to give an advantage to collective childcare services, but rather to allow parents to make their choice of childcare provision among different forms of supply while getting an equitable support from public authorities. It is a paradox that the current situation penalises collective forms of childcare, although they provide more guarantees in terms of training and recognised status for workers than individual childcare. Moreover, the most recent amendments to the law on family service jobs give the same tax advantages to households which use family service employment through enterprises as to those which directly recruit a domestic worker, but they do not take into account the associative forms of childcare. In other words, the initiatives of associations do not receive the same encouragement as those of private individuals and enterprises.

These statements also apply to home help, in which the superimposing of old forms of financing and new ways of direct help to users has made the procedures more complex. This has damaged the work of providers and detracted from the clarity of provision for users. Four formulas exist side by side: (1) benefits in kind, such as statutory, optional home help; (2) cash payments such as the compensatory allowance; (3) tax aid; and (4) exemptions from social contributions. This makes the system inextricable, as shown by the rapid development of the services of mandatory associations under the new arrangements. Associations which were already employers and now also operate under the new arrangements are seeing their employees – to whom they are bound by a contract corresponding to a collective agreement on home help – being also employed by several private employers as well under the agreement on family jobs. The result is that employment contracts and remuneration rules are different from one hour of the day to the next. This situation is damaging not just for employees, but also for the quality of the service.

In a way, it can be said that a 'poor quality bonus' has been established through the recent modes of mobilising resources on the demand side, favouring a payment per act. Instead of giving priority to quality standards, they have focused on level of price. The lack of a joint effort to structure supply means that the time allocated to training and co-operation between professionals and users is cut back in favour of 'productive' paid work alone. This is all the more serious since the nature of the services tends to lead to the isolation of employees and because opportunities to meet and discuss matters together are crucial for preventing the fragmentation and break-up of the services.

The end result is that associations, which are by far the biggest employers in the area of home help, are faced with an awkward dilemma, viz. either pay less attention to quality in order to remain competitive, or aim for quality and endanger their financial position. The rapid development of this area has strongly undermined their operations, and this does not help to promote managed change or openness to the needs of the user.

In contrast with traditional state regulation, which lumps users together into different administrative categories, competition-based regulation, be it of a market or quasi-market nature, takes account of the fact that proximity services are tailored to individuals. However, it ignores the fact that as well as producing private benefits for their immediate users, these services also produce collective benefits for the community; in other words they provide positive collective externalities. Moreover, it does not take into account the fact that proximity services can influence social links and citizenship. Regulation based on competition gives priority to support for consumption and employment, which, important as they are, cannot be the only aims of public action. Indeed, the public authorities may intervene in the regulation of childcare for many other reasons. As pointed out by Nyssens and Petrella (1996), they may intervene in the name of the principles of fairness chosen by society, which include the desire to give everyone access to this service; in order to produce positive externalities for the economy, for example the greater availability of women on the labour market and the educational role of childcare services; and to guarantee a high-quality service by the introduction of a set of standards in an area in which users find it difficult to assess the quality of the service provided.

To sum up, home help and childcare, which have long been thought of as collective services – in other words services which must be funded and controlled by the public authorities by means of state regulation – are increasingly coming to be considered to be private services in which consumers must be given freedom of choice and which can generate jobs. This evolution arises from a simplistic two-way opposition between collective and private services. In fact, proximity services cannot be considered to be exclusively collective or exclusively private. While it is true that they are services whose use is divisible, they are also services requiring public regulation, since they produce not only private benefits but also collective benefits which affect not just their users, and they also have effects in terms of social justice and equality.

Positive trends in regional policies

Taking into account this characteristic of proximity services to be both individual and quasi-collective is the aim of certain emerging forms of public intervention which are clearly distinct from the dominant tendency towards competition-based regulation. These efforts are gradually leading to a change in the objectives and methods of public intervention. This change contributes to a socio-economic development which mobilises society while, at the same time, ensuring that the principles of justice and the quality of life in society are respected.

A relevant example is provided by the policy adopted in July 1996 by the Regional Council of Nord-Pas-de-Calais which was 'designed to create a framework for professional jobs, and to ensure that these new activities are rooted in social reality', in order to 'promote the development of viable, lasting activities which are accessible to everyone'.[13] The main objective is to transform the local political and administrative system so that it can really encourage initiatives, since the region seems to be the most appropriate level for strengthening a locally based economy. This is being done, mainly, by involving networks of those engaged in the development and application of policy.

In this policy, it is assumed that proximity services may take the form of:

- private enterprises, for those services designed for specific groups of clients who have sufficient means, are convinced of the importance of paying for these services and have reliable information on their quality;
- public services which are in the general interest. Since they cannot be funded by market resources, they must be provided within the framework of

existing or new public utilities, which calls for negotiation between public or para-public authorities and institutions;

- social enterprises, which, with a view to creating a civil and solidarity-based economy, can achieve a lasting organisational balance by combining market resources (sale to users with resources), non-market resources (arrangements with public partners to ensure that the services are accessible) and non-monetary resources (voluntary commitments encouraged by local factors).

These are the basic lines along which proximity services can be institutionalised. In this perspective, the regional policy proposes new sets of measures comprising three stages: recognition of the right to take initiatives; strengthening and development of the existing range of services; and adaptation of methods of funding.

The recognition of a right to take initiatives is designed to remedy the inequality of a situation in which institutional support is provided only to entrepreneurs with financial resources or the right contacts. To this end, the public authorities undertake to fund the assets of projects which are designed to create lasting professional jobs with common-law contracts, and to contribute to the strengthening of social cohesion, on condition that the project organisers agree to work with professional support services which can help them to formalise the project. However, entrepreneurs sometimes have to stay unpaid during the months they organise the project, which results in *de facto* selection among the various promoters. The Regional Council intends to resolve the problem of the status of promoters by organising paid training for project organisers, so that they can be allocated a specific amount of working time in order to do all the work connected with the design of activities.

In addition to this assistance for project design and training, support is also provided for start-up, where one of the persistent difficulties is the funding of management posts during the first three years of operation because of the time needed (to establish trust with partners and clients) before the activity is up and running and because of the fact that various resources need to be mobilised (through negotiations with various partners). In order to discourage the use of stop-gap solutions, two forms of start-up resources are provided: resources tapering off over three years for the creation of management jobs and resources with the formation of working capital.

In order to strengthen and develop the existing range of services, it is necessary to provide recognised job status. The public authorities commit themselves to supporting measures to give recognised status to jobs on condition that these measures include an evaluation mechanism to improve knowledge of the operation of existing structures. The observations made during diagnosis and confirmed by an evaluation committee should be used in order to define, together with the services concerned, new forms of engineering and arrangements for on-the-job training measures that are appropriate to solving the problems identified. While jobs are being consolidated, voluntary commitment is being encouraged through the funding of measures to develop and give structure to voluntary work by promoting recognition of the role of users and the development of this role in establishing projects or diversifying activities. Rather than voluntary work replacing genuine jobs because of the lack of funds, the aim is to ensure that roles are divided up between paid professionals and responsible volunteers.

Lastly, as regards the adaptation of funding and the mobilisation of resources on the demand side and given the magnitude of these tasks, the Regional Council intends to establish limits for its action. It believes that the legitimacy of public action to mobilise resources on the demand side can only be guaranteed if this action is designed to promote the access of all categories of society to these services. The Regional Council therefore refuses to take part in measures to mobilise resources on the demand side that could contribute to the creation of new divisions in demand and could exacerbate inequality in access to the services. However, it is committed to providing assistance to experiments designed to guarantee the accessibility of services.

This regional approach is different from both traditional state regulation and competition-based regulation through the attention paid to the networks of associations. It has helped to create in the first two years of implementation several hundreds of jobs. But it has also contributed to promoting a public debate and to pointing out the associated implicit and explicit choices facing society in the area of new services.

Conclusions

Social enterprises represent a reaction against the phenomenon of institutional isomorphism that has affected various elements in the social economy.[14] To avoid taking on a quasi-administrative role, associations' promoters have sought to detach themselves from state supervision that has long dominated the associations. At the same time, they have assumed the associative legal status that is the easiest and the most flexible structure available to collective enterprises in France, although in its current form it presents a number of problems.[15] Like the co-operatives, social enterprises aim for a high degree of management independence, but unlike them they do not only have access to commercial resources since the social justice which they hope to promote and the collective benefits which they provide require public finance if they are to survive in the long term. Combining commercial and non-commercial resources on a permanent basis is not easy to achieve, because it requires complex partnerships and comes up against the compartmentalised institutional thinking inherited from the years of growth. Social enterprises cannot overcome these obstacles unless they can prove their ability to develop services through taking into account the real life experiences of the various stakeholders. This is true of childcare and home help, where supplementary resources, from neither the state nor the market, are brought into the equation and which draw on voluntary commitments made possible by their position in the personalised relationships of social networks. This characteristic feature has political implications. If we consider that the future of democracy is determined by a sense of belonging to a common world, the consolidation of production networks focused on social aims will support and strengthen it.

The ability to find innovative solutions developing out of the characteristic practices of both the state and the market has been the main advantage for the emergence of social enterprises in proximity services. Their future development will depend on their ability to negotiate a renewal of public policy, the thrust of which still works to their disadvantage. Among the necessary changes is an amendment of the legal structures available in France. Should the co-operative or associative structure be adapted, or do we need to introduce a new status? The topicality of this question in 1999 is shown by a number of investigations of social enterprises. These include: research about enterprises with a social purpose commissioned by the Minister for Employment and Solidarity; working group of the National Council of Co-operation on social co-operatives; working group of the Foundation for the Development of Associative Life. The social economy born in the nineteenth century is now looking for appropriate structures to take it into the twenty-first, but beyond the questions of status, their future is linked to the possibility of a more solidarity-based model of development. As Lipietz has said, this is part of the wider question of constructing 'a solidarity-based third sector of the economy' (Lipietz 1998: 3). The creation in 2000 of the first Ministry of the Civil and Solidarity-based Economy[16] shows how this question becomes a reality.

Notes

1 According to the law of 15 December 1981, which introduced the expression 'social economy' into the French legal system, setting up the Delegation for the Social Economy; see Vienney (1994).

2 The associations are non-profit organisations. Their origins are in joint voluntary actions, but they may employ staff; in fact more than 1 million people are employed by associations in France and 13 per cent of the jobs created between 1980 and 1990 in France were in associations. It therefore does not seem helpful to describe them as 'voluntary organisations' or to speak of a 'voluntary sector'. See Archambault (1996).

3 Insertion through economic activity has been broadly treated in previous publications, in particular Defourny, Favreau and Laville (1998).

4 An approximative translation in English of the French 'services de proximité' would be 'household and community services' but to preserve the specificity of the concept, the literal translation of 'proximity services' is used in the text.

5 Throughout this section, the 'state' refers, in general, to public or semi-public institutions involved to varying degrees in financing home help, e.g. departments, social assistance, sickness insurance funds, pension funds etc.

6 About institutional isomorphism, see also the contribution of Laville and Nyssens in this book (chapter 18).

7 Its objectives are: representation with the public authorities, creation of a network, promotion of new initiatives, research and experimentation within communities. For a fuller description of the *ACEPP* experience, see Combes (1989); Passaris (1984).

8 Ministère de la Santé publique et de l'Assurance-Maladie (1995).

9 The letters stand for *Écouter, Travailler, Rencontrer, Espérer* or, in English, 'Listen, Work, Meet, Hope'. *Etre* also means 'to be' in French.

10 For a fuller description cf. Laville and Gardin (1996).

11 This tax credit was raised from an initial 17,800 FF (2,744 Euro) in 1991 to 45,000 FF (6,860 Euro) in 1995.
12 This quotation and the following one are excerpts from a text published by the National French Employers' Council: Comité de liaison des services *CNPF* (1994: 24–44).
13 Excerpts from the report of G. Hascoët, Vice-President of the Regional Council of Nord-Pas-de-Calais (Hascoët 1996: 2).
14 It should be pointed out that in doing so, they have set off a debate within the co-operative production movement which led it to adopt, at their Lille Congress in October 1997, the following declaration: 'The co-operative movement will work to formulate a special status based on that of the Italian social co-operative movement allowing a new partnership between users, voluntary workers and employees.'
15 Including problems in raising own resources, the attribution of personal responsibility to the president, the absence of a clear tax regime, etc.
16 The State Secretary nominated is G. Hascoët who was responsible for the policy implemented by the regional council of Nord-Pas-de-Calais.

Bibliography

ACEPP (1996) *Manifeste de l'Association des collectifs-enfants-parents-professionnels, ACEPP*, Paris.

ALIX, N. and CASTRO, S. (1990) *L'entreprise associative: aspects juridiques de l'intervention économique des associations*, Economica, Paris.

ARCHAMBAULT, E. (1996*) Le secteur sans but lucratif – Associations et fondations en France*, Economica, Paris.

BERGER, A. and MICHEL, G. (1998) 'Des services de proximité? Oui, mais lesquels?', in *Topo-guide des services de proximité, ADSP*, Desclée de Brouwer, Paris, 15–35.

BERNIER, A. and ESTIVILL, J. (1997) *Des pratiques différentes, une volonté commune*, CNEI, Paris.

BIDET, E. (1997) *L'économie sociale*, Le Monde Éditions, Paris.

COMBES, J. (1989) *Les crèches parentales, lieux d'ancrage de réseaux de solidarité*, Département recherches-actions, *ACEPP*, Paris.

Comité de liaison des services CNPF (1994) *Les services à la personne. Services aux consommateurs et services de proximité: des marchés à développer par l'innovation dans l'offre et par le professionnalisme des intervenants, CNPF*, Paris.

CROFF, B. (1994) *Seules – Genèse des emplois familiaux*, Éditions Metailie, Paris.

DEFOURNY, J., FAVREAU, L. and LAVILLE, J.-L. (eds) (1998) *Insertion et nouvelle économie sociale*, Desclée de Brouwer, Paris.

DEMOUSTIER, D., HOFMAN, B. and RAMISSE, M.-L. (1996) 'Connaissance des associations du secteur sanitaire et social', Equipe de socio-économie associative et coopérative, Institut d'Études Politiques de Grenoble.

DI MAGGIO, P.J. and POWELL, W.W. (1983) 'The Iron Cage Revisited: Institutional Isomorphism and Collective Rationality in Organizational Fields', *American Sociological Review*, vol. 48: 147–60.

ENJOLRAS, B. (1996) 'Associations et isomorphisme institutionnel', *Revue des Études Coopératives, Mutualistes et Associatives*, vol. 75, 261: 68–76.

EVERS, A. (1993) 'The Welfare Mix Approach. Understanding the Pluralism of Welfare Systems', in EVERS, A. and SVETLIK, I. (eds) *Balancing Pluralism. New Welfare Mixes in Care for the Elderly*, Avebury, Vienna and Aldershot, 3–31.

FITOUSSI, J.-P. and ROSANVALLON, P. (1997) *Le nouvel âge des inégalités*, Le Seuil, Paris.

GIDDENS, A. (1994) *Beyond Left and Right, The Future of Radical Politics*, Polity Press, Cambridge.

HASCOËT, G. (1996) *Le développement des services de proximité*, Région Nord-Pas-de-Calais, Conseil Régional, Lille.

JEANTET, TH. (1995) 'L'économie sociale dans le contexte français', *Revue des Études Coopératives, Mutualistes et Associatives*, no. 256: 17–25.

LAVILLE, J.-L. (ed.) (1992) *Les services de proximité en Europe*, Syros-Alternatives, Paris.

LAVILLE, J.-L. and GARDIN, L. (1996) *Les services de proximité: un choix de société*, CRIDA-LSCI (CNRS-IRESCO), Paris.

LEPRINCE, F. (1985) *Accueillir les jeunes enfants*, CNAF, Espace et familles, résumé de thèse.

LIPIETZ, A. (1998) *L'opportunité d'un nouveau type de société à vocation sociale*, interim report to the Minister for Employment and Solidarity.

MANOA, J.-Y., RAULT, D. and VIENNEY, C. (1992) 'Les institutions de l'économie sociale en France. Identifications et mesures statistiques', in DEFOURNY, J. and MONZÓN CAMPOS, J.-L. (eds) *Économie sociale – The Third Sector*, De Boeck, Bruxelles, 57–106.

Ministère de la Santé publique et de l'Assurance-Maladie (1995) SES, *Info rapides*, no. 63.

NOGUES, H., BOUGET, B., TYMEN, J. and BROVELLI, G. (1984) *Politique d'aide ménagère en Loire-Atlantique*, Centre d'études des besoins sociaux, Faculté de Nantes, Nantes.

NYSSENS, M. and PETRELLA, F. (1996) 'L'organisation des services de proximité à Charleroi: vers une économie plurielle?', *Les cahiers du CERISIS*, 96/1, Charleroi.

PASSARIS, S. (1984) *La participation parentale dans les modes de garde de la petite enfance*, 4 tomes, CIRED, École des Hautes Études en Sciences Sociales, Paris.

VIENNEY, C. (1994) *L'économie sociale*, La Découverte, Paris.

6 Germany

Social enterprises and transitional employment

Adalbert Evers and Matthias Schulze-Böing

Introduction[1]

During the 1990s, the German economy could have been considered a poor performer with regard to employment. The new *Länder* (federal states) in the East faced a sharp decline in employment due to the severe restructuring associated with the transformation from a centrally administered to a market economy. Employment in the East decreased from nearly 10 million in 1990 to 6 million in 1993, and remained at this level in the following years. In the old western *Länder*, after a remarkable rise in 1991 and 1992 (the 'reunification-boom'), the number of people employed went down again to 28 million, a level which had already been achieved in 1990.

Unemployment reached a post-war climax at 11.4 per cent in 1997, with 4.4 million people registered officially as unemployed. The gap to full employment, including the number of those who were temporarily placed in public job-creation schemes and training programmes, or who belonged to the 'silent reserve' of those who were discouraged and had retreated from the labour market, was estimated at almost 7 million (European Commission 1998b).

When it comes to analysing the reasons for this unfavourable situation, the discussions become, in many respects, highly controversial. The explanations range from a comparatively inflexible labour-market regime and high taxation, to a missing dynamic in the service sector and the persistently heavy burdens of reunification and transformation in the East. Beyond that, there are emerging doubts about the assumption that the basic trend of shrinking demand for labour can be reversed at all. Potentially, in the future, participation in, and income from, paid work will not have the same significance for social participation as in the past. These doubts, raised in academic debates and among the public, have not really had an impact on public policies and official strategies so far. Such policies (1) aim at full employment and (2) equate, to a significant extent, problems of social exclusion with employment problems, i.e. they assume that problems of economic integration can be solved through employment and economic growth. While there are debates about urban neighbourhoods and rural landscapes marked by social disintegration and exclusion of various groups, these are still seen either as problems for social work and urban planning or as a challenge for job creation for young people or long-term unemployed.

Public employment policy has been relying to a large extent on the implementation of training and re-training measures on the one hand, and on a large number of job-creation schemes (*Arbeitsbeschaffungsmaßnahmen* or *ABM*) which are regarded as a publicly financed and 'second' labour market on the other hand. These measures[2] have prevented the more dramatic effects of social exclusion by unemployment from coming to the foreground. In Eastern Germany, the second labour market is in some regions – from a quantitative perspective – the most important segment of local employment. Nevertheless, the effectiveness of this type of centrally implemented policy in creating some temporary income and jobs is being questioned by a growing number of researchers and commentators. The failure to attain more, and especially sustainable, employment, as well as in fighting long-term unemployment and social exclusion, is obvious. As a consequence, job-creation programmes of the *ABM* type are progressively losing political support. The prevailing tone of the debate is that such programmes do not help with respect to the primary task of restructuring the 'first' labour market in a way that allows it to absorb more unemployed. A different type of critique that is seldom heard in Germany, even though it is not unusual at the European level, is based on the assumption that the complex nature of social exclusion may often require more complex answers than sectoral programmes for economic integration.

While a broad variety of alternative instruments are taken into consideration and implemented on an experimental basis, a turn to market and business-oriented instruments can be observed, with a stronger focus on reaching – within a short period of time – visible effects on people's integration in the 'normal' market economy. Consequently, new methods of job placement for disadvantaged target groups (*Maatwerk*-methodology) or 'job-rotation' training measures are increasingly preferred. However, at the level of central government, there is also a debate about introducing new forms of income mixes of transfers and earned income as a means of increasing the number of low-wage jobs in marketed services. Nevertheless, even after the political turnaround towards the left after the elections of 27 September 1998, problems of social exclusion are still mainly identified with the task of regaining full employment.

1   The third sector in Germany – a hidden potential for employment?

In contrast to a number of other European countries, the third sector as a relevant category in the formulation of employment policy has attained only a marginal position in Germany. This is true although the third sector represents a very important segment in terms of employment and economic relevance (Anheier 1997; Zimmer and Priller 1997). The big non-governmental welfare federations, which provide a large proportion of social, educational and health services in Germany, employ approximately 1.3 million. The two biggest, Caritas and Diakonie (bound to the Catholic and Protestant churches) have 400,000 and 330,000 staff respectively – more than the biggest commercial employer, Daimler-Benz, which has a workforce of 240,000. Legitimised by the principle of subsidiarity, which in Germany is laid down in the Constitution, these organisations play a central role in corporatist arrangements for social policy. They are mainly funded, not by contributions of their members (the churches or other independent sources), but by subsidies or remuneration for services by the state, municipalities or by social security state agencies. Ninety per cent of the income of the service providers run by the big voluntary organisations comes from state and social security funds, in return for usually highly standardised mainstream services. Therefore, creating more jobs in this area would just be a particular way of extending the public sector and traditional, non-innovative service provision.

However, there is also a more local, less visible part of the third sector, consisting of initiatives, projects and agencies which are not always components of the umbrella organisation of the big voluntary agencies. These have taken shape around less formalised social tasks and challenges such as urban decay, new social problems, concern for weak groups, unemployment and social exclusion. They are supported by less stable local funds, sometimes on time-limited programmes of the *Länder*, and they rely on local solidarity and a considerable degree of voluntary work and civic commitment.

Their legitimacy is backed by the fact that persistent unemployment and disillusionment with existing policies has led to a rising awareness of the need for new ideas on the potential links between the market and the state, which have been left aside by the mainstream strategies of the 1980s and 1990s. The relationships of these locally rooted associations and initiatives with the big traditional welfare associations vary. On the one hand, they are often seen as unwelcome competitors for scarce public resources; on the other hand, many of their innovative offers are not competing directly with existing services. Some of the big welfare organisations – especially the DPWV,[3] which is not aligned with one of the churches or the Social Democratic Party – welcome these new local initiatives as members. Thus, experiments and pilot-actions for the development of a local economy as well as new arrangements of public and private financing and of professional services and voluntary work are entering into the focus of research and political discussion. Models from other European countries, e.g. France, UK and Italy, are being studied and the guidelines and recommendations of the European Commission on the linking of employment promotion and local development are major stimuli for the ongoing process of reorientation of policy and strategy-formation.

In this context, the concept of the social enterprise can be studied as an example of the search for the hidden potential for local employment and social inclusion in the specific institutional, political and economic context of Germany.

2   Social enterprises and social capital – the conceptual framework

Even though the term social enterprise has emerged in the context of debates about employment-related goals and organisations, it should be understood as a concept which is valid for each and every third-sector organisation operating with an entrepreneurial approach for the public good. The term social enterprise suggests that organisations of this kind mix an entrepreneurial attitude and a certain degree of market orientation with social tasks and goals. Social enterprises can then be defined as a specific type of third-sector organisation. They differ from other civic associations and voluntary bodies to the extent that they also have a strong entrepreneurial and market element, which is counterbalanced by a specific set of social goals. Elsewhere in this book (see chapter 17 by Evers) it is made clear why we think that the potential for mobilising social capital – represented by the degree of trust, associability and sense of mutual co-operation in a civic and democratic society (Putnam 1995) – is a key feature of social enterprises as third-sector organisations. Summing up what is presented there, one can say that social enterprises as specific types of third-sector organisations are characterised as contributing to social capital formation in two basic ways: (1) as intermediate bodies, which use and balance a mix of resources from different sources including state, market, civil society and civic communities; (2) by merging various economic and social goals and purposes related to the public good in a single organisation. In this way, they produce added value to existing social capital, in the social as well as in the economic dimension, and follow a logic of social development (Midgley 1995) rather than simply the logic of either social policy or economic development.

What does this mean for those organisations and enterprises which we deal with here and which are concerned with social and occupational integration and job creation?

First of all, social goals can signify complementary yet different characteristics. 'Social' can (1) denote a special commitment towards the persons to be employed; it can (2) refer to the products and services to be produced; as well as (3) to the internal organisation of the working relationships. Social enterprises, which are directly linked with the tasks of creating or maintaining employment and access to labour markets, usually combine two types of social goals. On the one hand they strive for the social and labour-market integration of specific target groups, including long-term unemployed, disabled persons and socially disadvantaged young people. But at the same time they are focused on the improvement of the economic and social structures in a given social area of reference (for example, bettering the local material and civic infrastructure). Taking these two dimensions together, such social enterprises have a role in economic integration through employment but also a wider social role in social integration and development.

A second basic feature of local initiatives for occupational and social integration and job creation relates to the strong civic background and local embeddedness (Granovetter 1985) of these third-sector organisations being an important part of their resource structure. They have many links with the local environment, social movements, the forming of associations, solidarity and voluntary commitment. For integration, partners are needed in very different fields including the market sector and the families and neighbourhoods of young people at risk.

The potential for the creation and maintenance of social enterprises depends very much on the local environment and the extent to which social capital can be found there – represented by the attitudes of citizens and groups as well as of civic organisations, the nature of the business sector and the political and administrative organisations.

But these elements of social capital should be envisaged, not only in terms of existing conditions but also as elements still to be created. Local development can involve the mobilisation of social capital, while at the same time creating it for the local economy. By its very action, a social enterprise which takes in long-term unemployed helps to save or restore social networks and the means for integration in a community, while at the same time activating other components of local social capital such as the willingness of other organisations to form active partnerships. In other words, although the concept of social capital was originally introduced mainly as a given analytical category which has built up over a long time, from this perspective it can also be seen as an asset to be developed intentionally. As a consequence, the preservation and building of social capital may be considered as a key issue for social strategies (Gittell and Vidal 1998). Thus, links between social enterprises and networks of actors, such as partnerships for local development and employment, are very important, as suggested and illustrated in various EU documents (European Commission 1996; O'Conghaile 1997). Similarly, partnerships with ordinary enterprises and the creation of informal networks of committed local key persons are significant. Indeed, one of the common features of social enterprises is a multi-stakeholder structure (Pestoff 1996; Borzaga and Mittone 1997) in order to create and maintain the commitment of other organisations and institutions of civil society. Obviously, the tasks of keeping an active link to the local environment and safeguarding the mobilisation and constant use of solidarity resources make social enterprises both better suited and more fragile than the usual type of business organisation.

Given the fact that social enterprises as kinds of hybrids are unconventional organisations, legitimising a strong role for them and for complementary strategies like 'partnership approaches' in policies for social and occupational integration is important. A glance at developments, in the US for example, shows clearly that services for people at the margins can be carried out with some success by types of public–private partnerships, where public authorities subcontract exclusively to commercial providers. In that role, they can then carry out a great variety of social tasks. For instance, they not only run prisons but also training centres and employment agencies. So why should public authorities facilitate the emergence of social enterprises and give them a strong role as partners? Should this be only because – at least in Germany – they were the first to be there? From the line of argument developed so far, the answer is that their ability to combine a variety of goals – including social capital building – gives them a special advantage compared to public and commercial organisations insofar as:

- they can better create and make use of the commitment and trust of other social and economic partners (making use of volunteers and activating churches, trade unions and chambers of commerce) and thereby perhaps widen the scope of political options and programmes;
- they have better possibilities of building up services which depend on a close relationship in the local cultural context (e.g. building up household services and offers for home care);
- they are more credible as contacts and in regard to resocialising or reactivating a clientele – customers, trainees or employees – who might be passive or distrustful;
- they are better suited to meeting combined goals e.g. combining local development with labour-market integration for a specific group; ironically, precisely because their action is more diffuse, they produce by-products (e.g. the building-up of informal co-operative networks, closing the gaps between different organisations, social and policy sectors) which may be as important as the short-term goals of employment.

Whether these potentials are acknowledged by public policy-makers depends on their perspective. If social and occupational integration is seen as a clearly delineated job which can in principle be done by anyone who acts professionally – provided the public gives the resources – then there is no special need for social enterprises. It might, however, be different, once it is perceived that a strong civic commitment can be a key factor for doing better. And if the task is clearly and simply to reinsert individuals somewhere in the labour market, social enterprises might be redundant. They may, however, become more important, the more individual occupational reintegration is seen as a part of a broader strategy for social integration through making, by collective effort, (local) economic and social development more inclusive and changing the given economic and social framework wherein each person has to seek his or her individual chance.

3 Between social integration and business promotion – social enterprises in Germany

As a reaction to the persistent unemployment crisis, a variety of different types of initiatives have emerged in Germany roughly since the first half of the 1980s. Most of these have concentrated on training courses, offers of temporary employment and bridge building towards the conventional labour market. Many of them, however, try jointly to create enterprises that can offer additional employment, e.g. in the environmental and personal social service sector.[4] The following three types are translations of the respective German labels.

Social employment initiatives

Based mainly on local initiatives from churches, communities, welfare organisations, trade unions and others, special organisations have been founded in order to create employment for recipients of social welfare, the long-term unemployed and other target groups. Based to a large extent on funding through municipal workfare and *ABM* job creation schemes by the federal labour office, the jobs offered were mostly on a fixed-term basis and the range of activities was limited to (additional) tasks in the public interest, e.g. improvement of the local infrastructure, recycling and social services. The aim of producing something which can be considered as useful for the ecological, economic or social demands of the (local) community and/or for special groups, where collective purposes and individual needs meet, has a clear impact. Furthermore, many of these initiatives would not have been created without the mobilisation and utilisation of various types of social support, so these initiatives depended on social capital.

But the aim of creating places for training and/or temporary employment is the priority. This is particularly evident from the fact that the support provided to these initiatives by public programmes is not part of 'programmes for new services' but is provided by the Federal Institute of Labour under the headings of employment and training. In Germany, organisations of this kind are therefore rightly called 'social employment initiatives' (*Soziale Beschäftigungsinitiativen*). The contribution of their products and services to local social capital tends to be secondary to their employment role, which means that they may also lose their broader roots of social support. Moreover, because they have very limited access to the open market of products and services (being mostly forced to make 'additional' rather than competing offers), they are constantly endangered by a marginalisation trap – becoming a minor business in the machinery of integration policies instead of developing into an instrument which is able to activate and generate social capital. Walwei and Werner (1997) estimate the number of these initiatives at between 3,500 and 4,500,[5] with between 75,000 and 95,000 persons employed.

The associations for employment creation in Eastern Germany

In Germany, the 'employment creation and structural development associations' (*ABS, Gesellschaften zur Arbeitsförderung, Beschäftigung und Strukturentwicklung*) emerged exclusively in the new *Länder* after the reunification, mainly as a successor of state-owned companies closed down in the industrial restructuring process. The volume of employment is remarkable with 155,000 persons working in 400 *ABS* companies (Walwei and Werner 1997). Although their workforce was structured very differently from that of the social employment initiatives (generally an *ABS* company took over the complete staff of a former state-owned company, and was not oriented towards target groups), their limitations were in many respects similar to those of the social employment initiatives. As a consequence of tax and funding regulations, the *ABS* worked quite separately from the competitive market and failed to gain a stable economic basis of their own. As basically the outcomes of a central programme adopted by local political decision-making and administrative planning, they mostly failed to fit in with their social and economic environment. They had little contact with regular employers outside the *ABS* and failed to develop, as Knuth (1996) has put it, a concept for managing labour-market mobility.

In summary, one can say that with regard to the concept of social enterprise, as outlined earlier in the chapter, the types of employment initiatives and associations for employment creation just described show some important limits to their development as an integral part of social and economic life. This is caused by both the existing frameworks of politics and regulations and by the prevailing attitudes of many of their leaders and organisers. The main reasons for this are:

- restrictions caused by rules for taxation (the non-profit status restricts access to competitive markets);
- restrictions caused by funding schemes (many job creation schemes are strictly limited to tasks in the public interest and do not generate any profit or proceeds from the market);
- a social work perspective on the needs (real or assumed) of the target groups, which were not regarded as productive and stable enough to cope with the challenges of a competitive economy;
- little appreciation of the importance of a developmental concept which links these initiatives to the local social and economic environment. Even though such networking often played a role in practice, it was conceptually neglected and the potential role of social capital as a source and outcome of such initiatives was ignored.

All of this contributes to a process where employment initiatives can become trapped into a 'marginalist' orientation (European Commission 1996) focusing mainly on the weaknesses and deficits of their target groups and failing to structure themselves as elements of a local and regional economy.

As a consequence, the overall productivity of these initiatives is rather low. The percentage of costs covered by sales of products and services to private or public customers does not exceed 15 to 25 per cent (based on optimistic estimations). Public subsidies are the main financial basis and the resources generated in terms of supportive social capital usually get no special acknowledgement. They are generally not even mentioned as resources and potentials in government reports or in the literature of these organisations. Furthermore, critical evaluations of this type of social enterprise emphasise the fact that people employed in a social enterprise may endure the stigma of being pampered in a sheltering institution, lacking skills and unable to conform to the rules of conduct within the mainstream economy and a normal local working and service environment.

Organisations labelled as social enterprises in Germany

So far we have sketched two types of organisations which, under different labels, try to set up businesses and services out of a special concern with occupational integration and job creation. There is a third type for which the term 'social enterprise' (*Soziale Betriebe*) is commonly used in Germany. One should, however, remember that this label can be used in different ways. On the one hand, *Betrieb*, i.e. enterprise, can be associated primarily with issues like entrepreneurship and innovation. But it can, on the other hand, be also associated with 'enterprise' in the sense of a private market organisation, defined by the degree to which it finances itself by market sales – whatever its products and style of action. It is the latter association which is still dominant in Germany.

The explicitly so-called 'social enterprises' in North-Rhine-Westfalia, Lower Saxony and Sachsen-Anhalt are products of special development programmes associated with the labour-market policies of these *Länder*. Basically, all these programmes define social enterprises as a mixture of market-oriented initiatives and state-related temporary support. This support is given in order to link job creation and economic development with the function of integrating people into the labour market. State support, being temporary, creates social enterprises as transitional institutions, which are part of a transitional labour market (Schmid 1995). Basically, there are two ways of creating such a social enterprise. Firstly, it is possible to create a certain number of jobs for long-term unemployed in an existing firm working in the competitive labour market; secondly, it is possible to start up a new business with a certain proportion of new jobs for long-term unemployed. In both cases, state subsidies are provided to cover wage costs and other expenditures on the basis of a regressive scheme. The business has to be fully self-sustaining after five years. Available data show that a comparably small proportion of jobs have been created through this model – 1,500 jobs in 71 social enterprises.[6] Only a very few have already reached economic self-sustainability, so that further state subventions will be needed (Christe 1997).

It should be noted that this type of social enterprise links two functions – that of job creation/economic development and labour-market integration. However, it ignores the local and community integration dimension. Civic commitment, voluntary work and the moral support of other organisations and initiatives in the community may play a role in the founding phase of such social enterprises, but public programmes do not identify them as key factors and do not offer special rewards for activating such resources. The fact that the enterprise is required to reach the status of a normal business as soon as possible does not encourage the search for such resources and/or makes them look increasingly out of place. Furthermore, neither the products of such social enterprises, nor their mode of production require them to have a social dimension e.g. by addressing needs and demands in the local community. There is no gain in selecting a specific local social and public concern.

It has yet to be decided whether the dualism of social and economic goals can be balanced in a way which keeps these entities within the concept of social enterprises. Basically, a social enterprise concept that allows for potential transformation into an ordinary business can be an element (or instrument) of approaches which try to utilise the potential of third-sector organisations. The key question is whether such enterprises define themselves and aspire to be seen as part of a broader social development strategy for economic recovery, social integration and community development.

In summary, social enterprises, in the light of the German findings, can be seen as existing in two main variants – the 'social employment initiative' and the 'business type of social enterprise' (omitting the second type, the *ABS*, to be found in the new *Länder* only). From a conceptual perspective, both have specific strengths and weaknesses. The social employment initiatives work better in terms of activating and generating social capital, but the context in which they operate, and in some cases their own limited perspective, prevents them from seeing this important dimension of their resource and task structure. Most of these initiatives lack economic impact and outcomes in terms of economic integration effects through job creation. Furthermore, a public policy that perceives them only in terms of their immediate job creation effects restricts their potential as agents of local and social integration (e.g. through the services they create, their co-operative potential and the support they offer).

Those projects and initiatives which are explicitly called 'social enterprises' in Germany may be more successful in terms of their economic integration effects. But it is highly questionable whether they can contribute any more than normal business development action to addressing social exclusion, since their services and their overall orientation lack any specific development concept and community orientation. Perhaps the prevailing single goal/single organisation approach, which measures success only in terms of jobs created and people employed, must be overcome if public policy really wants to make use of the specific potentials of social enterprises. These organisations can have employment effects but they are not the right instruments for a policy solely concerned with occupational integration.

4   Social enterprises as part of a joint strategy for redevelopment and employment – the example of Duisburg-Marxloh

In the light of our argument so far, we want to take up in this section a concrete case of a type of policy development, which is giving more space to the unique possibilities of social enterprises. This example does not imply an easy positive alternative, but rather illustrates the difficulties entailed in a progressive perspective. The case we describe deals with two social enterprises whose development is interrelated with the implementation of an urban renewal programme set up by the government of North-Rhine-Westfalia and linked with various employment programmes of both the German authorities and the EU. It should be added that there is still a minor but increasing tendency to link occupational and local urban integration in a territorial approach.[7]

Duisburg-Marxloh (20,000 inhabitants) is a quarter of the municipality of Duisburg, in the Rhine-Ruhr area. It is still suffering from the effects of drastic changes from an industrial past to an uncertain future. In Marxloh, where more than 36 per cent of inhabitants are migrants (nearly all of them Turkish), unemployment is about 25 per cent; in Duisburg, it is about 18 per cent, and every fifth employee will be unemployed within the next decade.

Given these conditions, it is not surprising that Marxloh became one of the twenty-one city quarters addressed by the programme of the Federal State of North-Rhine-Westfalia (NRW) for 'city quarters with special demands for renewal'. This programme, which began in 1995, was designed in order to combine contributions from both urban and social policies of NRW to combat polarisation in cities. Since the beginning of 1996, this programme in Marxloh has also been supported by the EU URBAN programme for local development, which strengthens the economic and employment-oriented component. In this way, the question of social integration and employment is framed in Marxloh by a complex local development programme that, in its economic dimension, accentuates the stimulation of the local economy. Its social dimension aims to better the social infrastructure and strengthen the participation and social inclusion of individuals and associations. Finally, on the political level, the responsibility is with the municipality, which has created two semi-autonomous subcentres: a 'development organisation', concentrating on economic revitalisation and urban renewal and a 'city quarter project' concentrating on bettering the social services in Marxloh. Both organisations are eager to develop an enabling and co-operative style of working and they are both actors and points of reference for the use and integration of programmes for employment and qualification. Besides establishing these initiatives, the broader framework sketched here gives indirect support to single initiatives and projects by networking and activating, addressing local associations of all kinds in business, social and cultural life, stimulating the identification with Marxloh and recreating a sense of pride and belonging (e.g. by actions like a spring cleaning campaign). The economic programme, with its special link to the URBAN project, is still in the process of being worked out; it is concerned with developing a strategy for revitalising the local mall and shopping centre and taking action in addressing local banks through a regular get-together with German and Turkish local citizens setting up small enterprises.

As far as other initiatives for employment are concerned, the 'city quarter project' is an umbrella organisation for about 360 employees. Most of them participate in temporary training and qualification jobs which use the usual variety of employment and training funds on the state and federal level (the majority are sponsored by *ABM* funds). The majority of these jobs are to be found in the areas of city renewal and of the improvement and renewal of the often run down public places and social services (schools, centres, etc.). In general, these employment initiatives, operating in the framework of the developmental strategy, follow three principles: (1) 'Marxloh people work for

Marxloh', (2) the high percentage of migrants must be reflected in these programmes as well; (3) in 'matters of welfare', the central role of women must be taken into account.

Between occupational and social integration – the productivity of social enterprises

The two social enterprises to be sketched here are far from being spectacular. We have chosen them in order to demonstrate that the meaning given to the notion of entrepreneurial orientation is important. For some, categorising a non-governmental organisation providing social services as a social enterprise will denote creative and innovative action and will not strictly depend on the degree of income earned by market sales. For others, it is the latter that defines the difference between social enterprises and other organisations, public and private, which are non-governmental and not for profit. Securing one's income by market sales will then be the essential feature, and the innovative and entrepreneurial orientation will be secondary. The dilemma of the two social enterprises which are described below is that they are entrepreneurial mainly according to the first definition (pioneering and innovative), while the policy framework in which they operate mainly supports the second (maximising financing from market operations).

The two projects belong to a small group of projects and activities in Marxloh. At the time of our analysis they were intended to be transformed into elements of a more market and employment focused strategy. The idea was to reduce the considerable public funding and to strengthen the market component of these projects. Therefore, both cases are well suited to illustrating the tensions between a strongly employment and market focused policy and its understanding of an 'enterprise', and a policy for social integration which calls for a type of entrepreneurial orientation defined by a different type of public action and which focuses on the generation of social capital.

The first enterprise, a city quarter coffee shop, *Schwelgernstrasse*, is meant to be more than just another pub. It is an informal meeting point for those who are in any way near to the manifold urban and economic development projects in Marxloh. It also serves as a snack bar for people working nearby and it delivers hot meals for two schools in the surrounding area. Public institutions can order a buffet there and, together with an association of local businessmen and in co-operation with the Protestant church, it provides weekly meals for a small fee to people in need.

The second enterprise is a shop, called *Nahtstelle* (Interface), which has been established in the inner city of Marxloh. There one can buy toys and clothes for children, some of which are second-hand articles (collected, restored and repaired by the employees). Furthermore, the shop offers laundry services for senior citizens and all kinds of small clothes repair for institutions like schools, homes for children and for the elderly. Finally, the shop serves as an exchange centre for local services.

Both organisations can be called social enterprises due to the mix of resources on which they rely (state support, income by sales and various forms of social capital such as trust, commitment and voluntary work) and the way they mix economic goals and a concern for the public good. Yet admittedly, the market component is very limited. The approximately 15 women working in each of the two centres are paid through the *ABM* scheme, except the core personnel of two to three people, who work as leaders and trainers and are financed partly by a different training support programme. As far as the coffee shop is concerned, the income made by activities and sales in the profitable areas (e.g. the coffee shop) is used to pay part of the salaries of the core staff and to finance the deficits from social activities. In the *Nahtstelle* most of the income generated by sales has been used to repay the loans for the equipment.

However, the issue now is the future direction of development and the effects on these enterprises' socially integrative components, when taking them as projects which should clearly concentrate on the creation of market based jobs in the framework of the EU URBAN programme. For the *Nahtstelle*, it is proposed to further develop the tailoring of attractive children's clothes and the laundry services. It is estimated that this could serve as an economic base for two to three employees. As far as the city quarter café is concerned, the different concepts being negotiated at present mirror the different priorities of the partners for development and recovery. The representatives of the city quarter project would like to strengthen its character as a public institution to be subsidised further (perhaps to a high degree) for its neighbourhood-oriented services. However, the economic development agency would prefer to turn it into a commercial coffee shop, debating whether it should be sold to a private owner or carried on as a kind of co-operative by the women who work there and helped to build it up. In both cases one can see the difficulty of matching the goal of job creation on a commercial basis with social integration goals, e.g. by restricting the scope of services offered. Both the selection of employees and the establishment of roots in the neighbourhood and on local markets have built on social capital and helped to maintain it by giving solidarity and trust-related help and services. The question is to what degree can the process of using and regenerating social capital be upheld when the diversity of uses of the enterprises gets reduced to mere job creation.

5   Conclusions: the potentials of social enterprises – denied or realised?

The debate about social enterprises is situated at a crossroads. On the one hand, there is the debate about the degree to which occupational integration (by employment strategies) should be linked with developmental strategies especially at the local and regional level. On the other, there is the debate about the role of third-sector organisations as components and instruments of policies for occupational integration and local development.

Social enterprises have been presented here as third-sector organisations whose special potential stems from the very fact that they mix and intertwine resources and goals that are usually separated. While they share this feature with other organisations in the third-sector, social enterprises are different from them to the degree that they work as social entrepreneurs. If in their role as third-sector organisations, they are created or oriented to the aim of occupational reintegration and job creation, they can or should link such occupational goals with other purposes and contributions to the community. Operating that way, a variety of types of support, like trust, solidarity, voluntary commitment and partnerships are important factors which we have categorised as social capital.

As has been shown, social enterprises take specific forms, marked by the priorities of labour market and employment policies and programmes. So far, their strategies do not give special attention to the role of social capital – neither in their concepts for local development, nor in the way they understand and address social enterprises or third-sector organisations in general. At present, they frequently operate with a kind of reductionism, both concerning the problem of integration/development and the potential role of social enterprises:

- programmes against social exclusion are often equated with programmes for employment and job creation, and the latter items are often the only ones acknowledged by public policies which are eager to reach measurable goals in the short term;
- in such a narrow strategic framework, social enterprises are often supported by public policies only insofar as they seem to be special types of job-creating enterprises or training services in the third sector. The specific strengths of social enterprises are left aside, and due to this narrow way of addressing them, the development of social enterprises gets distorted.

Insofar as public policy is solely concerned with occupational integration and job creation, without challenging the type of (local) socio-economic development which has created social exclusion in the first place and destroyed local social capital, it cannot make full use of the potentials of social enterprises. However, social enterprises and third-sector organisations are not really effective as 'job machines' either. In order to flourish, they need concepts for a more inclusive approach to local and urban development which may entail a strong employment component but which should also appreciate the integrative effects of building social capital – effects which are however less easy to measure. Third-sector organisations should be encouraged to network and to balance various goals, e.g. by combining the development of new services and new jobs for the community. In the design of public support programmes, their efforts to activate social capital resources should become acknowledged as something which is good for the social enterprise itself but which also contributes to the public good.

Notes

1 This contribution is based on a more detailed study; see Evers, A., Schulze-Böing, M., Weck, S. and Zühlke, W. (1998).
2 For an overview, see Schulze-Böing and Johrendt (1994).

3 Like other welfare organisations, the DPWV does not have individual membership but has service-providing organisations as members.
4 For an overview, see Birkhölzer and Lorenz (1998).
5 For 1994, see also BAG Arbeit (1997).
6 Data for Lower Saxony: Walwei and Werner (1997: 14).
7 For Germany, see Alisch (1998); on the EU level, see European Commission (1998a).

Bibliography

ALISCH, M. (ed.) (1998) *Stadtteilmanagement. Voraussetzungen und Chancen für die soziale Stadt,* Leske und Budrich, Opladen.

ANHEIER, H.K. (1997) 'Der Dritte Sektor in Zahlen: Ein sozial-ökonomisches Porträt', in ANHEIER, H.K., PRILLER, E., SEIBEL, W. and ZIMMER, A. (eds) *Der Dritte Sektor in Deutschland,* Sigma, Berlin, 29–74.

BAG Arbeit e.V. (1997) *Soziale Unternehmen in Europa. Projekt zur Schaffung eines europäischen Netzwerks von Beschäftigungsgesellschaften,* Bundesarbeits-gemeinschaft Arbeit e.V., Berlin.

BIRKHÖLZER, K. and LORENZ, G. (1998) 'Allemagne. Les sociétés d'emploi et de qualification en appui à la réunification', in DEFOURNY, J., FAVREAU, L. and LAVILLE, J.-L. (eds) *Insertion et nouvelle économie sociale. Un bilan international,* Desclée de Brouwer, Paris, 127–58.

BORZAGA, C. and MITTONE, L. (1997) 'The Multi-Stakeholders versus the Nonprofit Organisation', Università di Trento, Dipartimento di Economia, Discussion Paper no. 7.

CHRISTE, G. (1997) 'Neue Ansätze erwerbswirtschaftlicher Orientierung in der öffentlichen Beschäftigungsförderung', in Friedrich-Ebert-Stiftung (ed.) *Arbeitsplätze zwischen Markt und Staat,* Forschungsinstitut der Friedrich-Ebert-Stiftung, Bonn.

European Commission (1998a) *Building Territories for the Millennium,* Project Catalogue, Adapt, Brussels.

—— (1998b) *Employment in Europe 1997,* GDV, Amt für amtliche Publikationen der Europäischen Gemeinschaften, Luxembourg.

—— (1996) 'Erster Bericht über lokale Entwicklungs- und Beschäftigungsinitiativen. Schlußfolgerungen für territoriale und lokale Beschäftigungsbündnisse', SEK (96) 2061, Brussels.

EVERS, A., SCHULZE-BÖING, M., WECK, S. and ZÜHLKE, W. (1998*) Soziale Betriebe als Element lokaler Beschäftigungs- und Strukturpolitik,* Gutachten für die Enquetekommission 'Zukunft der Erwerbsarbeit' des Landtags von Nordrhein-Westfalen, Frankfurt and Dortmund.

GITTELL, R. and VIDAL, A. (1998) *Community Organising. Building Social Capital as a Developmental Strategy,* Sage, London.

GRANOVETTER, M. (1985) 'Economic Action and Social Structure. The Problem of Embeddedness', *American Journal of Sociology,* vol. 91, 3: 481–510.

KNUTH, M. (1996) *Drehscheiben im Strukturwandel. Agenturen für Mobilitäts-, Arbeits- und Strukturförderung,* Sigma, Berlin.

MIDGLEY, J. (1995) *Social Development. The Developmental Perspective in Social Welfare,* Sage, London.

O'CONGHAILE, W. (1997) 'Die Rolle von Partnerschaften zur Förderung des sozialen Zusammenhalts', Paper presented at the International Conference on Partnerships for Social Cohesion, Institut für Gesundheitswesen, Wien, October 1997.

PESTOFF, V.A. (1996) 'Renewing Public Services and Developing the Welfare Society through Multi-stakeholder Co-operatives', *Journal of Rural Co-operation*, vol. 23, 2: 151–67.

PUTNAM, R.D. (1995) 'Bowling Alone: America's Declining Social Capital', *Journal of Democracy*, no. 1, 65–78.

SCHMID, G. (1995) 'Is Full Employment Still Possible? Transitional Labour Markets as a New Strategy of Labour Market Policy', *Economic and Industrial Democracy*, vol. 16, 429–56.

SCHULZE-BÖING, M. and JOHRENDT, N. (1994) (eds) *Wirkungen kommunaler Beschäftigungsprogramme*, Birkhäuser, Basel.

WALWEI, U. and WERNER, H. (1997) *Beschäftigungsinitiativen in Deutschland*, IAB-Werkstattbericht, 2/1997.

ZIMMER, A. and PRILLER, E. (1997) 'Zukunft des Dritten Sektors in Deutschland', in ANHEIER, H.K., PRILLER, E., SEIBEL, W. and ZIMMER, A. (eds) *Der Dritte Sektor in Deutschland*, Sigma, Berlin, 249–84.

7 Greece

Social enterprises responding to welfare needs

Dimitris Ziomas, Maria Ketsetzopoulou and Nikos Bouzas

Introduction

The social welfare system in Greece has failed so far to meet the demand for new social services, and it remains almost entirely restricted to the provision of traditional welfare services. Even today, and although certain positive steps have been taken by the state during the last decade, public provision of welfare and social services in Greece is dominated by monetary benefits and care in institutions, while facilities and programmes for open social care and protection are still limited. Besides, social welfare provision is still characterised by poor planning or even lack of planning. Consequently, in many sectors, needs remain unmet, while in other sectors there is a serious overlap in provision by multiple public or semi-public bodies (KEPE 1989; Kermalis 1990; Karantinos *et al.* 1993; Kavounidis 1996).

The recognition – though delayed – of the above-mentioned situation led, in September 1998, to the adoption of a new law for the reform of the social welfare system in Greece (Law no. 2646/1998). But it takes a long time before a law in Greece is actually enforced and becomes functional. Moreover, and especially in the light of the increasing situations of social exclusion and the persisting problem of unemployment, doubts are raised regarding the extent of the reform that these new legal arrangements may bring about.

Historically, in the field of social and welfare services, the Greek state has traditionally assumed a residual role, mainly aimed at filling the gaps left by the family, which, regardless of recent structural changes, still occupies the central position in the provision and distribution of welfare. In playing such a limited role in the provision of social services, the state has finally allowed private initiatives (private for-profit enterprises, charitable societies, church organisations) to take on the role of the other main agent (besides the family) in this field, along with a few semi-public nationwide organisations. The non-statutory provision exhibits a variety of forms ranging from formal institutions of the church and a number of large non-profit-making organisations (most of them with semi-independent status and under state surveillance) to small locally based associations, voluntary bodies, self-help and pressure groups. However, with the exception of the church and a small number of semi-public (semi-independent) organisations, their role has been very limited until recently.

Since the beginning of the 1990s, however, given the slowing down of the expansion of the public provision of services, in some cases due to public spending cuts in the area of social welfare, one notes that excess demand for such services is increasingly being met by the private sector. It is not so much transfer from the public to the private sector, or replacement, that can be observed, but rather the entry of private sector bodies, both non-profit and for-profit, to meet demand previously unsatisfied by the public sector. This is also congruent with the fact that the efficiency of informal systems (such as family support) has tended to decrease in recent years.

In particular, the role of the private for-profit sector in the provision of certain social services in Greece – such as childcare services and residential care for the elderly – has increased greatly over the last decade. This evolution manifests itself through the establishment of private limited liability companies governed by commercial law and to a lesser extent through the establishment of small family enterprises. This undoubtedly indicates the inability of public and private non-profit institutions to satisfy the demand for such services. Nevertheless, given the great potential that exists in this area, the intervention of the private for-profit sector in the provision of social services is considered to be still very limited, in terms of both its intensity and its range of activities.

In the case of work-integration activities, the private for-profit sector exhibits almost no involvement. However, since the early 1990s in particular, partly as a response to increasing situations of social exclusion, one may observe an increase in the emergence of non-profit organisations mainly concerned with addressing specific problems and covering recognised needs of certain vulnerable groups of society (disabled persons, immigrants, ethnic minorities, etc.) through the provision of training, job-finding support, psycho-social support, rehabilitation services, and so on. But given the lack of data and systematic research on the subject, it is very difficult to assess their relative weight in the provision of social and welfare services in Greece.

1 Social enterprises in Greece: lack of legal concept but presence of initiatives

It would be difficult to maintain that there has been in Greece any kind of systematic and in-depth academic discussion on the notion of 'social enterprises' since it has neither been precisely defined nor has it been accorded any specific institutional and legal form. Besides, this is congruent with the fact that the 'third sector of the economy' in Greece – the so-called 'social economy sector' – has failed so far to establish its importance with regard both to its performance in generating employment and to its relative contribution in the formation of the Greek GDP.

However, it appears that the term or concept of 'social enterprise' is now increasingly entering the vocabulary of academic and policy discussions in Greece. This recent development can be partly attributed to the necessity to deal with the problems arising from socio-economic changes and to the serious challenges at present facing the state in the social policy area. The recognition at the European level and in Greece that the social economy sector could well be a potential source of employment also helps to account for this evolution. In this context an array of non-profit organisations have been established in Greece in recent years to serve potentially the purpose of combating social exclusion, mainly through the provision of vocational training and work-integration activities.

The majority of these non-profit organisations have taken the legal form of 'associations' or 'civil law societies' (which are legal entities of private law as provided by the Greek Civil Code); only a few of them have been established as co-operatives. With the exception of the co-operatives, these legal configurations do not fulfil the criteria of combining together social solidarity and entrepreneurship which characterises social enterprise-type organisations. Consequently, the only initiatives in this area that can be considered as social enterprises, as defined for the purpose of this study, are those which have been established taking the legal form of a co-operative. There are two main types: on the one hand, the co-operatives established by persons with psycho-social disabilities and, on the other hand, the agritourism co-operatives established by women in rural areas. Both types have an explicit social purpose and are also characterised by an entrepreneurial capacity. They produce and sell goods and services and thus create jobs. No official records and relevant data exist, but the first-hand information that could be gathered indicates that the total number of such co-operatives today is estimated at around twenty-five.

However, note should be made of the fact that in May 1999 a law was passed (Law no. 2716/1999) that provides, among other things, for the establishment of 'limited liability social co-operatives'. This legal form can be adopted exclusively by initiatives aiming at the socio-economic (re)integration of persons with psycho-social disabilities. However, this new legal framework is expected not only to further promote the development and the efficient operation of the existing co-operatives in this field, but also to pave the way for similar legal arrangements to be made in order to facilitate the establishment of social co-operatives by other vulnerable population groups as well.

2   The labour-market situation in Greece

To understand the development of all the above-mentioned initiatives and the possible contributions of social enterprises, it is useful to have a quick look at the situation of the Greek labour market.

The Greek labour market still shows little resemblance to the well-structured and regulated labour markets of the EU northern countries. For, in spite of the significant changes that have taken place over recent years, it is still characterised by the following main features: a low percentage of people in waged employment (54.9 per cent in 1997), a high percentage of people employed in agriculture (20.3 per cent in 1996) and a relatively large scale of activity in the 'informal' economy (atypical forms of employment continue to have a strong presence in Greece due mainly to the existence of a large number of illegal immigrants – estimated at about 500,000 people).

Besides, the total employment rate in Greece appears to be at a stagnation point over recent years. It is close to 56 per cent, which is lower than the EU average rate. Women's total employment rate, although it has gone up by three percentage points over the period 1992–98 (from 37.2 per cent to 40.6 per cent), continues to be significantly lower than the EU average (51.3 per cent in 1998). As far as part-time employment is concerned, Greece continues to have the lowest percentage among the EU countries. In 1997, the rate of part-time employment was approximately 4.6 per cent – though recent legal arrangements on part-time work may have a positive effect on part-time employment.

However, the absence of any systematic study and monitoring of labour-market demand in Greece prevents us from having a clear picture of the demand side, and no official quantitative forecasts exist about future 'demand' developments. Nevertheless, on the basis of the data included in the Labour Force Surveys, the evolution of the structure of employment for the last fifteen years reveals that traditional sectors (i.e. agriculture and traditional manufacturing activities) have suffered from heavy job losses in contrast to the tertiary sector, which has exhibited significant employment gains – a trend which is expected to continue.

The service sector has the largest share in total employment and its importance keeps increasing: from 40.4 per cent in 1981, it rose to 50.2 per cent in 1991 and to 56.5 per cent in 1996. Particularly important was the rise in the employment share of the finance, insurance and real estate sectors and also of the 'other services' (which include public administration, education and health services). A large part of these increases over the last fifteen years can be attributed to an expansion in the number of people employed in the public administration and in enterprises and organisations controlled by the state, although, due to the restriction of hiring by the public sector since 1994, the rate of increase has slowed down in recent years. In contrast to the third sector, the primary sector's employment share has shrunk from 30.7 per cent in 1981 to 22.2 per cent in 1991 and to 20.3 per cent in 1996. The employment share of the secondary sector also shrank in the same period, from 29.1 per cent in 1981 to 27.5 per cent in 1991 and to 22.9 per cent in 1996.

As a result of the above-mentioned recent developments and in conjunction with the restrictive monetary policies that have been implemented in recent years, together with the considerable increase in the labour force participation of women in Greece, the rate of unemployment has increased considerably. It has reached record new heights in recent years: 7.9 per cent in 1992, 9.6 per cent in both 1996 and 1997. Moreover, the most prominent characteristic in recent years has been the relatively large share of long-term unemployed (twelve months and over) among all unemployed. The rise in the share of long-term unemployment between 1991 and 1997 has been significant: from 46.6 per cent in 1991, it rose to 58.2 per cent in 1996, with a slight decrease to 57.1 per cent in 1997. Accordingly, the long-term unemployment rate has risen from 4.96 per cent in 1993 to 6 per cent in 1997. Yet, the main features of the long-term unemployed remain the same over the years; they are young, graduates of general secondary education and mainly women.

The implementation of restrictive economic policies in recent years, in particular, while attempting to limit the public sector deficit, has caused cuts in public expenditure and especially in the social and welfare services. This, together with the continuous immigration flows to Greece from the Balkans and Eastern Europe since 1990, has triggered an increase in situations of social exclusion. Indeed, processes which lead to social exclusion have gained more and more ground over recent years in Greece. They affect, in various ways, different socio-economic groups and individuals, including: unemployed, persons with physical or mental disability, prisoners, ex-prisoners, ethnic or cultural minorities and women. Yet, the existing forms of public provision of social, welfare and support services are inadequate to meet the increasing needs in this area. Simultaneously, the existing mechanisms of matching supply and demand in the labour market, namely the Public Employment Services of Greece, are relying mainly on traditional measures and procedures which, under present conditions, render their role insignificant.

Undoubtedly work opportunities in the present unemployment situation have become even more limited for certain groups of population (including young people and women) and especially for those persons with physical or mental disabilities. Persons with disabilities, in particular, have had over recent years – and the situation is even worse today – to compete in the open labour market with the unemployed (who are frequently highly qualified) for positions traditionally taken by the former in the past. As a result, disabled persons tend to be among the first people to be excluded from the labour market because of their physical or mental condition, and this undermines their economic and social purchasing power. Under the present conditions of highly competitive open markets, the prospects for persons with disabilities to be taken on by the average productive firm for real training and job creation activities have been reduced drastically.

It follows, therefore, that with the existing unemployment problem in the country and the restrictive macroeconomic policies, new approaches to job creation and thus work integration are needed regarding both the economic activities and the operative structures in order to tackle the economic and social exclusion of certain vulnerable groups in society. A few initiatives that have emerged in Greece in recent years seem to be reflecting serious – although limited – attempts in this direction.

3   The types of social enterprises

As mentioned earlier, the main social enterprise types of organisations that have been established in Greece in recent years with the purpose of combating social exclusion (mainly through work-integration activities) are of two kinds: the agri-tourism co-operatives, established mainly by women in rural areas with potential in tourism, on the one hand, and the urban and agricultural co-operatives established by specific socially excluded groups of people (mainly persons with psycho-social disabilities), on the other hand.

Agritourism co-operatives

It can be said that the establishment of women's co-operatives constitutes the first and only structured model of the social enterprise type in Greece. Furthermore it may be said that this specific kind of co-operative constituted a 'pioneer' initiative in this kind of activity, even by EU standards. The legal framework used for the formation of the first agritourism co-operatives was the existing, antiquated, general framework for co-operatives (i.e. Law 921/79) which did not give much freedom to pursue social objectives nor to have a relative autonomy from the state in the management of the co-operative. Law no. 1541/85, which superseded Law no. 921/79, gave the agritourism co-operatives a much better legal framework to develop further. This relatively recent law introduced for the first time in the existing legal framework the social purpose for co-operatives, attributing to it equal weight to that of the economic purpose.

Since the mid 1980s a small number of such agritourism co-operatives have been established in various areas of rural Greece, but the most distinguished and more developed ones have been those agritourism co-operatives established by women. Their establishment and first stage of development were greatly supported by the General Secretariat for Gender Equality through subsidies and the provision of know-how and systematic training courses for women members. Existing empirical data reveal that nine women's agritourism co-operatives, with around 200 members, are in operation today. The main activities of such agritourism co-operatives are the provision of accommodation (with or without breakfast), the provision of various kinds of food and meals prepared according to local traditions, the production and sale of local agricultural products and handiwork (home-made or made in small workshops), etc.

Urban and agricultural co-operatives

A new approach to job creation for persons with psycho-social disabilities emerged mainly through the setting up of co-operatives operating both within and outside the mental hospitals. This activity was initiated through assistance under EU Reg. 815/84, which provided special aid to Greece for the creation of structures to promote psychiatric reform, including aid for the 'de-institutionalisation' of large mental hospitals. Other EU programmes including the ESF training and promotion of employment schemes and the Horizon initiative, have also funded these developments.

The legal framework provided for this type of co-operative is, in the case of the urban type, Law 1667/86, and in the case of the agricultural type, Law 1541/85 (the same as for agritourism co-operatives). These two laws were the only legal framework available for the initiatives established during the last few years by the mentally ill persons together with their caring personnel as well as by other specific groups such as women prisoners, ex-drug addicts and other categories of people with special needs. It should be noted that the dominant purpose of these organisations is more of a social and therapeutic nature and less oriented to economic viability, at least for the time being.

Although still in the development stage, the co-operatives established by people with psycho-social disabilities are operating both within and outside the psychiatric hospitals. A few of them are operating without having been formally established whereas the majority have been formally recognised as co-operatives with a special purpose, as provided for in the above mentioned laws. It is important to note that a number of these formally established co-operatives have been initiated by various 'civil law societies' involved in the field of mental health services. The co-operative was found to be the most suitable legal framework for the creation of alternative facilities for both vocational rehabilitation and work activities geared to the needs of people with psycho-social disabilities.

According to existing data, the number of such co-operatives that are in operation today (formal or informal) has gone up to fifteen with around 300 members (in total) involved. The main activities of this kind of urban co-operative with a special purpose are the small-scale production of various goods, the sale of products, the provision of services such as the running of cafeterias, the provision of cleaning services, photocopying services, etc. In the case of the agricultural type of co-operatives with a special purpose, the main activity is the production of agricultural goods.

4   The main characteristics of social enterprises

It should be stressed right from the outset that all the social enterprise-type initiatives which have emerged in Greece potentially serve the purpose of providing work opportunities for their members (who for certain reasons are excluded from traditional work arrangements) through the collective production and delivery of different goods and services. In other words, all these initiatives fall under the category of social enterprises that aim to combat social and economic exclusion, mainly through work-integration activities.

The social enterprise-type of initiatives considered are based on the legal framework provided for the co-operatives, which bears the following determining features: it requires the coming together of individuals with a common purpose or problem; it aims at the realisation of a mixture of economic and social objectives; it is not under state control but under collective control and democratic management through democratically elected (one member, one vote) organs; it can exercise entrepreneurial activities with emphasis on the production of socially useful products and services; and finally, the funding of its operation derives mainly from the selling of its products and services, but it can receive donations or state grants.

It appears, therefore, that both types of co-operatives considered are characterised by an entrepreneurial capacity, although to a varying degree. In the case of the agritourism co-operatives, this entrepreneurial capacity is greater than in the case of the urban and agricultural co-operatives established by specific socially excluded groups of people. The latter rely more on subsidies than the former type of co-operatives. The agritourism women's co-operatives are mainly financed through the market (i.e. selling of products and tourist services) and to a lesser extent by occasional state allowances. The economic and social objectives of both types of co-operatives stem from the principles of equal participation, solidarity and mutual aid among their members; they put equal weight on the social and the economic purposes. Among the objectives and activities of both kinds of co-operatives is the social and cultural development of their members, the fulfilment of social needs, the professional training of their members, and in certain cases the expansion of social tourism.

In particular, the operation of the co-operatives established by persons with psycho-social disabilities serves both therapeutic and entrepreneurial purposes. They provide the opportunity for their members to regain 'unused' skills or to acquire new ones, through on-the-job training and work experience. At the same time, members can learn to work on a collective basis and take part of the responsibility relating to the performance of the co-operative's activities. It is also worth emphasising that these co-operatives involve both disabled and non-disabled persons, thus avoiding the creation of a sheltered work situation. Moreover, they exhibit particular dynamism towards improving their entrepreneurial capacity. In the case of the agritourism co-operatives established by women in rural areas, these are characterised by a strong local dimension and they mainly serve the purpose of recouping the human and cultural resources that have been marginalised and of using them to enhance forms of alternative development. In doing so, they can generate an income and bring about social integration.

5   Resources mobilised by social enterprises

In social enterprises, both financial and human resources are essential to the success of the initiatives to be carried out. In Greece, a number of publicly run services and companies as well as banks have contributed financially to the setting up of a number of co-operatives, especially agritourism co-operatives, through the provision of subsidies and loans. Today, the financing of the co-operatives established by persons with disabilities rests mainly upon public subsidies, while a small part of their budget comes from the selling of products and services. It appears that the agricultural type of co-operatives have a much better economic performance, in terms of the income they make, than the urban type of co-operatives which implies that there is a need to link the activities of the latter more closely to the requirements of the market. On the other hand, the agritourism women's co-operatives are mainly financed through the market (i.e. selling of products and tourist services) and to a lesser extent by occasional state allowances.

Each member has the obligation – according to the relevant laws – to contribute financially in the co-operative's capital, the exact amount of which is determined by its constitution. But this requirement is not adequate to further promote the development of these organisations. Contributions in kind also exist, as shown by the example of the agritourism co-operatives, whose members are obliged to rent rooms in their own houses to tourists. This represents an obligatory contribution in kind. As a rule, one member of the agritourism co-operative works as a paid clerk; the hiring of paid staff (non-members) is usually an exception. The rest of the members are engaged in all other activities without a salary, receiving only their part of the co-operative's revenues. The members of these co-operatives are women of rural areas, while the users are visitors and tourists.

The members of the co-operatives established by persons with disabilities are both persons with psycho-social disabilities, mainly patients and ex-patients of the psychiatric hospitals (the majority) and non-disabled persons, mainly health professionals and workers. The users (clients) of the co-operatives' activities are mainly local residents and public and private organisations as well as the members themselves. The majority of the members of the co-operative are employees. In addition, the co-operatives may also employ a number of persons with psycho-social disabilities as well as other skilled staff who are not necessarily members. However, a provision allows the salaried workers to become members of the co-operative, if they so wish.

Overall, the experiences of co-operatives show that new innovative activities can become an important source of new job creation, provided appropriate help and guidance are offered. These also indicate that new jobs can be created without the need for much capital. In this context, there are indications that there are many unexploited possibilities in Greece for job creation, especially in activities related to tourism, artistic and cultural heritage, health and social services and various local services.

6   Achievements in the fight against social exclusion

Existing empirical data reveal that at present there are in operation some twenty-five social enterprises made up of: nine women's agritourism co-operatives (in which around 200 members are involved), fifteen special purpose co-operatives for persons with psycho-social disabilities (in which around 300 members are involved); and one special purpose co-operative for women ex-prisoners (with around thirty members). Given the lack of information, however, the possibility of more special purpose co-operatives of this type having been established during the last year or so should not be ruled out.

In the case of the agritourism co-operatives, it may undoubtedly be said that such initiatives reflect new ways of satisfying social needs (upgrading the social status of women living in rural areas) and, at the same time, they represent sources of new employment opportunities, thus generating income not only for the members themselves but also for the local community. It is important to note that the participation of women in these co-operatives means their participation in 'stable' work activity which generates certain income, the amount of which is subject to the performance of the co-operative in the market. Women's agri-tourism co-operatives serve the purpose of recouping and integrating, through employment creation, the human resources which have been marginalised. They also serve the need to make the best use of the local development potential such as tourism including, in particular, the preservation of traditional skills and prod-ucts. They thus have a strong local dimension and they support local development strategies.

With regard to the co-operatives established by persons with disabilities, their operation to date has already provided the opportunity for their members to regain social and 'unused' skills or to develop new skills through on-the-job training and work experience. The jobs created are a mixture of 'transitional' and 'stable' jobs, depending on the kind of economic activities carried out and the market conditions. It is also important to note that the operation of these co-operatives has helped the majority of their members, who were patients of the psychiatric hospitals, to leave the hospitals and lead an independent life, either in apartments or with their families. In addition, the facts that the activities of the co-operatives are located within the community and that the co-operatives regu-larly organise cultural events, have led to the sensitisation of the local society and consequently to the acceptance of persons with psycho-social disabilities as members of the community.

In addition, one observes that although the majority of these co-operatives are established by people with psycho-social disabilities in collaboration with mental health professionals, there is a growing interest in recent years among other vulnerable population groups supported by professionals in the social services to form such special purpose co-operatives. This interest arises mainly from the fact that European Social Fund programmes, especially those aiming at combating exclusion from the labour market, provide the funding for the devel-opment and promotion of such initiatives.

7 Weaknesses and barriers to development

One of the basic obstacles to the further development of the existing co-operative organisations has been the lack of financial resources. Another issue that has negatively affected the further development of the co-operative sector has been the fact that governments have changed quite frequently the relevant legal provi-sions regarding co-operatives. During the first two years of the enactment of Law no. 1541/85, the inherent weaknesses that were identified led to 114 modifica-tions of the Law.

Other factors impeding the effective operation of co-operatives in general in Greece have been:

- the non-maintenance of their independence, stemming mainly from polit-ical affiliations (members of the Management Board are usually elected on the basis of their political party affiliations);

- to some extent, the state's involvement and intervention, especially in terms of the bureaucratic procedures applied;
- the lack of specialised managers, in conjunction with the members' low level of knowledge about co-operative issues;
- the recruitment policies pursued, which have resulted in an excess number of staff, thus increasing total expenses;
- the lack of co-operation among co-operatives; and
- the difficulties in capital formation.

In general, the lack of properly organised activities of the non-profit sector (taking the form of social enterprises) in the provision of social services can be attributed mainly to the fact that the existing institutional and legal frameworks do not allow for such development. Nevertheless, some co-operatives have been established on the basis of the existing legal framework. They have encountered problems in their actual operation and functioning which result from both internal and external factors. More specifically, one of their main deficiencies has been the fact that almost none of them have developed according to real market prospects in productive activities and services. They have emerged in an *ad hoc* fashion that is not necessarily linked to the requirements of the market. Furthermore, no emphasis has been put on the improvement of training in skills specifically needed for management and business, and there is a total lack of supportive structures (i.e. advice and help with legal problems, marketing promotion, etc.) to encourage and promote their development. Any future attempts to introduce appropriate policy measures for the alleviation of obstacles against the establishment and operation of social enterprises/co-operatives should take serious account of all the above-mentioned problems.

Conclusions

As the foregoing analysis shows, a great number of social needs in Greece are not met or are met in an inappropriate manner, while the impressive record of private initiative (mainly for-profit), especially at the community level, indicates that, in the field of social services, there is a great potential for the development of new initiatives. In this context, social enterprises, i.e. collective private initiatives with a social purpose, should be able to make a valuable contribution. Yet there is not at present any specific legal framework in force that allows for such development. The recent far-reaching socio-economic changes in the European Union (and beyond) have generated a search for new pluralist approaches to welfare and a reappraisal of the role of non-statutory and informal provision in social policy. Furthermore, developments in the European Union following the Maastricht Treaty raise a new challenge for the role of social policy, i.e. to act as a major force for counterbalancing the inequalities and social costs that lie ahead. This places a high premium on new initiatives that promote social cohesion, while acting as the engine for development.

However, the policies pursued so far in Greece in this respect do not exhibit the rate of progress that one would expect, due to the rudimentary and uncoordinated nature of public and private provision of social services in the country. Nevertheless, the emerging problem of social exclusion, coupled with the European Union's policy orientations in this field, have already had an impact on the competent Greek authorities and the other parties involved in social policy. There are signs that they have begun to work for new ways, forms and partnerships, which are needed especially in the context of programmes aiming at combating exclusion from the labour market.

This tendency is reflected, in particular, in the recent law which provides for the establishment of social co-operatives by persons with psycho-social disabilities and which could be extended to all categories of people with special needs or even, with some modifications, to other population groups. Furthermore, it appears that a number of bodies implementing programmes to combat social exclusion in Greece are trying to find ways (formal or informal) to develop partnerships and co-operatives able to implement the multi-dimensional approach required by these problems. The need for a broader human resources infrastructure at local level and for a combined partnership involving non-statutory bodies has been, in recent years, an important development issue.

Overall one could conclude that in Greece, despite the lack of an appropriate legal framework, there exist pioneering attempts to form social enterprises undertaking activities in the social services sector. What precise form these social purpose collective organisations will finally take is an open question, depending on the socio-cultural, political and economic specificity of the country, as well as on the structure of its institutions. However, the quest for common experiences and for sharing expert knowledge among EU countries is gaining impetus in this field and is bringing its richness and diversity to the fore.

Bibliography

DELLASOUDAS, L.G. (1992) *I Idiki Epagelmatiki Katartissi*, Parousia Publications, Athens.

EMKE-POULOPOULOS, I. (1999) *I ilikiomeni polites stin Ellada: parelthon, paron kai mellon*, Ellin Publications, Athens.

European Commission (1997) *Employment in Europe*, DGV, Brussels.

IAKOVIDOU, O. (1992) 'O Rolos ton Gynekion Agrotouristikon Sineterismon stin proothissi tou Agrotourismou stin Ellada', *Sineteristiki Poria*, no. 27, 137–45.

KAPOGIANNIS, D. and TZOURAMANIS, Ch. (1989) *Sineteristikos Kodikas*, Sakkoula Publications, Athens.

KARANTINOS, D., KAVOUNIDIS, J. and IOANNOU, C. (1993) *Observatory on Policies to Combat Social Exclusion: Agencies, Institutions and Programmes: Their Interrelationships and Co-ordination in the Administration of Social Exclusion*, Institute of Educational and Vocational Guidance, Athens.

KARANTINOS, D., IOANNOU, C. and KAVOUNIDIS, J. (1992) *Observatory on Policies to Combat Social Exclusion: Social Services and Social Policies to Combat Social Exclusion*, National Centre of Social Research, Athens.

KAVOUNIDIS, J. (1996) 'Social Exclusion: Concept, Community Initiatives, the Greek Experience and Policy Dilemmas', *Diastassis tou Kinonikou Apoklismou stin Ellada*, National Centre for Social Research, vol. A, 47–79.

KEPE (1989) *Ekthessi gia tin Kinoniki Politiki, Pentaetes Programma 1988–1992*, KEPE (Centre of Planning and Economic Research), Athens.

KERMALIS, K. (1990) *Kinoniki Pronia*, Athens.

LAMBROPOULOU-DIMITRIADOU, B. (1995) 'Kritiki Theorissi tis Ellinikis Sineteristikis Nomothessias', *Sineteristiki Poria*, no. 38, 95–107.

National Statistical Service of Greece (1993–98) *Annual Labour Force Surveys*, Athens.

PAPAGEORGIOU, K. (1997) 'Makrochronia provlimata ton Sineterismon', *Sineteristiki Poria*, no. 48, 239–47.

   (1992) 'I antagonistikotita ton Ellinikon Sineterismon', *Sineteristiki Poria*, no. 27, 153–60.

TSARTAS, P. and THANOPOULOU, M. (1994) *Women's Agrotourist Co-operatives in Greece: A Survey Evaluating Their Function*, Mediterranean Women's Studies Institute, Athens.

ZIOMAS, D., KETSETZOPOULOU, M. and BOUZAS, N. (1998) 'Greece', in BORZAGA, C. and SANTUARI, A. (eds) *Social Enterprises and New Employment in Europe*, Regione Trentino-Alto Adige, Trento, 283–310.

8 Ireland

Social enterprises and local development

Patricia O'Hara

Introduction

In Ireland, the terms social economy and social enterprises have become part of policy and academic discourse only since the mid 1990s. This can be attributed primarily to the attention given to these concepts in the European Union in recent years and particularly to the identification of the social economy as a potential source of employment in EU documents.[1] The social economy – and social enterprises as used in this context – is thought of as a distinct sector, neither public nor private, which is generally involved in service provision, most usually in situations of market failure. In one of the first references to the sector in Irish policy discourse, the National Economic and Social Forum (NESF)[2] identified the social economy as 'concerned with meeting real demands which cannot be fully met by the market alone and are not provided by the public sector. It represents a continuum of delivery possibilities between fully commercial and public provision' (NESF 1995: 19).

The social economy is considered by the NESF to have a number of distinctive characteristics including a local focus in terms of market, ownership and operation; an income focus in terms of prioritising adequate and sustainable incomes for those involved; the pursuit of quality of life goals; and different forms of economic organisation. Subsequent discourse has emphasised different aspects of the NESF continuum involving varying levels of public assistance, trading income, voluntary activity, private support and user solidarity.

Kennelly and O'Shea (1998) have characterised the social economy as bridging the gap between the social needs of people, and the public and private resources available to meet these needs. They see social enterprises as most relevant in situations of market failure where needs and demands can be met through community, voluntary or co-operative forms of organisation rather than through the public or private for-profit sector (Kennelly and O'Shea 1998: 210). In recent commentary, three sub-sectors of the social economy have been identified – community businesses; deficient demand social enterprises, and enterprises based on public sector contracts.[3] The latter have not as yet developed to any significant extent.

In Ireland then, the terms social economy and social enterprises are generally understood to refer to initiatives involved in the production of goods or services but with social, rather than purely profit-making or commercial, goals. Perhaps because so many social enterprises are seen to be generally reliant on state support and not fully self-sustaining or commercial in orientation, there is a tendency to perceive social enterprises from both the supply and demand side, as primarily (but not exclusively) a response to problems of disadvantage or social exclusion. But before turning to the links between social exclusion, local development and social enterprise, it is important to set out the broad context of the social economy in Ireland. Although the concept itself is quite new, in practice social enterprises (as conceptualised for this research project) have existed in various forms in Ireland for a long time.

1   Social enterprises in Ireland – the broad context

It is not possible to construct a general typology of social enterprises mainly because information about 'third sector' or non-profit organisations is, at best, fragmented and unreliable. The classification of economic sub-sectors used in national statistics does not specifically delineate such enterprises, so the size and significance of the sector are unrecorded. The terms 'voluntary sector' or 'voluntary and community sector' are the most common concepts used to refer to non-profit organisations with social aims. One of the most recent surveys of the voluntary sector (Powell and Guerin 1997) does not refer to the concept of social economy or social enterprises at all, although it contains a detailed discussion of recent developments in civil society. Notwithstanding their lack of prominence in official statistics, institutions that generally correspond to the working definition of social enterprises adopted for the present study – that is, which incorporate entrepreneurial and social dimensions – are found under a range of classifications. Ireland has a considerable tradition of co-operative activity (dating from the late nineteenth century) and of self-help activity, particularly in the agricultural sector and in rural areas. Moreover, unlike some other northern European countries where the provision of social services is virtually a state monopoly, the non-profit sector has played a very significant part in the provision and delivery of health and personal social services.

Much of this is associated with, and has evolved from, the activities of religious organisations (particularly the Roman Catholic church) which have had a very considerable role in the establishment and operation of services in the fields of health, education and welfare. Religious orders have also been dominant or sole providers in the fields of mental and physical disability, residential childcare and care of the elderly. They have also had a very extensive involvement in education, and particularly in the provision of second level education.

This latter influence is evident in the present structure of the non-profit sector. Data from the Johns Hopkins Comparative Nonprofit Sector Project reveal that employment in non-profit schools accounts for more than half (54 per cent) of total jobs in the non-profit sector in Ireland so that the pattern of non-profit structure which Ireland exhibits is referred to in this study as 'education dominant'. Four-fifths of all non-profit employment are in the education and health sectors combined. The extent of the non-profit sector in Ireland ranks well below the European average in virtually all other fields of activity. This is most notable in social services where employment accounted for only 4.5 per cent compared to the European average of 26.4 per cent (Salamon *et al.* 1998).

Church involvement in social service provision is also reflected in the lay religious organisation, the Society of Saint Vincent de Paul, which has more than 1,000 local branches with some 11,000 members and operates as a kind of shadow welfare state by providing income support and welfare services to those in need. However, the decline in religious vocations and growing secularisation of Irish society has brought about structural changes. The numbers of religious personnel have declined and those who remain have increasingly withdrawn from involvement in institutional provision in the fields of health, education and welfare. Instead, many religious orders have deployed their resources in the provision of community-based services where they continue to have a significant involvement. One regional study of voluntary organisations found that more than half (57 per cent) of voluntary organisations had some form of religious involvement (Faughnan and Kelleher 1993).

The term 'voluntary sector' or 'voluntary and community sector' is used to describe organisations based largely on volunteer activity. Examples range from relatively large facilities providing health services, to professional associations, advocacy organisations and self-help organisations. Recent estimates suggest that there are about 500 voluntary organisations involved in such fields as social services provision, campaigning and advocacy, support and self-help, representation and co-ordination and cultural activity. Many such organisations have undergone significant professionalisation in the past decade. Those involved in advocacy and representation, for instance, have had to respond to the rapid modernisation of Irish society and the increasingly complex and inclusive policy-making process. As yet however, the impact on employment in this sector has not been assessed and there are no statistics or data which track employment in the sector. Unlike other European states, there is no federal structure that represents voluntary organisations. More than half of the voluntary and community organisations which exist in Ireland at present have been formed since the 1970s, and just under a third of the Irish population have been involved in voluntary organisations at some time, with around 18 per cent actively involved in 1995 (Ruddle and Donoghue 1995; Powell and Guerin 1997).

However, many voluntary organisations do not function in a participatory way in terms of involving stakeholders in the running of the organisation. Faughnan and Kelleher (1993) found that less than a third (31 per cent) of the organisations they studied had formal democratic representative structures. Powell and Guerin (1997) found that less than half (41 per cent) of voluntary bodies felt that their clients/users/members had a lot of influence within the organisation. Although the concept of democratisation was important to organisations, two-thirds of those studied believed that there had been no change in the level of democratic participation in the last twenty years, or since they were established.

2   Categories of social enterprises

Any attempt to delineate or categorise social enterprises in Ireland is, of necessity, rather arbitrary. There is no distinct legal definition of social enterprises; individual enterprises may select from a number of different options, which can provide them with a legal identity. Unlike the situation in other European states where legal regimes may actually encourage particular types of organisational forms, the legal context in Ireland generally exerts neither a facilitating nor inhibiting influence on the social economy. The emergence of social enterprises has not given rise to any specific legislative changes in recent decades.

Social enterprises may be limited companies, or industrial and provident societies, which is the legal form adopted by co-operatives. The company is the most common form of legal structure for business firms generally. Most commercial companies are limited by shares but companies may be limited by guarantee, and this is the form more commonly used by social enterprises. In order to omit the word 'limited' from its title such a company's profits or income must not be distributed among its members. Other legal forms adopted by social enterprises include co-operatives and trusts. Credit Unions have a separate legal status and are defined by statute.

In general then, we can distinguish social enterprises on the basis of their objectives, activities and operation rather than by their organisational form. According to the criteria for the definition of social enterprises adopted for the present study, five broad categories of social enterprises can be delineated. These are:

- work integration – social enterprises associated with insertion of members of excluded groups into the labour force;
- social enterprises concerned with housing provision;
- credit unions;
- social enterprises providing personal and proximity services; and
- local development organisations.

Obviously this is just one way of classifying social enterprises and the categories, particularly the latter two, are not entirely conceptually separate or mutually exclusive. Nevertheless, it is useful to delineate them because it is indicative of the way in which social enterprises have emerged and may develop in future. The first four are generally thought of as being part of the non-profit/voluntary sector and as the established or conventional social economy. Local development or community-based service organisations which provide innovative responses to the emerging needs of modern society are more typically characterised as being part of a new generation of social economy organisations. These will be examined in detail in the second part of this chapter. First, we look briefly at the enterprises in the more conventional social economy.

Work integration

Social enterprises categorised here as 'work integration' do not have a specific name or constitute a recognisable sector in Ireland, but all are concerned with providing work and labour-market integration for the socially excluded – usually for people with disabilities. The majority are run by voluntary, non-profit organisations in the disability field and provide training and employment in what are conventionally referred to as 'workshops' or 'sheltered employment'. Around twenty-six such organisations run enterprises which provide goods and services in nineteen different sectors. However, although they are commercially oriented, these enterprises rely to a very considerable extent on direct and indirect state support. Their parent organisations are financed through a combination of state subsidy, donations and commercial profit.

In 1994, the largest non-profit organisation in this area (Rehab Group) established a separate enterprise company to develop viable businesses. Building on the commercial base of some of the existing 'workshops', this has brought together seven companies from the food, textile, electronics and recycling sectors. This model has begun to be adopted in other enterprises established for on-the-job training for the long-term unemployed, in an attempt to reintegrate them into the workforce.

Housing

One of the most significant developments in the social economy in Ireland in recent years has been the increasing role of voluntary organisations in the provision of social housing. Substantial state assistance is available in the form of grants to approved voluntary or non-profit housing associations to assist in the provision of rented accommodation, particularly for those with special needs such as the elderly, people with disabilities and homeless people. More than half the social housing provision for elderly and disabled persons in the period 1988–1995 was accounted for by the non-profit sector. The main organisational forms in the non-profit housing sector are associations, trusts and co-operatives. There were 350 housing associations registered in 1996 of which 100 were affiliated to the Irish Council for Social Housing.

Credit unions

In some respects credit unions are the most easily recognisable social enterprises operating in Ireland. Credit unions are voluntary organisations whose members collectively save and lend to one another at a fair rate of interest. They are distinguished by the idea of a 'common bond', which can be either community, occupational or associational and is the basis for membership and solidarity. There were 435 credit unions registered in the Republic of Ireland in 1997 and about 90 per cent of these were community bond unions where the members live and work in the local area. Each credit union operates autonomously and profits are distributed to members in proportion to their transactions with the credit union, or may be used to provide additional services to members. The credit union movement relies heavily on volunteer workers but has become increasingly professionalised, particularly in larger communities. Credit unions employ more than 2,000 temporary and permanent staff. They are run on a commercial basis and receive no state subsidies.

Personal and proximity services

Non-profit organisations have traditionally provided a range of services in Ireland. Surveys of such organisations have shown that more than two-thirds of them are involved in the provision of services or self-help/mutual aid (Faughnan and Kelleher 1993; Powell and Guerin 1997). The elderly, the community in general (including children) and the unemployed are the most common client groups. The majority employ professional staff but rely heavily on volunteer input, generally from a small corps of fewer than twenty volunteers. The levels of state subsidy and dependence on donations differ greatly from service to service.

The services provided by these organisations include personal services such as community care, healthcare, childcare and counselling, or services to disadvantaged groups like travellers (gypsies) or the homeless, as well as environmental services such as recycling and food co-operatives. The enterprises may be structured as co-operatives and frequently have a strong commitment to egalitarianism. Their operations may not always conform to the definition of social enterprises adopted in the present study, but they have set the context for the emergence of what we have termed above the 'new social economy'.

Local development organisations

The final category of social enterprises outlined above are those that emerge in the context of local development initiatives. While these obviously overlap with the category just described, they are distinguished separately, and are the focal point of this chapter. This is because local development and community development have provided the context in which new social economy initiatives have emerged and were promoted in the 1990s.

3   Local development and the emergence of social enterprises in Ireland

Social partnership and social enterprises

In the mid 1980s, Ireland adopted a social partnership approach to national economic and social policy. This involved agreement among all the main interest groups or 'social partners' on strategies for economic and social development and was embodied in a series of national agreements for the years 1988 to 1999.[4] The partnership approach originated as a response to the worsening state of the economy, the public debt burden and widespread concern about unemployment and emigration in the 1980s. Part of the reorientation of public policy involved acknowledging that the existing centralised system for economic development and welfare provision was evidently ineffective in tackling persistent long-term unemployment and social exclusion. A key element in the new approach, therefore, was an emphasis on local development as a solution to the problem of long-term unemployment and the associated establishment of a support system for area-based and community development. Thus, in the 1990s, the concepts of partnership and area-based development have been central to the Irish approach to tackling social exclusion.

This reorientation of policy provided the context in which social enterprises have begun to emerge in recent years. Basically, there are two strands to the process: a series of policy initiatives which have facilitated and supported the emergence of social enterprises; and the gradual inclusion of community and voluntary organisations (now known as the 'fourth pillar') in the partnership process at national level. These strands have together provided both the impetus for the establishment of new social enterprises and for discourse about the social economy to which community and voluntary organisations have been the most prominent contributors. This entire process was also stimulated by the publication of the EU documents on growth, competitiveness and employment (1993) and on local employment initiatives (1995) and the identification of the social economy as a potential source of employment in European policy discourse.

EU and state support for local development activity

Ireland has a long tradition of local development but such activity received very little state support or acknowledgement until the 1980s when, as already pointed out, community development came to be seen as a strategy for combating unemployment at a local level. The establishment of a national Community Enterprise Programme in 1983 provided funded training programmes, development grants and commercial aids to community-based groups. By 1987 there were an estimated 300 community enterprise groups in Ireland, primarily in more disadvantaged areas, and they represented a core element of community development strategies for such areas (Donnison *et al.* 1991: 48).

However, studies of community enterprises in the 1980s revealed their precarious nature and their high dependence on state subsidies (O'Cinneide and Keane 1987; Collins 1991). Kelleher and Whelan's (1992) research on community enterprises in four disadvantaged Dublin communities concluded that it was extremely difficult to create viable businesses in economically disadvantaged areas. They found that projects were generally small-scale and undercapitalised and tended to experience ongoing cash flow problems, and generate low returns. In this context, they argued, it is inappropriate to attach conditions of actual or potential economic viability to support for such projects. Furthermore, funding agencies should support a whole range of activities and services for direct consumption by the community. Examples of socially useful activities that they suggested included community services, environmental projects and self-help healthcare. In the same vein, Donnison *et al.* (1991) argued that strategies for the promotion of community enterprise were much more likely to be successful if they formed part of a larger-scale effort to work in a more integrated way with all the actors and agencies in local communities. This point was strongly reiterated in a 1990 report to the government which recommended 'concerted, intensive programmes in small areas [which] can have an impact over and above the separate effects of individual programmes' (National Economic and Social Council 1990).

In 1991, the second partnership programme – PESP – took up this recommendation and included an area-based response to the problem of long-term unemployment whereby twelve partnership boards were established on a pilot basis. Each board had eighteen directors comprising six representatives respectively from the local community, the social partners and the state agencies in the area. The boards were legally constituted as limited companies. In 1992, the EU provided funding for these partnerships through a Global Grant under the Structural Funds to support local development and enterprise initiatives and to promote integrated economic, social and community development of local areas. An independent intermediary body – Area Development Management Ltd (ADM) – was established to administer the Global Grant and to provide support, technical assistance and funding.

This local partnership approach, involving a coming together of the public, private and community sectors at grassroots level, has given concrete expression to the idea of a 'bottom-up' approach to development. It has been considered a very successful way of stimulating innovative local responses to social exclusion by the OECD (Sabel 1996) and was extended in Ireland's National Development Plan 1994–99. The Operational Programme for Local Urban and Rural Development included support for area-based partnerships. This programme is supporting thirty-eight partnership companies and thirty-three Community Groups. Local development, in this context, is defined as a collective effort to improve local economic, social and environmental conditions through an integrated effort to counter disadvantage.

These partnerships are complemented by the EU LEADER programme for rural development, which also involves a partnership approach while not being specifically focused on social exclusion or collective effort. There are thirty-four LEADER Groups in the present programme. In addition, EU initiatives such as INTERREG, NOW, INTEGRA, URBAN and the Programme for Peace and Reconciliation directly and indirectly provide support for locally based development. Thus, in Ireland, the shape and direction of EU and national policy has brought about a renewed emphasis on, and support for, local development. This includes the establishment of a national Community Development Programme (CDP) to address social exclusion and poverty at the level of local communities. This support for local development has either helped to create the conditions for the emergence of new social enterprises or has afforded existing enterprises the opportunity to broaden or consolidate their activities through participation in such programmes.

The adoption of participatory strategies and their incorporation in recent national plans has also brought about significant changes in the institutional environment in which the goals and practice of local development are negotiated, and new participatory and consultative mechanisms incorporating the idea of partnership have been established. The National Economic and Social Forum, which has already been referred to, is one example, as is the addition of the 'fourth pillar' representing the community and voluntary sector in the negotiation of Partnership 2000 – the most recent national agreement between the social partners and the state (O'Donnell and Thomas 1998).

In this context, alliances between various interests with a specific focus on social exclusion have formed. These include a 'Third Strand' of NGOs representing women, unemployed, disadvantaged youth, older people, people with a disability, environmental interests and academics on the National Economic and Social Forum; the Community Platform, comprising national networks and organisations committed to combating poverty and social exclusion which formed part of the 'fourth pillar' in the Partnership 2000 negotiations; PLANET (Partnerships for Local Action), a network of area-based partnership companies; and the Community Workers Co-operative, a network of individuals and organisations engaged in community-based projects and initiatives. These coalitions of interests as well as ADM[5] have been the primary promoters of the 'social economy' concept in the second half of the 1990s.

Social enterprises and local development

Although primarily engaged in community development in the broadest sense, partnerships and community groups have been stimulated to search for appropriate responses to social exclusion at local level through creating or supporting social enterprises which respond to unmet social needs while simultaneously creating local employment. Social enterprises in this context are typically engaged in a range of social economy activities such as the provision of resource centres and the development and co-ordination of 'proximity services' such as childcare and community care for older people or people with disabilities, or transport, social housing, training and capacity-building. They might also be involved in environmental projects or culture and heritage activities. They are distinguished by a high degree of voluntarism and, as such, are significant users and reproducers of 'social capital' (Evers and Schulze-Böing 1997).

One small-scale study commissioned by ADM in 1996 involved the compilation of a list of groups 'engaged in either trading and/or service provision whether at a local or wider level' (Mallaghan *et al.* 1996). A total of 489 'social enterprises' were identified in this way and this is acknowledged by the authors to be an underestimation, since at least one region was known to be under-represented. A sample of ninety-seven of these social enterprises participated in a telephone survey of their activities. More than half (55 per cent) of these were located in rural areas and the same proportion had been established in the previous five years. Nearly three-quarters (72 per cent) were associated with area-based partnership companies. The company was the most common form of legal identity, accounting for just under two-thirds of the respondents. Of those who provided data on income sources, 23 per cent were totally dependent on the public sector while a further 24 per cent received more than three-quarters of their income from this source, mainly through their participation in various schemes and programmes. The remainder depended on public funding to varying degrees with only 22 per cent entirely independent of public sector support. The total annual income generated by all the groups in the sample was 20.9 million IEP (26.5 million Euro). Only a minority (22 per cent) were able to generate at least three-quarters of their income from trading activities, whereas almost two-thirds generated less than a quarter of their income from trading. Social enterprises provide opportunities for women, who accounted for almost half (48 per cent) of management employees and 85 per cent of the workers. They were effective in targeting their recruitment in that 73 per cent of workers were previously unemployed.

A further sub-group of twenty-seven were designated as 'community businesses' based on the criteria of: open membership; democratic control (one member, one vote); focus on economic welfare/development of a specified community; and profits for the benefit of the community and not individual members. These were evenly split between rural and urban, and tended to be longer established, have a lower reliance on public sector support and generate more income from trading. These 'community businesses' generated a total annual income of 4.7 million IEP (6 million Euro).

Aside from these data, there have been no other systematic attempts to catalogue the range and breadth of social economy activities being undertaken by local development organisations, although they are referred to in broader studies of locally based development in Ireland (O'Hara 1998; O'Hara and Commins 1998; Walsh et al. 1998). NGOs and interest groups such as ADM, PLANET and the Community Workers Co-operative have recently published documents which identify the strategies and policies to develop and support the social economy.[6] However, these bodies give the social economy a definition of their own, associating it specifically with the regeneration of local economies and describing its distinguishing features as resourcing the local economy, promoting ownership within the local community, and developing local control of and benefit from local resources.[7]

Many social enterprises have only recently been established and are in the early or pilot stage of development. They range across a broad spectrum of responses to social exclusion and include food co-operatives, advice and information centres, community businesses, personal or proximity services such as counselling, childcare, elder care and healthcare, or specific services to disadvantaged groups such as women, lone parents, the long-term unemployed, travellers (gypsies) or the homeless. Such enterprises have a high volunteer input but also employ paid workers. The levels of state and EU subsidy and dependence on donations vary greatly and social enterprises in a local development context are often developed under the aegis of an organisation that also provides a range of supports for private enterprise. One local area partnership has established a Social Economy Unit (which is itself a social enterprise) in order to promote social enterprises.

Two case examples are outlined below in order to provide illustrations of the kinds of social enterprises that are emerging in a local development context in Ireland. The first of these is essentially a village-based initiative in which women's domestic skills are being commoditised in order to respond to a set of local social needs. In the second, an employment creation initiative in a small town has evolved to a partnership with a national agency to create a social enterprise involving people with disabilities.

4 Case examples

Tulsk Parish Services

Tulsk is a small village in the west of Ireland made up of 570 households. Tulsk Parish Services (TPS) was established in 1994 in order to address local problems of exclusion and isolation through the development of sustainable employment and training opportunities, especially for women. The second objective was to provide services and facilities that are accessible and flexible, particularly for the elderly and for young families. Having set up a voluntary management committee, TPS received start-up funding from ADM and the regional health board and later received EU funding under a special European programme (B2–605) that supported pilot actions for the long-term unemployed. This enabled the recruitment of a co-ordinator and a group of fifteen women who would provide the service. TPS is registered as a company limited by guarantee and has charitable status.

Home care and transport were the services offered by TPS initially. The home care service provides care for the elderly living alone or whose families are absent during the day and for mothers with young children. The range of services offered includes meal provision and delivery, replacement care and night care for the ill, hairdressing, childminding, baby-sitting and home help of all kinds.

Services are provided 'on demand' and, in the first year, were provided to seventy-five local people, mainly in their own homes. The charge to the 'customer' pays for the wages of the service provider while the 'overheads' (co-ordinator, training, administration, premises etc.) are met through grants. Members of TPS have attended various training courses to enhance their skills and professionalism. These include courses in social care and community development, catering and hospitality, basic nursing care and computer skills as well as personal and community development. Following members' attendance at catering and business innovation courses, TPS has established a local catering service, which is being run on a fully commercial basis.

In 1996, TPS was awarded funding from the EU Social Fund for training for older women (aged over forty) wishing to enter/re-enter the workforce and for the establishment of a Resource Centre incorporating a kitchen, laundry, meeting rooms, office and crèche from which an expanded social care service could be operated. A project manager was appointed and additional women were recruited and undertook a training and work experience programme.

Plans for the future envisage the provision of five services: laundry, catering, care, advisory and secretarial. The laundry and catering services are a rationalisation and expansion of the services already being provided by TPS, whereas the advisory and secretarial services are new ventures for which TPS has identified a local market. It is anticipated that the seven full-time and nine part-time jobs in the service will become ten full-time and six part-time jobs by 2000.

Both in its direct focus on social exclusion and in the nature of the services it offers, TPS is relatively unusual. Its existing services combine a sensitive and much-needed response to the needs of vulnerable sections of the local population with a strategic response to the inclusion needs of rural women through skills training, part-time employment and confidence building. The service offered is flexible and tailored to the needs of the customers. It is often very personal, being delivered in clients' homes and, in order to be effective, calls for a high degree of sensitivity, understanding, discretion and personal commitment on the part of the carer. It is, in effect, a kind of commercialisation of old networks of caring and neighbourliness which no longer operate as effectively or spontaneously as in the past.

TPS has been particularly successful in attracting funding, which has allowed it to grow relatively rapidly. The leadership, management and negotiation skills of a few key women in the core group have been critical to its success. They are highly motivated, well organised and committed to the development of the project. However, these very elements will also influence its ultimate sustainability. The project is highly dependent on the skills and commitment of voluntary time by a small group of women. Those women who become highly skilled and experienced in what is effectively a quasi-commercial service (with marginal pay rates) may move on to full professional employment. While this is not undesirable, it could present problems in staffing the service. Finally, it is not clear whether TPS could survive if operated purely on a commercial basis, particularly as the services are demand-led and this demand may be diminishing. Social enterprises of this nature may find it necessary to diversify and respond to shifts in demand and to the emergence of new service opportunities.

The Mill Social Enterprise

Mountmellick is a small town of 3,500 residents in the midlands of Ireland. The Mountmellick Development Association (MDA) purchased a disused mill in the town in order to develop an enterprise centre to create employment. In 1994, as a result of contacts between the project manager and the area manager of the National Training and Development Institute (NTDI), the NTDI agreed to lease part of the enterprise centre to establish a social employment business, on condition that MDA would refurbish the Mill. MDA got an unsecured bank loan of

142,000 IEP (180,000 Euro) and a grant of 47,000 IEP (60,000 Euro) from the County Enterprise Board to finance the refurbishment. A ten-year lease incorporating industrial space, a restaurant and offices was signed in 1995. In 1996, additional space for training rooms, consultation rooms and stores was leased for 2 years and 9 months. Through MDA, the local community has now invested about 394,000 IEP (0,5 million Euro) in the enterprise centre.

The Mill Social Enterprise was established in 1996 as a partnership between the NTDI and MDA. Around 130 people in total are employed by the enterprise. Training and support are provided to around thirty people with disabilities in order to enable them to make the transition to independent worker status. In addition, the enterprise provides employment for 100 people from the local community and is the largest single employer in the area.

There are three main businesses. The first one, 'Subcontract Services', involves assembly, packaging and labelling of products from a local factory on a sub-contract service basis, supported by management, warehousing, inventory control and transport. This enterprise operates to 'just in time' principles, an arrangement which means that labour intensive or non-core activities are offered to an industry at a rate which makes it worthwhile for them to contract them out. The second business, which is smaller, is a sports bag manufacturing enterprise. It provides a customised sports bag manufacture and a screen printing service to clients such as clubs and marketing companies. The third business is the 'Old Mill Restaurant', which provides high quality meals as well as outside catering services. The Mill Social Enterprise project is also supported by the INTEGRA strand of the EU Employment Initiative, which funds support services for people with disabilities who are employed there.

By mid 1997 there were 134 people employed in the Mill and there is potential for expansion, the main limiting factor being space at present. Both the sub-contract services and the restaurant enterprises are commercially viable.

The Mill Social Enterprise is considered to be the major achievement of MDA, which has evolved, over a period of fifteen years, into a respected development organisation. The success of the Mill Social Enterprise is related to the organisation's ability to form a strategic partnership that would realise economic and social objectives, and to its success in attracting EU and state funding to underpin its social objectives.

5 Conclusions and policy implications

The need to address social exclusion, particularly the persistence of long-term unemployment, has led Ireland to adopt a development strategy which, *inter alia*, involves strengthening local capacity by supporting development partnerships. One of the recognised values of this 'partnership' approach is its capacity to effectively address a combination of economic and social issues simultaneously (Sabel 1996). It is in this context that social enterprises are emerging, as local groups search for effective and appropriate responses to social exclusion. Since social enterprises can provide both job opportunities and services, they are seen as a particularly effective response to social exclusion. The 'social capital' they generate includes the creation, in disadvantaged areas, of a local labour pool with good management and business skills, improving the confidence, self-esteem and knowledge of the individuals involved, and the development of local solidarity and capacity to effectively represent the local needs.

NGOs and interest groups involved in local development are promoting the social economy as an important contribution to the regeneration of local areas where social enterprises can provide services in situations of market failure. Thus, in Ireland, the impetus for development of the social economy and the promotion of social enterprises has come primarily from those involved in local and community development through their various networks and representative bodies.

The social economy concept has been incorporated into contemporary development discourse and the various NGOs and coalitions of interest are negotiating with the state for greater support for social enterprises. Indeed, most of the discussion and documentation regarding the social economy has been initiated and published by the NGOs involved in local development.[8] Largely as a result of pressure from the Community Platform, the state established a Social Economy Working Group as part of the Partnership 2000 agreement. The Working Group comprised representatives from various government departments, employers, trade unions and other relevant interest groups. Indeed, such groups had a strong input into the Working Group, and its report – published in 1998 – draws heavily on their publications.

One of the key conclusions of the Group was that the main state support to the sector has come in the form of a labour subsidy through the various labour-market integration programmes. The second significant source of state support is through programmes to combat disadvantage and social exclusion. The Group set out a series of recommendations for developing the social economy as a means of combating disadvantage and regenerating communities. They recommended that specific financial and institutional supports should involve a reorientation of existing supports and funding, rather than the creation of new ones. The report contained neither estimates of existing employment in social economy organisations nor any assessment of its possible employment potential. Nor did it address the issue of public service contracts for social economy organisations.

While the state has created a supportive environment and responded to pressure from the 'community sector', the Report of the Working Group is relatively limited and avoids tackling some of the most fundamental issues in the sector. At the most basic level there is a need to establish the circumstances in which social enterprises are an appropriate and successful response to social exclusion. Some communities have been particularly effective in this field and the reasons for this need to be established and support mechanisms for encouraging social entrepreneurship put in place. Social enterprises face formidable barriers in attracting finance and investment capital, and state support could take the form of loans, grants, credit facilities, training and technical support.

In Ireland, labour-market programmes are a crucial way of subsidising labour to social enterprises and the key state support to the sector. Indeed expenditure on active labour-market policies in Ireland at 1.8 per cent of GDP is exceeded only by Denmark and Sweden in the OECD. This evolved in the context of high and intractable unemployment and the issue of the creation of a secondary labour market is quite obvious. Moreover, as economic growth continues and job opportunities in the Irish economy generally continue to improve, labour is diverted from the social economy to the private sector, and there is evidence of the labour pool for social enterprises becoming depleted. Already the sector relies to a considerable extent on female labour, both professional and voluntary. As women's labour-market participation patterns evolve, the pool of voluntary and part-time female labour on which many social enterprises depend is likely to decrease.

It is also necessary to address the extent to which state support is essential in order for social enterprises to maintain a social orientation and respond to particular needs. This includes establishing the appropriate mix between earned income and state support in order to ensure sustainability. As yet, social enterprises in Ireland have not become involved to any significant extent in providing services under contract to the state. If this is to be the way forward, it also involves addressing the most appropriate relationship between the state and social enterprises in order to ensure the effective delivery of services at local level.

The issue of quality is also important, i.e. whether social enterprises can deliver a 'quality' product in the area of personal services and whether this is best organised and delivered at local level. From the demand side, it is necessary to consider the most effective way of supporting low-income consumers so that they may have access to the services provided by social enterprises or participate in solidarity organisations on an equal footing.

Finally, as Ireland becomes an increasingly prosperous society, it seems likely that social enterprises may come to be seen as an effective and appropriate means of providing services to socially excluded groups. The local development experience of the 1990s may provide a model of how this can best be achieved.

Notes

1 Commission of the European Communities (1993, 1994, 1995).
2 The NESF was established in 1993 as a mechanism for achieving a wider national consensus on social and economic matters in Ireland. It is one of four social partnership institutions which negotiate economic and social policies in Ireland (see National Economic and Social Forum, 1997).
3 PLANET (1997); ADM (1998); Community Workers Co-operative (1998); Social Economy Working Group Report (1998).
4 These social partnership programmes were: Programme for National Recovery (PNR) 1988–90; Programme for Economic and Social Progress (PESP) 1991–93; Programme for Competitiveness and Work (PCW) 1994–96; and Partnership 2000 for Inclusion, Employment and Competitiveness 1997–99.
5 Area Development Management Ltd is an independent intermediary company, designated by the Irish Government in agreement with the European Commission to

oversee the Local Development Sub-Programme of the Operational Programme for Local Urban and Rural Development in Ireland.
6   See PLANET (1997); Community Platform (1997); ADM (1998); Community Workers Co-operative (1998).
7   PLANET (1997); Community Workers Co-operative (1998).
8   See ADM (1997, 1998); Planet (1997); Community Workers Co-operative (1998).

Bibliography

ADM (Area Development Management Limited) (1998) *Financial Supports for Social Economy Development*, Report for the Community Enterprise Advisory Committee prepared by the Social Economy Unit Tallaght, ADM, Dublin.
—— (1997) *Partnerships: Making a Difference in People's Lives*, ADM, Dublin.
COLLINS, T. (1991) 'Community Enterprise: Participation in Local Development', unpublished Ph.D. thesis, National University of Ireland, Maynooth.
Commission of the European Communities (1995) *Local Development and Employment Initiatives*, Brussels.
—— (1994) *European Social Policy: A Way Forward for the Union*, Brussels.
—— (1993) *Growth, Competitiveness, Employment – The Challenges and Ways Forward into the 21st Century*, Brussels.
Community Platform (1997) *Achieving Social Partnership: the Strategy and Proposals of The Community Platform in the Partnership 2000 Negotiations*, Community Platform, Dublin.
Community Workers Co-operative (1998) *Strategies to Develop the Social Economy*, Strategy Guide no. 2, Community Workers Co-operative, Galway.
DONNISON, D. *et al.* (1991) *Urban Poverty, the Economy and Public Policy*, Combat Poverty Agency, Dublin.
EVERS, A. and SCHULZE-BÖING, M. (1997) 'Mobilising Social Capital. The Contribution of Social Enterprises to Strategies against Unemployment and Social Exclusion', paper for an EMES Seminar, Barcelona.
FAUGHNAN, P. and KELLEHER, P. (1993) *The Voluntary Sector and The State: A Study of Organisations in One Region*, CMRS, Dublin.
HART, M. and MACFARLANE, R. (1996) 'The Role of Community Enterprise in Local Economic Development in Ireland', paper presented at the ADM Conference on Community Business and the Social Economy, Dublin.
KELLEHER, P. and WHELAN, M. (1992) *Dublin Communities in Action*, Community Action Network/Combat Poverty Agency, Dublin.
KENNELLY, B. and O'SHEA, E. (1998) 'The Welfare State in Ireland: A European Perspective', in HEALY, S. and REYNOLDS, B. (eds) *Social Policy in Ireland*, Oak Tree Press, Dublin, 193–220.
MALLAGHAN, A., HART, M., MACFARLANE, R. and CONNOLLY, E. (1996) *A Study of Community Business within the Social Economy in Ireland*, Report of a Study for Area Development Management Ltd., Dublin.
National Economic and Social Council (1990) *Strategy for the Nineties: Economic Stability and Structural Change*, NESC, Dublin.
National Economic and Social Forum (1997) *A Framework for Partnership – Enriching Strategic Consensus through Participation*, Government Publications, Dublin.
—— (1995) *Jobs Potential of the Services Sector*, Government Publications, Dublin.
O'CINNEIDE, M. and KEANE, M. (1987) *Community Self-Help Economic Initiatives and Development Agency Responses in the Mid-West of Ireland*, Social Sciences Research Centre, University College Galway, Galway.

O'DONNELL, R. and THOMAS, D. (1998) 'Partnership and Policy-Making', in HEALY, S. and REYNOLDS, B. (eds) *Social Policy in Ireland*, Oak Tree Press, Dublin, 117–46.

O'HARA, P. (1998) *Action on the Ground: Models of Practice in Rural Development*, Irish Rural Link, Galway.

O'HARA, P. and COMMINS, P. (1998) 'Rural Development: Towards the New Century', in HEALY, S. and REYNOLDS, B. (eds) *Social Policy in Ireland*, Oak Tree Press, Dublin, 261–84.

PLANET (Partnership for Local Action Network) (1997) *Building the Social Economy: New Areas of Work, Enterprise and Development*, Planet, Dublin.

POWELL, F. and GUERIN, D. (1997) *Civil Society and Social Policy*, A&A Farmar, Dublin.

RUDDLE, H. and DONOGHUE, F. (1995) *The Organisation of Volunteering: A Study of Irish Voluntary Organisations in the Social Welfare Area*, Policy Research Centre, National College of Industrial Relations, Dublin.

SABEL, C. (1996) *Ireland: Local Partnerships and Social Innovation*, OECD, Paris.

SALAMON, L.M., ANHEIER, H.K. *et al.* (1998) *The Emerging Sector Revisited*, Johns Hopkins University Institute for Policy Studies and Center for Civil Society Studies, Baltimore.

Social Economy Working Group Report (1998) *Partnership 2000*, The Stationery Office, Dublin.

WALSH, J., CRAIG, S. and MCCAFFERTY, D. (1998) *Local Partnerships for Social Inclusion?*, Oak Tree Press in association with Combat Poverty Agency, Dublin.

9 Italy

From traditional co-operatives to innovative social enterprises

Carlo Borzaga and Alceste Santuari

Introduction

In Italy, there is neither a specific legal concept nor a legal definition of 'social enterprise'. The term is more and more used in both political and scientific debate to define those third-sector organisations that supply, in a stable and entrepreneurial manner, services aimed at combating social exclusion and, more generally, personal and community services. The term social enterprise came into use from the beginning of the 1990s with the approval of the law that recognised and defined social co-operatives. Its use has been growing with the impressive development of these new co-operatives providing both social services and promoting work integration.

To understand the development of social enterprises in Italy, it is necessary to take into account the main features of both the Italian welfare system and the Italian non-profit sector as they developed after the Second World War. The Italian welfare system, measured in terms of public expenditure, grew especially after the 1970s, reaching the EU average in the 1990s, but was mainly oriented to money transfers, with a poor supply of social services. The Italian non-profit sector, on the other hand, was mainly playing an advocacy role, having the state as its counterpart. Given this context, the development of social enterprises (especially of social co-operatives) can be understood as an innovative way of meeting the growing and unsatisfied demand for social services.

This chapter describes and interprets this development. After providing a summary of the different types of social enterprises in Italy (section 1), we briefly analyse the context in which they developed (section 2) and describe the birth, the evolution and the main characteristics of social co-operatives (sections 3 and 4). Finally, we attempt to evaluate the functions of social co-operatives (section 5) and their prospects for development (section 6). The analysis is limited to social co-operatives providing social services and does not give attention to work-integration social co-operatives.[1]

1 Social enterprises in Italy

The production of services to counter social exclusion is nowadays carried out by organisations with various legal forms. These can be identified as follows:

- social co-operatives, as defined by Act 381/1991. In 1998, this category comprised around 4,500 organisations supplying social services (about 70 per cent) or engaged in work-integration activities (about 30 per cent);
- around 20 per cent of the 10,000 voluntary organisations defined by Act 266/1991. According to this Act, voluntary organisations, although they are engaged in combating social exclusion, should not deliver social services on a stable and regular basis, and they should be staffed mainly by volunteers. In fact, the constraints imposed by the Act are rather generic, and this explains why there are at least 2,000 voluntary organisations which can be effectively included in the category of social enterprises, both because of the kind of services that they supply, and because these services are supplied on a steady and ongoing basis;[2]
- some hundreds of associations other than voluntary ones, which fall within the provisions of the Civil Code of 1942. These associations perform activities mainly or exclusively for the benefit of their members. Stating their precise number is more difficult since little data are available. In this case too, given that the provisions of the Civil Code state that associations must pursue an 'ideal' (i.e. non commercial) aim, stable commitment to the production of services would be contrary to the legal provisions (even though court decisions tend to deliver a rather flexible interpretation of the law);
- some traditional co-ops provided for by the Act of 1947 which actually operate in sectors of collective interest, and which are similar to social co-ops, although they do not call themselves such. In this case too, the available data are scant. However, the number of these organisations can be estimated at between 1,000 and 1,500;
- some charitable and social care public institutions (*IPAB*, *Istituzioni Pubbliche di Assistenza e Beneficienza*), particularly those which have transformed themselves from public institutions into private foundations according to a recent law.[3] In spite of the legal and bureaucratic difficulties in retrieving precise data at the national level, the number of *IPAB* can be estimated at roughly 800, of which only one in four has become private;
- a few joint-stock companies.

Of all the aforementioned organisational forms, the one that best meets all the characteristics of a social enterprise, and which displays them on a stable basis, is the social co-operative. In fact, voluntary associations are prevented by law from undertaking the stable provision of services. Moreover, both associations and voluntary organisations, which are mainly unregistered entities, do not allow limited liability for their members. Associations and ordinary co-operatives do not necessarily pursue a social aim; rather they pursue a mutual one. Finally, *IPAB* still largely belong to the public sector, since their boards of directors and most of their decisions must be directly endorsed by public authorities. It follows that the present chapter will only deal with social co-ops, and specifically with those co-ops that supply social and educational services.[4]

2   The context

The first social co-ops were established towards the end of the 1970s. Together with voluntary organisations, they are among the most innovative legal and organisational forms of (and in) the modern Italian non-profit sector. In order to understand the birth of these new organisations and their characteristics, therefore, one must analyse what occurred in that period, with regard to the evolution of both the non-profit sector and the welfare system.

In Italy, charities and voluntary organisations (the historical ancestors of modern not-for-profit organisations) freely developed until the end of the eighteenth century. Social work, healthcare, elderly care, and education were all areas of private charitable activity. A significant contribution to such development was made through the action of the Catholic church for the benefit of the weakest classes in the society. From the end of the eighteenth century onwards, and following the French Revolution, charities in Italy, as in other European countries, were the object of growing suspicion and hostility. They were regarded as belonging to extraneous powers that should be countervailed because they represented a third party between the government and individuals. Indeed, these were the only two subjects that the ideology of the Enlightenment recognised: the state was the supreme interpreter of the people's will and no other established body should exist, because citizens had to strengthen the authority of the state in order to widen and protect their individual rights. The liberal form of the state affirmed by the French Revolution implied the isolation of individuals from the state. Accordingly, the legitimacy of intermediate bodies was to be denied, since freedom only related to single individuals, not to social groups such as corporations, foundations and associations. In Italy, therefore, the action of charities and voluntary organisations was progressively replaced by the direct intervention of public authorities, as in the case of the *IPAB*. This attitude towards non-profit organisations was strengthened between the First and the Second World Wars by fascism and, subsequently, by the building of the public welfare system.

Italy followed the same line of growth as most European welfare systems, which were mainly public, with regard both to redistribution (social security, social care, and so forth) and to the provision of services. This caused the transformation into public agencies of many social institutions that had always been privately run, and created the dependence of the non-profit organisations that were allowed to keep an autonomous status (especially those belonging to the Catholic church) on public funds and decision-making.

This evolution makes it clear why, at the beginning of the 1970s, non-profit organisations were relatively few and confined to advocacy functions, mainly for the benefit of their members. There was little room for non-profit organisations carrying out productive activities. Not-for-profit organisations were either incorporated into the public sphere, or they were constrained to produce in a manner that was closely dependent on the public authorities. The only private enterprises with a social aim were co-operatives, but these had to restrict their social benefits to their members.

The Italian welfare system built after the Second World War was based more on the redistribution of monetary resources than on the provision of services.[5] The only social services provided on a large scale by the Italian welfare system were education and healthcare – both supplied mainly by public institutions.[6] Later on, while demand for services increased, the Italian welfare system endeavoured to match the new needs by supplying transfers, particularly through the social security pension system. This was so much so that in 1997, although Italian social expenditure was lower than the European average with respect to GDP, social pensions expenditures amounted to 15.8 per cent of GDP, as opposed to the European average of 12 per cent.

It is therefore in this gap between types of public intervention and needs, that from the 1970s onwards, the development of the third sector is to be located. In a few years, third-sector organisations:

• superseded their mutual dimension. The newly established not-for-profit organisations were created mainly to meet the demands of individuals other than their members;
• increased the provision of services, albeit in the conviction that they were substituting for the public authorities for a short period of time. Indeed, many of the new organisations were formed by people who regarded the difficulties of the welfare system in dealing with the new needs as temporary, and therefore considered their role to be merely the provisional replacement of public intervention. These organisations were initially established in the form of associations and were largely based on voluntary work. However, already towards the end of the 1970s, the first co-ops were created, the members of which were both volunteers and paid workers.

3   Birth and evolution of social enterprises

The coming into being of social co-ops

The use of the association form to produce services, and of the co-operative form to work mainly for the benefit of non-members, collided with the Italian legal system and its clear distinction between the First Book and Fifth Book of the Civil Code. In the former, associations and foundations, which are the only two non-profit organisations provided for by the Civil Code, were conceived as pursuing ideal purposes, i.e. they should not have economic goals and activities or, at most, only marginal ones. By contrast, companies and corporations, which also include co-operatives, were entrusted by the Fifth Book with commercial and industrial activities, the aim of which was to secure profits or benefits for their owners. The Civil Code does not envisage the carrying out of productive activities, such as the provision of social services, by using a not-for-profit organisational form.

Despite the numerous applications of the associative form, it often appeared clearly that associations, and to a certain extent also foundations, were ill suited to the stable and entrepreneurial supply of services. As a consequence, while the new organisations producing social services stepped up their activities, they began to assume the organisational form of the co-operative society. This use of the co-operative form, though in contrast with the common expectation that co-ops should identify with mutuality, has been made possible by the facts that:

- the Italian Constitution (which is subsequent to the Civil Code) did grant co-operation a social function, although the concept was not clearly explained. This enabled the early social co-ops to defend their activities for the benefit of disadvantaged people, as a broader application of the mutual principle and as 'mutuality' among volunteers, so much so that the term 'extended mutuality' came into common use;
- the capital required to establish a co-op was very small – not higher than that required to establish an association.

Furthermore, co-ops were granted a separate legal personality and the limited liability of their members, and they were required to manage their initiatives democratically, according to the one-person-one-vote principle, which should theoretically have made co-ops more democratic than associations.

Thus, little by little, amidst many difficulties[7] and despite the sceptical position of the co-operative movement, the co-operative form began to be used in the provision of social services. Several voluntary or advocacy organisations transformed themselves into co-ops, or they established co-ops. From the first research on this kind of co-op, carried out in 1986 (Borzaga 1988; Borzaga and Failoni 1990) it appears that of the 496 co-ops surveyed, 22.6 per cent had been formed by voluntary organisations and 15.9 per cent by associations. Only 50 per cent of co-ops had been established as co-ops from the outset. With regard to members, only 27 per cent were paid workers, whereas the rest were volunteers directly engaged in the activity, and more generally, supporting members. Only 21 per cent of the co-ops surveyed did not have volunteers in their membership (in the northern regions, this proportion was 10 per cent).

A phenomenon therefore emerged with distinct features, and it defined itself as the 'social solidarity co-operative'. It began to develop its own organisational strategy, especially by forming consortia at the local level and one consortium at the national level. It also began to exert pressure within the co-operative movement and within Parliament to obtain legal recognition of its own specific aspects.

Legal recognition: the Act of 1991

Legal recognition of social co-ops was attained in 1991 with the passing of a specific Act. The Italian social co-operative society, as provided for by the Act of 1991, represents an important innovation at both the domestic and international levels. The most significant aspects of social co-operatives are the following:

- the beneficiary is above all the community, or groups of disadvantaged people within it, even if they are not members. Indeed, the Act of 1991 provides that social co-ops have to carry out their activities 'for the general benefit of the community and for the social integration of citizens';
- membership may consist of various kinds of stakeholders, such as:

  - members who perform an activity in the co-op and earn a monetary compensation from it (workers, managers),
  - members who benefit directly from the services provided by the co-op (elderly people, the handicapped),
  - members who work voluntarily for the co-op in 'a personal, spontaneous and free manner without any profitable aim' and who cannot constitute more than 50 per cent of the total workforce, according to the Act of 1991,[8]
  - financing members and public institutions.

The Act divides social co-operative societies into two categories, which correspond to two types of activity:

- co-ops that carry out activities in the area of health, social or educational services (A-type co-ops);
- co-ops that act as agencies for integrating disadvantaged people in the labour market (B-type co-ops).

A further distinctive characteristic of Italian social co-operatives is their particular and privileged relationships with local and national authorities – relationships that are often governed by special agreements.

Finally, contrary to the rule that applies to non-profit organisations in general, the Act of 1991 does not prevent co-ops from distributing profits, but it imposes restrictions on this distribution. Indeed, the Act states that the amount of profits to be divided must not exceed 80 per cent of the total; that the rate of profits for each share cannot be higher than 2 per cent of the rate applicable to the bonds issued by the Italian Post Service; and that no assets can be distributed should the co-op be wound up. Of course, social co-operative societies are free to choose, in their deed of settlement, not to divide any profits among their members.

The Act of 1991 was passed after ten years of parliamentary debate[9] which involved both the political parties and the co-operative movement. The co-ops in favour of the Act were mainly those belonging to the Catholic tradition and the Christian Democrats, whereas the Socialist and Communist Parties and those co-ops that identified with these two parties were against the Act. The latter were particularly opposed to the inclusion of volunteers among the members of co-ops. In this respect, the final text of the Act is a compromise insofar as volunteer members are allowed, but their presence is not compulsory and it is limited. Their name also changed: instead of 'social solidarity co-ops', these new organisations were called 'social co-ops'.

Consolidation

After their legal recognition, social co-ops began to spread throughout the country. The Act of 1991 gave greater visibility to the social co-op model and encouraged its acceptance by all courts. The social co-operative movement, which was already structured and organised, managed to start a wide-ranging debate on the Act and its implementation, which in turn helped to give social co-ops greater visibility. Legal provisions enacted by regional governments subsequent to the national Act also fostered the growth of social co-ops.

The development of social co-operatives was also influenced by a closer attention to social services by the public authorities, especially local ones, which gave rise to contracting-out policies. Under pressure from the demand for social services, local authorities increasingly began to contract out these services, particularly the newest ones, to social enterprises. This trend made it possible for public authorities to increase the supply of services without boosting the number of civil servants, and contrasted with the previous welfare model which allocated even the production of services to the public administration.

Finally, the progressive acceptance of social co-operation by the co-operative movement, part of which realised that it was a good opportunity to revive co-operation as a whole, gave further support to the diffusion of social co-ops.

The economic and employment dimensions[10]

In 1991, when the Act was passed, social co-ops numbered just under 2,000. By the end of 1997, the number of social co-ops in Italy was estimated at around 4,500. Social co-ops currently represent about 4 per cent of the total number of co-operatives and 10 per cent of total co-operative employment. Seventy per cent of social co-ops are of A-type and 30 per cent are social co-ops whose purpose is to integrate disadvantaged people into the labour market.[11] This means that the co-ops carrying out personal services number at least 2,800 to 3,000.

By drawing on different statistical sources, a total number of at least 100,000 members of social co-ops, of which about 9,000 are volunteers and 75,000 are paid workers can be estimated. Social co-ops providing social services have about 75,000 members, of whom 6,000 are volunteers and 60,000 are paid workers. The other members, who cannot be classified as paid workers, nor as volunteers (because they do not work systematically in services provision) are referred to as supporting members. These supporting members often guarantee the linkage with the local community; they also sometimes participate in the executive board or take part in the work to help the co-operative on specific tasks. The number of users served by social co-ops can be estimated at 400,000 (*CGM* 1994, 1997).

The average size of social co-ops is between 40 and 50 members, including an average of twenty-five paid worker members (in social co-operatives, workers are usually also members). About 90 per cent of social co-ops have fewer than 100 members, and 70 per cent of them fewer than fifty. There are only a few large social co-ops, with some hundreds of worker members. In 1995, the average turnover was about 900 million lira per year (464,811 Euro).

The predominantly small size of social co-ops seems to be consistent with the tendency of these organisations to restrict their activities to limited territorial areas. In 1986, 35 per cent of the social co-ops surveyed operated only in the municipality in which their premises were located, whereas 49 per cent operated at the provincial or regional level (*CGM* 1997). Although there are no data available for the following years, it is likely that the situation did not change significantly. Only in some particular cases did these co-ops grow in size. From 1992 to 1994 the annual average increase was 1.8 to two employees. This tendency to control the size is mainly the result of a planned strategy, and particularly to keep a high level of trust among members and with the community.

Contrary to the situation that the surveys carried out in the 1980s revealed, the membership of social co-ops today consists mainly of workers. In 1996, more than half of the co-ops examined did not have volunteer members (*CGM* 1997). Where these were present, they rarely numbered more than ten. In co-ops for which data are available for both 1993 and 1996, the number of volunteer members halved in the three-year period, and the increase in their number of members (from fifty-two to fifty-four on average) was entirely due to the entry of new worker members. This change in the composition of membership was favoured by the Act of 1991, and it is the consequence of the remarkable growth of social co-operation in the 1990s.[12] The increase in the demand for services from the public authorities induced the fast creation of new co-operatives; and this generally involved greater reliance on paid jobs than on volunteering, because the mobilisation of volunteers is usually the result of long-term investments in social capital and cannot be achieved within a very short time. This indicates that the entrepreneurial dimension of social co-ops has been strengthening, while their social function and relations with local communities may have diminished. The presence in the membership of consumers who are benefiting from the co-op's services is still limited; indeed, fewer than one hundred co-ops state that their membership includes their consumers.

Social co-ops initially developed mainly in the northern regions of Italy, where social capital was abundant and the enterprise culture was widespread.[13] Later on, social co-ops spread also in the South of Italy, though to a more limited extent. In the South, many co-ops were formed as a way to combat unemployment, and few of them included volunteers as members. In 1996, about 60 per cent of social co-ops had their offices in the northern regions, whereas the remaining 40 per cent had theirs in the central and southern regions, where the majority of co-ops supply social and healthcare services. The lesser development of social co-ops in the South is due both to smaller demand for social services (which are still largely supplied by families), and to the more limited attention paid to social problems by the public authorities. In recent years, moreover, social co-ops in the southern regions have been sometimes misused in order to support the purely social-care activity of local authorities. However, most recently, the national organisations of social co-operatives (especially *Federsolidarietà* and *CGM, Consorzio 'Gino Mattarelli'*) have made notable efforts to create new social co-ops in the South consistent with the co-operative tradition and with the legal provisions of the Act of 1991. The success of this action bodes well for the achievement of a more balanced spread of social co-ops across the national territory.

4   The characteristics of social co-operatives

Services supplied

Data from a survey carried out by CGM^{14} show that, in 1994, almost half of social co-ops provided services to more than one type of user, and that the same proportion provided several kinds of services (for example, home care and residential care). These data give an idea of the complexity of the production process in social co-ops. The users of these co-ops were mainly elderly (47.1 per cent), juveniles with problems (44.1 per cent), handicapped (39.8 per cent), drug addicts (9.9 per cent), mentally ill (9.6 per cent) and disadvantaged adults (14.7 per cent). Comparison with the data from a survey carried out in 1986 reveals a change in the types of clients served by social co-ops. In 1986, 32 per cent of the co-ops provided services to handicapped people; only 18.8 per cent had the elderly as their users; 15.9 per cent served juniors and 11.5 per cent drug addicts. These changes may be viewed as the consequence of an evolution in both the needs and the funding policy of public authorities, which tend to give priority to policies in support of the elderly. The survey revealed that the principal form of service provision was residential care, i.e. the service was delivered on the co-op's premises.

Human resources and their composition

Social co-ops may have, as already stated, mixed memberships, but this is not legally compulsory. Consequently, there are social co-ops formed by consumers (or users) only, by worker members only, by workers and volunteers or by consumers and volunteers. The only legal obligation, as already mentioned, is that volunteers do not exceed 50 per cent of the total workforce. Legal entities, particularly city councils (although this possibility has seldom been taken up), and financing members (individuals or legal persons) may also become members of social co-ops. Many co-ops also comprise members who actually do not take part in their activities (neither as workers nor as volunteers), and rarely take part in the decision-making process.

Given this situation, the data on the characteristics of the individuals involved in social co-ops may vary according to the definition of 'volunteer member' adopted by the statistical database (i.e. whether volunteers are required to actively and continuously take part in the co-op's activities). According to the audit proceedings collected by the Italian Ministry of Labour on 1,134 co-ops, in 1994 these had 66,363 members (about fifty on average in each co-op), of whom 45.2 per cent were inactive members. Ninety-one per cent of active members were worker members, 8.4 per cent were volunteer members, 0.4 per cent

Table 9.1   Changes in composition of the membership of 260 social co-ops

Type of members	When set up	Average number of members		
		1990	*1992*	*1995*
Worker members	2.7	15.6	18.2	24.8
Volunteer members	9.4	14.1	14.3	12.3
Members who are neither workers nor volunteers	6.8	30.9	34.4	35.8
Total number of members	18.9	60.6	66.9	72.9

Source: *CGM* (1997)

financing members and 0.3 per cent legal entities (of which some were city councils). However, this source of data uses a very restricted definition of volunteer member. According to figures issued by the *CGM*, which refer to a smaller but more homogenous sample of social co-ops, inactive members accounted for 24 per cent of the membership, and volunteer members for 26 per cent in 1996.

Examination of all the sources, however, suggests that there is a generalised tendency towards a reduction in the proportion of volunteers. This results in particular from the fact that the growth in the total number of active members has been almost completely due to the entry of worker members. This decline in the proportion of volunteers has not been counterbalanced by an increase in the number of user members, who are present in only very few co-ops. Finally, a significant percentage of co-ops (42.8 per cent) hire workers and volunteers who are not members. A clear picture of this evolution is provided in Table 9.1, in which data collected in 1995 on a sample of 260 social co-ops (*CGM* 1997) are summarised.

Financial resources and their composition

The overall turnover of Italian social co-ops in 1994 was estimated at 2,500 billion lira (1,291,142,248 Euro), with an average value by co-op of about 900 million lira (464,811 Euro), of which 880 million (454,482 Euro) was derived from the supply of services to public authorities or private individuals and 20 million (10,329 Euro) from public funds (*CGM* 1997). The principal clients of A-type social co-ops are public authorities (77 per cent), followed by private individuals (4.7 per cent), other non-profit organisations (5.9 per cent) and private for-profit companies (3.1 per cent). Of course the composition of users also depends on the type of service supplied.

Most of the funding from public authorities is obtained from participation in competitive tenders, or is assigned according to the quantity of services provided. More than 61 per cent of the 75.6 per cent of turnover which social co-ops derive from public authorities is obtained in this way compared to 14.4 per cent granted in the form of public subsidies. Local authorities intending to contract out a service to a social co-operative often compare the tenders submitted by several co-ops (or by different non-profit or for-profit organisations). They then choose either on the basis of straightforward cost parameters or according to a more complex set of criteria where particular attention is paid to the quality of the project, the services to be supplied, and the co-op's capacity to mobilise volunteers. Local authorities then undertake a contract with the co-operative or organisation that has been selected. This contract sets out the rules on how the service is to be organised and paid for. The voucher system is little used in Italy.

Social co-ops derive the financial means they need to manage their activities almost entirely from private sources. These consist mainly of members' shares, and to a significant extent of reserve funds. By taking the capacity of self-financing as indicator, the ratio between financial resources and liabilities is on average higher than 40 per cent.

The organisation

Since their earliest development, one of the main strategies of social co-ops has been to avoid increasing an individual co-op's size to match the growing demand for services, but rather to spin off new initiatives,[15] thus pursuing a specialisation strategy. Co-ops also reap the advantages of large size by grouping into local consortia. The integrated entrepreneurial system developed over recent years is now characterised by a three-level structure as follows:

- the first level consists of the single co-ops;
- the second level is constituted by the local, mainly provincial, consortia. These function as strategic support in the contractual relations between co-operatives and public authorities, often acting as general contractors. They also provide marketing development, administrative counselling, training and development of human resources, organisational and managerial counselling of the partners and of the newly established organisations. The first provincial consortium of social co-ops was established in 1983 in Brescia. As of 30 June 1997, there were at least seventy local and territorial consortia throughout the country, with a particular concentration in the northern part of Italy, especially in Lombardy (seventeen consortia);[16]
- the third level, which is represented by the national consortium *CGM*, performs long-run strategic functions, such as research activity, training of the managers and trainers of the local consortia, counselling and developing activities. Moreover, when possible and necessary, the *CGM* also assumes the role of general contractor with respect to actions at the national level. It was established in 1986, and as of 1 October 1997 it grouped together forty-two territorial consortia, which in turn comprised around 700 co-ops, of which at least 450 supplied social services.

The composition and structure of social co-ops and consortia grouped into the *CGM* are summarised in Table 9.2.

Table 9.2 The *CGM* composition and structure

Data available on
545 social enterprises, of which:
339 (62%) A-type social co-ops
201 (37%) B-type social co-ops
5 (1%) non-social co-ops
19,833 members, of which:
10,064 workers members
2,997 volunteers members
2,607 user members
1,343 disadvantaged workers
2,822 supporting members

Source: *CGM* (1997)

The *CGM* has a small superstructure with only fifteen full-time workers and collaborators. A much larger number of trainers, consultants, research fellows and social entrepreneurs come from the territorial consortia members and act within specific projects of the *CGM*. As a whole then, the consortium system tends to appear as an enterprise network that develops itself in a conscious way, according to a given project, and which is characterised simultaneously by the independence of the different organisations and by their considerable integration. This last characteristic is strengthened and assured by specific company obligations.

5 Evaluation of the functions of social co-ops

Contribution to the fight against social exclusion

The main contribution of social co-ops to the fight against social exclusion is that they have proved that the private provision of services aimed at social cohesion is possible, and that otherwise unavailable human and financial resources can be directly involved when working in the framework of social enterprises. By demonstrating that some specific needs can be better satisfied by providing services, rather than by monetary transfers, social co-ops have helped to transform the Italian welfare system. They have proved better able to create social cohesion. Moreover, many of the services supplied are for the benefit of particularly needy groups (drug addicts, former inmates, and so forth). These services, as well as voluntarism, have also enhanced political awareness of the problems connected with social exclusion. Furthermore, the contribution of social co-ops to innovation in the field of social services has been very important. Many new ways of fighting social exclusion through service provision have been created for the first time by social co-ops and voluntary organisations.

Social co-ops have also increased the efficiency of the supply of services to public authorities. The greater flexibility and more rational use of resources made possible by the trust relationships that characterise social co-ops yield greater efficiency. With the same amount of public money, a larger number of people are served when the supply of services is ensured by social co-ops rather than by other kinds of organisations.

Strengths

Among the main strengths of social co-ops are the following:

- firstly, social co-ops are enterprises – they are legal entities with limited liability on the part of their members that can appeal to the financial market just like any other enterprise;
- secondly, since they are usually small in size, they are rooted in the local territory in which they operate and are therefore close to the needs of local people. Consequently, they have a remarkable ability to take advantage of and create social capital. Moreover, grouping into local and national consortia gives social co-ops the advantages of both small and large sized firms;
- thirdly, they have been able to bring together highly qualified human resources, thanks to the involvement of volunteers, and to their capacity to employ altruistic people;
- finally, social co-ops display a great innovative capacity with respect to the services supplied. This derives from a good level of independence of public authorities in decisions regarding the entrepreneurial strategies. In this respect, it is noteworthy that a significant proportion of new social services in Italy have been pioneered by social co-ops.

Weaknesses

The negative aspects of social co-ops may be summarised as follows:

- they have developed too fast insofar as the growing demand for services requires an organisational form to which not all social co-ops are able to adapt;
- they are increasingly dependent on public authorities which means that they serve more the needs of public administration than of individuals;
- many of them have no volunteers, and accordingly have fewer human resources, entrepreneurial skills, and relations with the local community than those co-ops which are able to mobilise volunteer work. True, the trend towards co-operatives consisting only of worker members is not per se dele- terious; social co-operatives may select motivated workers, who therefore ensure that attention is paid to users' needs, to quality and to efficiency. Nonetheless, the lack of volunteers makes the social enterprise model more fragile, increases the dependence of co-operatives on external (especially public) funding, and undermines the important role of monitoring the quality of the services provided.

One can see today that several different models of social co-ops are developing, with differing membership, degrees of user and/or volunteer control of the decision-making process, relationships with public authorities and probably with various levels of fragility.

6 Prospects for development

There are many factors which indicate that social co-operation will continue to grow substantially in the next few years:

- the tendency of local authorities to entrust social co-ops with the production of social services is still strong, and it is growing to include new services such as kindergartens;
- new tax exemption policies concerning private demand for services and the granting of vouchers are being promoted. These policies should lead to a further increase in the demand for services;
- a recently enacted law providing for tax exemptions for private donations to non-profit organisations, including social co-ops, and the granting of tax benefits for those who buy 'solidarity bonds' issued to finance non-profit activities;
- political interest in social co-ops is very high and increasing;
- there are very few private for-profit organisations that intend to compete with social co-ops. True, there is competition, but mainly with workers' co-ops and among different models of social co-ops.

These prospects for development may accelerate the identification of social co-ops with other co-operative forms. However, such an evolution might be countered by:

- a more precise definition (either statutory or by ethical codes) of the organisational form. This should prevent, over the years, the loss by social co-ops of their capacity to produce positive externalities. This means to discourage the development of social co-ops consisting of worker members only;
- a different way of assigning public contracts to social co-ops. Competitive tenders, especially those in which price is given the greatest if not exclusive importance, tend to favour those co-ops formed by worker members only (or for-profit firms), in which the main strategy is to reduce labour costs. From this perspective, the competition policy set out by the European Union, which is based on the idea that all markets should be subject to competition rules, is having a negative effect;
- the development of a culture of social enterprise, in order to increase awareness among social co-operatives of their specificity and of the link between this specificity and the efficiency and effectiveness of their work. In this respect, one notes that the national federation of social co-operatives (*Federsolidarietà*) belonging to one of the three national co-operative

federations, the *Confederazione Italiana delle Cooperative* (*Confcooperative*), linked to the Catholic movement, has recently introduced an ethical code which binds co-operatives to specialisation, to small size, to an emphasis on voluntarism, and to equity towards workers;

- the development of a policy to encourage the more innovative social co-ops to operate in new fields of activities, not only in those of interest to the public authorities.

Conclusions

The experience of Italian social co-operatives demonstrates that it is possible to create enterprises pursuing a social aim instead of a purely economic one and that the introduction of laws that clearly recognise and identify these enterprises can give strong support to their development. At the same time, the Italian experience shows that the entrepreneurial model of social enterprises is fragile and that social enterprises can easily transform themselves into more traditional forms of enterprises. Specific policies aimed at improving the entrepreneurial model are needed. Among the most important are policies aimed at the provision of consistent legal forms, a better organisation of the quasi-market for social services and the development of an entrepreneurial and managerial culture tailored to their needs.

Notes

1 For an analysis of work-integration social co-operatives in Italy see Borzaga (1998).
2 According to a recent survey carried out by *Fondazione Italiana per il Volontariato* (Italian Foundation for Volunteering) in 1998 (Frisanco and Ranci 1998) out of 10,516 voluntary organisations, 1,031 (9.8 per cent) of them stated that they supplied social services on a steady and ongoing basis. They employed 2,083 paid workers, while the conscientious objectors working for them numbered 1,279 and the volunteers 53,529. More than 65 per cent of these organisations funded their activities solely or mainly by means of private incomes (supply of services).
3 These are organisations that date back to the Middle Ages, when they were established mainly in the form of private foundations. Later, in the nineteenth century, with the passing of the Act of 1890, these entities were absorbed into the public administration, thus becoming public bodies subject to the body of laws, powers and responsibilities of public authorities. Since 1988, *IPAB* have been allowed to transform themselves back into private non-profit organisations and thus reacquire their original legal and organisational form.
4 These are the social co-operatives defined by law as A-type co-operatives. B-type co-operatives are work-integration social co-operatives (see Borzaga 1998).
5 Social services were mainly provided by families.
6 Some figures may help to give an idea of the characteristics of the Italian welfare system. In 1970, the ratio of public expenditure for transfers and GDP was 15.4 per cent compared with a ratio of public expenditure for final consumption and GDP of 12.9 per cent. In Sweden, the same ratios were 15.8 per cent and 21.5 per cent respectively, while in UK they were 13.9 per cent and 17.9 per cent.
7 Many Italian Courts would not grant incorporation to these new co-ops, because they did not respect the mutual principle, traditionally regarded as entailing benefit for the co-op's members only.

8 This constraint, which did not apply to social co-operatives established prior to the Act of 1991, was introduced due to the fear that an excessive number of volunteer members would deprive social co-ops of their 'entrepreneurial nature'.

9 Indeed, the first bill was tabled in Parliament in 1981.

10 At the moment, there is no research based on a census of social co-ops, regarding either social co-ops as a whole or A-type co-ops. Nevertheless, several studies based on samples are available. The one that includes the largest number of social co-ops was carried out by examining the auditing minutes. Other studies on smaller samples have been carried out directly in the field. This chapter uses data from the studies available, specifying each time the number of co-ops involved in the survey.

11 According to the data supplied by the National Institute for Social Security which is responsible for insuring disadvantaged people, by the end of 1996 there were 754 B-type social co-ops. They employed 11,165 workers, of whom 5,414 were disadvantaged people.

12 It should, however, be stressed that there are a remarkable number of co-ops with volunteers who are not members.

13 This concentration in the northern regions is a common feature of the Italian co-operative movement.

14 *CGM* (1997). The survey encompassed 726 co-ops.

15 This strategy was named the 'strawberry field' strategy.

16 Besides territorial consortia, others have been established, which are characterised either by their greater specialisation in particular activities (training, project management funded by the EU, management of services for elderly people, and so on) or by a close link with associative experiences (such as the *Solaris-Acli Consortium, Compagnia delle Opere, Apicolf*).

Bibliography

BORZAGA, C. (1998) 'Italie: L'impressionnant développement des coopératives sociales', in DEFOURNY, J., FAVREAU, L. and LAVILLE, J.-L. (eds) *Insertion et nouvelle économie sociale. Un bilan international*, Desclée de Brouwer, Paris, 99–126.

—— (1988) 'La cooperazione di solidarietà sociale: prime riflessioni su un settore emergente', in CARBONARO, A. and GHERARDI, S. (eds) *I nuovi scenari della cooperazione in Italia: problemi di efficacia, efficienza e legittimazione sociale*, Sociologia del Lavoro, no. 30–31, Angeli, Milano, 266–301.

BORZAGA, C. and FAILONI, G. (1990) 'La cooperazione di solidarietà sociale in Italia', *Cooperazione e Credito*, no. 128, 273–97.

BORZAGA, C. and SANTUARI, A. (eds) (1998) *Social Enterprises and New Employment in Europe*, Regione Trentino-Alto Adige, Trento.

CGM (1997) *Imprenditori sociali. Secondo rapporto sulla cooperazione sociale in Italia*, Fondazione Giovanni Agnelli, Torino.

—— (1994) *Primo Rapporto sulla cooperazione sociale in Italia*, CGM ed., Milano.

FRISANCO, R. and RANCI, C. (eds) (1998) *Le dimensioni della solidarietà. Secondo rapporto sul volontariato sociale italiano*, Fivol, Roma.

SANTUARI, A. (1997) 'Uno sguardo di insieme sulle esperienze straniere', in VITTADINI, G. (ed.) *Il Non Profit Dimezzato*, Etas Libri, Milan, 71–95.

—— (1997) 'Evoluzione storica, aspetti giuridici e comparatistici delle organizzazioni non profit', in GUI, B. (ed.) *Il Terzo Settore tra economicità e valori*, Gregoriana Libreria Editrice, Padua, 169–211.

10 Luxembourg

Work-integration social enterprises in an emerging third sector

Paul Delaunois and Eugène Becker

Introduction

Given the particular employment situation in Luxembourg as the last European Union country in which full employment is still the rule, and the repercussions this has for the development of structures and organisations in the third sector, and for labour-market insertion in particular, we shall start by describing the labour-market situation in the country and its particular features. We will then try to explain the emergence of the third sector in Luxembourg, before going on to focus on the structures for insertion and their importance, roles, manner of operation and results.

1 Luxembourg: an employment situation unique in Europe

Unlike other countries in the European Union, the Grand Duchy of Luxembourg has so far avoided mass unemployment, although since the mid 1990s the number of persons seeking employment has risen above 3 per cent of the working population and continues to rise appreciably despite continued growth in internal employment.

The Luxembourg labour market has a number of unique features insofar as the supply of internal employment has known a period of uninterrupted growth lasting more than twenty years, and the number of available jobs in Luxembourg itself has grown by an average of 6 per cent a year for the last five years, with 44,000 new jobs bringing the number today to 238,000.[1] The country's job market is attractive to frontier workers, given both the high rates of unemployment in the surrounding regions – 7 per cent in the Belgian province of Luxembourg, 10 per cent in Lorraine, 5.7 per cent in Rheinland-Pfalz and 9.1 per cent in the Saar (Gengler 1998) – and the markedly higher levels of pay offered in Luxembourg compared with its neighbours. For these reasons, 32 per cent of jobs in Luxembourg are held by frontier workers (Hausman 1999).

The education system, particularly in Luxembourg, has many repercussions on the labour-market situation. The system in Luxembourg is based on a thorough knowledge of two foreign languages, French and German, and is highly selective. In the absence of full university courses or many higher training courses, the Ministry for National Education has imposed a very demanding educational programme because the authorities want to make sure that students reach a level which is sufficient to gain entry to universities in neighbouring countries. This leads to large-scale failure in Luxembourg schools. The most recent available statistics show that more than half of pupils (52 per cent) leave school without qualifications (Kollwelter 1998). The proportion rises steeply for the children of migrant workers, particularly from the Portuguese community, which is by far the largest immigrant community in Luxembourg. Luxembourg has rates of enrolment in secondary and higher education which are 2–3 per cent lower than the average in the European Union (Kollwelter 1998).

Luxembourg's education system is, today, unable to ensure a sufficient output in terms of people with qualifications to maintain and develop the country's economic well-being. In a competitive labour market, young people are at a particular disadvantage compared with their peers from surrounding frontier regions.

Unemployment among young people under the age of twenty-six (aged 17–26) is running at almost 10 per cent[2] and represents a quarter of all unemployment, despite the fact that a high proportion of these young people are the beneficiaries of active insertion measures aimed at enabling them to find work relatively easily. As long as young people do eventually find work, the situation is not desperate, since the rate of unemployment is still at an acceptable level. But this situation could deteriorate rapidly if there were to be a serious economic crisis. Job seekers living in Luxembourg are mainly unqualified people, or people whose qualifications do not match the profiles sought in the labour market.

To these characteristics, we must add the profound socio-economic changes which have taken place in the country since the mid 1970s, with the decline of the two major pillars of the economy at that time, viz. the iron and steel industry (including iron ore extraction) and agriculture. These two industries – which, between them, employed one worker in four in 1974[3] – now account for only 4 per cent of global employment.[4] Employment drifted towards the service sector, where it has grown by 300 per cent in the same period; this sector now employs seven workers out of ten.

Against this background, successive governments have striven since the 1960s to introduce initiatives to diversify the economy and avoid dependence on a single sector of activity. Following the crisis of 1973, when the iron and steel industry, at that time the largest employer in the country, began to feel the effects of the international fall in demand for steel products, significant unemployment made its first appearance. It was to creep slowly upwards and was not to be curbed. The government reacted in 1975 by drawing up and adopting the law of 26 July 1975 giving itself powers 'to take measures aimed at preventing redundancies due to economic conditions and guaranteeing full employment'. This law opened the way for a changing legislative framework allowing sectoral or individual measures to be taken through government orders. A year later, this first law was supplemented by the 'creation of a fund for employment and the regulation of the payment of unemployment benefit', thus setting up a framework for the application of measures to fight unemployment. It must be said that these 'passive measures' served to manage existing unemployment rather than to reduce it.

After 1978, government policy changed in both analysis and approach, and a number of measures promoting youth employment were introduced. The law of 27 July 1978 set up a pool of temporary workers (the *Division d'Auxiliaires Temporaires*) which could be used for tasks of public or social utility or cultural value proposed and carried out by the state or by local authorities. This law also established an enterprise-based work experience scheme guaranteeing a practical introduction to young job seekers and easing the transition between education and the beginning of working life. These two measures were complemented in 1983 by a further work experience scheme aimed at providing alternating periods of practical experience and theoretical training.

Following views expressed by the Economic and Social Council and the Labour and Employment Commission of the Chamber, stressing the need to focus on young people and the long-term unemployed in the fight against unemployment, the law of 12 May 1987 provided measures aimed at helping registered job seekers, mainly through training and vocational guidance.

Since 1992, the growth of unemployment has taken a more worrying turn, increasing by around 1,000 persons a year (Borsenberger 1996); the unemployment rate rose from 1.2 per cent (1,800 persons) to 3.2 per cent (6,400 persons) between 1992 and 1998. This has led the government to introduce further and more diverse measures, more targeted on young university graduates (the creation in 1995 of a 'pool of assistants' to work in secondary education), women and the long-term unemployed. By 1996 almost half of unemployed young people were covered by one or other existing measure (Kollwelter 1998).

Finally, the active part played by Luxembourg in organising the first European employment summit in Luxembourg in November 1997 forced the government to produce a 'national action plan' for employment which was particularly ambitious, if scarcely original. The new legislation renews the earlier proposals by reorganising, co-ordinating and adding to the existing body of measures. However, it goes further. Job seekers aged over thirty are offered trainee posts with a view to re-entering the world of work, the schools are opened up to adults[5] and a 'second chance' school is to be provided for young people excluded from the education system.[6]

As a number of politicians and economic agents have pointed out, national unemployment is caused by the mismatch between supply and demand and not, as in other industrialised countries, by a lack of vacancies. The employment policies followed by the Luxembourg government have succeeded in diversifying the economy; they have introduced new specialisation into existing sectors, including the iron and steel industry, and developed the role of the financial sector; and they have also created a variety of measures to prevent mass unemployment.

2 From voluntary social aid to the state-contracted voluntary sector: the birth of a third sector

Until the end of the 1960s, the care of the poor and sick in Luxembourg depended for the most part on the religious orders which took care of the needy and of disabled people. The church was responsible for all the schemes providing both healthcare and social support. Apart from the social security provided by the state, all social work, including the provision of accommodation for children, hospitals and the care of the elderly, was almost entirely dependent on private initiatives and was run by the religious orders (Als 1991). However, without financial resources, given the almost complete absence of financial assistance from the state, the infrastructures were often outdated, and the concept of care, based exclusively on the voluntary service of monks and nuns, was out of touch and no longer corresponded with the real needs of society.

Social changes at the end of the 1960s, such as the rise in women's employment and the breakdown of the traditional family, together with the growth in state resources, led the government to better take public needs into account. From 1968 on, the state agreed contracts taking responsibility for the operational and staff costs of certain religious groups in order to improve professional standards in existing support structures and to modernise outdated buildings and infrastructure (Als 1991). After 1975, because of the flexibility of these arrangements, such contracts were to become the most common approach adopted by ministries for the creation of new social, family or healthcare services. Since then, the state-contracted voluntary sector has grown in importance as the agent responsible for carrying out the tasks which arose as the welfare state took over from religious institutions.

Currently, there are about 5,000 salaried employees in the social, family support and therapeutic sectors, about half of whom are paid by the state under conditions similar to those of civil servants (recognition of salary scales, comparable social advantages etc.), and the costs represent 2.6 per cent of the total state budget – 4,440 million LUF (110 million Euro) in 1998 – or ten times the figure for the early 1980s.[7] The third sector in Luxembourg has been built on just this basis of state support and involvement.

Through contracts with the Ministries of Health, Labour, and Social Security, the Ministry for the Family and Solidarity and the Ministries for Women's Affairs, Culture and Youth, a number of schemes have been introduced over the last thirty years, mostly in the form of non-profit associations (*Associations Sans But Lucratif*). This has encouraged significant rates of participation by citizens in the associative sector. In 1997 more than one adult in six claimed to carry out some voluntary work in an associative movement, and many people are involved in two, three or even four voluntary activities on a weekly basis. Volunteers are attracted to cultural, sporting, social and humanitarian activities. They devote an average of five hours a week to this unpaid work (Le Jealle 1998). However, it must be noted that most of these initiatives enjoy a full subsidy for their expenses and run no financial risks. The norm in Luxembourg is thus that the public authorities alone support almost all social provision and contribute significantly to the provision of cultural and sporting activities and other voluntary work.

Although the voluntary sector is very prevalent, the concept of a third sector as such remains undeveloped in Luxembourg compared to other European countries, except in certain organisations active in the social and vocational insertion of the unemployed and of people with few qualifications. It is therefore not surprising that, unlike other countries in the European Union, Luxembourg has no legal or regulatory framework for the third sector, other than the concept of 'aid to employment of socio-economic utility', which appears officially in the law of 1983. This law makes it possible to support new projects for creating jobs reserved for disadvantaged unemployed workers, specifically those who can only make the transition towards normal employment through socio-educational guidance.

3 The social community approach underlying initiatives for insertion through economic activity

It was at the end of the 1970s and beginning of the 1980s that the first active measures to promote integration really developed. This period saw the birth of a number of associations which brought a new perspective to social assistance – the social community approach. Unlike traditional social work, which continues to be generally applied in the various social assistance services and which consists of providing the available aid according to certain criteria, the community approach prefers to tackle the source of the problem through structural change.

Of course in Luxembourg, where the unemployment rate has stuck at 3–4 per cent of the population, the question of combating exclusion is not posed in the same terms as in neighbouring countries. However, structural unemployment (which is not due to economic conditions) does affect a part of the population. Before the introduction of the minimum guaranteed income (*RMG, Revenu Minimum Garanti*), 8 per cent of households were living in very precarious conditions, and a further 18 per cent were on the threshold of poverty.[8] The law of 26 July 1986, which established the right to an *RMG*, enabled some to fight back against poverty, but by no means eliminated it.

Following a study of the inhabitants of two districts in the town of Luxembourg, the Grund and the Pfaffental, then considered to be districts at risk, concerned social workers decided to become involved in projects for integration through work and in the fight against delinquency. At the end of the 1980s the following three associations appeared almost simultaneously:

*   the *Inter-Action Faubourg* association, which set up several other structures including *Inter-Actions Asbl, Polygone Sarl*,[9] *B4 Construction Sarl* and *Ecotec Sarl*;
*   the agricultural association *Co-labor* which would later assume co-operative status;

- the *Nei Aarbecht* association which is directly answerable to the National Committee for Social Defence attached to the Ministry of Justice.

(Georges and Borsenberger 1997)

These three initiatives were to be a source of inspiration for other associations and today there are approximately forty initiatives working in the field of reintegration, and half of these have developed commercial activities. These initiatives for integration through economic activities are active in areas such as the environment, agriculture, forestry, building, waste management and restoration.

Despite the small size of the territory and the rather small number of organisations, there is a great diversity of Luxembourg structures active in integration, all having their own characteristics in terms of their activities, the nature of their target groups, their objectives and their mode of operation. This diversity can be explained by the particular method of state subsidy, which has sought to support specific pilot projects.

4 Integration initiatives: some examples

Most of these initiatives have opted for the non-profit association status (*Asbl*) and have a unitary structure covering all their services which include social support, training, workshops or production services and accommodation where necessary.

Particularly original is the approach of the *Inter-Actions* association, which has taken the unusual step of setting up a socio-economic support structure composed of three limited liability enterprises (*Sarl*) alongside the social/educational structure. In this way the association has positions available in the normal labour market for young unemployed people who are difficult to place (Nottrot 1999).

Target groups

The help offered by the various organisations is generally targeted on a particular public. Among those targeted are: people with a physical, mental or psychological disability, people receiving the guaranteed minimum income, women, and former prisoners. However, it should be noted that, while most of the active measures to fight unemployment introduced by the state are aimed at young vulnerable unemployed people under the age of thirty, structures developing commercial activities are also targeting this group. This is partly in response to the expectations of the state and the ministries with regard to contractual arrangements, and partly so as to benefit from two subsidised forms of contract, viz. the 'introductory traineeship' and the 'temporary assistantship'. These contracts were set up by the Employment Department, which assumes responsibility through the Employment Fund for 50 per cent of the allowance paid (which may be 80 per cent or 100 per cent of the minimum social wage, i.e. 46,270 LUF (1,147 Euro per month)), as well as for all the employers' costs.

These integration schemes are thus keen to employ their beneficiaries under this kind of contract, which compensate both for the reduced profit levels, which are inevitable when employing disadvantaged people who need extra support, and for the effort which these services put into the provision of vocational training and social skills.

Apart from the financial aspect, the use of these schemes also has consequences for the length of contracts offered, which is restricted to eighteen or sometimes even twelve months. This means that the help given has to be concentrated into this period. This limitation on the duration of contracts emphasises the role of these structures as a gateway to employment for the young. In a country where full employment is the rule, it remains fairly easy for those responsible for social follow-up and integration to find a trainee position or other job for these young people reaching the end of their contracts. However, a young person who is insufficiently prepared cannot fully avail of the opportunity offered.

It appears that only the co-operative *Co-labor* stands apart from the other initiatives in this area. This co-operative, active in the field of horticulture and environmental management, offers permanent jobs to about thirty people who have experienced exclusion (out of total staff of seventy). Although its staff turnover varies between 15 and 30 per cent annually, the co-operative achieves more lasting results in integrating people into the labour market than other systems (in which the insertion period is limited in time), because employees move on to a new position without the pressure of a deadline (*Co-labor* 1998).

Economic aspects

Through the contracts concluded with their supervising ministries, integration bodies enjoy economic and financial stability, at least for their activities in providing socio-economic support and training. Some have also benefited from substantial subsidies for co-financed measures under Objective 3 and other EU initiatives. During the period 1995–2000 no less than 102 million Euro have been shared among the different organisations (Calmes, Hartman-Hirsch and Pals 1997).

In terms of the organisations which are developing commercial activities, it has to be stressed that generally speaking, in Luxembourg, initiatives which have launched business activities have not encountered problems, and even though there are wide variations, the launching of business activities is generally followed by an increase in turnover. Subsequently, as one might expect, the situation stabilises in most services. The founders of integration initiatives with commercial activities almost all came from a background in social work and they were consequently ill prepared for the world of business and the economy, sometimes even having an outright aversion to it. They often got off to a difficult start in business management and, without state support, most of these initiatives would probably have run into trouble.

The development of insertion organisations has evolved towards a greater reliance on market resources which has led to an increase in technical demands, due to the economic compulsion to accept always more complex rules. This, together with a certain degree of competitive pressure, coming *inter alia* from frontier companies, has led the management of these enterprises to recruit more qualified staff, including business managers. This phenomenon clearly shows in the variations between the proportion of the target public (the people to be integrated) to qualified workers employed in the business. In every case this proportion has fallen over the past ten years from four out of five, to three out of four, to less than one half.

There has been a gradual shift away from management by volunteers, as was traditional in associations, to an increasingly professional management approach, with very positive effects. Today the long-standing enterprises have overcome their teething problems and the newest can benefit from their experience, since in such a small geographic space contacts and discussions are particularly lively.

The results

Overall today, slightly more than 1,500 people are beneficiaries of these various schemes in Luxembourg. About one third (550 in 1997) have a recognised physical, mental or psychological disability (Calmes, Hartman-Hirsch and Pals 1997). Apart from services for the disabled, there are six schemes operating on a somewhat larger scale, providing jobs for more than thirty people – the other associations being rather smaller.

All these schemes benefit from broad state support, which may be as high as 100 per cent of their costs except in the case of organisations which have developed commercial activities. In the latter case, the proportion of state aid, which is restricted to the social and educational activities carried out under contract, is reduced as the importance of the commercial business expands.

Services working with young people generally record reintegration rates ranging from 50 to 70 per cent. Given the fact that the social and economic situation in Luxembourg is such that unemployed young people are particularly hard to place,[10] these initiatives may be regarded as extremely successful.

5 Which way next?

Since unemployment in Luxembourg continues to grow, it can be expected that the third sector will also develop further during the next few years. Although we continue to deplore the absence of a legal framework for the social economy, the Minister for Family Affairs stated in the periodical *Forum* that the debate is now open in our country regarding the need for a legal framework enabling the state to intervene financially in the social economy. New needs have been identified in a number of areas, including the environment, local development and neighbourhood services. Legislation should be able to adapt to these new situations and make it possible to meet present and future needs. Any public intervention must of course be based on transparency. A qualitative and quantitative assessment of the projects and their results seems to be of paramount importance in justifying the use of public money. The debate should also consider the particular situation in Luxembourg and the different kinds of public targeted by the social economy (Jacobs 1999).

So it seems that concerted moves between the ministers concerned and representatives of existing organisations could lead to the creation of a post of inter-departmental minister with responsibility for the social economy. This would certainly enable the needs and special circumstances of the whole sector to be better taken into account.

The recent involvement of the two major national trade unions in activities relating to local development and integration will undoubtedly open the way to a greater appreciation of the needs of people most removed from employment. However, there is a danger that these two organisations, which are involved in social negotiations at national level (the tripartite negotiations), may tend to take all the credit to the detriment of existing structures, as happened when EU subsidies under Objective 3 were distributed. Stricter and less political government arbitration would preserve the existing balance and protect the development of the whole sector.

Finally, a special effort should be made to train project developers, who are the vital links in creating new structures and new sectors of activity.

Notes

1 *Bulletin Luxembourgeois de l'Emploi* 09/98, 11/98 and 04/99.
2 *Bulletin Luxembourgeois de l'Emploi* 09/98, 11/98 and 04/99.
3 STATEC (1990).
4 *Bulletin Luxembourgeois de l'Emploi* 09/98, 11/98 and 04/99.
5 The 'dual system', within some professional formations, allows apprentices to work in an enterprise with a specific real worker's contract while undertaking complementary theoretical training for about 200 hours per year (one day per week) in a technical school.
6 *Loi du 12 février 1999 concernant la mise en oeuvre du plan d'action national en faveur de l'emploi 1998 Mémorial A no. 13 du 23 février 1999*, page 190.
7 *Rapport de la Commission de la Famille et de la Solidarité Sociale sur le projet de la loi dite 'ASFT', 2 juillet 1998 – document no. 3571 de la Chambre des Députés, session ordinaire 1997–1998*, Luxembourg.
8 See the report referred to in note 7. One of the main factors accounting for this figure – which could seem surprisingly high for a country in which the unemployment rate is particularly low – is the definition of the threshold of poverty. A family whose income is lower than half of the mean income in the country is considered under the threshold of poverty. As a consequence of the fast development of the service sector, especially the financial sector, which practises a policy of raising wages (policy which has also been followed by the governmental and other public sectors), the mean income in Luxembourg has grown significantly.
9 *Sarl, Société à responsabilité limitée*, that is limited liability company.
10 In general, young people find a job quite easily; but those who do not are usually people with serious problems, for whom it is very difficult to find a job. In other words, although the unemployment rate is very low, the proportion of people with a low employability among the unemployed in general is high.

Bibliography

ALS, G. (1991) 'Histoire quantitative du Luxembourg 1839–1990', *Cahiers économiques*, no. 79, STATEC, Luxembourg.

BORSENBERGER, M. (1996) *Mesures sur l'Emploi*, CEPS/Instead, Luxembourg.

Bulletin Luxembourgeois de l'Emploi (1998–1999) nos. 09/98, 11/98 and 04/99, Administration de l'Emploi, Luxembourg.

CALMES, A., HARTMAN-HIRSCH, C. and PALS, M. (1997*) Rapport d'évaluation pour le Grand-Duché de Luxembourg*, Rapport au Fonds Social Européen, Ministère du Travail et de l'Emploi, Luxembourg.

Co-labor (1998) 'Rapport d'activité sociale 1997', *Co-labor*, Luxembourg.

GENGLER, C. (1998) 'Grande région Saar-Lor-Lux: un exemple pour l'Europe', *Le Jeudi*, supplément du no. 46/98.

GEORGES, N. and BORSENBERGER, M. (1997*) Répertoires des associations actives dans le domaine de l'emploi*, CEPS/Instead, Luxembourg.

HAUSMAN, P. (1999) 'La situation des résidents sur le marché du travail', *Population et Emploi*, no. 1/99, CEPS/Instead, Luxembourg.

JACOBS, M.-J. (1999) 'La législation devra s'adapter', *Forum*, no. 190, mars 1999.

KOLLWELTER, R. (1998*) Pour une école de la deuxième chance au Luxembourg*, Rapport de la Mission parlementaire – Chambre des Députés, Luxembourg.

LE JEALLE, B. (1998) 'Le travail bénévole au Luxembourg', *Population et Emploi*, no. 01/98, CEPS/Instead, Luxembourg.

Loi du 12 février 1999 concernant la mise en oeuvre du plan d'action national en faveur de l'emploi, Mémorial A no. 13 du 23 février 1999, p. 190.

NOTTROT, J. (1999) 'Wirtschaftlichkeit und soziale Eingliederung: Ergänzung statt Gegensatz', *Forum*, no. 190, Luxembourg.

Rapport de la Commission de la Famille et de la Solidarité Sociale sur le projet de la loi dite 'ASFT', 2 juillet 1998, document no. 3571 de la Chambre des Députés, session ordinaire 1997–98, Luxembourg.

STATEC (1990) *Statistiques historiques 1839–1989*, STATEC, Luxembourg.

11 Portugal

Co-operatives for rehabilitation of people with disabilities

Heloísa Perista

Introduction[1]

Poverty is deeply rooted in social and economic structures in Portuguese society. Recent figures still place Portugal at the top of the European Union member states in terms of the poverty rate. According to European Community Household Panel data for 1994, more than one in every four households (around 27 per cent of individuals) was living below the poverty line.

Specific groups in the population have been identified as particularly affected by (or vulnerable to) poverty and social exclusion. These are: old-age pensioners, low income farmers, low income workers, precarious workers and workers in the informal sector, ethnic minorities (not necessarily of foreign nationality), lone-parent families, homeless people, unemployed, and young people with low qualifications looking for their first job, among others.

The high incidence of poverty and social exclusion goes along with a late and slow development of the welfare state in Portugal. Full juridical and institutional acknowledgement of the Portuguese social security system came only after the Portuguese Revolution of 1974, with the enlargement of social rights and the improvement of welfare policies. The increasing social pressure in favour of the centrality of the role of the state, in terms of the provision of social protection to citizens, occurs in a broader context of national and international economic recession and of crisis in the welfare state.

The Portuguese system of social security is thus based on a pluralist model, where responsibilities are shared between the state and civil society i.e. the non-governmental and non-profit sector. The constitution recognises the right of private social solidarity institutions to develop, replacing or complementing state action for social security purposes and especially for social action activities – these being regulated, fiscally controlled and financially supported by the state, through co-operation agreements. The setting of a common strategy of co-operation between the institutions of the social sector which pursue social solidarity-oriented aims, the central administration and the local and regional administrations was designed in the 'Covenant on Co-operation for Social Solidarity' (*Pacto de Cooperação para a Solidariedade Social*), agreed and signed on 19 December 1996. In terms of a legal framework, we must also refer to the National Action Plan for

Employment, which emphasises the potential of job creation in the 'social employment market'[2] and aims, among other things, at stimulating the social economy, especially as a means of promoting participation in employment of groups who have been excluded or who are more vulnerable to poverty and social exclusion.

It may be interesting to compare the attribution of responsibilities to private social solidarity institutions at the legal level with the perception that these same institutions have about themselves and their competencies. Different studies (Baptista *et al.*, 1995; Capucha *et al.*, 1995; Pereirinha, 1999) have shown that these social solidarity organisations tend to attribute the major responsibility in the fight against poverty and social problems to the state. However, when asked about their evaluation of the performance of different organisations, it clearly appears that social solidarity institutions have a negative vision of state action, and a very positive one of their own performance. Actually, the so-called social sector is largely responsible for the supply of social protection in a number of fields, and social sector organisations have been growing and diversifying, penetrating new areas and developing new forms of response. But there are still needs – traditional needs and needs of a new kind – to be satisfied in nearly all fields and there is a clear margin for the development of supply, namely in terms of proximity services.

1 Overview of the social economy in Portugal

The Portuguese third sector covers a wide range of organisations, including: *misericórdias*, mutual benefit associations, Private Social Solidarity Institutions (*IPSS, Instituições Particulares de Solidariedade Social*), co-operatives and integration enterprises.

Misericórdias

These organisations have existed for centuries. The Portuguese *misericórdias* were created in the fifteenth century by a queen, Dª. Leonor. Traditionally, *misericórdias* provided health assistance, but they have recently diversified their social action. They support children, elderly people, the disabled; they provide professional training; and they fight unemployment and social exclusion. These institutions, which in most cases were related to the Catholic church, used to be self-funded, mostly on the basis of large donations and legacies from individual persons. Nowadays, given their role of social services providers, *misericórdias* are mostly funded by state transfers, through co-operation agreements.[3] In 1998, there were 326 *misericórdias*, running 571 services and/or establishments of social action, with nearly 65,000 users (*RSESS*/98).

Mutual benefit associations

Mutual benefit associations in Portugal have also existed since medieval times. However, the first mutual benefit association with an economic activity dates back to 1840, when a credit organisation – *Caixa Económica, Montepio Geral* – was created. This organisation is today among the largest banks in Portugal. The history of mutual benefit associations reveals a decrease in their number, especially after 1930, with, on the one hand, the creation of the official system of compulsory insurance and, on the other hand, the prosecution of mutual benefit associations by the fascist regime. In 1921, there were 865 mutual benefit associations; in 1930 there were 527; in 1964 there were 133; and in 1998 there were 88. There were over 818,000 associates, more than 2,154,000 indirect users, 965 full-time employees and 599 part-time employees. Mutual benefit associations are self-funded through their own associates. Among the economic activities developed by mutual benefit associations, we can identify healthcare (four medical clinics), social pharmacies (seven), credit unions (five), social support to children and elderly (twenty-four services and/or establishments, with over 1,000 users).[4]

The IPSS sector in general

Both the *misericórdias* and the mutual benefit associations are covered by the juridical frame of *IPSS*, which also covers social solidarity associations, volunteers associations for social action and foundations of social solidarity. The *IPSS* sector as a whole represents around 70 per cent of the social action in the country (measured in terms of total cost). *IPSS* activities are funded through cooperation agreements with the state. This generates a strong relationship between *IPSS* and the state as well as financial dependency (Hespanha 1999). However, a recent study concludes that *IPSS* tend to be more responsive to demand, or to social needs, than state organisations (Variz 1998).

In the last few years 800 new institutions were registered, although in a somewhat arbitrary and uncoordinated way (Hespanha 1999). The number of volunteers engaged in *IPSS* is around 53,000 people (32,000 of which are on management boards).[5] In 1998, there were 2,539 *IPSS* developing social action activities (not including *misericórdias*), with nearly 265,000 users (*RSESS*/98) and the sector is likely to grow. According to social security statistics for 1997, during that year alone, the management of thirty-four establishments (thirty of those in the area of children and youth) was transferred from the state to *IPSS*. This clearly illustrates the still increasing role of the third sector in the field of social action.

Co-operatives

Co-operatives have existed in Portugal since the nineteenth century, but they only experienced significant development after 1974. Also, co-operatives develop social activities, especially the Co-operatives for the Education and Rehabilitation of Disabled Children (*CERCIs*), the first of which was created in Lisbon in 1975. More recently, in 1996, the Second Co-operative Code created a new branch of co-operatives of social solidarity (mainly covering *CERCIs* but also other co-operatives). This Code establishes the existence of multi-sectoral co-operatives. In 1999, a specific programme (PRODESCOOP) introduced for the first time state funding for the co-operative movement. All this will be referred to in detail in the subsequent sections of this chapter.

Integration enterprises

When discussing the Portuguese third sector, we must also refer to integration enterprises, which were included in the 'social employment market', introduced in 1996, and in the government strategy for the eradication of poverty and social exclusion. The first integration enterprises were created in June 1998. They aimed at the social and employment reintegration of the long-term unemployed and of those at a disadvantage in the employment market. The integration enterprise status is granted by the Social Employment Market Commission upon application by the enterprise. In one and a half years, 375 integration enterprises were created, generating around 3,500 jobs. It is still too soon to assess the real impact of integration enterprises, as monitoring and assessment data are not yet available.

2   Social enterprises in Portugal: the case of *CERCIs*

The social enterprise concept is not yet stabilised in Portugal. There is an on-going discussion about the meaning and the contents of this concept among the representative unions of the third-sector organisations. However, referring to the definition of social enterprise adopted for the purpose of the present EMES study, we can identify various types of organisations within the third sector that can be labelled as 'social enterprises'. A clear example is provided by the 'Co-operatives for the Education and Rehabilitation of Disabled Children' (*CERCIs, Cooperativas para a Educação e Reabilitação de Crianças Inadaptadas*), on which this section will focus.

The evolution of CERCIs

CERCIs were born within the scope of the social and political movements generated after the Revolution of 25 April 1974. People were then highly motivated by associative and co-operative ideals and the many needs which had been left unmet. This was so in the case of mentally disabled children, for whom there were no services either in regular schools, from which they were excluded, or in private schools, which were scarce and very expensive. A group of parents of these children, together with some professionals, then organised themselves and created the first *CERCI*, in Lisbon, in 1975. The movement spread throughout the country and, during the first year, three other *CERCIs* were created, to be followed in the second year by a further ten. Most *CERCIs* were established in the period up to the early 1980s. *FENACERCI*, the national federation of *CERCIs*, was created in 1985.

The promoters of *CERCIs* met a lot of financial difficulties and were faced with a lack of legislation within which to frame their activity. Volunteer work, donations from various companies and organisations, together with public fund-raising played a very important role in the creation of *CERCIs*. They also had the collaboration of the Ministry of Education, which financially supported the schools and their personnel. In addition, the Ministry of Social Security created a new allowance for special education. There was also important sensitisation work done in local communities, in order to break the resistance and the preju-dices against mentally disabled children.

CERCIs started as special education schools, mainly providing for children who had mild mental handicaps or learning difficulties; but these children grew up and *CERCIs*' users got older – those who remained were usually the ones with severe, profound or multiple handicaps. Moreover, older users (beyond school age) represented a significant part of the new admissions. *CERCIs* therefore faced a challenge to diversify their activities. They then started creating occupa-tional centres for young adults and promoting professional training. This raised new needs in terms of funding, since *CERCIs* had to build new facilities. The problem was finally solved with a legal change in 1993/4, which enabled *CERCIs* to enter into agreements with the Ministry of Social Security in order to accede to specific funding (until then only available to *IPSS*). Since then, *CERCIs* have experienced a boom in the development of new activities and new facilities. They now provide services to mentally disabled people from birth to death as follows: occupational activities (forty-three *CERCIs* out of forty-seven), profes-sional training (thirty-nine), 'early intervention'[6] (nineteen), residential units (thirteen), sheltered employment (eight), and home-care (five). On the other hand, the demand for special education may decline, due to the new orientation to inclusive education in regular schools, but forty-six *CERCIs* still run this kind of service.[7] *CERCIs* also play a growing role in the social employment market, supporting job creation for disabled people through the promotion of small enterprises. Due to their origins and evolution, many *CERCIs* have now become 'Co-operatives for the Education and Rehabilitation of Disabled Citizens' (*Cooperativas para a Educação e Reabilitação de Cidadãos Inadaptados*).

The approval of a new Co-operative Code, in 1996,[8] represented the creation of a new co-operative branch – co-operatives of social solidarity[9] – in which *CERCIs* were included. This implied an adjustment in their legal status, since they had been classified as teaching co-operatives, according to the previous Co-operative Code (Co-operative Code of 1980). Co-operatives of social solidarity include not only *CERCIs*, but also some other co-operatives providing social support to other disadvantaged groups, such as children at risk and old people, as well as co-operatives active in the field of proximity services. There are sixty co-operatives of social solidarity of which forty-seven are *CERCIs*.

CERCIs' *internal organisation*

CERCIs have experienced an increasing professionalisation of their manage-ment boards, which has accompanied their development as more social enterprises. Decision-making is formally governed by the principle of democratic management. Usually the board of directors, which is composed of professionals and some parents,[10] works closely with a consultative technical-pedagogical council and oversees the co-ordinators of different units. A recent study on *CERCIs* concluded that the leadership styles in the organisations under analysis are a symbiosis between the authoritarian and the democratic style. Leaders decide and define real objectives; they delegate technical authority to the unit's co-ordinators, although keeping to themselves decisions about the best administrative and financial criteria, even to the detriment of more convenient solutions from the technical and pedagogical point of view. However, although all global policies are defined by the leaders, the pedagogical organisation of work within the units is freely defined by consensus between the co-ordinators and the other members (Veiga 1999).

Some of the paid workers, as well as most of the parents, are members of the co-operative. Some users, but not many, are also members, and there is now a project (headed by *FENACERCI*) aiming at the promotion of self-representation of mentally disabled people within the *CERCI* movement.

The growing diversification of services and users has been paralleled by an increase in *CERCIs'* workforce. Besides paid employees, who are a significant part of those with long-term contracts, *CERCIs* also make use of special employment programmes, such as occupational programmes and subsidised jobs for disabled people. Part of the teaching staff is provided by the Ministry of Education, as part of the existing formal agreement.

CERCI s' *resources*

CERCIs sell part of their products in the market. Products of their professional training centres are sold at a low price, mostly to individuals, while products of the small enterprises for job creation for mentally disabled people are sold at a market price to other enterprises (for instance in the area of catering). *CERCIs* also have contracts with public institutions. For instance, *CERCI Lisboa*, under an agreement with the Ministry of Foreign Affairs, provided cleaning services for the official cars in the occupational centres during the Portuguese Presidency of the EU.

Among non-market public resources, *CERCIs* have formal agreements with the Ministry of Education and the Ministry of Work and Solidarity in order to access subsidies for their activities. Subsidies for professional training come through the Institute for Employment and Professional Training, a public body under the Ministry of Work and Solidarity. These state subsidies represent the major source of funding for *CERCIs*, which also receive subsidies from local authorities, mostly for occasional actions.[11] Among public resources, one should also mention the fact that, in special education schools, users aged sixteen to eighteen years are subsidised and this subsidy is paid to the *CERCIs* which run these schools. This might be considered as a form of indirect subsidies to *CERCIs'* activities.

In some cases, *CERCIs* receive private gifts and sponsorships, including resources in kind, such as computers or raw materials given by enterprises, and donations and legacies by individuals or foundations. Every year *CERCIs* promote a large public fund-raising campaign, the so-called *Pirilampo Mágico* campaign.[12] Most *CERCIs* also run specific projects (for instance in the field of professional training) funded by national and/or European programmes, such as *Ser Criança* ('Being a Child', run by the Ministry of Work and Solidarity), *Integrar* ('Integrating', nationally run with EU co-funding) and the Employment Initiative (a European Social Fund initiative). Volunteer work is especially important at the management level. There is also some volunteer participation in occasional tasks, such as fund-raising.

Finally, *CERCIs* also benefit from two recent government initiatives specifically aimed at the promotion of co-operatives. These are: a specific fiscal status for co-operatives, more favourable to job creation, which was approved in 1998[13] and a specific programme to support co-operative creation and development, the PRODESCOOP (Programme for Co-operative Development), which came into force in January 1999.[14] This latter programme was included in the National Action Plan for Employment[15] as part of the measures aimed at job creation in the social economy, and specifically in the co-operative sector.[16] PRODE-SCOOP is both an instrument of employment policy and of co-operative promotion. As an instrument of employment policy, the programme includes active measure such as support for the recruitment of young people looking for their first job, long-term unemployed, guaranteed minimum income recipients, disabled people, as well as young qualified staff. It also offers an award for equal opportunities, available to co-operatives creating new jobs for both men and women (i.e. at most, people of either sex occupy 60 per cent of the jobs created). As an instrument to promote co-operation, the programme complements other systems of financial and technical assistance for the creation and consolidation of co-operatives, and especially for job creation.

The specific contribution of CERCIs to addressing social exclusion

CERCIs have created a significant number of jobs. For example, *CERCI Lisboa* started with ten workers; it now has 150. At the national level, around 3,000 jobs have been created and *CERCIs* have about 7,239 users, while around 1,030 additional people are on a waiting list to become users. Among the young people assisted by *CERCIs* since their creation, a significant number (about 911) are now integrated into the labour market. These co-operatives have also invested in terms of the professional training of their personnel, in order to provide better services.

These services would be out of reach for a large proportion of the users, due to their high costs, if *CERCIs* did not exist. But their existence is only made possible by the strong social commitment of all those who work in these institutions. Their specificity and comparative advantage is thus based on this social capital, used, reproduced and multiplied, especially at the local community level. Some of the users even become co-producers of the services provided by

CERCIs, due to job creation processes and recruitment policies. More generally, people's empowerment is a major purpose of co-operatives. In terms of collective externalities, *CERCIs* stimulate local partnerships, formal or informal, which contribute to community development. This is a permanent concern of these co-operatives, 'to work in the community and for the people from the community' (*CERCI Lisboa*).

CERCIs' *weaknesses*

One of the main weaknesses of *CERCIs* arises from the lack of entrepreneurial leadership. Many of those involved have not yet realised that *CERCIs* are not assistance institutions but social enterprises, demanding an entrepreneurial commitment and management.[17] The lack of adequate facilities is also a major problem for most *CERCIs*. Lack of space, difficult accesses and lack of adequate housing are some of the main deficiencies (Veiga 1999).

Financial vulnerability and sensitivity to political cycles also weaken the performance of *CERCIs*. According to a survey of *CERCIs* in March 1994 conducted by INSCOOP (Paiva 1997), the most serious problem *CERCIs* had to face was insufficient state support, followed by delays in the transfer of funds or subsidies. This pointed to a significant financial dependency on the state.[18]

Relations between CERCIs *and public authorities*

The relations between *CERCIs* and public authorities have been changing from a disposition of begging for subsidies to partnerships (for instance with regular schools) and collaboration. However, there is still a long way to go. One of the fields where interactions between *CERCIs* and public policies worked best is the social employment market, insofar as *CERCIs* were listened to on this issue and their proposals were retained and even included in the National Action Plan for Employment.

3 Future perspectives and conclusions

In the field of the mentally disabled, as well as in many other fields of social protection, there are still a large number of needs to be satisfied. Therefore, *CERCIs* still have scope to grow, to multiply and to diversify their services. However, there is currently a trend towards the increasing absorption of mildly and moderately mentally disabled children and youngsters by regular schools. Consequently, the main users of *CERCIs* in the future may be mostly either children with severe and multiple handicaps or adult disabled people.

Since most *CERCIs* are geographically concentrated in the coastal areas, and in and around large urban centres, the extension of this kind of co-operative to the inner and less developed regions of the country – thus contributing to local development and job creation – might be desirable.

In terms of the organisational model, the dominant perspective among the most active leaders of the *CERCI* movement indicates a reconciliation between co-operative principles and the growing need for a strategic and professionalised management of resources (Veiga 1999) in a social entrepreneurship perspective. The interactions with public policies have improved in recent years and it seems that the conditions exist for *CERCIs* to progress in a positive way. Following the legal recognition of social solidarity co-operatives, recent state initiatives favouring co-operatives within a strategy of job creation mostly for disadvantaged groups are a sign of this trend. The creation of a National Council for Social Economy, at ministerial level, is now under preparation. This could lead to a better interaction between social enterprises and public policies, particularly in the area of the fight against social exclusion.

Notes

1 The author thanks Susana Nogueira for her collaboration. Given the relative lack of research and published data on these issues, the updated and full picture of the main types of social enterprises within the third sector as well as the in-depth analysis on *CERCIs* would not have been possible without the collaboration of a number of key persons and organisations. Among these we are particularly grateful to: Acácio Catarino (Observatory of Employment and Professional Training); Gertrudes Jorge and Hélia Lisboa (National Commission for the Social Employment Market); José Martins Maia (Union of *IPSS* – Private Social Solidarity Institutions); Julieta Sanches (*CERCI Lisboa* – Co-operative for the Education and Rehabilitation of Disabled Children); Maldonado Gonelha, Paula Guimarães and Odete Duarte (Union of Portuguese Mutual Benefit Associations); Manuel Canaveira de Campos (INSCOOP – António Sérgio's Institute for the Co-operative Sector); Manuel de Lemos (Union of Portuguese 'Misericórdias' – Church Welfare Organisations); Rogério Cação and Ana Rita Martins Peralta (*FENACERCI* – National Federation of *CERCIs*).
2 *Mercado social de emprego*, i.e. 'a diversified series of solutions, which aim to integrate or reintegrate the unemployed, in both social and employment terms, through activities to meet social needs that are not met by the normal operation of the market' (Instituto do Emprego e Formação Profissional, 'The Social Employment Market').
3 According to the chairman of the *Union of Portuguese Misericórdias*, Melícias, quoted by Barros and Santos (1997: 335), it would be more correct to speak about state funding of the institutions' activities, not of the institutions themselves.
4 Data for 1998 provided by the Union of Portuguese Mutual Benefit Associations.
5 According to an estimation made by the chairman of the Union of *IPSS*.
6 By 'early intervention', we refer to the action developed by *CERCIs* which is addressed to children at risk – either newborn babies who have a prenatal indication of mental handicap or children who present some development problems.
7 In the recent past, this trend generated some negative reactions from the *CERCI* movement, but it has now gained the support of *CERCIs*, which are even collaborating with some regular schools.
8 Law 51/96 (7 September 1996). This new Co-operative Code also allows the constitution of multi-sectoral co-operatives, which may be advantageous to *CERCIs*, since these may combine their traditional activities with activities classified in other branches of the co-operative sector, such as culture, handicraft, services, etc, without loosing their social solidarity co-operative status.
9 Whose juridical regime was defined through Decree-Law 7/98 (15 January 1998). The rights, duties and benefits, at the fiscal level, of *IPSS* were extended to co-operatives of social solidarity, through Law 101/97 (13 September 1997).

10 The participation and commitment of parents in the management of *CERCIs* has weakened significantly, especially parents from socially and culturally disadvantaged groups. On the one hand, it is difficult to convince them to sit on a board of directors and, on the other hand, the presence of parents is often seen by professionals as a source of conflict and internal problems (Veiga 1999).

11 It should be stressed that the relations between *CERCIs* and local authorities may vary from one municipality to another; in some cases, the local administration represents a major support to *CERCIs'* activity, in others there is a negative relationship (Veiga 1999).

12 The quotas paid by *CERCIs'* members and the users' monthly payments are another source of funding, although mainly symbolic, given their reduced weight in *CERCIs'* budget.

13 Law 85/98 (16 December 1998), changed by the Decree-Law 393/99 (1 October 1999).

14 Statutory Instrument 52-A/99 (22 January 1999).

15 Cabinet Resolution 59/98 (6 May 1998).

16 By the end of 1999, according to the Interim Report on the National Action Plan for Employment, about 178 applications from co-operatives to PRODESCOOP were under analysis.

17 According to Julieta Sanches, *CERCI Lisboa*.

18 It is estimated that, on average, state and EU subsidies cover between 75 per cent and 85 per cent of the total yearly expenses of *CERCIs* (Veiga 1999). But these average figures should not hide the great diversity that prevails in reality among *CERCIs*. For example, the financial autonomy rate of the five largest *CERCIs* varies between 12 per cent and 71 per cent (INSCOOP 1999a).

Bibliography

AZEVEDO, M. (1992) 'Respostas Institucionais, Limites e Virtualidades. As Misericórdias', 1ª Jornadas Nacionais de Acção Social, 6–8 November, Centro Regional de Segurança Social, Braga.

BAPTISTA, I., PERISTA, H. and REIS, A.L. (1995) *A Pobreza no Porto: Representações Sociais e Práticas Institucionais*, Cadernos REAPN no. 1, REAPN, Porto.

BARÃO, M.G. (1992) 'Economia Social', 1ª Jornadas Nacionais de Acção Social, 6–8 November, Centro Regional de Segurança Social, Braga.

BARROS, C.P. and SANTOS, J.C.G. (1998) *O Mutualismo Português: Solidariedade e Progresso Social*, Editora Vulgata, Lisboa.

——(1997) *As Instituições Não – Lucrativas e a Acção Social em Portugal* – Estudos e Pesquisas Multidisciplinares Sobre o Sector Não-Lucrativo – I, Editora Vulgata, Lisboa.

CAPUCHA, L. and CORDEIRO, O.L. (1998) 'Les Entreprises d'Insertion au Portugal', in *Les Politiques Sociales – Entreprendre Autrement*, vol. 57: 53–9.

CAPUCHA, L., AIRES, S., QUINTELA, J., REIS, A.L. and SANTOS, P.C. (1995) *ONG's de Solidariedade Social: Práticas e Disposições*, Cadernos REAPN no. 2, REAPN, Porto.

CATARINO, A. (1998) 'Mercado Social de Emprego: Esboço de Introdução Conceptual', *Sociedade e Trabalho*, no. 2, 6–13.

——(1992) '*IPSS* – Limitações e Virtualidades', 1ª Jornadas Nacionais de Acção Social, 6–8 November, Centro Regional de Segurança Social, Braga.

HESPANHA, P. (1999) 'Em Torno do Papel Providencial da Sociedade Civil Portuguesa', *Cadernos de Política Social*, no. 1, 15–42.

INSCOOP – Instituto António Sérgio do Sector Cooperativo (1999a) *As 100 Maiores Empresas Cooperativas*, INSCOOP, Lisboa.

—— Instituto António Sérgio do Sector Cooperativo (1999b) *Anuário Comercial do Sector Cooperativo*, INSCOOP, Lisboa.

Instituto de Gestão Financeira da Segurança Social/MTS (1997) *Estatísticas da Segurança Social – Acção Social*, Lisboa.

Instituto do Emprego e Formação Profissional, 'The Social Employment Market – Combined Action and Shared Responsibilities', mimeo.

ISCTE/SAE (1996) *Proximity Services in Portugal. Main Trends and Characteristics (a First Evaluation)*, ISCTE, Lisboa.

Ministério do Trabalho e da Solidariedade / Secretaria de Estado da Inserção Social (1998) *Pacto de Cooperação para a Solidariedade Social*, União das Mutualidades Portuguesas, Lisboa.

Ministério do Trabalho e da Solidariedade/DEPP – Departamento de Estudos, Prospectiva e Planeamento (1999) *Plano Nacional de Emprego 99 – Portugal e a Estratégia Europeia para o Emprego*, Lisboa.

PAIVA, F. (1997) 'CERCIS – Cooperativas de solidariedade social', in BARROS, C.P. and SANTOS, J.C.G., *As Instituições Não – Lucrativas e a Acção Social em Portugal*, Estudos e Pesquisas Multidisciplinares Sobre o Sector Não-Lucrativo – I, Editora Vulgata, Lisboa, 139–57.

PEREIRINHA, J. (ed.) (1999) *Exclusão Social em Portugal: Estudo de Situações e Processos e Avaliação das Políticas Sociais*, CISEP/CESIS, Lisboa.

PERISTA, H., BAPTISTA, I. and PERISTA, P. (1999) *Collection of Information on Local Initiatives to Combat Social Exclusion – Final Report*, CESIS, Lisboa.

ROSENDO, V. (1996) *O Mutualismo em Portugal. Dois Séculos de História e suas Origens*, Multinova, Lisboa.

RSESS/98, Ministério do Trabalho e da Solidariedade/Secretaria de Estado da Inserção Social/Direcção-Geral da Acção Social, Lisboa.

União das Mutualidades Portuguesas (1999) *VIII Congresso Nacional de Mutualismo – 1998 – Conclusões*, União das Mutualidades Portuguesas, Lisboa.

VARIZ, P.E. (1998) *Fundamentos Económicos e Sociológicos das Instituições Particulares de Solidariedade Social*, Editora Vulgata, Lisboa.

VEIGA, C.V. (1999) *Cooperativas de Educação e Reabilitação de Crianças Inadaptadas: Uma Visão Global*, Secretariado Nacional para a Reabilitação e Integração das Pessoas com Deficiência, Lisboa.

12 Spain

Social enterprises as a response to employment policy failure

Isabel Vidal

Introduction[1]

To understand the phenomenon of social enterprises, it is necessary to look back in history since these initiatives are often the product of evolutionary development of old organisational forms. Although the scope of this chapter is confined to the more recent steps taken within civil society generally, it is noteworthy that during the twentieth century some forms of social enterprises have arisen in matters that hitherto were confined to the family. Examples include the services devoted to the handicapped or, more recently, to persons with newer social problems such as those related to drugs and AIDS. Historically, the church has been vigorously engaged in traditional activities to alleviate poverty – an international example of this being *Caritas*. More recently, lay initiatives have taken over from religious action, especially with regard to the handicapped. The parents' associations of handicapped children organised and created the first special work centres and the first residences in the 1960s and 1970s. Later, in the 1980s, with the emergence of the welfare state in Spain, these private initiatives were reinforced by public sector initiatives. But the consistent historical pattern is that in the first stage, private initiatives, both religious and lay, predominate. Then, at a later stage, public initiatives take responsibility and make the activities developed by the social private sector more professional, or start to finance them on a more regular basis.

This process is interlinked with the evolution of welfare expenditures between 1975 and 1997. In 1975, public spending in Spain represented 25 per cent of GDP, while the average across the countries of the European Union exceeded 40 per cent. This shortfall in public funds encouraged the development of social enterprises in the fields of health, social services, education, culture and leisure, often under the legal form of associations and foundations. By 1997, public spending represented 43 per cent of GDP. During the period of strong growth in public spending, the government often opted to contract out the management of the public services. This option encouraged the rapid growth of the third sector in Spain, in the form of associations and foundations, as management arms of public authorities in the provision of personal public services. In 1995, there were 226,658 associations and foundations in operation. They employed

500,000 persons (4.5 per cent of the employed population). They also mobilised 4 million volunteers, and their budget was about 16,828.3 million Euro (4.5 per cent of GDP).[2] Among the new organisations developed during the last twenty years, the work-integration social enterprises are particularly innovative and entrepreneurial, especially in terms of the services supplied.

1   The Spanish labour-market context: a brief overview

Before tackling the specific subject of this chapter, it is necessary to highlight some general aspects of the Spanish economic system and, especially, of the labour market. The industrial crisis of the 1970s and the subsequent financial crisis of the state deepened the problems linked to the then-prevailing entrepreneurial development model and to the state. Two negative consequences followed: the insufficient demand for labour coming from traditional enterprises – which may be described as market failure – and the insufficient capacity of the state to respond to the growing demand for personal services of value to the community – state failure. These two failures forced civil society to invent new answers – among which were social enterprises – to meet unsatisfied social demands.

In Spain, the industrial crisis of the early 1970s coincided with the political process of transition to democracy. Whilst GDP had grown during the 1960s by a cumulative 7 per cent per annum, this figure was down to just 1.6 per cent for the period from the mid 1970s to the mid 1980s. This spectacular downturn in economic growth was accompanied by runaway inflation. Inflation reached a high point of 24.5 per cent in 1977, while average inflation for the period 1975–1985 was 15.6 per cent.

Employment was hit especially hard. Spain recorded a net loss of 2.13 million jobs between 1975 and 1985, i.e. a decrease of 16.5 per cent in employment. By 1997, the number of jobs in Spain had returned to the levels recorded in 1977, but with the active population having grown by 3 million during that twenty-year period, the unemployment rate in 1998 reached 18 per cent. In 1999, the level of unemployment went down to 15.4 per cent. Nowadays, employment in Spain is increasing very fast.

In the 1970s, unemployed workers or those employees in danger of losing their jobs on account of company closures, initiated jointly owned enterprises under two different legal formulas: the traditional form of workers' co-operative and the employee-owned company. Both workers' co-operatives and employee-owned companies aim at creating and sustaining employment. The main difference between the two forms lies in their legal definition, insofar as the co-operative is an association of persons, while the employee-owned company is an equity business in which the majority of the share capital belongs to the workers. Until 1986, the legal form of the employee-owned company was better suited to the workers' needs than the co-operative form because if a co-operative was closed down, its workers were not entitled to unemployment benefit. This caused many unemployed workers and workers in danger of losing their jobs to prefer the employee-owned company form. When the law on co-operatives eventually changed in 1986, employee-owned companies already constituted a strong movement, which gained official recognition that same year with the passing of the first law on employee-owned companies. This development helps to account for the co-existence of two distinct legal forms of worker-managed enterprises, both considering themselves as part of the social economy in Spain.

In the last quarter of 1999, there were 22,331 workers' co-operatives in operation, employing 241,719 workers, and 9,080 employee-owned companies providing 73,526 jobs.[3] In total, a group of 31,411 jointly owned enterprises have created 315,245 jobs at a time when traditional enterprises have been shedding jobs. These are enterprises whose role is to provide their members with employment. They are mainly small enterprises, based on relations of mutual trust between their members and on a horizontal organisational structure, which makes it possible to practise economic democracy. Business decisions are taken according to the overriding objective of maintaining employment.

Although they appeared in the same period as workers' co-operatives and employee-owned companies, work-integration enterprises differ from these in that they are not a form of mutual-help organisation, initiated by the unemployed or by workers threatened with unemployment. Work-integration enterprises aim at employing those who are systematically excluded from the labour market – persons with physical or mental disabilities or the socially excluded. Promoters of these initiatives are not the users themselves; they are usually relatives of the users, in the case of enterprises aimed at persons with disabilities, or the parochial community or neighbours, in the case of enterprises aimed at the socially excluded. Usually, work-integration enterprises choose the association or the foundation legal form, rather than the co-operative or the employee-owned company form.

2   The focus of the analysis

The present section focuses on social enterprises active in the field of social integration through employment of persons systematically excluded from the ordinary labour market. In other words, this kind of social enterprise tries to reduce the failures of the labour market that the state fails to solve with its bureaucratic and standardised approach.

Two main categories should be distinguished within the group of persons systematically excluded from the ordinary labour market: these are persons with disabilities and the socially excluded. The former include people with physical or mental handicaps. The latter include young persons who have failed at school, young persons with a criminal record, single mothers, migrants – in short, the long-term unemployed with negligible or zero levels of employability.

Social enterprises active in the social integration of persons with disabilities can benefit from the job creation measures for workers with disabilities set out in Royal Decree 145/1983, which governs selective employment and measures to promote the employment of people with disabilities. It provides incentives for the hiring of disabled workers in the form of subsidies for each contract concluded, significant rebates on the social security charges, subsidies for the adaptation of workplaces, and the granting of resources for personal safety and vocational training. The Royal Decree 145/1983 also governs employment workshops, the aim of which is the integration into the labour market of all those persons with a disability. They are production units with an average of 150 workers. In some areas, they are currently the enterprises with the largest work-force or those that have created most jobs over the last twenty years.

By contrast, there are still very few traditional enterprises employing disadvan-taged workers. The *Report on the Situation of Persons with Disabilities and Proposals for Getting them Back to Work* of the Economic and Social Council (*CES, Consejo Económico y Social*) recognised that 'the number of registered contracts making use of job-creation procedures shows that enterprises have not taken up this incen-tive-based way of providing access to employment' (*CES* 1995: 96). This suggests that for the most part, social enterprises involved in the employment-led integra-tion of persons with disabilities have been virtually the only employers of disabled people and the only users of the measures intended to promote the employment of persons with a disability. An interesting development among these enterprises is the establishment of 'enterprise groups', which is dealt with later on.

On the other hand, social enterprises involved in the integration of socially excluded persons are more recent and smaller in scale, with lower production capacities, a lower level of professionalism and a greater number of voluntary workers. They did not receive any extra resources for providing jobs for the socially excluded until 2000. The Law 55/1999 allows companies and non-profit-making bodies who offer contracts to unemployed workers in a situation of social exclusion to receive 60 per cent subsidies on their social security insurance payment in the first twenty-four months of the work contract.

These enterprises appeared at the beginning of the 1980s. Their main promoter was the Catholic church, through *Caritas*, but little by little, small projects initiated by parochial communities and by neighbourhood associations have also been developing, independently of *Caritas*. Although the whole move-ment still retains a strong religious influence, it may become more secular in the coming years, as enterprises that are active in the field of work integration of persons with social disabilities may, with the advent of Law 55/1999, develop a stronger entrepreneurship movement. Twenty-two initiatives operating in the field of social exclusion were analysed by CIES (1998, 1999). Without receiving any institutional support or reductions in social security contributions, these schemes had taken on, in 1997 and 1998 respectively, 401 and 540 persons who otherwise would have little chance of finding employment.

Although these are two different types of social enterprise, it has been decided to examine them together for two reasons. Firstly, because it is felt that social enterprises employing people with disabilities will act as a point of refer-ence in relation to the entrepreneurial future of social enterprises working in the field of social exclusion. Secondly, because there is the possibility that with the recognition of social exclusion by the Spanish government, social enterprises that are currently involved with people with disabilities only would extend the profile of their users. In other words, their objective would be the integration through employment of any person, irrespective of his/her profile and of the legal recognition of the disability.

3 Methodology and sample

There are no records or statistical information available on social enterprises active in the field of social integration of persons who otherwise would have little chance of finding employment. Thus, the following two approaches were adopted:

- interviews were conducted with the general managers of ten enterprises employing persons with disabilities or the socially excluded;
- twenty-two enterprises, members of the *Asociación Española de Recuperadores de la Economía Social y Solidaria (AERESS)*,[4] took part in a survey carried out in 1997 and 1998. Information was collected about employees, income and funding sources, expenditure, investment, the economic value of the productive capacity and the productive activity.

Six of the general managers interviewed worked to integrate persons with disabilities. Among the enterprises from which they come is the *Asociación Atzegui – Grupo Gureak*. This is the most important organisation in the field of social integration through employment of persons with disabilities in Guipuzcoa (Basque Country). To achieve its work-integration goals, the *Asociación Atzegui* (parents' association, founded in 1972) developed an enterprise called *Talleres Gureak* (Gureak Workshops) in 1982, which comprises fourteen employment centres; it also created eight other enterprises which are legal entities in their own right. *Talleres Gureak* is a joint stock company; the other eight enterprises are limited liability companies. Atzegui parents' association is the main stakeholder in these enterprises. In 1997, they provided 2,008 jobs, of which only 174 were for persons who did not have disabilities. Another example is the *Asociación AMICA* (founded in 1984), which, in 1990, established *SOEMCA*, a limited company, whose capital is wholly owned by the *Asociación AMICA*. It is the leader in the field of social insertion through employment of persons with disabilities in Cantabria. It started up in the industrial laundry sector. Its customers are hospitals, hotels and restaurants. In 1997 *AMICA* had a total of 571 members and *SOEMCA* had 163 workers with contracts of employment.

The other four general managers who were interviewed came from enterprises in the field of work integration for the socially excluded. The *Fundación Engrunes-Cooperativas Miques* (established in 1982) operates in Catalonia with trading activities based on the selective collection of urban waste, construction, rehabilitation of buildings and sale of second-hand products. The *Fundación Deixalles* (1986) operates in the Balearic Islands, and its activities focus on the selective collection of solid urban waste, its sorting, recovery and subsequent sale. The *Traperos de Emaus San Sebastian* (founded in 1980) operates in the Basque Country; its activities focus on sales of second-hand products and it provides services to the socially excluded such as accommodation, healthcare and clothing, work guidance, training and acclimatisation to work, career guidance and workplace integration. The *Traperos de Emaus Nafarroa*, in the autonomous community of Navarra, is also involved in trading based on the selective collection of solid urban waste.

These last four enterprises did not benefit from institutional recognition until year 2000. They are members of *AERESS*, and belong to the group of 22 work-integration enterprises which took part in the survey, conducted in 1997 and 1998, which constitutes the second source of information (besides the interviews) used for the purpose of the present study. The study focused on innovative behaviour that could inject a new energy into integration enterprises. This presentation therefore concentrates on the most outstanding aspects and obstacles or difficulties facing the leading integration enterprises in Spain today.

4   The specific nature of leading enterprises in social integration

The promoters

All social enterprises that were involved in the interviews and survey are bottom-up initiatives. The social groups promoting a work-integration organisation differ according to the target group of people who are to be integrated into the labour market. If the target group is made up of persons with disabilities, the promoters are associations of parents and relatives. If the group to be integrated is the socially excluded, the promoters are usually Christian communities and neighbourhood associations.

The prevailing legal form is the association. In the disabilities sector, parents' associations have developed significantly from the 1970s onwards. The associations engaged in the field of social exclusion began to appear in the 1980s, when Spanish society became aware of the social consequences of structural unemployment. The decision to opt for the association is generally taken not so much on account of its significance as a non-profit and democratic structure, but because this is the form that involves the lowest formal establishment and running costs.

It is important to stress that in all the projects that have made the leap to efficiency-based, market-orientated entrepreneurial business, the key factor has been the presence of a leader. The leaders have introduced an entrepreneurial culture to their organisations. The economic and social results achieved by these enterprise groups cannot be explained without taking into account the vital role played by these social entrepreneurs. A large majority of the latter has had prior business experience in the traditional private sector. They are able to apply and adjust the techniques of enterprise management and the strategies of private sector firms to the mission of the social enterprise.

The productive choice

Social enterprises were created with the explicit objective of integrating into the ordinary labour market persons who are systematically excluded from it. To achieve this objective, social enterprises have to develop an enterprise culture radically different from that of business organisations. They might choose the same activity and they might be competing in the same market, but the reasons for choosing this activity and this market will be different. In the decision taken by social entrepreneurs, the interests of the user – the person with disabilities – take precedence, whilst in the decision taken by the leader of a conventional enterprise, the overriding criterion is the return on capital invested.

This same analysis can be applied to the production process that each of these enterprises chooses. Social enterprises working with disabled people use labour-intensive production processes in order to fulfil their role. On the other hand, a conventional enterprise uses a more capital-intensive production process. The result is higher productivity per worker in the conventional enterprise. However, the total production costs are not necessarily higher in a social enterprise than in an ordinary enterprise because of a completely different wage structure and capital costs. Moreover, social enterprises generate positive externalities and increase social capital by strengthening civic cohesion where they operate.

The organisational form: enterprise groups

The enterprise group is the most usual form adopted in Spain by work-integration social enterprises aiming to provide integrated services, such as training, employment and accommodation. Within the enterprise group, the legal form of each enterprise depends on the productive activity being carried out. The constituent group enterprise carrying out activities that can be defined as a public service (such as healthcare or residential care for persons with disabilities) usually takes the legal form of a non-profit body, i.e. association or foundation. On the other hand, the group enterprise responsible for those activities that are carried out in the conventional market alongside traditional businesses most often takes on a legal form appropriate to a capitalist company, i.e. joint-stock company (*sociedad anónima*), limited company (*sociedad limitada*), or employee-owned company (*sociedad laboral*). In a few cases, the form of co-operative society (*sociedad cooperativa*) is chosen. The association remains the main or sole shareholder of the enterprises it promotes. In some cases, the association becomes a foundation, while in others the associative form is retained.

The source of finance partly determines the legal form that the enterprise group uses for the organisation providing the service. Also, the legal form is considered as a way to communicate information to the public. The form an organisation chooses will thus vary according to its main customer and to the message it wants to give to external entities. If the main customer for a particular service to be supplied is a public agency, the legal form chosen will very probably be that of a non-profit organisation. If funding stems mainly from the market, as is the case with initiatives involved in job creation and labour-market integration, the legal form chosen will be the form usually preferred by the commercial sector, because of the organisation's desire to be considered as able to compete with commercial enterprises. A specific feature of the work-integration social enterprises surveyed is that a single entity or enterprise group is responsible for co-ordinating the provision of the range of services needed by any one user, thus increasing levels of efficiency and utility compared with those which would exist if different suppliers, with perhaps different entrepreneurial cultures, provided the various services

The evolution from long-term enterprises to 'bridging' enterprises

One current topic of discussion in Spain is whether the most appropriate enterprises for people with low levels of employability are those providing transitional jobs, so-called 'bridging' enterprises, or those enterprises which typically provide employment to a person with disability throughout his/her working life. And to complicate matters further, the behaviour of work-integration social enterprises for persons with disabilities differs from that of enterprises for the socially excluded.

Enterprises employing workers with disabilities

Until very recently, the employment workshops (RD 145/1983) preferred to regard themselves as 'long-term' enterprises. This perspective has resulted in contracts of employment being of indefinite duration. However – and this is a novel feature in this sector – in some sheltered employment workshops, the managers are beginning to regard the enterprise as a tool for training and apprenticeship, and merely as an intermediary step after which its beneficiaries will be able to move into the open labour market. They feel that the insertion into the open market marks a further stage of improvement and adjustment for the individual. The result of this approach is that, in enterprises that think in this way, short-term contracts of employment are preferred. The beneficiary knows that his/her job is temporary, i.e. it is a transitional period that will end with his/her absorption into the open labour market.

These employment workshops, which their managers see as bridging enterprises for persons with disabilities, have a department acting as an employment agency. The professionals working in this department fulfil two mutually complementary roles. One role consists of contacting conventional enterprises, explaining the tax advantages of hiring a person with a disability, giving support during the initial stages of work integration, and guaranteeing that the individual can return to the special employment workshop if he/she is not happy in their new job. The other role consists of training the person with a disability and providing the professional and psychological skills that will ease the individual's integration into the wider labour market. According to these associations and employment workshops, the logistical support that the employment agency provides makes it possible to integrate a greater number of people with better contracts than if this support did not exist.

Enterprises employing the socially excluded

Social enterprises targeting the socially excluded have always set themselves up from the outset as transitional enterprises, never as 'long-term' enterprises. They know that they should not turn themselves into repositories of persons with a low level of employability. They are sensitive to avoiding the ghetto phenomenon and are well aware that the real integration of these persons into society will occur when they find a job and stability in the open market. However, such enterprises do not yet have a department functioning as an employment agency, as in some special employment workshops.

There are two reasons for this situation. First, they lack the financial resources for setting up such a department. It has to be remembered that the institutional recognition of enterprises active in the field of integration of the social excluded came only in January 2000. In the near future, as this institutional recognition increases, it may allow the creation of structures and services such as those which enterprises active in the field of social integration of persons with disabilities already have. The second reason – more important because of its innovative character – is that integration into the ordinary labour market is achieved on the basis of productive activities that give the individual the opportunity to come into contact with ordinary enterprises. Enterprises which employ the socially excluded co-operate with traditional enterprises for the execution of the work, and this co-operation makes it easier, whenever the ordinary enterprise needs a worker, for the integration enterprise to 'lend' it one of its workers. In the case of a person with a criminal record, the issue is his curriculum vitae, not his level of productivity. The integration enterprise offers him a contract of employment and the opportunity to be in contact with conventional businesses. These are two key factors that should make it easier for the individual to secure a job in the ordinary labour market.

Resources mobilised

As to the resources available for social enterprises, one can distinguish between:

- monetary resources derived from:

  - public authorities,
  - the market (sales of services),
  - private donations, in money or in kind;

- volunteering.

The role of public and market resources

As far as resources coming from public authorities and from the market are concerned, in 1997, enterprises engaged in the activity of work integration of persons with disabilities had average sales of 300 million pesetas (1,803,036 Euro). The most successful enterprises reached more than 1,000 million pesetas of sales (6,010,121 Euro). The survey and interviews revealed that sales in the market represented 70 per cent of turnover and that subsidies relative to total sales have dropped progressively over the last three years of operation.

Enterprises active in the field of work integration of socially excluded persons invoiced an average of 150 million pesetas (901,518 Euro), with some projects recording twice this amount. CIES (1999) shows that in a total of twenty-two sample sets of accounts for the 1997 and 1998 financial years, the private market provided 45 per cent of income of which retail accounted for 35 per cent, and wholesale for 10 per cent. The public market represented 32 per cent of income. If we add together the public and private markets, we have 77 per cent of income coming from market-related activities. Of the remainder, subsidies represented 18 per cent of income, whilst private donations accounted for 5 per cent. Staff costs in those enterprises qualifying under Royal Decree 145/83[5] represent around 35 per cent of the total production costs. In enterprises employing the socially excluded, this figure was 74 per cent before Law 55/1999 was passed.

In the period 1997 to 1998, the group of twenty-two enterprises – all members of the *AERESS* Group – which took part in the survey, paid 448 million pesetas (2,692,534 Euro) in the form of social security contributions for their workers. These enterprises received, for the integration task they performed, subsidies amounting to 400 million pesetas (2,404,048 Euro). The difference, 48 million pesetas (288,486 Euro), represents the net income to the public sector. Consequently, it can be said that integration enterprises for the socially excluded generated a net income for the public authorities.

Such enterprises have solicited exemption from social security contributions for their users. The reasons put forward to justify this demand include the fact that they are labour intensive with a low-skilled workforce, that they employ workers with health problems, and that, consequently, they have a very low level of productivity. Furthermore, the leaders of work-integration enterprises consider that the fact of being market-oriented has a therapeutic effect on their workers. Their claim for institutional recognition is not motivated by a wish to obtain higher subsidies. They simply want to get tax exemptions, justified by the fact that they produce positive externalities through their commercial activity. In Spain Law 55/1999 is a first step in the process of institutional recognition of integration enterprises targeted at the socially excluded.

The role of donations and volunteers and their impact on the organisation

A distinction can be made between three different types of donations: in cash, in kind and in time. Donations in cash are not very significant. In 1998 around 5 per cent of the income of enterprises for the socially excluded came from donations (CIES 1999), and donations did not figure at all in the income of enterprises active in the field of disabilities. Donations in kind are more important, particularly donations of second-hand clothes and other goods in enterprises for the socially excluded that are active in economic activities relating to the collection of solid urban waste.

Donations in time have a number of possible features, such as availability of volunteers, extra working hours not being paid for, and lower wages. The main donation is the time that the managers set aside to take part in the various bodies that make up the political/administrative structures of the entity. Employers responsible for managing the enterprise group do so free of charge. As regards the voluntary resources mobilised by these social enterprises, it should be noted that the more precarious the economic situation of the enterprise, the greater the level of voluntary resources it uses. As and when the enterprise manages to carve out a space for itself in the market and becomes professional, the importance of these voluntary resources decreases and is eventually reduced to the participation of the employers or partners in the enterprise's decision-making structures.

Another dimension of the voluntary nature of this work is the low salaries paid to the leaders and managers of the initiatives. This form of voluntary work is common in enterprises for the socially excluded. One result of this is a narrow wage range. Cases have been recorded of enterprises in which the ratio between the salaries of a worker and his or her general manager is 1:1.5; i.e. the most senior manager earns 50 per cent more than the most recently recruited person who has suffered social exclusion. The fact that enterprises involved in the integration of persons with social disabilities can do the work they are doing is because of this form of voluntary involvement of their leaders and managers.

In the special employment workshops (RD 145/83), there are no volunteers in the technical/productive structure. Moreover, the wage levels of the professionals working there are higher than in the case of those working in enterprises for the socially excluded.

To sum up, voluntary resources are mobilised in all enterprises active in the field of work integration. These voluntary resources commonly take the form of donations in time. However, it should be noted that the greater the institutional recognition, the more the presence of volunteers is reduced. When they were first set up, all the entrepreneurial integration schemes recorded high levels of voluntary work. This then gradually decreased as and when institutional recognition enabled the enterprises to achieve their social objectives by using the productive resources available in the commercial field and by replacing the resources used in the non-trading or voluntary field by subsidies. This replacement is regarded as positive, and reflects the taking on of responsibilities by civil society at large.

The representation structures of social enterprises

Theoretically, social enterprises are entrepreneurial initiatives that are intended to be part of the third sector or the social economy. In fact, the associations, foundations and enterprises that are engaged in the field of disabilities, with the exception of the National Organisation of Spanish Blind People (*Organización Nacional de los Ciegos Españoles*), do not take part in the representative structures of the social economy in Spain. Neither are they regarded as belonging to the social economy, nor have they been concerned to create a common front with all the bodies and organisations which provide services to communities of interest.

Since the mid 1970s, with the development of a welfare state in Spain, and the necessity for public contracting for the provision and management of services, public authorities have promoted vertical organisations for each target group. As a result, each target group – the physically or the mentally disabled, the deaf, drug addicts, abused women, etc. – is, although to a varying extent, organised in a representation structure of its own. For their day-to-day running, these representative structures depend mainly on public subsidies, not on the contributions of their members. Consequently, their members see them more as top-down 'drivers' than as bottom-up communication channels.

The leaders of these representative structures have not considered it necessary to create horizontal links among themselves. The result is that, unlike the situation with representative organisations for more conventional enterprises, the representative organisations for the different lobbying groups work without any kind of horizontal co-ordination. It has also to be stressed that the different groups of organisations that work in the field of disabilities, drug addiction or poverty do not see themselves as part of the third sector or the social economy – or perhaps, do not regard such a reference as useful. Of course, the situation might change, as funding for representative organisations changes and may be reduced.

Moreover, it is even possible to find examples of leading social enterprises that are members of traditional enterprise organisations. This is because they identify more with the dynamic of such entities, and above all for reasons of symbolism and external communication. They want to be considered as normal, everyday businesses that can relate to their conventional counterparts because this is the most effective mechanism for integration into the ordinary market. Other social enterprises have created small structures with local friendly enterprises with which they can exchange views and jointly negotiate with the regional authorities. The large majority of these social enterprises have opted to create genuine private enterprise groups, enabling them to reach a sufficient size and therefore have the capacity to establish direct dialogue with the competent public authorities in the sectors in which they operate.

Work-integration enterprises for persons who are socially excluded are more willing to be identified with the social economy. However, social economy leaders nowadays do not accept work-integration enterprises as members of their political representation structures. The 'old' social economy representatives have a defensive attitude. As a result, in 1998, work-integration enterprises active in the field of social exclusion set up a third-degree representative structure or confederation whose members are district federations. This organisation is called the

'Federation of Integration Enterprises' (*FEDEI, Federación de Empresas de Inserción*). Its founding members include *Caritas, AERESS, Traperos de Emaus España*, the 'Madrid Association of Integration Enterprises' (*Asociación Madrileña de Empresas de Inserción*) and the Catalan Social and Solidarity-based Association of Recovery Companies *(ACERESS, Asociación Catalana de Empresas Recuperadoras de la Economía Social y Solidaria)*. The *FEDEI* groups together the principal and longest-standing bodies working for the integration of the socially excluded.

In short, there is no general representative organisation bringing together all enterprises with social objectives in Spain, and there is no single forum for representatives of social enterprises. There are various organisations which channel and support the interests of these initiatives and of their managers, but these lack co-ordination among themselves.

5   Risks for social enterprises

There is a risk that enterprises active in the field of social integration through work may abandon their role as bridging enterprises and become long-term enterprises. The risk remains even in enterprises whose leaders or promoters clearly understand that the organisations they are managing must be transitional or bridging enterprises for the user. There are various factors that help to explain this. One factor, external to the enterprise, is the difficulty currently faced by integration enterprise users when trying to find employment in the ordinary labour market, due to their social profile. Factors internal to the enterprise include, *inter alia*, the fact that integration enterprises provide the user with an employment contract in order to give his activity more recognition, and in so doing, they create vague expectations of permanence, even though the contract is temporary. The risk of the enterprise becoming long term for the user increases if this user participates in the decision-making structures of the enterprise. One is thus presented with the irony that the greater the internal democracy in an enterprise, the greater the risk that the enterprise will become long term for the user.

Another reason why this may happen is related to the internal management of human resources. There is, in fact, a contradiction between the role of the enterprise and the immediate production needs of workshop managers. The role of the enterprise is to integrate its workforce with improved qualifications into the labour market. This leads to a continuous loss of human resources which workshop managers may try to prevent because of its effects on productivity – particularly in the case of a social enterprise whose productive activity depends on its competitiveness in the open market.

One of the major risks work-integration enterprises have to face originates in their own leaders. The purpose of an integration enterprise is to resolve or at least relieve the problem of social exclusion. But many leaders have difficulties in associating this purpose with the concept of enterprise. As a matter of fact, very few leaders consider the enterprise as an instrument that, if properly used, can help them achieve their social objectives. The social or religious environment from which leaders come, combined with the negative image of enterprise which prevails in Spain, result in a feeling of aversion towards the concept of enterprise. They thus have a contradiction to resolve insofar as they do not want their organisations to be considered as enterprises because enterprise is associated with exploitation. At the same time, they must develop a productive activity that can be sold on the market if they want to systematically contract persons excluded from the labour market. There is thus an urgent need to develop a discourse that would promote the positive aspects of enterprise and help in broadening the understanding that it can be used to achieve social purposes. However, the concept of enterprise has gained legitimacy in recent years, and where the leaders are young people who did not experience the decade of the 1970s, they are more open to this type of discourse and to the need for professionalisation and training. Still, there is a need for new leaders in the field of work-integration enterprises. They must be persons who have already discovered that the enterprise, if well managed, produces positive externalities and reinforces social cohesion.

6   Interaction with public policies

Social initiatives in the field of disability were being taken prior to the establishment of the welfare state in Spain. When the welfare state was set up, family associations had already created special schools, employment centres and residential accommodation for their relatives. With the development of the welfare state, family associations achieved institutional recognition for the disabilities of their relatives and managed to transform the services they had set up into public services. Consequently, there was a transfer of control from the private sector to the public sector, which included the integration of the special education schools into the public school network. For employment and residential services, an intermediate formula was chosen in that the state financed the employment or residential place but the parents' association continued to act as owners and managers. It is true that in the early days of the welfare state, public authorities invested in new residential accommodation, but in many cases, the preferred route was that of co-operation between the public sector and the organisations of civil society.

In the case of initiatives for work integration of the socially excluded, the partnership between the public sector and the third sector is just beginning to develop and it is still very early to forecast the level of collaboration that public authorities and social enterprises may reach in order to achieve official recognition. An example of lack of collaboration is to be found in regard to public contracts dealing with selective collection of solid waste in large cities. This is an economic activity, which was rediscovered by enterprises for work integration in the 1980s as an economic activity that was well suited to the capacities and skills of persons with social problems. In those years, this was an activity of very little market importance. The major conventional solid waste disposal companies scorned this potential market, and allowed enterprises for work integration to develop. But during the 1990s, social and cultural developments have increased environmental awareness, and the selective collection of solid waste has turned into a large and attractive market for local authorities and traditional businesses. As a consequence, work-integration enterprises lost this market largely because local authorities preferred to give contracts to established companies, since they proposed to mechanise the process. The result is that selective solid waste disposal is now mainly carried out mechanically. In short, when it came to awarding contracts, local officials did not take into account the other added value which social enterprises working in the environmental field provide i.e. the integration of hard-to-place persons.

7   Future perspectives and conclusions

Social enterprises engaged in the field of work integration are business organisations with a social objective, namely, the integration of groups of persons who are systematically excluded from the traditional labour market. In Spain, the leaders of work-integration enterprises who have achieved the best results from their social action are those who understand that the social integration of a person of working age is very often achieved through his/her integration in the ordinary labour market. These leaders are persons who have designed and created enterprises meant to serve such persons. They have noted the therapeutic effect of the execution of a labour contract between the enterprise and the user. They have also noted that if they manage their operation as if it were an ordinary enterprise, open to market competition, their results in their integration activities are better. In fact, these leaders have become entrepreneurs in order to be able to develop their social objectives with greater efficiency. But it has to be emphasised that social leaders of this kind are still very scarce due to the deeply rooted belief that enterprise and social action are somehow incompatible. Even in this sector, concepts of charity from another time still prevail, and although the present work focuses on innovative behaviours on the part of integration enterprises, it has to be remembered that, in this field like in any other, conservative behaviours are still predominant.

As shown by Thake and Zadek (1997), creative and energetic leaders play a vital role in job creation in society. However, our society does not often acknowledge that role, and does not recognise the qualities and the contributions that these leaders make. Very rarely are their efforts supported. On the contrary, institutions often work against them. This is the situation in which social enterprises and their leaders find themselves in Spain. They have no name, and no status. There is no economic information that endorses their successes. They are not part of a single collectivity, and they do not identify with the conventional social economy. They work in isolation, acting as troubleshooters throughout society. Social enterprises have closer relations with their foreign than with their domestic counterparts. Indeed, European initiatives have played a key role for these enterprises and their leaders. They have made it possible to set up cross-border forums through which key ideas on organisational forms and working methodologies can be exchanged. They have contributed – and this is important – towards the raising of awareness of these experiments in Spain.

Spain is a country which is 'democratically young', with a small and only recently developed social services sector. This sector is expected to progressively increase its presence in society as the country's wealth increases. However, its development must adjust to new schemes. The sharing of responsibilities between conventional enterprises and the state has to be redefined and both have to evolve. On the one hand, enterprises must not only be competitive and produce wealth and employment; they must also be open to new entrepreneurial approaches that create more social cohesion. On the other hand, the state must reconsider its role as direct manager of services when these have had unsatisfying results in the fight against the negative effects of unbalanced economic development. Public authorities and society at large must discover that the promotion and consolidation of social enterprises may be an instrument to solve state and market failures. Of course, it is true too that the civil support to social enterprises will be determined by their legitimacy. In this respect, the legal form is not the most important element. What is important is the trust of citizens in these enterprises. In order to achieve this trust, the adoption of a multi-stakeholder structure seems to be of particular importance. Enterprises that solicit institutional support and a favourable tax regime must be able to take into account all those who are involved in one way or another in their activity. Moreover, it is important that enterprises are easily evaluated, and for this reason clear accounting practices are necessary and social audit schemes might be useful. Finally, it has to be stressed that there is still a long way to go before the potential of social enterprises is fully recognised. If it remains undiscovered, an opportunity to advance social well-being will be lost.

Notes

1 This study has been granted financial support from the I+D National Plan of the Science and Technology Inter-ministerial Committee of the Spanish Government (SEC97–1309).
2 Fundación Banco Bilbao Vizcaya, *Proyecto Comparativo del Sector no Lucrativo. España, El País*, 4 de noviembre de 1998.
3 Ministry of Labour and Social Security, Companies registered for Social Security, third quarter of 1999.
4 *AERESS* is a federation which represents twenty-two businesses devoted to the integration, through employment, of persons with negligible or zero employability. The main trading activity of *AERESS* enterprises is concentrated on the selective collection of solid urban waste (paper, glass, clothing, tins and cans, bulky items and batteries), its sorting, recovery and subsequent sale. In 1998, twenty-two enterprises were providing employment to 540 persons who, through their work, achieved a turnover in excess of 1,500 million pesetas (9,015,182 Euro).
5 As already mentioned, this decree governs selective employment and measures to promote the employment of people with disabilities.

Bibliography

BALLET, J. (1997) *Les entreprises d'insertion*, Presses Universitaires de France, Coll. 'Que sais-je?', Paris.

BORZAGA, C. and MITTONE, L. (1997) 'The Multi-Stakeholder versus the Non-Profit Organisation', Discussion Paper no. 7, Dipartimento di Economia, Università degli Studi di Trento.

CES (*Consejo Económico y Social*) (1995) *Informe 5 sobre la situación del empleo de las personas con discapacidad y propuestas para su reactivación*, Madrid.

CIES (1999) 'Informe Socio-Económico de las empresas miembros de la Asociación Española de Recuperadores de la Economía Social y Solidaria 1997–98', Barcelona, (mimeo).

——(1998) 'AERESS Report', Barcelona, (mimeo).

DEFOURNY, J., FAVREAU, L. and LAVILLE, J.-L. (eds) (1998) *Insertion et nouvelle économie sociale. Un bilan international*, Desclée de Brouwer, Paris.

GAGLIARDI, P. (ed.) (1991) *Le imprese come culture. Nuove prospettive di analisi organizzativa*, ISEDI-ISTUD, Turin.

HIRSCHMAN, A.O. (1970) *Exit, Voice and Loyalty*, Harvard University Press, Cambridge, MA.

LEVI, Y. (1997) 'Rethinking the For-Profit vs. Non-Profit Argument: a Social Enterprise Perspective', International Research Centre on Rural Co-operative Communities, CIRCOM, Israel.

PESTOFF, V.A. (1998) *Beyond the Market and State – Social Entreprises and Civil Democracy in a Welfare Society*, Ashgate, Aldershot.

——(1997) *Social Enterprises and Civil Democracy in Sweden. Enriching Work Environment and Empowering Citizens as Co-Producers*, School of Business, Stockholm.

THAKE, S. and ZADEK, S. (1997) *Practical People, Noble Causes. How To Support Community-based Social Entrepreneurs*, New Economic Foundation, London.

VIDAL, I. (1998) 'Espagne: Une nouvelle économie sociale encore mal connue et reconnue', in DEFOURNY, J., FAVREAU, L. and LAVILLE, J.-L. (eds) *Insertion et nouvelle économie sociale. Un bilan international*, Desclée de Brouwer, Paris, 229–44.

—— (ed.) (1996) *Inserción social por el trabajo. Una visión internacional*, CIES, Barcelona.

13 Sweden

The emergence of work-integration social enterprises

Yohanan Stryjan

Introduction

It is commonly thought that the Swedish third sector is not very developed because of the existence of an extensive welfare state, but reality differs from this widespread perception. In fact, the Swedish third sector consists of some 200,000 organisations that manage an aggregated input of nearly 400,000 man-years of paid or voluntary labour – a volume that is fully comparable with that of other Western European countries (Lundström and Wijkström 1998). However, the sector's activity profile and the associations which characterise it differ from their European counterparts. Traditionally, Swedish third-sector organisations engaged primarily in the fields of culture, leisure, adult education and interest representation. Relatively few organisations were engaged in actual production of goods or welfare services (Stryjan and Wijkström 1996). The institutional roots of this situation will be outlined in the opening sections of this chapter.

The crisis and transformation of the 'Swedish model' from the 1980s onwards prompted the emergence of new populations of organisations, and a gradual reorientation of traditional ones. Emergent third-sector organisations account for a significant part of service provision within child day-care (Pestoff 1998) and care for the seriously handicapped. This chapter will focus mainly on organisations working in the field of employability. This is the newest field of third-sector expansion, marked by the strong growth dynamic of an emerging population of social co-operatives on the one hand, and the changing attitudes and features of the public administration on the other. It is marked by a high rate of social entrepreneurship and organisational innovation, but also by a high degree of legal and conceptual ambiguity.

1 Defining the field: state, welfare and charity

The particular composition of the Swedish third sector and its societal positioning arose in an institutional development path that involved the (re)positioning of state, welfare and charity within the emerging welfare state. In pre-Reformation Sweden charity was, as in most European countries of the period, a prime concern for the church. By coupling church and state, the Swedish Reformation indirectly introduced the idea of public administration of welfare. Poverty relief and, eventually, public health and education as well were entrusted to the parish councils (Gullstrand 1930), thus laying the conceptual and legal foundations for a future public sector.[1] An emerging urban artisan and middle class introduced mutual social insurance arrangements in the beginning of the eighteenth century. Charitable societies entered the field of poverty relief as well, from 1810 onwards. Their contribution was soon contested by other agencies, namely by the parish councils evolving into local government organs with a rudimentary welfare agenda, and by emerging social movements with a strong emphasis on mutuality and self-help. The first of these emerging social movements was the temperance movement in the early 1830s. The trend culminated, from 1870 on, in the formation of the major popular mass movements and new associations, including the free churches, the labour movement, consumer co-operatives, the sports movement, and the adult education institutes.[2] All these laid the foundations for a strong third sector. The broad array of welfare services initiated, and originally run by these organisations, played a central role in the evolution of the welfare state.

The lines of demarcation between the state, popular movements and voluntary/charitable organisations were redrawn in the twentieth century. Many social welfare activities previously carried out by philanthropic organisations declined in importance with the advent of mutual-help initiatives and the expansion of public welfare programmes. Central welfare activities were eventually taken over by the state, not infrequently on the initiative or with the approval of the organisations themselves. This was particularly the case for co-operative organisations that saw in the emerging welfare state a superior implementation of the principle of mutuality. This realignment was accomplished in a largely smooth manner.[3]

The mature Swedish societal model's best-known characteristic is that of a universal and comprehensive welfare state, with a broad array of welfare services administered and produced by the public sector (Stryjan 1994). Underlying this model is a basically corporatist division of tasks among the organised societal sectors: the state, the business community and the popular movements. In this division, the business community (*näringslivet*) stands for production and accumulation (Erixon 1996); the state administers (re)distribution (Abrahamsson and Broström 1980) and this increasingly came to encompass production of welfare; and the popular movements are expected to focus on the articulation of interests, and on central aspects of consumption. Their direct role in the provision of services was traded, as it were, for an institutionalised position of influence over the ongoing expansion of the public sector. Already identified and sanctioned needs were, in most cases, handled by the public sector. The tacit assumption was that third-sector organisations would, of their own accord, identify and mobilise to meet whatever social need had not yet been met, acting as a pathfinder and a corrective, and managing activities that, by their nature, were difficult to regulate in detail. New movements established in the post-war period, such as immigrant organisations (Bäck 1983) and organisations for medical patients and handicapped persons (Holgersson 1992), positioned themselves within these pre-established lines.

2   Organisational and legal forms

Key terms: public benefit versus charity and non-profit

The term 'charity' does exist in Swedish, but is used solely to denote social welfare (Blennberger 1993; James 1989; Kuhnle and Selle 1992; Qvarsell 1993). The Swedish usage has clearly negative connotations (Qvarsell 1993; Stryjan 1994). This derogatory attitude, initially propagated by the labour movement, and outspokenly shared by the movement of the handicapped, has obviously been internalised by the charitable organisations themselves. A recent survey of voluntary organisations (Lundström and Wijkström 1994) shows that, though nearly 8 per cent of all respondents could have denoted themselves (by internationally accepted criteria) as charitable organisations, none chose to do so. Even internationally oriented charitable organisations eschew the charity label, and prefer to be regarded as part of a social movement. Hardly surprisingly, the category 'charitable organisations' is normally lacking in Swedish statistics (Boli 1991, 1992).

Typically, the term 'non-profit' has no direct correspondent in Swedish. In the absence of any sort of preferential tax or contracting rights, the need to define boundary specifications for non-profits never arose in Sweden. Instead, a concept of general/public benefit (*almännytta*), also applicable to semi-public undertakings (e.g. in the field of public utilities), is applied in Swedish legislation. Organisations that provide benefits to their members may, according to this rationale, be considered as providing a public benefit if they observe the rule of openness. The term 'popular movement' (*folkrörelse*), often assumed by larger third-sector organisations, implicitly connects with this perception.

Legal forms: association and foundation

Three legal incorporation forms are commonly resorted to by organisations within the Swedish third sector: (1) foundation (*stiftelse*),[4] (2) *ideell* (or non-profit) association; and (3) economic association (Stryjan and Wijkström 1996). Co-operatives do not exist as a distinct category of legal entity. Generally, co-operatives incorporate under one of the two association forms, most commonly as economic associations. It would be possible to incorporate a co-operative as a joint-stock company (Stryjan 1989) and, theoretically, even as a foundation, though these alternatives are rarely resorted to.

An association is created when a number of individuals (or legal entities), in organised forms and for a set period of time or until further notice, co-operate towards a common objective (Hemström 1992). The Swedish legal notion of an association has a stronger collectivistic emphasis than other legal traditions (Boli 1991, 1992). There is no common legal definition of an association in Swedish law (Mallmén 1989) and it is necessary to distinguish further between two categories: the economic and the *ideell* (roughly voluntary) association.

The Law on Economic Associations[5] defines an economic association as a joint endeavour of natural and/or legal persons/members with the aim of promoting the economic interest of the members through economic activity in which they participate as consumers, suppliers, providers of their own labour, service recipients, or in any other appropriate way.[6] The Rochdale principles of open membership, one-member-one-vote democracy, limited return on invested capital, and dividend by members' patronage were assimilated into the law (Rodhe 1988). Most co-operatives adopt the legal form of economic association, and the terms economic association and co-operative are used in a nearly interchangeable manner by co-operators and politicians alike.

The term *ideell förening* could roughly be translated as private non-profit association (Hemström 1972). Generally speaking, an association that does not meet the twin criteria of: (1) engaging in business activity; and (2) economically benefiting its members, is automatically regarded as an *ideell* association. The Swedish system treats both trade unions and associations of employers as *ideell* associations (Bäck 1980). This association form is not regulated in existing law. In actual legal practice, however, legislation on economic associations is applied as a default norm for all associations. Thus, for instance, the one-member-one-vote rule would be assumed to apply to an *ideell* association unless there is evidence/explicit provision to the contrary in the association's articles/charter.

The two forms of association are suitable, in principle, for co-operative organisations. However, only the economic association form provides the protection of a limited liability provision.[7] This makes it a natural choice for any co-operative with sizeable economic activity. The economic association form does not in any way enforce a non-profit constraint, nor does it impede commercial for-profit operations. In fact, it explicitly endorses it insofar as an association that fails to specify the economic interests that it is intended to promote, may even be denied registration. Some of the central features of the three forms are summarised in Table 13.1.

As the table illustrates, the legal system can be neatly divided between social and economic (risk-taking) objectives. Co-operatives are seen as fully-fledged business actors but, generally, they are not considered as serving the general interest. *Ideell* associations, on the other hand, are expected to refrain from entrepreneurial activity.

Tax exemptions, whenever awarded, are activity specific. An association may thus be entitled to tax exemptions (from corporate profit tax and property tax) on activities that are judged as salient to its core activity, and be fully taxed on activities that are judged as purely entrepreneurial. Until the last decade, these rules effectively precluded the formation of social enterprises, and channelled the resourcefulness of organisations within the sector (with the exception of the most affluent ones) into economically low-risk fields, such as political action, or the articulation of group demands and interests.

Table 13.1   Characteristics of foundations and associations

		Legal form	
Characteristics	*Foundation*	*Economic association*	*Ideell association*
Legal definition	Yes	Yes	No
Capital required	Yes	No	No
Members	None	Required	Required
Articles/charter	Yes	Yes	Yes
Democratic governance	No	Mandatory	Encouraged
Registration	Necessary	Necessary	Optional
Limited liability provision in commercial operations	No	Yes	No[a]
Profit aim	No	Yes	No
Priority/exclusivity for social/charitable aims	Yes	No	Yes

Note: [a] In practice, this means that in a case of bankruptcy due to unsuccessful business operations, the members of the board may find themselves personally liable

3   The third sector and employment

A few years ago, third-sector organisations employed about 100,000 persons – a little less than 2.3 per cent of the country's labour force.[8] Employment in the third sector is estimated at 83,000 FTE (full-time equivalents).[9] The direct contribution of most established organisations to the employment of excluded groups and to labour-market insertion is, none the less, rather low. The overwhelming majority of those employed by third-sector organisations are, on the contrary, professionally trained personnel, and less skilled tasks are often carried out by voluntary labour. Significantly, the volume of voluntary work is estimated at 300,000 FTE, i.e. over three times the volume of employed personnel (Wijkström 1994). This situation results from, and reflects, the conviction that voluntary organisations should keep their involvement in the labour market as low as possible.

The Swedish traditional division of responsibilities in the employment field acknowledged the role of two, and only two, actors: the government as a facilitator of job creation and the business community (*näringslivet*) as an actual creator of jobs (Stryjan and Wijkström 1998a). This division of labour virtually cut off voluntary organisations from job creation in the ordinary sense of the term, and from state support for such initiatives on the sector's behalf. While state interference in industrial crises – through direct support, subventions and local governments' business-friendly policies – was routinely motivated by job-creation arguments, support for third-sector organisations was largely conditional on it *not* generating any jobs. Subsidised workers were, in principle, not to be used for tasks that could have been carried out by commercial organisations. Organisations using subsidised labour, it was argued, would be distorting competition. In other words, a job within the sector could be publicly financed (wholly or partly) only if it was possible to prove that it was not really in demand. Throughout the 1970s and the 1980s, social enterprises' impact in the field of job creation was confined to marginal cases and non-market jobs, mostly under various temporary job-placement programmes for the long-time unemployed, such as *ALU*-placements (acronym for working-life development). Küchen (1994) notes that associations resorted to such manpower programmes to a much higher degree than did other organisations. The highest rate (1.1 *ALU* placement job per one regular employee) was observed in organisations of interest groups. In other words, commercial enterprises were clearly less motivated to avail themselves of the available manpower, subsidies notwithstanding. Significantly, a government report of the period (Statskontoret 1994) considers this high rate of job placements as a token of inefficiency and of dependence on state support, rather than as an expression of a social commitment and willingness to employ the otherwise unemployable.

The fairly rigid societal division of tasks and domains described above has been somewhat eroded in the course of the last two decades. Grassroots involvement led to the appearance, in the early 1980s, of the first social enterprises in the field of local development. Towards the mid 1980s, a national network of co-operative development agencies emerged, aided by a growing involvement of the established popular movements (Stryjan and Wijkström 1998a). From the mid 1990s onwards, this infrastructure has proved instrumental in the development of initiatives aimed at new – or newly acknowledged – problem groups, namely residents of problematic suburbs, young unemployed, and immigrants (*SOU* 1996). Rather than integration or job creation in the narrow sense of the term, these initiatives are geared towards creating a blend of voluntary labour and regular jobs, often within emergent small businesses. In keeping with the Swedish organisational tradition, a strong emphasis is placed on mutuality and self-reliance. The growth pattern followed is, generally, that of proliferation rather than expansion (Stryjan 1996), i.e. it facilitates the formation of new organisations in emerging fields, rather than the expansion and diversification of established ones.

4   Social co-operatives

A new and highly interesting field for co-operative activity, which will be outlined below, is the rehabilitation and employment of those excluded from the labour market due to mental illness or other functional impairments. A closer examination of the relationship between exclusion and unemployment in the Swedish model can help to clarify some of the features of this field, and the fact that it has not previously been claimed by other organisations. Full employment was (and in many respects, still is) a central element in the normative core of the Swedish model (Stryjan and Wijkström 1998a), linking, as it were, welfare entitlements that are employment-based with a norm of general welfare. The existence of permanently unemployable groups could not be easily accommodated into the model (Stryjan and Wijkström 1996) and unemployment was programmatically seen as a frictional phenomenon or – at the individual level – as a passing affliction, to be remedied by the labour market policy organs.

The welfare state thus assumes a double role in the field of employment. Primarily, it is responsible for facilitating (re)integration in the labour market for those (implicitly) deemed employable, a function that originally also included the creation of sheltered workplaces and wage-subsidised placements for the handicapped. An array of measures, ranging from hospitalisation to long-duration sick-leave and early retirement, for those still marginalised, inadvertently institutionalises the exclusion of those who were not deemed employable. These measures, while guaranteeing subsistence, also bar or penalise the options of creating one's own income, or of re-entering the labour market. It could thus be said that the system enshrines having a job as a keystone of individual identity while at the same time excluding some categories from ever attaining it.

The problem became increasingly visible in the mid 1980s, as the public sector embarked on an ambitious policy of mental healthcare reform including the phasing out of big mental health institutions. Emancipatory aspirations and growing militancy on the part of patient organisations correlated well with advances in the field of psycho-pharmaceutics and with growing concerns for hospitalisation costs. Laudable intentions notwithstanding, the effort and resources invested in creating alternative frameworks for the released patients were quite insufficient. At about the same time, the admission practices of *SAMHALL* (the public sheltered workplace system) became increasingly selective, further reducing the options available for patients with mental illnesses. Though ensuring physical subsistence, the authorities thus generally failed to provide an acceptable social context for the persons involved. For the first time in the Swedish model's history, a highly visible problem group was (re)created and released into society.

A first effort to address this issue by organising worker co-operatives for patients with mental illnesses was initiated in 1989 by persons involved in the field of mental health care, including care personnel, patients and ex-patients. Typically, a co-operative consisted of five to fifteen users and one to two instructors each.[10] The *Psyk-Ädel* reform of mental care, which transferred responsibility for psychiatric care from county authorities to municipalities, created a new situation. The municipalities, now in charge of psychiatric outpatient care and of ex-patients' rehabilitation, were less bound by mental healthcare traditions and by budget allocation regulations and, as a consequence, they were also more open to new solutions. At this juncture, the idea of promoting co-operative forms as a means of social reintegration and empowerment was taken over by institutional actors within the third sector. These were the co-operative development agencies – *LKUs*, organised in a national association, *FKU* (Stryjan and Wijkström, 1998a) – mental health organisations (which engaged in propagating the co-operative model among prospective users/members) and the folk high schools (*folkhögskolor*) movement. The latter started local courses in co-operation for potential participants, in partnership with *LKUs*. The social co-operative model was also advocated, with considerable success, in the organisations' contacts with municipalities and with labour-market authorities.

At the moment, there are about seventy functioning social worker co-operatives for former mental patients and the functionally handicapped throughout Sweden. The number of members is estimated at about 900.[11] The exact organisational details and the degree of binding to the respective municipalities, as well as the financing structures, vary greatly from case to case. Some of the basic features of these organisations are discussed below.

Organisation and governance

All co-operatives in this field of activity are incorporated either as economic associations or as *ideell* associations.[12] New organisations are often established on a project basis and may lack, to start with, any incorporation whatsoever (the potential and limitations of the project format will be discussed in section 5).

Typically, a co-operative would consist of one to two tutors (*handledare*), and five to six users per tutor. Considerable deviations from this standard exist. The ratio may be as low as 1:12, and as high as 1:3, depending on the orientation and the type of activity. At least one co-operative (*Vildrosen* in Växjö), manages its activity without any tutors at all.

A considerable proportion of the members are former mental patients. However, the tendency has increasingly been towards recruitment on the basis of life-situation rather than medical diagnosis. The forms of initial recruitment vary from case to case, depending on whether the co-operative emerged spontaneously or on an external initiative. Once established, co-operatives generally take in new members by vote, usually after a trial period. In many cases, tutors are expected to apply for membership.

In accordance with Swedish legislation on associations (see above), the co-operative's finances, recruitment and internal affairs are managed by an elected board. The 'one member-one vote' rule applies. Tutors may not be elected to the board, but they are often appointed to management positions. In at least one case, a double governance structure was created, with a co-operative of users commissioning the services of a worker co-operative of tutors.

Entrepreneurial features

The co-operatives in the group produce a broad range of goods and services, including the running of a staff restaurant in a medium-sized company, renovation of windows, cleaning, and industrial assembly. Handicraft is consciously avoided by most co-operatives.[13] Work is normally organised in work groups supported by tutors. The turnover of the enterprises' commercial operations varies considerably, from about 1.26 million SEK (150,000 Euro), for the most entrepreneurially oriented, to a few thousand, for those whose chief emphasis is on providing a social context.

The definition and comparison of economic performance encounter a number of technical problems insofar as an enterprise can be seen as a nexus of contracts and transactions. Transactions that are carried out through this nexus can be said to be included in the enterprise. Those transactions that bypass the nexus (e.g. direct transfer payments to participants, rather than to the enterprise) would, obviously, not be included in the enterprise's balance sheet. Sales revenues and material costs are two elements that are handled in a conventional business manner by all social co-operatives. Other major components that may be included in the enterprise's resource package are members' income/wages, tutors' wages, disposal of surplus, and rental of premises. They are included in some cases, and omitted in others.[14] The considerable local variation in the ways that such boundary lines are drawn foils any effort at providing aggregated or comparative economic statistics across the population of social co-operatives.

Most social co-operatives aspire to remunerate their members' work with regular wages. However, only a minority attains this goal. Existing regulations inhibit direct conversion of individual transfer payments (such as sick pay, retirement, etc.) into wage supplements payable to members via the enterprise. In most cases, members' incomes have thus to be provided for by income guarantee payments which bypass the co-operative. Existing rules preclude the payment of part-time wages as well and a member's personal income may actually decrease due to the threshold effects that the rather inflexible rules generate.[15] The economic thresholds that this rule regime establishes are insurmountable for any but the best performing enterprises.

In a large portion of the cases, tutors are municipal employees on municipal payrolls. Tutors may also be self-employed through a worker co-operative that is directly contracted to the municipality. In the cases where tutors are employed by the co-operative, the municipality reimburses between 50 per cent and 100 per cent of the expense, with the balance being covered either by the co-operative's surplus or by funding from other public bodies.

Premises are normally rent free, which is to say that rent is paid directly to the landlord by the local authority. In one of the cases studied, premises were provided by a private company.[16] In another case (*Vildrosen*, Växjö), the municipality covers only a part of the rent; the balance is covered by revenues generated by the co-operative. Other cost-sharing arrangements (both permanent and project-based) exist.

As the foregoing illustrates, both the co-operatives' economic results and the financial support they receive are largely a matter of definition. For the time being, there is no ready institutionalised model for financing the operation, or for defining its component parts. Existing co-operatives are run on an *ad hoc* basis and mobilise support in different forms and from various sources. Support for a co-operative may be explicit – as reimbursement of expenses – or implicit.

Explicit support may be granted for expenses directly borne by the co-operative. Thus, a co-operative that pays wages may be eligible for wage-supplement funds from the labour-market authorities. Similarly, co-operatives that pay rent for their premises are likely to receive reimbursement, primarily from municipal authorities, for all or part of the expense they incur. The same applies to tutors' salaries. Incoming support (or the corresponding fee for rehabilitation services) would naturally be reflected in the enterprise's turnover.

Implicit support is rendered if the expense is directly borne by another actor, wholly bypassing the co-operative (e.g placing the tutors on the municipal payroll, or providing premises free of charge). Implicit support leaves no trace in the co-operative's balance sheet and indirectly diminishes the operation's visible economic scope. A prospective donor's choice between different forms of support may be swayed by taxation considerations.[17]

Naturally, the definition of economic results is contingent on the way the co-operative's expenses and sources of income are defined. In the existing rule system, a path of lesser resistance is often chosen insofar as members receive no wages, and the surplus generated is spent either on common undertakings, on investments or (within strict limits) as an income supplement. Since the enterprises discussed here are, as a rule, labour intensive, the shadow wages received (in the form of subsistence grants directly awarded/paid by the authorities) distort information on economic performance, and make comparisons to other enterprises difficult.

Relationship to the local community

The social co-operatives' contribution to the local community and to the formation of social capital varies from case to case. Available descriptions indicate, however, that most co-operatives concentrate on services to the local population[18] or to other SMEs in the immediate surroundings. They may for example run a workplace canteen or a cafeteria in an industrial park. Relations to customers are, in this case, clearly personalised, and contribute to the creation of social links between the co-operative and its social environment.

On the whole, commercial activity is not aimed at large businesses, and hardly at all towards the public sector. Whether deliberately or by default, their strategy seems to be focused on generating a tighter social network for the co-operative and its members. *Projektet arbetskooperativ* in Norrtälje (which recently evolved into a cluster of co-operatives) provides one of the most interesting examples of such strategies.[19] One of the project's groups, *servicepoolen*, offers auxiliary services (cleaning, repairs, building maintenance, etc) to farmers, house owners and small firms in the small town and vicinity. *Servicepoolen* originally consisted of three teams, each with an (employed) team leader. The three team instructors are tradesmen and former small entrepreneurs that had to leave the labour market for health reasons.

A customer survey[20] showed that most customers learned about *servicepoolen* primarily through personal contacts. All but two (of twenty-two) respondents found the quality of services good or very good and would contact *servicepoolen* again on similar occasions. In about one third of the cases, the job in question would not have been done at all had *servicepoolen* not been available. It is difficult to determine whether this statement proves the co-operative's competitive advantage or is an illustration of community support. Keeping in mind the reserved attitude to charity in Swedish society, this ambiguity may well be intentional, and deliberately maintained by all parties in the relationship.

5   Problems and prospects

Social co-operatives are a relatively recent and not yet fully established newcomer to the expanding population of third-sector organisations that operate in the borderland of the Swedish public sector. The development paths adopted and the problems encountered by this group (the latter were touched upon in a previous section) closely resemble those met (and partly overcome) by earlier entrants into this field, such as parent co-operative kindergartens, Independent Living co-operatives etc. The trends discussed in the closing sections are, therefore, relevant to the entire population.

Prospects for future expansion

The social co-operative organisational form has now made its first steps on the path to institutionalisation, as the isolated local initiatives that gave rise to the first social co-operatives gradually link together into a network. An essentially similar strategy was pursued by other emergent groups, from the 1980s onwards. A national association, connecting the social co-operatives and providing a channel for exchange of experiences and a base for further expansion is presently being established. In parallel, a national education project, developed jointly by *FKU* (the national association of *LKUs*) and *RIFS* (a foundation established by two major mental patients' organisations)[21] started in 1998. The project is also supported by the national association of municipal governments, and has been joined by over thirty municipalities. The project contracts local branches of adult-education movements to develop and administer schooling programmes for would-be co-operative members/users on the one hand, and for municipal administrators in the fields of health and welfare on the other. The project marks an important step in the dissemination of the model among users and administrators alike, and provides an arena for discussing – and experimenting with – the reform of the existing rule systems.

Rule systems

Social co-operatives operate at the intersection of the market and the public sector and are, to a high degree, influenced by the rules that regulate transfer of resources between the two spheres. Co-operatives in the field of welfare attained the right to convert welfare entitlements (which, in the Swedish welfare system generally are disbursed in kind, as services delivered by public institutions) into monetary ones[22] that may be pooled together by the users. Social co-operatives are seldom allowed to accomplish this transformation since social security entitlements (even when monetary) are strictly individual and situation bound, rather than transferable and needs bound, and cannot be capitalised or pooled together under existing regulations. The result is somewhat anomalous to the extent that in most social co-operatives the users are the only participant category that contributes voluntary labour, while tutors receive wages, and other stakeholders relate to the co-operative through contractual/market agreements. In other words, the symbolic transformation of resources – from need to entitlement, and from entitlement to funding of a more acceptable societal status[23] – effected by the co-operatives, has been less than complete. Co-operative members did attain the right to work and to engage in entrepreneurial activity, but only a minority attained the more central right to receive wages for their labour. Welfare-service co-operatives, such as parent co-operative kindergartens and co-operatives for the seriously handicapped, did manage to overcome similar limitations in the 1980s. Whether the social co-operatives, with their limited resources, will make such an impact remains an open question. Ongoing experimentation with new ways of implementing existing regulations within municipal governments and labour-market authorities gives some room for optimism on this count.

Project organisations

Many of the social co-operatives were initially started as projects. Some of them still maintain this status. In the field of social services, the project form has traditionally been perceived as an exception to the norm, while the status of permanent organisation was seen as the objective to be eventually attained by successful projects. The *STIL* co-operative, for example, which implemented an innovative way of managing individual entitlements, initially emerged as a project but was granted permanent status after two years' operation (Stryjan 1994). The same path has recently been followed by the Norrtälje project, discussed above. The general trend is, however, towards increased prominence of the provisional status, i.e. a growth in the population of strictly time-limited projects and an increasing reliance on project tenders on the part of permanent organisations. This proliferation of temporary organisations (Lundin 1998; March 1995) is perhaps the most significant feature of the field at present. To some extent, this trend towards the project format is facilitated by the fact that temporary organisations are increasingly feasible, as information technology and the increasing institutionalisation of the organisational field both contribute to lower the transaction costs of establishing and winding down organisations (Stryjan 1996). There are also weighty institutional forces driving this development insofar as projects proliferate mainly because they are the form of organised activity that authorities are most willing to finance at present.

The project format is a convenient vehicle for transcending administrative limits, without having to formally modify them. Consequently, it is often employed as a mechanism for testing novel administrative routines. It creates something of an institutional safe haven from conventional budgetary time constraints and (in the case of social co-operatives) rigid pension and social security rules, and permits more flexible task specifications – an important advantage for innovative initiatives. Unlike conventional organisations, projects have a pre-programmed date of expiry. This localises risk and provides a degree of control over the organisational product, and no overt (and potentially politically embarrassing) action by administrators is required to terminate undesirable results. Project organisations provide a compromise between the administrative conceptions of time (as circular and budget-ruled), entitlement (as strictly universal and rule bound) and risk and those which are socially engendered. Thus, the project format enables social initiatives to transcend some important limitations of the public financing system and opens new perspectives for the development of social co-operatives.

These advantages are, however, achieved at a price, both for the social initiatives involved, and for the system as a whole. The shift to project formats means that the recurring uncertainty inherent in periodic budget negotiation is being replaced by a relationship that is unambiguous, but strictly time limited. Uncertainty is not eliminated, but traded off for discontinuity, i.e uncertainty of a higher order, as it were. The implications of this trade-off may be far-reaching. The potential comparative advantage of social enterprises normally lies in their embededdness in the surrounding community. Embeddedness, in its turn, generates trust and presupposes continuity and credibility in the belief that rendered services could be reciprocated in the future. The provisional, discontinuous nature of project undertakings largely negates this dimension.

As the present cohort of projects and experimental organisations approaches the end of their project lives, they may be allowed to graduate into a permanent status – a solution that may involve some modification of the established administrative routines. Conversely, they may simply be phased out and give way to a new batch of projects. Depending on which of the competing scenarios are pursued, current development may give rise to a new and growing population of social co-operatives. Alternatively, they may transform the field into an emerging project (quasi) market, in which social initiatives would be stripped of their unique advantages, and reduced to a format in which public authorities and corporate actors compete for project funding. The key comparative advantages in such a market would be administrative resources and institutional connections, rather than trust and embeddedness. Such a scenario may lead to a commoditisation of the field of reinsertion and job creation, giving rise to a quasi-market for labour-market services, in which public organs and for-profit companies engage in cherry-picking and compete for lucrative projects and the most promising participants. In such a market, the core activity of future social entrepreneurs may be the spawning and administration of projects.

6   Conclusions and implications

The field of social co-operatives is evolving rapidly and the organisations now being founded exist in different institutional set-ups to their predecessors, and are substantially different from them. Projections of future trends that are based on surveys of existing organisations are not fully reliable. Case studies are an important instrument for the assessment of possible future and emerging trends.

The major forces that shape the field at present are the strong growth dynamics of an emerging population of social co-operatives on one hand, and the changing attitudes and features of public administration on the other. This highlights the importance of not only educating activists within the sector but also of educating public administrators. The introduction of the project form and of market mechanisms into the field facilitates the creation of more flexible and innovative solutions, but it also carries a risk of (re)marginalising precisely those actors whose interests this development was intended to promote. The outcome of the ongoing process will depend, to a great extent, on whether successful experiments will be allowed to crystallise into stable organisations. Those public organs that will be acting as gatekeepers in the process will require new, more comprehensible auditing and evaluating tools, criteria and practices.

Notes

1 The emergence of the parish (*socken*) as the basic unit of local government, and administration of welfare/charity (Gullstrand 1930), is highly illustrative in this respect. The reorganisation of local government in the mid-nineteenth century was initiated by the Committee on Poverty Relief (*Fattigvårdkommitéen*) of 1837. The differentiation of local self-government and parish organs was accomplished first in 1862.

2 The labour movement as well as consumer co-operatives were formed just before 1900. The Social Democratic Party was founded in 1889, and the Swedish Trade Union Confederation ten years later.

3 Stryjan and Wijkström (1996). Exceptions exist though: some services run by non-profit organisations were forced out of business (Qvarsell 1993); others remained, despite central government's aspirations (Stenius 1995).

4 See Norin and Wessman (1993). The total number of foundations in Sweden is estimated at about 50,000. They represent a considerable amount of accumulated wealth. It has been estimated that they control assets of nearly 50,000 billion SEK (about 5,950 billion Euro) (Lundström and Wijkström 1998).

5 Law on Economic Associations (Lag 1987: 667 *om ekonomiska föreningar*).

6 Economic associations active in the financial sector are governed by special legislation, and are not relevant to the concept of the non-profit sector (Hemström 1992; Mallmén 1989; Rodhe 1988).

7 *Ideell* associations are covered only conditionally. If the association engages in purely commercial operations, board members may be personally liable for the association's debts.

8 This figure does not fully discount extremely short part-time assignments, and probably overestimates the sector's labour-force share somewhat.

9 Lundström and Wijkström (1998). These figures do not include the commercial operations of consumer and farmer co-operatives.

10 At its height, the group numbered twenty-five co-operatives. Many of these were, however, therapeutic rather than enterprising, and only eight survived the *Psyk-Ädel* reform of psychiatric healthcare in the 1990s. For a brief description of the first of these co-operatives, *Samverkarna*, see Stryjan and Wijkström (1996).

11 Information from Eva Laurelii, Kooperativ Konsult, Gothenburg, February 1999.

12 Information from Eva Laurelii, Kooperativ Konsult, Gothenburg, Eva Johansson, KIC Stockholm, and Bosse Blideman, KUR.

13 Among the motives given were the fact that the added value was low and the wish to distance oneself from typical occupational therapy activities.

14 No information is available on investments in production equipment.

15 According to early-pension rules currently in operation, pensions would be reduced by 25 per cent once earnings exceed a minimum amount that lies well below 25 per cent of the pension. Reporting a small income may thus result in a direct income loss.

16 The company is *Marks Pelle Vävare* in Borås, whose canteen is run by the *Gryningen* co-operative.

17 For example, donations in kind are *de facto* tax deductible for firms, but not for individuals. Monetary donations are not tax-deductible, while sponsoring is, etc. The arithmetic becomes even more complex where VAT and payroll taxes are involved. For authorities, a budgetary allocation for wages is 33 per cent higher than for a pension of the same amount, etc.
18 For example second-hand bookstore, car washing, dog-kennel.
19 This information is based on own interviews, information from Bosse Blideman, then at KUR, and documentation (in draft) prepared by *Biometri Ek. För.*
20 By *Biometri Analys Ek. För.*, in draft.
21 *RSMH*, the National Association for Social and Mental Health, and *IFS*, *Intresseförbundet för Schizofreni.*
22 The procedure applied in the case of co-operative kindergartens was discussed in Stryjan (1994).
23 A transformation of this type, from handicapped client in need of assistance to employer was described in Stryjan (1994).

Bibliography

ABRAHAMSSON, B. and BROSTRÖM, A. (1980) *The Rights of Labour*, Sage, Beverly Hills, London.

BÄCK, H. (1983) *Invandrarnas riksorganisationer*, Liber, Stockholm.

——(1980) *Partier och organisationer i Sverige*, Liber Förlag, Stockholm.

BLENNBERGER, E. (1993) 'Begrepp och modeller', in *SOU* (*Statens Offentliga Utredningar*, Public State Reports), no. 1993: 82, Allmänna Förlaget, Stockholm.

BOLI, J. (1992) 'The Ties That Bind: The Non-profit Sector and the State in Sweden', in MC CARTHY, K.D. *et al.* (eds) *The Non-profit Sector in the Global Community*, Jossey Bass, San Francisco, 240–54.

——(1991) 'Sweden: Is There a Viable Third Sector?', in WUTHNOW, R. (ed.) *Between States and Markets. The Voluntary Sector in Comparative Perspective*, Princeton University Press, Princeton.

BRUNSSON, N. and BENGT J. (eds) (1982) *Lokal mobilisering. Om industriers kommunalpolitik och kommuners industripolitik*, Doxa, Lund.

ERIXON, L. (1996) 'The Golden Age of the Swedish Model. The Coherence Between Capital Accumulation and Economic Policy in Sweden in the Early Post-war Period', Department of Economics, University of Stockholm.

GOUGH, R., BJUHR, M. and PALM, P. (1991) *Inget självständigt liv utan personlig assistans*, Arbetslivscentrum, Stockholm.

GULLSTRAND, R. (1930) 'Svensk kommunalkunskap', in *Kunskap*, Bonniers, Stockholm, 380–415.

HEMSTRÖM, C. (1992) *Organisationernas rättsliga ställning. Om ekonomiska och ideella föreningar*, Norstedts juridik, Lund.

——(1972) *Uteslutning ur ideell förening*, PA Norstedt and Söners Förlag, Stockholm.

HOLGERSSON, L. (1992) *Socialtjänst – Lagtexter med kommentarer i historisk belysning*, Tiden, Stockholm.

JAMES, E. (1989) 'The Private Provision of Public Services: A Comparison of Sweden and Holland', in JAMES, E. (ed.) *The Non-Profit Sector in International Perspective. Studies in Comparative Culture and Policy*, Oxford University Press, New York, 30–61.

KÜCHEN, T. (1994) 'Ny kooperation och den offentliga sektorn', in ALÉX *et al.* (eds) *Kooperation och välfärd*, Kooperativa Studier, Stockholm, 53–68.

KUHNLE, S. and SELLE, P. (1992) *Government and Voluntary Organisations*, Avebury, Aldershot.

LUNDIN, R.A. (1998) 'Temporära organisationer', in CZARNIAWSKA, B. (ed.) *Organisationsteori på svenska*, Liber Ekonomi, Malmö.

LUNDSTRÖM, T. and WIJKSTRÖM, F. (1998) *The Swedish Non-profit Sector*, Manchester University Press, Manchester.

——(1994) 'The Swedish Non-profit Sector', EFI Research Report, Ekonomiska Forskningsinstitutet, Stockholm.

MALLMÉN, A. (1989) *Lagen om ekonomiska föreningar*, Norstedts Förlag, Stockholm.

MARCH, G. (1995) 'The Future, Disposable Organizations and the Rigidities of Imagination', *Organization*, vol. 2 (3/4): 427–40.

NORIN, M. and WESSMAN, L. (1993) *Stiftelser – den nya lagstiftningen, redovisning, beskattning*, Ernest and Young, Stockholm.

PESTOFF, V.A. (1998) *Beyond the Market and State. Social Enterprises and Civil Democracy in a Welfare Society*, Ashgate, Aldershot.

QVARSELL, R. (1993) 'Välgörenhet, filantropi och frivilligt socialt arbete i en historisk översikt', in *SOU (Statens Offentliga Utredningar)*, 1993: 82, Allmänna Förlaget, Stockholm.

RODHE, K. (1988) *Föreningslagen – 1987 års lag om föreninga*, 8th revised edition, LTs Förlag, Stockholm.

SOU (Statens Offentliga Utredningar) (1996) *Kooperativa möjligheter i storstadsområden. Underlagsrapport från storstadskommittén*, 1996: 54, Allmänna Förlaget, Stockholm.

—— (1988) *Mål och resultat – nya principer för det statliga stödet till föreningslivet*, 1988: 39, Allmänna Förlaget, Stockholm.

Statskontoret (1994) *Utblick mot frivillig verksamhet*, Rapport 1994: 19.

STENIUS, K. (1995) 'From Common to Anonymous. State, Local Government, Third Sector and Market in Swedish Alcohol and Drug Treatment', mimeo, Stockholm School of Business.

STRYJAN, Y. (1996) 'Competing with Concepts. A Note on Co-operators, Corporate Strategy and Computer Fads', *Review of International Co-operation*, vol. 89, 2: 75–81.

—— (1994) 'Co-operatives in the Welfare Market', in PERRI, 6 and VIDAL, I. (eds) *Delivering Welfare*, CIES, Barcelona, 305–41.

—— (1989) *Impossible Organisations*, Greenwood Press, New York, Westport CT, London.

STRYJAN, Y. and WIJKSTRÖM, F. (1998a) 'Des agences de développement coopératif pour pallier les failles récentes du système', in DEFOURNY, J., FAVREAU, L. and LAVILLE, J.-L. (eds) *Insertion et nouvelle économie sociale. Un bilan international*, Desclée de Brouwer, Paris, 183–206.

——(1998b) 'Sweden', in BORZAGA, C. and SANTUARI, A. (eds) *Social Enterprises and New Employment in Europe*, Regione Autonoma Trentino-Alto Adige and DG V, Trento, 461–90.

——(1996) 'Co-operatives and Non-profit Organisations in Swedish Social Welfare', *Annals of Public and Co-operative Economics*, vol. 67, 1: 5–27.

WIJKSTRÖM, F. (1994) 'Den ideella sektorns roll', in ALÉX, P., NORMARK, P., SCHÖRLING, I., STRYJAN, Y. and WIJKSTRÖM, B. (eds) *Kooperation and välfärd*, Föreningen Kooperativa Studier, Stockholm.

14 The Netherlands

Neighbourhood development enterprises

Piet H. Renooy

Introduction

In the Netherlands, the borderline between the social economy and other sectors is a vague and dynamic one. The *raison d'être* for social enterprises as well as their characteristics (legal form, organisation of employment, etc.) are dependent on formal institutional arrangements. As a result of institutional changes, various activities in the social economy have been taken on by private for-profit or public entities, while activities originally initiated in the informal sector have shifted into the social economy.

For a good understanding of the emergence of social enterprises in the Netherlands, we will, in the first section, sketch the general context in which the Dutch non-profit sector has developed. In doing so, we will focus on two main topics namely, the history and development of the non-profit sector in Dutch society, on the one hand, and Dutch labour-market policy, on the other. In the second section, we will analyse the emergence of social enterprises in the Dutch context. The third section will focus on one specific type of social enterprise, particularly interesting in the context of this study, namely the so-called '*BBBs*' (neighbourhood development schemes).

1 The Dutch non-profit sector[1]

In terms of employment, the Netherlands has the largest non-profit sector in the world. In 1995, over 12 per cent of the Dutch labour force worked in the non-profit sector, especially in the fields of education, healthcare and welfare (Burger and Dekker 1998), while in the same year the average share of non-profit employment in developed countries was estimated at about 7 per cent. However, Dutch non-profit organisations are not characterised by a high degree of autonomy, which is one of the criteria set in the Johns Hopkins Comparative Non-profit Sector Project. An explanation for the size of the non-profit sector and its dependency on government funding can be found in the specific history of the Dutch non-profit sector.

The development of the Dutch non-profit sector

The 'pillarisation' process

The development of the Dutch non-profit sector can only be explained in the light of the so-called 'pillarisation' process. Pillarisation is the process by which groups of citizens organised themselves along religious and political lines. Catholics, Protestants, Liberals and Socialists each founded their own political parties, labour unions, housing associations, newspapers, schools, broadcasting associations, sports clubs, hospitals and so on. The pillarisation was not confined to the non-profit sector, as every town or neighbourhood had its own Catholic and Protestant shops.

Pillarisation is said to have had a great influence on the emancipation of different population groups.[2] It was the way for the Catholic, Calvinist and Socialist minorities to achieve full citizenship. Scholars tend to point out the effect of the social control exercised through the pillar organisations. Through the pillars, the norms and values of the religious communities were reproduced and, for a long time, differences among pillars were sharpened. At the same time, however, the elites (leaders) of the pillars could work very well together to maintain the status quo (and in so doing, their own positions). They respected each other and realised that none of them could ever claim a majority. Therefore in government they also had to co-operate in coalition cabinets. Because the elites had a great interest in keeping all the pillars satisfied, funding of the pillar organisations through government money grew. Since pillarisation was so pervasive, it led to a vertical segmentation of Dutch society.

In the twentieth century, and especially after the Second World War, all kinds of service-providing organisations were set up along the lines of the pillars. In the fields of education, healthcare, welfare and housing, private non-profit pillar organisations developed rapidly. These organisations, most of them foundations and associations, were financed by collective arrangements. This development can be understood by recognising two leading principles in the politics of the elites, namely a limited and subsidiary government and equal treatment of all pillars.

The principle of a limited government was agreed on by Catholics, Protestants and Liberals. In the Protestant community, the principle of sovereignty in one's own circle was primary. According to this principle, in important areas of the society, such as the family, education, religion and even business, the role of government should be minimised. The Catholic principle of subsidiarity has the same effect in that it states that the government should only interfere in everyday life when family, community or the church cannot handle it themselves. Of course, Liberals also were averse to government interference. Pillar organisations thus started their own schools, healthcare institutions, welfare organisations and so forth.

The principle of equal treatment made it possible for government subsidies to be granted to comparable organisations in the different pillars. This principle was most evident in the field of education. Equal financial treatment for public and private education was enshrined in the Dutch Constitution.[3] Through this proportional distribution of facilities and of benefits among the different segments of the population, the non-profit sector grew steadily.

After the Second World War, the foundations of Dutch welfare society were laid by the elites. Several corporatist structures were set up to smooth the path to economic prosperity. Well-known and very important in the field of agrarian production are the product and industry boards, created as public-law institutions. The most important corporatist body is the 'Socio-Economic Council', (the *SER, Sociaal Economische Raad*), in which labour unions, employers' organisations and the government (independent experts) each have one-third of the seats. The *SER* has the right to advise the government on important socio-economic issues. Agreements in the *SER* and in the 'Foundation of Labour' (*Stichting van de Arbeid*), where employers and employees meet, are said to be important conditions for continuing economic growth in the Netherlands (the Dutch socio-economic system has become known as the 'Polder-model'). New corporatist structures are still being established. Less than ten years ago, employment services were 'tripartised' – the former directorate general of the Ministry of Social Affairs was privatised and put under the management of employers, employees and government. And even these days, in restructuring employment and social security policies, tripartite bodies are created.

At the turn of the millennium, the Netherlands still has an extensive non-profit sector. It functions in important spheres of society like healthcare, education and housing. Private non-profit organisations are mostly publicly financed and they perform public tasks, but in their way of operating, they do not merely carry out government policy. As the Johns Hopkins study clearly points out, it is often a two-way relationship in that government regulations are frequently designed after extensive consultation with the representatives of the various fields (Burger *et al.* 1997). Nevertheless, many of these non-profit organisations are subject to government rules and regulations. Schools, for example, are not free to set their own salaries or to define their own curriculum, and housing corporations have to comply with national rent levels. Because of the requirements they have to fulfil, the non-profit organisations have had to professionalise, with little room for voluntary activities.

The future of the Dutch non-profit sector

As stated above, Dutch society still has corporatist characteristics. The various corporate bodies, however, have been under fierce criticism. These organisations were accused of being soft and the social partners are seen as not being sufficiently conscious of the limitations of the public purse. This is associated with a cry for more market influences in the different spheres where non-profit organisations are active. This would result, for instance, in other ways of financing, with hard contracting instead of more or less open activity subsidies.

The influence of the pillars is diminishing as a result of secularisation. As a matter of fact, pillarised organisations are getting a more secular character and are freer in their operations. Simultaneously, their natural groups of clients are disappearing. A Catholic is no longer automatically a member of the Catholic broadcasting organisation, and Protestants schools are frequently attended by children from Socialist or Liberal families.

This does not mean that the non-profit sector is diminishing. What is noticeable is that many of the older non-profit organisations are reorganising and are becoming more market oriented. They are responding to demand with well-defined products, they are budgeting more strictly, and they have a more professional policy on personnel (human resource management). Some of the older pillarised organisations are losing members. This is the case, for example, with religious welfare organisations that work with many volunteers. But, on the other hand, some big organisations that use volunteers are growing rapidly, especially foundations and associations that are active in fields such as environment protection, human rights and international solidarity.

One can also see new types of non-profit organisations coming into being. For instance, in the field of reintegration of the long-term unemployed or of the partially disabled, many private foundations offering services to municipalities have been set up. The city of Amsterdam has, for example, established a non-profit business corporation (a limited company) to organise and execute part of the city's policy on reintegration of the unemployed. 'The Work Ltd.', as it has been called, is still in operation and is expanding its activities to foreign countries.

Finally, there is a lively debate on the strengthening of civil society. With the diminishing influence of the pillars, in their role in the reproduction of norms and values and in the social control they exert, and with the growing importance of the market and of individualisation, a new need is felt for integrating structures. New non-profit organisations are reacting to this demand. An example is the neighbourhood development schemes, that are aimed at bringing back social cohesion in neighbourhoods, at stimulating local economies, and at keeping neighbourhoods clean and safe while creating jobs for the unemployed. But before focusing on these organisations (which we will do in section 3), we will discuss another important feature of Dutch society with regard to the development of social enterprises, namely the Dutch active labour-market policy.

The Dutch active labour-market policy

As already mentioned, the Dutch welfare system has proved sufficiently specific to be considered as a model in its own right and has achieved significant results in the fight against unemployment. It aims at combining flexibility with a high degree of social security. The active labour-market policy is one of the policies implemented in the framework of this model, and it is of particular importance in understanding the emergence of social enterprises in the Dutch context. It will thus be examined in this section.

The Dutch government has been pursuing the so-called 'active labour-market and social security policy' for some years now. According to this policy, social security must increasingly focus on the re-entry of the unemployed into the labour market or, if this is not feasible, into activities which will prevent social exclusion. The local social services departments together with the job centres make special efforts to achieve this.

To implement this policy, the central government has developed several measures. The most recent legislation is the 'Jobseekers Insertion Law' (*WIW, Wet Inschakeling Werkzoekenden*). The *WIW*, introduced in 1998, is aimed at the long-term unemployed and all unemployed youth under twenty-three years of age. The measure offers local authorities a range of possibilities to tackle these people's employment problems. For those furthest removed from the labour market (with a low employability), the instrument of 'social activation' allows the unemployed who are not able to move on to the regular labour market in the short term to do a range of (quasi-work) activities without losing their social security benefit. Possible activities include volunteer work, resocialisation programmes and the like. The main purpose of these programmes is to avoid and to combat the social exclusion of the long-term unemployed.

People with a slightly better labour-market position can be put to work with the municipality through subsidised jobs. They will be able to earn up to 120 per cent of the legal minimum wage, and will be seconded to private enterprises or institutions. Initially, these jobs are for two years, but they can be converted into permanent appointments. Those closer to the labour market (with a higher employability, but still long-term unemployed) can, under the *WIW*, be employed in so-called 'work-experience jobs'. The local government is in a position to offer a very substantial wage cost subsidy to those firms willing to create work-experience jobs for the long-term unemployed.[4] The unemployed can stay in these jobs for a maximum of one year and, after that, they are expected to move on to regular jobs without further subsidy. It is estimated that, in 1998, some 55,000 unemployed had been re-employed in either a secondment job or a work-experience job. Among those 55,000 are all the people under 23 who have been unemployed for six months.

The *WIW* replaced two important former schemes for the unemployed, i.e. the 'Jobpoolscheme' (*Regeling Banenpools*), for the long-term unemployed, and the 'Youth Employment Guarantee Act' (*Jeugd Werkgarantiewet*), which was meant for the unemployed up to twenty-three years old. In 1999, the *WIW* also incorporated projects which up to then were administered under the so-called 'Melkert-2 Scheme'.[5] This scheme, officially called 'Experiments Activating Benefit Money' (*Experimenten Activering Uitkeringsgelden*), encompassed various experiments where social benefit money is used to create jobs. Projects that were approved by the Ministry of Social Affairs and Employment receive a subsidy of 8,000 Euro per job created. This amount equals the central government's contribution to unemployment benefit (90 per cent of the benefit). More than 20,000 jobs were created in this way. The majority of Melkert-2 projects have been transferred to the *WIW* work-experience jobs programme.

Besides the *WIW*, another important job-creation plan, the 'Melkert-1 Scheme', has been in operation since 1995. The scheme is officially called 'Extra Employment Scheme for the Long-Term Unemployed'.[6] The essence of the scheme is the creation of 40,000 jobs, paying up to 120 per cent of the minimum wage in the public sector. This scheme is funded, in part, through social expenditure that would otherwise have been spent on unemployment payments to the participants. The jobs are meant for the long-term unemployed and are in the care sector (including hospitals, and homes for the elderly), in day nurseries, in public safety/supervision jobs, in schools and in the sports sector. The intention of the government is to create normal jobs i.e. the unemployed should get regular labour contracts. The only 'peculiarity' of the jobs is their financing. By mid 1998, about 30,000 of these jobs had been created. After a study which explored the possibilities of enlarging the total number of Melkert-1 jobs[7] the government announced further subsidised jobs under this scheme. Some of these new jobs will pay up to 150 per cent of the minimum wage.

Finally, for those people who, as a result of physical and mental handicap, are unable to obtain a job in the usual ways the Netherlands introduced, in 1967, the 'Social Labour Provision Act' (*WSW, Wet Sociale Werkvoorziening*) under which the local authorities are responsible for the organisation of work. Currently local authorities have established 102 units (the so-called sheltered or social work-shops) where work is carried out within the *WSW* context. The majority of these units are public corporations, and some are foundations. Among the *WSW* enterprises, we can distinguish five different groups of activities:

- heavy manufacturing industry (metal, electrical and printing);
- light manufacturing industry (assembling, packaging);
- outside activities (horticultural);
- secondments;
- other activities.

A little over half of the 85,000 people engaged in *WSW* enterprises are active in manufacturing. Basically, these jobs are so-called 'last resort jobs', meant to prevent the handicapped from becoming socially excluded. The costs incurred by *WSW* institutions were originally almost fully reimbursed by the government, but in 1989 a system of budget financing was introduced. Since then, the activities of *WSW* enterprises have become increasingly market oriented.

2 The Dutch context and the emergence of social enterprises

The above-described measures are all part of an all-encompassing approach. Not one long-term unemployed person was to be left alone; a plan should be drawn up (by local authorities) leading to some kind of activity, be it a paid job, voluntary activities, schooling or training. In the middle of 1998, the Netherlands had around 500,000 unemployed (excluding handicapped) of whom approximately 50 per cent were long-term unemployed. By this time, more than 100,000 jobs had been created within the framework of the above-mentioned schemes: 30,000 in Melkert-1, 21,000 in Melkert-2 and 55,000 in the *WIW* schemes.

This all-encompassing approach of the Dutch government leaves little room for fully independent local initiatives, like there were in the 1970s and the 1980s. In those years, numerous small enterprises and projects operated on both an ideological and a not-for-profit basis, yet were market oriented and made payments to their participants. In 1984 and 1989, these initiatives were described in the 'Atlas of Local Initiatives'. There were three kind of activities that more or less matched the EMES definition of social enterprises: the so-called 'service and aid schemes', the sheltered workshops and certain job schemes. In 1988, the Netherlands had 541 of these initiatives, employing over 25,000 people.

Over the past years, many of these initiatives and enterprises have been incorporated in either the public or the private sector. Banks, formal support organisations and larger firms recognised the possibilities offered by certain small-scale ideological enterprises and supported them or even took them over. Other initiatives were absorbed by government measures against unemployment, in which case, they can still be formally independent associations or foundations. Their existence, however, is fully tied to the government, both financially and through rules and regulations. For many of the existing projects and for new ones, participating in the government-steered programmes is a logical decision in that by doing so, they gain access to subsidies for wages and often for organisational costs. For the unemployed, it represents a way to get work experience at a relatively good wage. It is also in line with the history of non-profit organisations in the Netherlands, as described above.

As a consequence, however, almost no project can meet the complete set of entrepreneurial and social criteria defining social enterprises. Economic risk is reduced and is substituted by a certain degree of dependency on government. Furthermore, the organisations are never fully autonomous. They have to meet a number of criteria set by the government and they have to comply with certain rules concerning their market behaviour (e.g. no 'unfair' competition). True enough, the labour is paid for, but mostly through government subsidies. Besides, at least part of the initiators are employees of municipalities, paid to start up these kinds of initiatives, and the organisations involved are not always democratic organisations with participation of multiple stakeholders.

What does characterise many new Dutch initiatives fighting unemployment and social exclusion is that they make use of contributions from different sources. As stated above, many initiatives are oriented towards the market but are using state subsidies at the same time. The third source many initiatives turn to is social capital.[8] Trust, civic spirit, solidarity and the like are resources which are used extensively by initiatives which are, in turn, reproducing these resources by their activities. These activities are not only for private consumption, but they generate and enhance collective externalities.[9]

The way in which these various resources are mixed within the initiatives differs according to local or national contexts. From country to country, access to state resources will differ, and from region to region (or even from neighbourhood to neighbourhood) the possibilities of using social capital will differ. One can, following Lambooy (1981) and Renooy (1990), speak of a production environment for social enterprises.

We will now turn to a specific Dutch type of social enterprise, the neighbourhood development schemes.

3 Neighbourhood development schemes

One of the most interesting examples of new initiatives are the so-called neighbourhood development schemes – in Dutch, *BuurtBeheer Bedrijven*. The abbreviation *BBBs* will be used hereinafter to refer to these schemes.

History

BBBs were inspired by the *Régies de Quartier* in France. They can be described as independent enterprises where local residents are given the opportunity to work part time for pay, doing simple maintenance jobs on houses and the living environment or providing social services for other neighbourhood residents. In 1992, feasibility studies were carried out for four *BBBs*, to be set up in neighbourhoods in the cities of Rotterdam, The Hague, Almere and Maastricht. One year later, these *BBBs* had actually started. The goals that these initiatives defined for themselves were:

- enlarging participation of the residents in the management of the neighbourhood;
- improving the income position of people on minimum incomes;
- breaking the social isolation of certain groups (long-term unemployed, migrants, the elderly);
- improving the daily upkeep of the neighbourhood.

An important initiator of the *BBBs* on the national level was the 'Dutch Foundation for Experiments in Housing', (the *SEV, Stuurgroep Experimenten Volkshuisvesting*). The *SEV* more or less imported the concept of the French *Régies de Quartier*. At city level, it was mainly professionals (social workers) who took up the idea and mobilised the inhabitants of the neighbourhoods. These first social entrepreneurs managed to activate more than 150 residents, but experienced some start-up problems. The most serious were the following:

- potential customers (housing corporations) hesitated to make use of the services offered by the *BBBs*;
- municipal (maintenance) departments feared loss of jobs;
- municipalities had already started other schemes to combat unemployment;
- social security laws hindered an easy entrance of the unemployed into the *BBBs*;
- rules on subsidised labour (for example Jobpools) restricted the type of activities that the unemployed could undertake and forbade part-time jobs;
- entrepreneurial skills had to be developed.

The problems encountered by the Dutch *BBBs* reveal an important difference from the circumstances under which the *Régies de Quartier* came about. In France, the social benefit payment was lower than in the Netherlands, but people on benefit were allowed to work part-time (for six months) despite their benefit. This meant that the unemployed could enter *Régies* on a part-time basis more easily than in the Netherlands. Of course, this is not the only difference between the Dutch and French situations. In French cities, for example, at the time *Régies* came about, there was more work to do to improve living conditions than in the Dutch case, where public housing schemes, in most cases, ensured a good standard of maintenance. In this context, some speak of 'a stimulating backlog' for the French initiatives (*SEV* 1998a). *BBBs* also differ from the *Régies* in their legal framework. Whereas the *Régies* are democratic associations, *BBBs* are either foundations or limited liability companies, i.e. more entrepreneurial legal forms.

One year after their start-up, the first four *BBBs* employed seventy-eight persons (of whom forty-two were through a government scheme as described above) and had a turnover varying from 80,000 NLG (36,000 Euro) to 251,000 NLG (about 113,000 Euro). In 1998, these four *BBBs* employed, in one way or another, around 200 persons.

Diversity

In 1998, there were twenty-four *BBBs*, all more or less fitting the description given above and all pursuing the goals stated above. But within this unity in definition and goals, a great variety can be observed in the ways they are operated. In the following sections we will elaborate on different characteristics of the *BBBs*. When possible, an overall picture will be given and the diversity will be illustrated with examples.

Legal form and organisation

All of the *BBBs* use the foundation as the legal form. The simplest organisations have a board with representatives of the neighbourhood, the municipality or welfare foundations, a managing director for daily management and one or more product groups or activity fields, which may in turn have co-ordinators. Two *BBBs* also make use of the limited company as a legal form. *BBB Schilderswijk*, in The Hague, for example, operates its commercial activities through four limited companies and its non-commercial work through a foundation.

The use of foundations and limited companies as legal forms results in fewer possibilities for the inhabitants of the neighbourhood to influence the policy of the *BBBs*. To enhance the participation of inhabitants in the *BBBs*, the concept of neighbourhood shareholdership has recently been put forward. The idea is to make it possible for tenants to buy a share in their neighbourhood by paying 10 NLG (4.5 Euro) a month to a community-fund. This fund can finance the repair, construction or maintenance desired by the shareholders. Housing corporations (i.e. highly professionalised corporations of tenants supplying housing) in the town of Capelle aan den IJssel are seriously thinking of introducing this plan.

Activities

BBBs undertake a wide range of activities. At the core of their work are the maintenance of housing blocks, the cleaning of public spaces, small repairs, etc. While some *BBBs* confine themselves to these tasks, others have expanded considerably. The already-mentioned *BBB Schilderswijk*, for example, has four limited companies for commercial activities. These activities include the management of a swimming pool and of sports facilities, the supervision of exams at a Polytechnic in The Hague and the organisation of activities for events in the city (*Urban Fun Ltd*). This *BBB* argues that they get what they can, if only to compensate for losses in non-commercial activities. A growing market for the *BBBs* is the field of personal services, such as cleaning, baby-sitting and the like.

BBBs' activities can be classified into three categories. The first is commercial activities through which social goals are achieved. A second category consists of so-called 'additional work'. Additional refers to the fact that the activities are not carried out by regular firms and thus do not raise any problem of unfair competition although government subsidies are used to pay the workers. Examples are: collection of waste paper, recycling centres, running of bicycle stores, collection and disposal of injection-needles (for drugs), garden maintenance and graffiti removal. The main goal of these activities, however, is to provide services for the neighbourhood. The third category of activities includes those in which the emphasis lies more on providing work experience, or even offering a way out of social isolation, than on the delivery of services in itself. These activities can be carried out using government schemes like the *WIW*, but they can also be done voluntarily.

Financing/customers

Just as the activities vary, the types of customers differ among *BBBs*. Local authorities and housing corporations are almost everywhere important consumers of *BBBs'* services. Next to these, private households, schools, shops and regular enterprises are the main users. The *BBB's* capacity to sell its services determines its degree of dependency on (local) government subsidies. Examples of income from assigned work and from subsidies in five *BBBs* in 1996 are set out in Table 14.1.

It should be underlined that the *BBBs* have rather substantial turnovers. Between 1994 and 1996, the mean turnover tripled from 312,000 NLG (141,579 Euro) to 1,034,968 NLG (469,565 Euro).

The ratio of income from assigned work to subsidies differs greatly between *BBBs*. This variation is related to the different types of activities that are undertaken by the *BBBs*. In Rotterdam, for example, where 85 per cent of the income is derived from subsidies, many activities are meant to offer work experience to

Table 14.1 Income of BBBs, 1996

Income source	Rotterdam	The Hague	Maastricht	Almere	Glanerbrug	Mean
Assigned work	160,000 NLG (72,605 Euro) (15%)	2,347,950 NLG (1,065,453 Euro) (94%)	329,819 NLG (149,665 Euro) (58%)	540,000 NLG (245,041 Euro) (90%)	92,600 NLG (42,020 Euro) (20.5%)	694,074 NLG (314,957 Euro) (67%)
Subsidies	900,000 NLG (408,402 Euro) (85%)	150,000 NLG (68,067 Euro) (6%)	234,473 NLG (106,399 Euro) (42%)	60,000 NLG (27,227 Euro) (10%)	350,000 NLG (158,823 Euro) (77.4%)	338,895 NLG (153,784 Euro) (33%)
Other	(0%)	(0%)	(0%)	(0%)	10,000 NLG (4,538 Euro) (2.1%)	
Total	1,060,000 NLG (481,007 Euro) (100%)	2,497,950 NLG (1,133,520 Euro) (100%)	564,292 NLG (256,065 Euro) (100%)	600,000 NLG (272,268 Euro) (100%)	452,600 NLG (205,381 Euro) (100%)	1,034,968 NLG (469,648 Euro) (100%)

Source: SEV (1997)

Table 14.2   Income and expenditure of *BBBs*, 1996

	Rotterdam	Maastricht	Almere	Glanerbrug
Income	1,060,000 NLG	564,292 NLG	600,000 NLG	452,600 NLG
	(481,007 Euro)	(256,065 Euro)	(272,268 Euro)	(205,381 Euro)
Expenditure	980,000 NLG	629,085 NLG	429,000 NLG	438,800 NLG
	(444,705 Euro)	(285,466 Euro)	(194,672 Euro)	(199,119 Euro)
Result	80,000 NLG	–64,793 NLG	171,000 NLG	13,800 NLG
	(36,302 Euro)	(–29,401 Euro)	(77,596 Euro)	(6,262 Euro)

Source: *SEV* (1997)

long-term unemployed. The Hague, on the other hand, with 94 per cent of the income coming from assigned work, has a very commercial approach, with mostly commercial activities.

The flipside of income is of course expenditure. In Table 14.2, income and expenditure are compared for those *BBBs* for which figures are available. Except for Maastricht, the *BBBs* appear to conduct their businesses profitably, and even with low reliance on subsidies, a *BBB* can be successful. If we divide the turnover by the number of workers in the *BBBs*, it appears that a mature *BBB* is able to generate around 20,000 NLG (9,000 Euro) per full-time worker per year.

Contracting

BBBs are increasingly faced with commercialisation and professionalisation pressures. Assignments are becoming less 'open' and *BBBs* are forced to compete on price and product with other market participants. As Spear puts it, 'hard contracting' is replacing 'soft contracting' (Spear 1998). This development is not without consequences. More attention to strictly defined performance means higher demands on productivity, which in turn means that there will be a tendency to hire only the 'better' unemployed; in other words, this trend induces a process of 'skimming' (or 'creaming'), as it is called in the Netherlands. The fact that hard contracting implies tangible, specifiable goods and services means that more intangible goals like improving living conditions or (social) safety are pushed to the background in the tasks of the *BBBs*.

Despite the increasing importance of hard contracting, it is obvious that, in the case of the *BBBs*, one cannot speak of a real market. On the one hand, the price of labour is highly subsidised. On the other, the *BBB* is supposed to create societal benefits (collective externalities) which are never taken into account in the simple cost-benefit analyses that underlie the so-called hard contracts. It is difficult to measure these societal benefits, but neglecting them amounts to neglecting the specific character of the *BBB* as a social enterprise.

Workers

In Table 14.3, we present the total number of workers in *BBBs* in 1997.[10] If we take into account the five *BBBs* that could not produce accurate figures, we may conclude that around 600 people are working for the *BBBs*. It is clear that

Table 14.3   Workers in *BBBs*, 1997

	Regular	Subsidised	Voluntary	Total
Part-time	56	53		109
Full-time	74	311		385
Total	130 (24.1%)	364 (67.4%)	46 (8.5%)	540

Source: *SEV* (1998a); Prantl (1998)

subsidised labour is crucial for the running of a *BBB*. Even the commercial *BBB* in The Hague has more than 50 per cent subsidised workers. It is notable that *BBBs* mostly employ men. The fact that part-time jobs are scarce in the *BBBs* could be one of the reasons for the under-representation of women (Prantl 1998).

The original idea that *BBB* workers should live in the neighbourhood does not seem to be adhered to. While *BBBs* attempt to recruit their personnel from their neighbourhoods, they are often forced to seek employees from other parts of town. The only selection criteria that the *BBBs* strictly adhere to are motivation and a basic knowledge of the Dutch language. Of course, this has some repercussions for the quality of the work.

The kind of subsidised labour varies and workers engaged in all types of government schemes are to be found in the *BBBs*: *WIW* jobs, Melkert-1 and Melkert-2 jobs, *WSW* (disabled workers) jobs and people under different sanctions (young offenders). Besides these, several *BBBs* work with volunteers. The use of subsidised labour helps the *BBBs* to offer their services for relatively low prices. One of the main challenges that *BBBs* are facing is the simultaneous achievement of two important goals which are sometimes difficult to reconcile. On the one hand, they seek to provide good-quality, professional services, while on the other, one of the main goals of subsidised labour schemes is to have the former unemployed move on to regular jobs, and consequently the best subsidised workers usually leave the *BBBs* first. The very achievement of their reintegration goal can thus make it difficult for *BBBs* to attain their economic goal. In other words, a *BBB* with good results in terms of reintegration of the unemployed into the labour market will also, as a consequence of the constant turnover of workers, experience more difficulties in achieving its economic goals. These difficulties should thus not be considered as a sign of failure, but as a logical consequence of the social goals of the *BBB*.

Participation

One of the main goals of *BBBs* is the stimulation of the participation of residents in the upkeep of their own neighbourhood. On the whole, results on this criterion cannot be seen as very positive. As already stated, the legal framework, the foundation, is in itself not very democratic, and the possibilities for residents' involvement in the management of *BBBs* are limited. In practice, besides the people working for the *BBBs*, participation is confined to a small, permanent group of people. There are several reasons for this low rate of participation.

First of all, as a result of the Dutch employment schemes, working part time is almost impossible. This impedes the active participation of many people. Another reason is that *BBBs* concentrate on work. Neighbourhood festivities or other social events are seldom organised by *BBBs* (unlike the situation with French *Régies*). A third explanation could be that *BBBs* are professionalising. Some *BBBs* are expanding their territory and are strongly market-oriented. This reduces the identification with the *BBBs* on the part of neighbourhood residents. Finally, participation is often low because social cohesion, trust and solidarity are low. For example, in neighbourhoods in Rotterdam and The Hague, cultural heterogeneity is very high, people lead individual, atomistic lives and frequently have an almost fatalistic attitude. The feeling of being a community is absent.[11] As much as a *BBB* is needed to produce social capital, it can use social capital as a specific resource in these areas only to a limited extent.

4   Conclusions and lines for the future

BBBs are probably the most prominent type of social enterprises in the Netherlands. An examination of their characteristics reveals that, although achievements of most *BBBs* in terms of participation and the mobilisation of other than public resources are not very impressive, they effectively contribute to the improvement of living conditions and standards in certain neighbourhoods insofar as streets are cleaner and houses are better maintained. But their most positive results are certainly those achieved in their work with the long-term unemployed. For these people, *BBBs* constitute a way to gain work experience or to just escape from social isolation. On the whole, *BBBs* can be said to make a valuable contribution to local development in the broader sense of the word.

In summary, several factors contribute to low participation of residents in *BBBs*. These include: unfavourable existing legal forms; the fact that Dutch social laws leave little possibility for innovative solutions involving, for example, part-time jobs for the unemployed;[12] an emphasis on work and production activities on the part of the *BBBs*, with little attention to the socialising effect on the neighbourhood.[13]

Finally, and maybe more fundamentally, one could also argue that it is not necessary for *BBBs* to achieve a high participation rate, since it appears that a low participation rate does not impede the achievement of their reintegration goals. As already mentioned, the low participation rate can be considered as the normal result of *BBBs*' success. This is because when the unemployed reintegrate into the 'classical' labour market, there is a rapid turnover of workers, and participation is affected.

As far as their resources are concerned, some *BBBs* are deliberately turning to the market in order to reduce their dependency on government subsidies for labour. In doing so, hard contracting increases and consequently, social goals and the identification with the community diminishes. It appears that *BBBs* which are undergoing such a development are confronted with a difficult choice: if they turn to the market, the possibility of relying on social capital as a resource is reduced, but they can still be successful employment schemes. If, on the other hand, *BBBs* are still seeking social capital as an important resource besides government subsidies, and some money from the market, they need to find ways to mobilise residents, and this is often incompatible with market-oriented policies. Seeking co-operation with Dutch organisations for voluntary work and utilising Dutch active labour-market policies are possibilities for the *BBBs* which choose the second alternative. A national support organisation could also be of great help to *BBBs*. In France, the *Régies* have their national organisation, the *Comité National de Liaison des Régies de Quartier*. Such a structure is still missing in the Netherlands, although plans for a national network have been drawn up.

It is difficult to evaluate the actual prospects for the development of *BBBs*. Generally, one could say that social enterprises, as a way of mobilising and reproducing social capital, could play a very useful role in the Netherlands. Indeed, there is a growing awareness that after years of budget cuts in the collective sector and rationalisation in the market sector, Dutch society has something which could be called a 'social deficit'.[14] Stimulating social enterprises, as new types of organisations within the non-profit sector, could be a way to combat this.

Notes

1 This paragraph is based on the study 'Defining the Non-profit Sector: The Netherlands', which is part of the Johns Hopkins Comparative Nonprofit Sector Project (Burger *et al.*, 1997).
2 In recent years, there has been a plea for an Islamic pillar in Dutch society to speed up the integration of Muslims into the society.
3 This can sometimes lead to ridiculous situations. When, for instance, a window was broken in the public school, all schools received a new window. This has changed.
4 Depending on the job security offered, 9,780–12,000 NLG (4,400–5,400 Euro) per year.
5 Ad Melkert was the Dutch Minister of Social Affairs and Employment during the period 1994–1998. He initiated several job schemes.
6 *Regeling Extra Werkgelegenheid voor Langdurig Werklozen.*
7 See Homburg and Renooy (1998).
8 See the contribution of Evers in this book (Chapter 17).
9 See the contribution of Laville and Nyssens in this book (chapter 18).
10 Figures represent nineteen of the twenty-four *BBBs*. For the other five, no figures were available.
11 See, for example, Kroft *et al.* (1989).
12 It could be said that, until recently, certain initiatives of the unemployed were smothered to death through social laws; the new law, the *WIW*, now offers more possibilities for flexible use.
13 In the Netherlands, the organisation of social activities has traditionally been the responsibility of professional social workers. In recent years, however, the social work sector has been confronted with very serious budget cuts, which has led to a decline in its activities.
14 This term was used by P. Rosenmöller of the Dutch Green party in the election campaign of 1998 to counter the continuous use of the budget deficit as an argument for government policy.

Bibliography

ABRAHAMSON, P. (1991) 'Welfare for the Elderly in Denmark: From Institutionaliza-tion to Self-reliance?', in EVERS, A. and SVETLIK, I. (eds) *New Welfare Mixes and Care for the Elderly*, Eurosocial Report 40/2, European Centre, Vienna, 35–63.

BORZAGA, C. (1997) 'The EMES Network: the Emergence of Social Enterprises in Europe', ISSAN, University of Trento.

BURGER, A. and DEKKER, P. (1998) 'De grootste non-profit sector ter wereld', in *ESB*, 11 December 1998, no. 4, 181: 945–6.

BURGER, A., DEKKER, P., VAN DER PLOEG, T. and VAN VEEN, W. (1997) 'Defining the Non-profit Sector: The Netherlands', Working Papers of the Johns Hopkins Comparative Non-profit Sector Project, no. 23, The Johns Hopkins Institute for Policy Studies, Baltimore.

HOMBURG, G. and RENOOY, P. (1998) *Nieuwe banen in de collectieve sector*, Ministerie van Sociale Zaken en Werkgelegenheid, Den Haag.

KROFT, H., ENGBERSEN, G., SCHUYT, K. and VAN WAARDEN, F. (1989) *Een tijd zonder werk*, Leiden, Antwerpen.

LAMBOOY, J.G. (1981) *Economie en ruimte*, Van Gorcum, Assen.

PRANTL, S. (1998) 'Buurtbeheerbedrijven', Master's thesis, University of Wageningen.

RENOOY, P. (1993) 'Een nieuwe welzijnsmix in Europa', *Facta*, no. 3, 10–14.

—— (1990) 'The Informal Economy – Meaning, Measurement and Social Significance', Netherlands Geographical Studies, 115, Amsterdam.

SEV (Stuurgroep Experimenten Volkshuisvesting) (1998a) 'Eindadvies inzake het experimenten-thema Buurtbeheerbedrijven 1992–97', Rotterdam.

—— (1998b) 'Kerngegevens Buurtbeheerbedrijven', paper for Congress on Buurtbe-heerbedrijven, April, Den Haag.

—— (1997) 'Nieuwsbrief BuurtBeheerBerichten', Juli, SEV, Rotterdam.

SPEAR, R. (1998) 'Contracting for Welfare Services', Draft for an EMES Seminar.

15 United Kingdom

A wide range of social enterprises

Roger Spear

Introduction

Social enterprises in the UK cannot be examined without an historical perspective which shows how the whole third sector evolved. That is why in this chapter we first look at the main traditional components of the social economy as a basis for examining the social enterprises which emerged more recently. Organisations in the UK that might be termed social enterprises (this category is quite large) are then examined; they have quite diverse legal forms, and even within each legal category there is considerable variety. Next the range of sectors where social enterprises are found is looked at. We then go on to examine social enterprises in the welfare sector, looking in particular at some case studies and the role of local government in contracting. Finally, an analysis of some specific features of social enterprises is developed.

1 Third-sector organisations in historical perspective

Analysis of the emergence of third-sector organisations has been dominated by theories of the non-profit sector stressing state and market failures (demand side theories), the role and profile of entrepreneurs (supply side theories) or the dynamics of institutional choice (historical and contextual factors, embeddedness, etc.).

In spite of their limitations, these kinds of approaches can be used to differentiate traditional third-sector enterprises and new social enterprises in terms of the changing nature of state/market failures that they responded to, the changing patterns of entrepreneurship and the very different contexts from which they emerged.

Traditionally, the third sector, also called the social economy, may be considered as comprising co-operatives, mutuals and voluntary organisations (which include charities and foundations). These categories include older organisations, some of which were formed in the last century and many of which are large enterprises, as well as new organisations, many of which are small or medium-sized, but which may have a stronger value base. In terms of overall employment, third-sector organisations play a significant role in the economic landscape.[1] Co-operatives employ about 131,971 employees, mutual organisations provide work for some 27,500 people and voluntary organisations for 1,473,000 people, i.e. the social economy accounts for a total of approximately 1,684,500 jobs.

Looking first at the co-operative sector, its origins lie on the one hand in market failure in the provision of good quality products and lack of state regulation in the retail sector, leading to the rise of the Rochdale pioneers. But the subsequent proliferation of new retail societies owes as much to the dynamic entrepreneurial activity associated with a vibrant social movement bridging working-class and lower-middle-class interests. The co-operative sector is still dominated by consumer societies, with 9.2 million members, and 104,000 staff. Among these, the Co-operative Wholesale Society (by far the largest retail society particularly after its current merger with the second largest society) also owns very successful co-operative financial services which were initially an extension of the range of services provided to retail customer/members, but have now grown beyond that. In a similar vein, the growth of mutuals in financial services may be seen as a response to the excessive market power and profits of private providers in the last century.

The agricultural co-op sector, with its 300,000 members and 12,243 employees, was built on a spirit of self-help in a context of growing urban markets, and on the need to counter the emerging economic power of wholesalers, and a growing class of retailers. It has moved to a certain extent towards more privatised forms of ownership.

While it is clear that many of these traditional social enterprises have suffered some degree of degeneration in their guiding values, it is also the case that many of the market/state failures they emerged to counter have since altered due to changing market dynamics. These are the older, more traditional sectors and they have faced declining market share and threats of demutualisation. However, alongside this decline, there is continued market leadership in other sectors e.g. funerals, travel and insurance, while the co-operative bank has been a market leader in ethical trading.

This varied performance has had two kinds of social impact: the retail societies, although declining economically, have a good record of retaining shopping outlets in a wide range of communities; the CIS (Co-op Insurance Society) has a network of local community-based representatives who perform a similar function. On the other hand, the Co-operative Bank has strong ethical and environmental policies, and sponsors a number of ethical projects that support disadvantaged groups. And although, until recently, CWS (Co-op Wholesale Society) and other retailer societies have suffered a degeneration of values, there is currently a regeneration underway in the sector, which is developing a community shopping strategy, strengthening community-based activities and building social capital.

Voluntary organisations form the largest part of the third sector in terms of staff employed (paid and volunteers). An examination of contextual factors in the UK can be made using Esping-Andersen's characterisation of types of welfare state regimes, i.e. liberal, corporatist and social democratic. The UK is usually referred to as 'liberal' with relatively low expenditure, the use of means testing, and strict rules of entitlement. Due to a relatively early formation of the state, the national Protestant church plays a much smaller role in welfare compared to the Catholic church in corporatist models. However, the post-war creation of the National Health Service was very much informed by social democratic ideas (universalism and non-market provision). The effect of this has been a very small voluntary sector presence in the health sector, but a relatively large voluntary involvement in social services, education and research, and culture/recreation sectors.

The newer co-operative and mutual organisations are more closely linked to the voluntary sector in terms of commonality of activities. They operate in a range of sectors responding to failures in state housing provision, labour-market failures (leading to exclusion), failures in macro-economic policies leading to high unemployment, and local government failures to manage community development (multi-racial/ethnic, inner city, and rural areas). But the largest area arises from welfare failures, and restructuring arising from the breakdown of the post-war consensus on the welfare state.

New sector social enterprises also parallel their nineteenth century forerunners in combating market failure in retailing (especially in new products, such as organic and whole foods, radical books, etc.); and similarly the formation of new enterprises was closely linked to the social movements of the 1960s. By the same token, market failures and state regulatory failures in the retailing of financial services (exclusion of many combined with highly exploitative private loan shark operations) have been major factors in the rise of credit unions.

2   Overview of social enterprises in the UK

The term social enterprise is only occasionally used in the UK but its meaning is not obscure; it has a general meaning, usually associated with the idea of a trading enterprise having a social purpose e.g. rewarding those at risk from social exclusion rather than shareholders.

UK law is not tailored particularly to the idea of social enterprise. There is no law for co-operatives or specifically for mutual or voluntary organisations, which are the forms usually adopted by social enterprises in most countries. On the other hand, the law is quite flexible with regard to such enterprises. There are two relevant types of law – company law and industrial and provident (I&P) society law. Social enterprises (whether co-operatives or voluntary organisations) would usually be formed as companies limited by guarantee under the former, and as I&P societies under the latter. The Registrar of Friendly Societies, which caters for I&P societies, offers more protection to bona fide co-operatives than to entities registering under company law. I&P societies allow shareholding by members but they are democratically controlled, since members have only one vote each. The usual form of registration under company law is a company limited by guarantee, where the company is controlled by members (one person, one vote) with (usually) nominal shareholding and liability is limited to the

amount initially agreed to be provided by the member if the company is liqui-
dated. It is also possible to register social enterprises under the branch of
company law where a company is limited by shares. Social enterprises (voluntary
organisations) can also be registered as charities with the Charities Commission
under the Charities Act 1992/3. Charitable status exempts the organisation from
corporation tax, but this must be balanced against value added tax which cannot
be reclaimed. During the past year or two there has been considerable interest in
developing co-operative legislation, which resulted in the drafting of a law, not
yet scheduled for parliamentary time.

Despite the lack of a specific legal status, several types of organisations may
be identified as social enterprises.

New co-operatives and mutuals

Worker co-operatives

Worker co-operatives have always been a small but influential part of the UK
co-op sector. Since the 1980s they experienced a substantial growth (from 279
in 1980 to over 1,100 in 1992). They operate in many sectors, and are especially prevalent in the service sector. They are typically small firms with an
average size of ten workers. A large part of the success of these worker co-
ops is due to the network of small locally based co-operative development
agencies (CDAs) that exist to help set up co-ops, often by working with the
unemployed and with disadvantaged groups. It is difficult to judge what
proportion of co-ops come from these categories, but a majority emerges from
initiatives to create jobs for the unemployed or to save the jobs in failing businesses. A substantial minority comes from initiatives to help the long-term
unemployed, women returning to work, ethnic minority groups, and people
with disabilities.

Social co-operatives

It is important to differentiate between two types of social co-ops – social care
co-ops providing services like home care, and social employment co-ops that
provide employment for disadvantaged groups. These categories may overlap so
that social care co-ops may employ people with disabilities or disadvantages.
Social co-ops are similar to worker co-ops, but with some differences. Firstly,
because of the nature of the service (personal), users may have some level of
participation in the affairs of the co-op, though this may often be consultative
rather than formal. Secondly, in the social employment co-ops, the status, terms
and conditions of employment of people with disabilities is problematic and
tends to be different to other members because of the risk of losing their state
benefits. In some cases they are volunteers and in others employees, but in
neither case are they paid normal wages. They are usually paid only expenses
because otherwise they would risk losing their benefits if they were ever made

unemployed. Although, in some co-ops, there are clearly different types of stake-holders e.g. volunteers or associate member workers and employed member workers, or sometimes support staff as members, there is still no evidence of the creation of consumer/user co-ops.

The number of home-care and nursery co-ops has continued to increase since 1993, but the exact figures are difficult to establish (about fifty care co-ops, and thirty nursery co-ops). There are a certain number of doctors' co-ops which provide emergency healthcare services to general (medical) practices in local communities. There are about thirty to forty social employment co-ops in the manufacturing and retail sectors in the UK. Co-ops have a good record as employers of people with disabilities. The best-known successful examples are: Daily Bread, a wholefood retailer and wholesaler employing people recovering from mental illness; Pedlars Sandwiches, a catering co-op employing people with mental illnesses; Adept Press, a printing business employing people with hearing impairment; Rowanwood, which employs people with learning disabilities producing wooden panelling products; and Teddington Wholefood Co-op, which grew out of a London day-care centre and employs people with learning disabilities.

Social firms[2]

Social firms are enterprises with a social purpose that try to provide real jobs for people with disabilities. These firms are oriented to the market, and their main client group has been people with mental illnesses. There are about thirty to forty social firms in the UK and they have been sponsored or developed through public and voluntary sector partnerships, often with EU funding.

Mutual organisations

There are some new examples of mutuals often much more radical than the traditional established ones, for example in ethical investment and social invest-ment. They result in new employment and might be important in developing strategies to help address financial exclusion.

Trading voluntary organisations

Trading voluntary organisations are adapting towards a contracting culture, and increasing their role as service providers in a range of areas including welfare, training and enterprise development. There is a strong trend to professionalisa-tion and the acquisition of managerial competencies in the sector. Voluntary organisations are active in a number of sectors, particularly culture/recreation, education and training, and welfare, as well as housing, and some social/envi-ronmental sectors such as recycling of clothing for fundraising. Voluntary organisations carrying out non-traded advocacy and redistribution activities are not considered social enterprises.

Voluntary organisations may be charitable trusts, in which case they either rely on fundraising or endowed assets – financial or buildings. They may also be instruments for development activity, as in the case of development trusts, which are quite numerous, and some form the core of community businesses. Major charities are playing an increasingly important role in providing welfare services – they already run residential homes, day centres, and domiciliary services such as 'meals on wheels'. Charities and other voluntary organisations often specialise in supporting a particular target group, and this may be regarded as a traditional strength of the voluntary sector.

Intermediate labour-market organisations

In the UK recently there has been considerable interest in intermediate labour markets. These are 'waged or salaried, full or part-time jobs with training, which are only available to unemployed people for a limited time period, and where the product of their work has either a direct social purpose or is trading for a social purpose where that work or trading would not normally be undertaken' (Simmonds and Emmerich 1996). A famous example is Glasgow Works, which in 1999 was coordinating twenty projects employing 400–500 people.

The key features of these intermediate labour-market (ILM) organisations are that: they are intermediate (i.e. leading to the normal labour market); they pay the rate for the job; they provide a temporary job; they trade for a social purpose and provide added value (i.e. avoiding substitution/displacement effects). It could be argued that such initiatives are a development of the Community Programme,[3] but the differences are that training is more integral, they are more closely and overtly linked to the local social economy and they have more community control.

Community businesses

Community businesses share many of the principles of co-operatives but they are usually non-profit. They first started in rural areas, most notably in the Highlands and Islands of Scotland. They were highly successful there as a way of mobilising local communities to provide services such as transport and shops. Members of the community take a share in the community business and thereby own and control it. The overall community business then spawns various projects, which are accountable to the community business. This idea which first developed in rural areas was then successfully transferred to inner-city areas, most extensively in Glasgow. It has been taken up to a certain extent in the rest of the UK, as an approach for addressing problems in the most severely disadvantaged inner-city areas, in order to establish and strengthen community structures and services. It has also been used elsewhere in initiatives that might benefit from a sense of community ownership. Community businesses have gradually increased in number and are seen by many as an attractive structure for initiatives in the welfare sector.

Major features of new social enterprises

In the UK, social enterprises appear as independent trading organisations with social dimensions, selling user-oriented services privately in the market or contracting with the state. The main new social enterprises are voluntary organisations, co-operatives/mutuals, ILMs, and community organisations.

Volunteers tend not to be used in co-ops and traditional mutuals, but tend to be more readily used in voluntary organisations (but not in residential care), and in community business and trusts. If one were to visualise enterprises on an economic/social spectrum, volunteers would more likely be used at the social end rather than the economic end. Also, in the case of public contracts, legal liability tends to limit the use of volunteers. Members are clearly specified in many social enterprises, but users are not usually specified in their legal structures.

Social enterprises have varied sources of finance. Most do not receive donations, although voluntary organisations, settlements (via trusts), and some community businesses do. Those with endowed assets (e.g. settlements) have more stable operations. Most of these organisations are almost, by definition, trading in the market, but this may be the quasi-market of state contracts as in the case of residential care. Public subsidies used to be more common, but they now tend to take the form of a contractual relationship with the public authority paying for the delivery of a 'public' service. The term 'service agreement' is also frequently used.

3   Overview of new social enterprise sectors

When considering the sectors in which the new social enterprises operate, it is important to relate them to new market/state failures, and to reflect on the different dynamics operating. Social enterprises respond to failures in state housing provision, labour-market failures (which result in exclusion), failures in macro-economic policies (in particular high unemployment), local government failures in the management of community development (multi-racial/ethnic, inner-city and rural areas), and of course the large area of welfare failures. With regard to the dynamics of social enterprises in relation to market, state and community, it is clear that some sectors are quasi-markets, while some are conventional markets with services paid by the consumer/user (though voucher schemes or benefit systems may complicate the picture). In addition, there are associative relations (reciprocity) and, in many cases, there will be mixtures of these varied types of exchanges.

In the following sections the sectors where social enterprises have emerged and the types of social enterprise found in them are reviewed.

Work integration and employment services

The following types of labour-market integration initiatives may be identified:

- work initiatives (with training) for people with disabilities, often run by charities serving that group;
- work initiatives (with training) for people recovering from mental illness, often by charities serving that group;
- community regeneration projects creating jobs (full and part-time), often run by development trusts;
- work projects run by multi-project community-based organisations (such as settlements);
- employment, training and advice projects run by housing associations.

Current UK labour-market policy trends are towards making the market work better, with a smaller role for labour-market integration measures. Employment services are particularly emphasised in the UK, since these represent a low cost method of providing assistance to a large number of people. But the potentially unfavourable inflationary effects of inactive or excluded people (their exclusion reduces the number of people available on the labour market) are likely to result in some measure of continuing support for labour-market integration, particularly for youth and long-term unemployed. In addition, as large voluntary organisations move increasingly into the area of developing 'real' jobs for people with disabilities and those recovering from mental illness, the profile and effectiveness of such initiatives will be raised. The state funds numerous schemes through contract-like arrangements or through partnerships.

Co-operatives continue to offer the most economically viable model for such initiatives, but other initiatives have different strengths. For example, community businesses are best at targeting disadvantaged communities, voluntary organisations for assisting the types of groups they specialise in supporting, while intermediate labour-market organisations have a well-defined philosophy for giving transitional support to both communities and disadvantaged groups.

Although UK labour-market policy is marked by an emphasis on placement and job search, the labour-market integration initiatives described here achieve some degree of support because it is recognised that they are effective with the more disadvantaged in society. Given the complexity of the policy framework and the support required for these initiatives, a development function often needs to be established through a support structure, since it fulfils an important role in overcoming barriers, and projects may also be managed through holding structures (as in the case of community business).

Projects to improve labour-market functioning fall into three main categories, all aimed at improving the matching of people to jobs and vacancies: placement, job search and promoting equality of opportunity, for example to women, youth and ethnic minorities. Typically an initiative might involve a club that provides training in writing a CV and in interview techniques, free use of telephones for responding to job advertisements, etc. A club also serves to reduce isolation and to facilitate informal learning. The voluntary sector is the major operator here after the state. It is particularly well placed to serve special groups, since it tends to specialise in supporting certain target groups. Thus while there are state schemes covering the first two areas (placement and job search) for all groups, the voluntary initiatives often specialise in servicing the needs of one target group.

Housing

Low cost housing is increasingly provided by housing associations rather than local authorities. A relatively small part of this provision is through over 500 housing co-ops. A large proportion of these housing associations operates in the social housing market for disadvantaged groups. This sector continues to grow in size and in terms of the services provided. Sheltered or supported housing for people with special needs has increased substantially in the 1980s and 1990s. There is an increasing amount of interest and projects which focus on providing services for the most disadvantaged people in a housing association, and such employment projects are becoming a more and more important part of housing association activities. Most schemes are for the single homeless, young people, and people with disabilities or mental illness.

Local development

Local development includes a wide variety of social enterprises. Primarily concerned with community economic and social development, it covers some of the other categories as well as community services, environmental improvement/ development, cultural development (media and entertainment), transport services with a local orientation and special educational services (e.g. for ethnic minorities). All types of initiatives are found here, especially worker co-ops, trading voluntary organisations and community businesses.

There are over 160 development trusts, i.e. 'enterprises with social objectives which are actively engaged in the regeneration of an area – a valley, a housing estate, a town centre or a wasteland – whilst ensuring that the benefits are returned to the community'. They are partnership organisations often involving public, private and community partners in funding and governance. They promote and manage a variety of types of projects, including managed workspaces for small enterprises, environmental improvement, community transport, training and advice to small businesses, housing improvements and city farms.

Another interesting area of development activity can be seen in the work of settlements. These are multi-purpose organisations committed to tackling poverty and injustice in urban and inner-city areas. They are trusts governed by trustees, and many have been established for over 100 years, having been endowed with a large property to house their projects and provide some income. They carry out a wide range of projects, some of which are related to training and work integration. Many operate in poor inner-city areas and support ethnic minorities among others.

Credit and exchange

There is enormous interest in micro-credit schemes for individuals, as well as credit/finance schemes for enterprises. There has been some development of such schemes and increasing development of credit unions for assisting disadvantaged groups and communities. Credit unions have a relatively recent history in the UK but they are now growing fast, although employee schemes are much stronger than community-based schemes.

There has also been innovative development of mutual guarantee societies among SMEs for assisting in the raising of financial capital. Many of these initiatives prepare the ground for employment generation, and indeed may be vital to the sustainability of social enterprises, but they are not currently significant employers.

Finally, several hundred LETS schemes (local exchange trading systems) have been developed for assisting disadvantaged groups. LETS operate through a barter system that allows a large number of people to make exchanges (buy or sell goods but usually services). Thereby they facilitate economic development from a low base and they keep money or exchanges within the community.

Ethical trade

A number of ethical trading organisations are social enterprises. These have strong ethical trading statements, as is the case with Traidcraft, the Christian non-profit enterprise that imports goods from developing countries and sells them through their own network of volunteers, and through charity shops. It has development aims linking the third world and developed world. It is difficult to estimate the size of this subsector, but some of the enterprises are quite large and successful.

Welfare and personal services

Considerable changes have taken place since the early 1990s in the British welfare state. A major policy shift in welfare services was brought about through the Health Services and Care in the Community Act, implemented in 1993. The main policy impact of this Act was that there should be a move away from caring for people (older people, mentally ill, physically disabled people and those with learning disabilities, etc.) in large institutions towards more community-based care, either in people's own homes or in smaller local units or day centres. This has resulted in de-institutionalisation, for example closing down large mental hospitals and providing local community or home-based services. A second important feature of the Act was that there should be a transfer of direct responsibility for funding these welfare services from the central Department of Social Security to Local Authority Social Services Departments, and that they would contract out most of the services required.

State benefits have played an important role in the development of social enterprises providing welfare services. During the 1980s, the take up in benefits increased substantially. Between 1979 and 1992 the numbers claiming invalidity benefit rose from 600,000 to 1,585,000, attendance allowance from 265,000 to 830,000 and mobility allowance from 95,000 to 1,090,000. Benefits have an important role in helping people to pay for welfare services, such as home care, but they may also have a negative influence on the possibility of individuals (e.g. people with disabilities) moving into employment. For example they can create a poverty trap preventing people with substantial benefits from getting a job.

Alternatively, conditions associated with benefits may make the transition to work difficult or risky. The Blair government is reviewing the whole benefits system, but so far only minor changes have been made.

The outcome of the major policy shifts has been growth of the private, voluntary and co-operative organisation provision in the welfare sector. Growing private sector provision has been particularly pronounced in the residential care sector, and more recently it has developed a growing presence in the home-care sector. The voluntary sector has reacted to these policy changes and has itself undergone major changes in the last few years, with a greater professional and market orientation. Social enterprises in the form of large voluntary organisations, and small co-operatives, have expanded their service provision activities and taken on contracts for services (usually to supply services previously supplied directly by the public sector). However, relative to the private sector this has been quite slow, and in general market share has been lost. Co-operative provision has not developed as quickly as anticipated, while voluntary sector provision has focused on its strength of serving specific target groups, and has consolidated or developed complementary domiciliary services, such as meals on wheels (a home delivery service of meals using a high proportion of volunteers). In some cases such services also make use of other facilities in the social economy such as voluntary sector transport provision, i.e. community transport.

4   Social enterprises in welfare services

After this overview of the main sectors where social enterprises operate in the UK, we will now focus more specifically on social enterprises active in the area of welfare services. This is a particularly interesting area when analysing the evolution of social enterprises as a response to evolving market/state failures. In this section we review some of the background to the development of a mixed economy of care in welfare services in the UK, and look specifically at how market contracting operates for social enterprises. A specific sector – home-care services – within the general category of welfare services is analysed, but many of the principles revealed are common to other kinds of welfare services operating in such market-like conditions.

Public sector contracting

Public sector purchasing is becoming more and more widespread. Social services departments are not the only organisations that contract services. Other contractors include health authorities, local authorities (e.g. for warden services, or sheltered accommodation), the probation service (alcohol advisory services, drugs services, marriage guidance, community programmes, etc.), and the educational services in prisons. Some private sector companies are contracting out counselling and crèche provision to voluntary sector and co-operative organisations.

Contracting usually results in the award of an external contract or service agreement, and thereby forces a new kind of relationship that focuses attention on the deal or exchange between the purchaser (e.g. local authority) and the provider. It involves greater clarity and more explicitness about each of the processes involved. Securing a contract or service agreement is likely to involve going through a variety of steps, partly determined by the provider selection process, but also by the purchasing arrangements in each local authority.

The terms of contract are quite a crucial area in determining the pressures on social enterprises – there have been clear examples of externalising uncertainty, by specifying contract limits within which the public authority will operate, leaving it to the social enterprise to manage variable demand. These are 'call off' contracts. In these, the local authority social services department specifies an hourly rate for twelve months and the maximum number of hours per week. The local authority varies demand from week to week, and it can withdraw from this contract at any time with a month's notice.

State policy is central in determining the size of the market, and the proportion of independent provision as opposed to public sector provision. Public authorities have not always selected providers on price, but clearly this is one of the most important criteria. Sometimes their criteria for selecting providers are not transparent, and providing agencies may be faced with sudden reductions in contracts, or no contracts at all, as a result of the tendering process once a year. On the other hand local authorities have played a part in helping social enterprises become established, both through help in the provision of premises, and through management assistance in the early years.

Social enterprises in the welfare sector often get part of their income from private clients, but, as outlined above, such clients are usually drawing state benefits in order to pay for the services. Thus the benefits system and changes to it influence the size and operation of the sector. In addition there are local authority contracts to provide services. One example is the contract with the Walsall Home Care Co-operative that, in 1997, had 2,800 hours of contract work per week. This work was carried out by many of its 150 carers, some of whom also had private clients provided through the co-op.

Examples of state contracting for welfare services

To illustrate public sector contracting in the field of welfare services, we now turn to two different local authority areas, one a medium size town and the other an inner-city borough.

Table 15.1   Commercial possibilities and type of provider

Concentration of business	Type of provider
High – commercial possibilities	Private (for-profit) vs. large national voluntary organisations
Low – little commercial possibilities, strong mutual/self-help character	Voluntary/self-help organisations only

In one area studied (population 200,000) the state contractor had no formal classification system for welfare services, although there were budgetary classifications usually based on user needs (e.g. mental health, disability, older people). However, an examination of contracting practice showed that there were about thirty block contracts for substantial amounts of a service (e.g. several thousand hours of home care) and 200 'spot' or framework contracts (usually for individuals). Block contracts were used for more standardised services. These contracted services could be classified as follows: residential care (private for-profit sector dominant, but voluntary organisations as minor players); home care; carer oriented services (e.g. respite); day-care services; meals (lunch clubs, home deliveries); mutual support; specialist rehabilitation (e.g. for visually impaired); advice and counselling.

The choice between providers was determined to a large extent by who was in the market. So in the residential care sector, the strong presence of the private sector ensured that they gained the majority of contracts. In other service areas the presence of strong national organisations, such as Age Concern and Mind, with established reputations and services, ensured that they received contracts. In other service areas, there was not sufficient volume of business to warrant private enterprises becoming established, and voluntary organisations (such as support organisations for drug/alcohol abuse) were the only credible options, since they demonstrated a capacity of strong responsiveness to user need. In some cases, such as meal delivery, there was a combination of private and voluntary provision differentiated by activity – cooking (private) and delivery (voluntary organisation). Thus a differentiation could be identified, as shown in Table 15.1.

The additional important factor in choice of provider was the policy of the local authority. In the area studied, the local authority favoured in-house provision where possible, but there are severe central government constraints on this currently. Moreover, the contribution of specialist partners (i.e. social enterprises) was more valued than for-profits (who might make a profit from care).

In another area studied, an inner-city area with considerable ethnic and religious diversity, the most prominent characteristic of organisations in the welfare sector was again the capacity of strong responsiveness to user need, on the part of voluntary organisations, but in this case along religious and ethnic lines. There were large numbers of relatively small voluntary organisations of this type, building on the ethnic/religious associative dimension of communities.

Home care – the sector and cases

There are currently about fifty home-care co-ops in the UK. They have an average size of about thirty carers, and provide an average of over 600 hours of care per week. Most of their staff/members are women, often with families, working part-time. The public sector is still a prominent player in the market, with the private sector having had the highest growth rate, and large voluntary organisations also being active. Social care (home-care) enterprises have the advantage of requiring relatively few resources initially for central administration. They often make use of community resources for office space or use facilities provided by the local authority. Once trading they draw their income both from state contracts and from people who pay with their state benefits, as illustrated by the following cases.

Walsall Home Care Co-operative

The Walsall Home Care Co-operative, in the West Midlands, started at the instigation of a community care officer from the Department of Social Services who asked some women if they would like to care for and visit some elderly people in the area. As the work grew, twelve carers increased to twenty-eight and, in February 1989, they set up a co-operative. The six people initially on the management committee did all the administration, as well as doing part-time caring. As the business grew, the administrators had to give up their care work. Nowadays, the administrative work is carried out by five office staff, two of whom are part-time carers. In 1992 there were 250 carers but this has since declined to 150 carers as competition has increased (from two private competitors in the early days to about twenty now). All the carers are members of the co-operative. They are provided with advice and support and all have to undergo a one-week training course.

The co-operative is committed to delivering a high quality service. Finding a good match between carer and client is seen as important. Where possible, the co-operative tries to ensure the same carer keeps with the same client. The carers provide care for any age group, in people's own homes. They serve people who are mentally and physically disabled, elderly people and children. They also care for terminally ill people, usually in association with Macmillan nurses (terminal care specialists). They provide a domestic service of cleaning, washing, washing up and a personal care service of helping people to get dressed, have their meals, get up, go to bed, etc. They do not provide nursing care. They also help people get the benefits required to pay for the care. Many of their clients pay for care through benefits while some have private means.

The majority of the co-operative's work (approximately 2,800 hours/week) now comes from contracts with the local authorities. For contract work, the local authority social services department insists on the co-op employing the carers. In most of their other work, the carers are self-employed but the co-operative acts as an agency, and the client pays the carer, who in turn pays the co-op a commission of 17.5 per cent. The Walsall Home Care Co-operative members have been quite innovative in trying to establish formal training schemes, diversifying their care services to cover, for example, work at day-care centres and at further education colleges for people with learning disabilities.

Wrekin Home Care Co-operative

The Wrekin Co-operative was set up in 1991/1992 as a result of a Wrekin Council initiative, similar to the Walsall Home Care Co-operative model. The initial ten members/carers rapidly grew to fifty-one in 1992, and to eighty-one carers working about twenty hours per week in 1999. Potential future carers are asked for two referees and are police checked. Those who are deemed suitable must attend a training course that covers most aspects of what is required of them, including being a co-operative member.

All carers are self-employed except for local authority contracts. They are paid a flat hourly rate directly from clients, and they then pay the co-op a £1 (about 1.6 Euro) per hour levy. The two full-time staff – a manager and a co-ordinator – are paid from this levy and they carry out most administrative tasks. The management committee members are elected at the annual general meeting. They meet once a month. An informal meeting also takes place once a month where any member can come and air views, complaints, etc. Regular social events are held for carers on a monthly basis. Decisions are mostly taken by consensus.

Carers provide home-care services on a seven days a week, twenty-four hours a day cover and operate mostly in urban areas in and around Telford. They are not able to meet all the demand and keep turning business away. Their clientele are mostly older and disabled people on benefits. They do not advertise their services and get most of their business through word of mouth and referrals from statutory services. When they set up the co-operative, they received a start-up grant of £10,000 (about 15,900 Euro), but they are now financially self-sufficient and clearly viable.

The co-operative's members believe that there is a limit to its effective size in order to maintain the quality of care they have developed, based on individual assessment and matching of carer to client. They have been innovative in developing a broad range of care services, and have opened a day-care centre largely for council contract work. As in the case of Walsall Home Care Co-operative, for contract work, the carers have to be employed by the co-op.

Specific features of social enterprises in the welfare sector

Social benefit and social capital

Analysis of contracting practices and types of social enterprises in a few areas has revealed a strong responsiveness both to user needs and ethnic/religious diversity. This strong responsiveness may be seen on the one hand as ensuring access for such communities to a public good, and on the other as facilitating the specialisation of what is often a standardised bureaucratised service to match better the specific needs of these segments of the community. In this respect it may be regarded as a way of combating exclusion, thus producing a social benefit. The strength and capacity of voluntary organisations to respond in this way is due to their matching with the associative dimension of such community groups. In other words, these organisations mobilise and reproduce social capital among their user groups.[4] Such social capital will also be useful in establishing similar types of associative activity within ethnic groups and between ethnic groups and local government.

In the case of home-care co-ops, participatory structures allow integration of carers into the business with an associated development of skills. The organisations also have a strong commitment to social integration of the carers through regular social events which they organise. They may thus be a path back to better employment.

User involvement is more problematic in home-care co-ops because of the lack of mobility of users. This is overcome by involving the more active ones in some cases, by ensuring good user contact and quality control, by making use of representative bodies (such as Age Concern) and involving them in governance structures or consulting them on key issues. The home-care co-ops vary in their approaches to this issue, but generally take some significant steps. This represents a way of combating social exclusion of users.

Externalities

The nature of the constructed quasi-market places important limits on the extent to which a social enterprise may make a distinctively different value-based contribution to welfare services and exclusion. In general terms, in case of hard contracting, i.e. when discrimination is largely based on price in competitive markets with little regulation of quality and diversity of services, the potential for value added services, generation of social capital, and the inclusion of externalities is squeezed out. On the other hand, this potential is much greater in case of soft contracting, i.e. when service level agreements allow the valuing of such value-added services. But such considerations apply largely to services where there is a substantial market. In service areas where there is not the volume of business required for a commercial enterprise (sub-market services), social enterprises have a clear and dominant role to play.

Conclusions

As explained in the introduction of this book, social entrepreneurship has much to do with innovation. The examination of social enterprises in the UK has confirmed that feature, especially in the welfare sector. Indeed, there has been a great degree of innovation in the whole sector.

Firstly, there has been economic innovation in that the services provided by the private (both for-profit and non-profit) sector have often replaced rather bureaucratic state provision which was not very flexible. As a consequence, services are now more varied, cover a wider range, and are often cheaper. One also witnesses attempts to develop vertical or horizontal integration of services.

There has also been social innovation, although this may not always be intentional; a move towards proximity services might be due to the small size and local nature of a service. Social innovation might include better support for the informal sector, or making more use of volunteers. It often means involving more of the social partners in an initiative, thus helping to increase the level of social integration in an area. One social function that is not always recognised is the ability to provide help to clients, not only in terms of care, but also in helping them to secure finance (e.g. benefits) in order to pay for that care.

In this chapter a brief consideration of theories on the origins of social enterprise has helped explain the sectors in which they operate, by reference to market and state failures. This approach has also reflected the advantages of social enterprises and their requirements in terms of support for the entrepreneurial or development function. The contribution of social enterprises to combating social exclusion has been revealed by examining the process by which social capital is generated and reproduced, how externalities are generated, and the extent of innovation – but this is greatly influenced by the nature of the market contracting process which may – or may not – allow the space for negotiating these kinds of outcomes.

Notes

1   Data from Eurostat (1997), reports from co-ops and co-op federations in each sector and the Johns Hopkins Comparative Non-profit Sector Project (Kendall and Knapp, 1996).
2   Social firms are included in the section on new co-operatives because their activities are very similar to social employment co-ops, but they are more properly considered as trading voluntary organisations.
3   The Community Programme was one of the largest government employment creation programmes utilised in the UK during the Thatcher era; it supported temporary work and training.
4   See the contribution by Evers in this book (chapter 17).

Bibliography

BATSLEER, J., CORNFORTH, C. and PATON, R. (eds) (1991) *Issues in Voluntary and Non-profit Management*, Addison-Wesley, Wokingham.

BORNAT, J., PEREIRA, C., PILGRIM, D. and WILLIAMS, F. (1993) *Community Care: A Reader*, Macmillan with Open University, Basingstoke.

BUTLER, R.J. and WILSON, D.C. (1990) *Managing Voluntary and Non-profit Organisations: Strategy and Structure*, Routledge, London.

Co-operative Working 1, 2 and 3, Learning Packs from LMSO, Open University, Milton Keynes.

CORNFORTH, C., THOMAS, A., LEWIS, J. and SPEAR, R. (1988) *Developing Successful Worker Co-ops*, Sage, London.

Directory of Co-operatives (1993) Co-ops Research Unit, Open University, Milton Keynes.

Does Employee Ownership Improve the Quality of Service, A Case of Home Care for The Elderly in New York (1989), Job Ownership Ltd, London.

EUROSTAT (1997) *The Co-operative, Mutual and Non-Profit Sector in the European Union*, DG 23, European Commission.

GRIFFITH, Sir Roy (1988) 'Community Care: Agenda for Action. A Report to the Secretary of State for Social Services', HMSO, London.

HOYES, L. *et al.* (1993) *User Empowerment and the Reform of Community Care*, School of Advanced Urban Studies, Bristol University.

KENDALL, J. and ALMOND, S. (1998) *The UK Voluntary (Third) Sector in Comparative Perspective*, PSSRU, University of Kent.

KENDALL, J. and KNAPP, M. (1996) *The Voluntary Sector in the UK*, Manchester University Press, Manchester.

KENDALL, J., FORDER, J. and KNAPP, M. (1998) 'The Voluntary Sector in the Mixed Economy: Care for Elderly People', CIRIEC Study on Associations and Services to Elderly People, Liège.

National Health Service and Community Care Act (1990), HMSO.

PHARAOH, C. and SMERDON, M. (eds) (1998) *Dimensions of the Voluntary Sector*, Charities Aid Foundation, West Malling.

RAMON, S. (1991) *Beyond Community Care – Normalisation and Integration Work*, Macmillan with Mind Publications, Basingstoke.

SIMMONDS, D. and EMMERICH, M. (1996) *Regeneration through Work*, CLES, Manchester.

Social Firms (1997) Echo Project, European Commission, Garant, Leuven.

SPEAR, R. and VOETS, H. (1995) *Success and Enterprise*, Avebury, Hants.

SPEAR, R., LEONETTI, A. and THOMAS, A. (1994) *Third Sector Care*, CRU, Open University, Milton Keynes.

Strategic Management in the Social Economy – Learning and Training Pack, CRU, Open University, Milton Keynes.

THOMAS, A. and CORNFORTH, C. (1994) 'The Changing Structure of the Worker Co-operative Sector in the UK: Interpretation of Recent Trends', *Annals of Public and Co-operative Economy*, vol. 65, 4: 641–56.

Part II

Social enterprises

A theoretical perspective

16 Social enterprises as incentive structures

An economic analysis

Alberto Bacchiega and Carlo Borzaga

Introduction

In recent years, the third or non-profit sector (as opposed to the private for-profit and public sectors) has attracted increasing attention from policy-makers and public opinion. The reasons for this are twofold. On the one hand, the organisations that constitute the third sector have operated successfully in industries (health, cultural, leisure and welfare) which have experienced considerable growth in recent years.[1] On the other hand, these organisational forms have undergone a constant process of evolution, which has enabled them to meet part of the growing demand for social, community care and collective services.[2] Since the 1980s, third-sector organisations have gradually acquired a productive and entrepreneurial role. Productive third-sector organisations providing services have become, especially in Europe, increasingly active in areas previously dominated by governmental or charitable intervention, such as social services and the work integration of disadvantaged people. In countries where the provision of these services was scarce and mainly undertaken by public institutions (e.g. Italy and Spain), the emergence of third-sector entrepreneurial organisations is an almost entirely new phenomenon. In other countries (e.g. France and Belgium), where private third-sector organisations were already involved in the provision of welfare services, the trend has been towards their greater autonomy from the public authorities.

The term 'social enterprise' has come into use to distinguish the new entrepreneurial forms from more traditional third-sector or non-profit organisations. The distinction underlines the growing involvement of the new organisations in the production of services and it is this which differentiates them from traditional charities. It is also necessary, because the non-profit distribution constraint – the characteristic of third-sector organisations most stressed in the economic literature – does not seem to be crucial to distinguish them from the private for-profit enterprises. Indeed, although all social enterprises pursue objectives other than profit maximisation, not all of them are subject to a non-profit distribution constraint.[3]

The key feature of social enterprises seems to be their ability to strengthen the fiduciary relationship within and around the organisation, and to mobilise resources from individuals and from the local community (social capital). They do so using institutional and organisational mechanisms that rely, *inter alia*, on the forceful and broader representation of the interests of stakeholders, on a participatory and democratic governance system, and on the use of volunteer labour. As a consequence, the simple dichotomy between for-profit and non-profit, so widely used in the economic literature, does not suffice to explain the emerging organisational differentiation within the third sector, and particularly the evolution of social enterprises as described above. In our view, this dichotomy stems from the emphasis in this literature on a very specific organisational form – the foundation – and its insufficient use of the insights offered by the institutional approach to the study of organisations. We believe that there should be reconsideration of the nature of third-sector organisations, bearing in mind that the sector is made up of a plurality of organisations far richer and more complex than the homogeneous entities described by the non-profit distribution constraint alone.

We will argue that social enterprises implement a number of institutional arrangements whereby the objectives of the organisation (to serve the community or a specific group of people, and to promote social responsibility at the local level) give rise to original incentive and relational systems involving donors, consumers, public authorities, volunteers and employees. Relations of trust with the local community, the users, volunteers and workers are guaranteed by the involvement of different stakeholders, and by democratic management.

We first develop a general framework for the analysis of social enterprises from an institutional point of view, and then concentrate on a specific aspect that has been neglected by existing studies, viz. the place of workers in the organisation. We will argue that, in social enterprises, incentives for workers are not based exclusively on monetary rewards; rather, they derive mainly from workers' involvement in shaping and sharing the organisation's goals and mission. As a consequence, opportunistic behaviour may be reduced and the functioning of the organisation improved.

The chapter is organised as follows. A brief introduction to the institutional approach to organisations is presented in section 1. The purpose of this section is to summarise the main elements of the theory of institutions. The shortcomings of existing theories in analysing the recent evolution of the third sector are considered in section 2. The peculiarities of the markets in which social enterprises operate are highlighted in section 3. In section 4, the institutional specificities of social enterprises are analysed, and in section 5, a view of social enterprises as original incentive systems is proposed, and the main strengths and weaknesses of these organisations are highlighted.

1   The firm: production function versus co-ordination mechanism

The neo-classical and institutional approaches

In this subsection we briefly compare the neo-classical view of the firm and the view based on the (neo-) institutional approach. Neo-classical theory seeks to explain resource allocation as a process guided by prices (Demsetz 1997). The relevance of the firm to the understanding of the economy is marginal; once the available technology and the prices of inputs and outputs are given, there is no discretion in the production process. With perfect competition, the entrepreneur needs only to choose the best technology among well-known alternatives, go to the market to buy the machines (whose price is known), hire the workers (at the wage established in the labour market), and sell the goods produced (at the price determined on the market). Technology is also the determinant of the firm's size.

Whatever happens inside the firm is of no interest because there are no particular decisions to be taken, and any rational agent would act in the same way. The firm is a 'black box', a production function in which resources go in and goods come out. There is no need to open the black box, because nothing of interest is inside; all the interesting things happen in the market. Indeed, it is in the market that all relevant contracts are stipulated and that transactions take place.

The neo-classical view has been challenged by those theorists[4] who consider the firm to be more than a mere production function. Firms involve more than the transformation of inputs into outputs alone. They are institutions which co-ordinate and manage costly transactions. Firms rely only partially on price signals and contracting, and base their internal relations on other co-ordination mechanisms (hierarchy, communication, ownership, and so on). Firms may therefore constitute a more efficient institutional setting than markets for the conduct of some economic activities.

Moreover, firms may enable transactions to take place when price mechanisms do not convey the actual value of goods and inputs (i.e. when markets fail). The market institution is costly insofar as there are costs involved in finding a suitable partner for the transaction, in drawing up the contract, and in specifying the relevant clauses.[5] The costs of using the price system are greatly increased if information is asymmetrically distributed and if the future is only imperfectly known. In the latter case, it is extremely difficult to devise contracts that foresee all possible eventualities, and the co-ordination of transactions within the firm becomes comparatively cheap.

Firms may be able to reduce the costs of using the market, or the costs of contracting. This is because relations within firms do not have to foresee all possible eventualities; they need only define the scope of the co-ordination to take place between agents. For example, a labour contract would contain the maximum number of daily working hours, the wage and a rough description of the tasks to be performed, leaving the entrepreneur free to determine the specific content of the job.

However, relations within firms involve costs as well. There are the costs of setting up and running the organisation, of delegating tasks and controlling subordinates, of collective decision-making (when, as is often the case, more than one agent shares authority), and of bearing the risk involved in the enterprise. These costs can be labelled 'co-ordination costs' or 'costs of ownership'. As Hansmann (1996) puts it, the institutional choice between markets and firms for the relevant transactions depends on the relative size of the 'costs of contracting' versus the 'costs of ownership'.

It is worth noting that the firm as a co-ordination mechanism is a much more flexible concept than the firm as a production function. While the latter leaves no room for diversity (all firms, given prices and technology, are the same), one can imagine a great number of possible co-ordination structures. The entrepreneur making decisions within the contractual limits is a way of co-ordinating transactions, but this does not exhaust the range of options.

We may, accordingly, say that institutional theory is better able than neo-classical theory to explain the variety of organisational forms that exist in reality. In fact there is no such thing as 'the firm'. Rather, there are a number of institutional arrangements that substitute for the price system in governing transactions (e.g. investor-owned firms, customer-owned firms, worker-owned firms, and non-profit firms).[6] The organisational form that most efficiently performs a given type of transaction in a given environment is the one that is able to minimise transaction costs, i.e. the sum of contracting and ownership costs (Hansmann 1996). From this point of view, each organisational form is a particular institutional answer to a situation in which the markets do not guarantee an optimal solution, with its own costs and benefits. According to Arrow (Arrow 1963: 947), 'when market fails to achieve an optimal state, society will, to some extent at least, recognise the gap, and non-market social institutions will arise attempting to bridge it'.

The idea of the firm as an institutional alternative to the market is closely bound up with the idea that the main and most pervasive market failure is due to the imperfect and asymmetric distribution of information. This applies both to knowledge about technology and the price system and to the division of labour within firms. Thus, the co-ordination role attributed to the entrepreneur has been justified in terms of his/her ability to deal with imperfect information. Alchian and Demsetz (1972) claim that the role of the entrepreneur is to control the effort of the other contractual parties when the contribution of each to the final output cannot be attributed clearly. In order to motivate the entrepreneur in this endeavour, he/she is given ownership of the firm, including the right to co-ordinate all contractual relations with other agents, and the right to retain the residual earnings after all contracts have been honoured.

The firm as a nexus of contracts

Co-ordination within the firm is not per se an alternative to market contracting. The firm may be viewed as a nexus of contracts where the agents voluntarily accept the co-ordination role performed by the owner, but give him/her no authority or special rights apart from those explicitly stated in contracts (Demsetz 1997). Under this approach (sometimes called the new-institutional theory), the rationale for the existence of the firm is not the superiority of internal co-ordination with respect to the price system, but the need to have someone to monitor the behaviour of numerous different agents in complex production processes. One assumption of this approach is that all agents are able to optimally process all the available (asymmetrically distributed) information at the time when they write contracts. Contracts are thus optimal, in the sense that given the available information, the (second) best outcome is achieved.

This new institutional theory views the firm not as an antagonist to the price system but as an organisation which fully incorporates the price system into its contracts, in an environment characterised by information asymmetries among agents. From this point of view, new-institutional theory bridges the gap with neo-classical theory. The entrepreneur, however, still has an important role to play in co-ordinating contracts. The diversity of organisational forms can be explained under this approach in terms of the diversity of the systems of contractual arrangements within firms. Owners may exercise their right to co-ordinate contractual arrangements personally, or they may appoint other agents (the managers) to act on their behalf. An organisation may pursue a variety of objectives, and it may use different types of contract to motivate agents to take part in production.

The firm as an alternative co-ordination mechanism to the market

The contractual view of the firm considered in the previous section has been criticised by those economists who view the nexus of contracts as nothing more than the reintroduction of the market system into production processes. According to the institutional approach, organisations cannot be reduced to a web of prices and contracts; they are fully fledged alternatives to the market. Organisations are defined not only by the co-ordination of different agents and by the rewards that they obtain from participation in production (price mechanism); they also entail authority and trust relations among agents, and the identification of agents with the organisation and its goals (co-ordination mechanism).

It is possible to identify two main interrelated objections against the view of organisations as simple nexuses of contracts. The first is based on bounded rationality, and the second on the incompleteness of contracts. These will now be considered in turn.

Bounded rationality challenges the idea that agents in firms write optimal contracts. Empirical observation shows that actual contracts within firms are much simpler than predicted by optimal contracting theory. The bounded rationality approach maintains that this is because, in reality, agents do not have the computational and rational abilities that the new-institutional theory requires in order to derive optimal contracts. As a consequence, relations within firms cannot be understood solely by relying on self-interested interactions among perfectly rational agents. In particular, the participation and motivation of workers in organisations cannot be studied within the usual principal–agent framework. They depend on a larger set of variables, which Simon (1991) summarises as authority, reward, identification and co-ordination. While authority, reward and co-ordination can be explained through optimal contract theory, identification with the goal of the organisation does not seem compatible with the assumption of maximising, self-interested individuals.

The identification with organisational goals is, according to Simon, closely related to the idea that agents do not behave as maximising individuals; instead, they display bounded rationality. Imperfectly rational agents internalise the objectives and values of the organisations in which they work. Simon (1993) shows that boundedly rational agents with a certain degree of 'docility' (i.e. they are ready to accept the values of the organisation as their own, even if these values do not affect their utility function) are, from an evolutionary point of view, more resistant than purely self-interested individuals.

The contract incompleteness approach to the study of organisations is relatively recent.[7] Like the bounded rationality approach, it starts from the empirical observation that actual contracts are usually strikingly simple – contrary to the predictions of optimal contract theory. Incomplete contract theory suggests that this is so because there are prohibitive costs to writing optimal contracts. Even when it is possible to envisage all future events and their associated probabilities, giving exact contractual specification to all of them entails costs. Even assuming that these costs are not particularly high, it may still happen that a third party (e.g. a court that must decide whether the contract has been fulfilled) is unable to verify important events that can be observed by the parties involved in the contract. For this reason, contracts are often incomplete insofar as they do not specify all possible events but instead specify who has the authority to take decisions (i.e. who possesses 'control') in situations not covered by the contract. The incomplete contract approach therefore regards the firm as a truly alternative co-ordination mechanism with respect to the market institution. At the same time, it leaves room for diversity among organisational forms in the ways in which authority can be distributed within an organisation.

As noted above, the rationale for choosing a particular organisational form resides in its capacity to reduce transaction costs. Both bounded rationality and contract incompleteness provide a theoretical foundation for the comparative study of organisations as institutions that seek to minimise the costs of contracting (i.e. the costs of carrying out transactions in the marketplace) and the costs of ownership (i.e. the costs of carrying out transactions within the firm). In the sections that follow, we shall mainly use the conceptual categories of incomplete contract theory (assuming that workers are rational, although not purely self-interested) to analyse the existence, the evolution, and the diversification of third-sector institutions. However, it should be noted that incomplete contracting and bounded rationality are, to some extent, complementary in the theory of organisations.[8] Very similar conclusions to ours could be reached starting from an approach based on bounded rationality.

2   The institutional approach and third-sector organisations: existing theories and their limitations

Economists have drawn largely on institutional theory to explain the existence of third-sector organisations and, more generally, of organisations and enterprises owned by stakeholders different from investors. A very brief review of the economic literature on third-sector organisations may help to illustrate this point.[9] This literature has focused principally on four explanations for the existence of such organisations:

- Hansmann (1980) considers mainly non-profit organisations, and interprets them as less liable to exploit consumers than their for-profit counterparts when producers have an informational advantage on the quality of the product;
- Ben-Ner (1986,) extending his analysis to include other third-sector organisations, stresses the role of consumer control on output production in overcoming the asymmetric information problem;[10]
- Weisbrod (1977) considers third-sector production to be the private response to a public failure to satisfy heterogeneous demand for public goods. This theory has since been integrated with Hansmann's (Weisbrod 1988);
- the role of entrepreneurs and managers in shaping the objectives of third-sector organisations is stressed by Young (1983, 1997) with regard to entrepreneurial preferences, James (1989) who considers religious and political beliefs, Rose-Ackerman (1987) who analyses cross subsidisation of preferred non-profit activities through market production, Glaeser and Shleifer (1998) who describe the choice of a non-profit organisation as a rational entrepreneur's commitment to soft incentives.

To a large extent, these interpretations of the economic role of third-sector organisations are compatible (Anheier and Ben-Ner 1997; Krashinsky 1997), and they have often been used jointly. For example, Hansmann and Weisbrod explain why consumers may want to buy from non-profit organisations, while Ben-Ner and the 'entrepreneurial approach' explain why people may decide to set up a third-sector organisation. Not all the theories consider the non-profit distribution constraint to be crucial for understanding the phenomenon. However, the most influential explanation, which is almost universally accepted, is the one proposed by Hansmann. As a consequence, the 'non-profit-distribution constraint' has become the most important characteristic used to define the organisational typology.

In Hansmann's theory, the non-profit distribution constraint coincides with the absence of agents formally identified as *owners* of the organisation. The importance of this characteristic can be better understood if we recall the two principal formal rights associated with ownership, (1) the right to select, sign and co-ordinate contracts with the agents that establish a relation with the organisation, either as suppliers of inputs or as purchasers of the goods or services produced, and (2) the right to appropriate the residual income of the organisation, once all contractual relations have been honoured.[11]

The fact that these are formal rights obviously means that it is not necessary for them to be directly exercised by owners. In several organisational forms some ownership rights are delegated to some other agents. In particular, the right to decide on contracts to be signed is often delegated to managers, who thus have *effective control* over the organisation. The owners retain a *right to exercise control*[12] over the actions of the managers.[13]

In his early works, Hansmann (1980) focused mainly on the right to the residual income of the organisation, disregarding the issue of the allocation of control rights. The essence of the non-profit distribution constraint is, in fact, the formal recognition that nobody is entitled to the residual income of the organisation. This view was expressed by Hansmann in the following way: 'a non-profit organisation is, in essence, an organisation that is barred from distributing its net earnings, if any, to individuals who exercise control over it' (Hansmann 1980: 838). Since the organisation cannot distribute profits, the owners gain no advantage from exploiting any superior information that they may possess on product quality in order to maximise profit. Consumers are therefore somewhat protected against contractual failure.

In this approach, third-sector organisations have very often been identified solely with this highly specific allocation of residual income: the non-profit distribution constraint. As a consequence, the complexity of the third sector has been reduced to a simpler set of organisations, namely non-profits. Many of the other interesting features of third-sector organisations have been neglected as a result of this reliance on the non-profit distribution constraint in defining the sector.[14] This is particularly the case in many European countries, where the non-profit distribution constraint is not the main characteristic of most third-sector organisations, as the contributions to this book show.

More recently, Hansmann (1996) argued that non-profits arise when both the costs of contracting and the costs of ownership are too high for some category of patrons. In this case, defining specific owners for the organisations is inefficient and the control role is substituted by a fiduciary relationship with the managers, who possess effective control over the organisation, so that 'the non-profit form abandons any benefit of full ownership in favour of stricter fiduciary constraints on managers' (Hansmann 1996: 228).

However, it is not clear what the origin of the fiduciary relationship is, nor how it actually takes place, nor what factors guarantee that it will be respected. Implicitly, a great deal of importance is once again given to the non-profit distribution constraint, as the mechanism that prevents opportunistic behaviour by managers. The theory rests on two main assumptions. The first is that the absence of agents formally entitled to the residual income effectively protects consumers against opportunistic behaviour. The second is that for-profit firms do not have an incentive to establish a reputation as being non-exploitative of consumers. However, neither assumption seems particularly robust (Ortmann 1996). In fact, the non-profit distribution constraint has proved highly ineffective in preventing the onset of opportunistic behaviour and the exploitation of consumers. If the fiduciary relationship cannot be enforced, and in the absence of explicit residual rights of control, organisations seem unable to prevent the exploitation of their resources by the agents who hold effective control, they therefore fail to operate efficiently.

Moreover, the economic literature has focused mostly on the relationship between organisations on the one hand, and the donors or the customers on the other. The relations among agents within organisations have not been thoroughly analysed. For example, little attempt has been made to interpret the motives that induce workers and managers to supply their labour to third-sector organisations and to behave in accordance with the goals of their founders. In other words, attention has concentrated on the capacity of third-sector organisations to cope with failures in the product market, while their ability to remedy failures in the control of managers and workers (agency costs) has been neglected.

This theoretical weakness is all the more evident when the theory seeks to explain the more recent forms of third-sector organisations, those that engage in the production and sale of social services to government agencies or directly to the public. In many of these services, in fact, both consumers and government agencies are able to exert some control over quality, while the for-profit provider is able to overcome information problems by investing in reputation (Ortmann 1996). Indeed, Hansmann himself recognises that his theory is mainly a theory of donative non-profits. He admits that, when non-profits produce private goods or services, the problems of asymmetric information 'are inadequate to explain why investor owned firms do not have an even larger market share in these industries than they already do. The non-profit form is a very crude consumer protection device' (Hansmann 1996: 234–5). Hansmann's conclusion is that the main strength of non-profits which produce goods or services is often their being well-established incumbents in the market, since they do not gain significant comparative advantages from mitigating the cost of contracting. This conclusion highlights the difficulties that beset the view of third-sector organisations as based on the non-profit distribution constraint when it seeks to explain the complexity of the phenomenon and its recent evolution.

For a more general theory, it should be borne in mind that third-sector organisations can assume a plurality of roles including: advocacy for a particular group of citizens or for certain rights; redistribution of resources among individuals, groups, or activities; and the stable and continuous production of social and collective services. In a given period of time, an organisation may more actively engage in one of these activities and, in many cases, entirely specialise in it. The contributions to this book clearly identify a trend in third-sector organisations towards the production of services, with an increasingly entrepreneurial orientation in the marketplace. Often, social enterprises have developed out of already existing consumer or volunteer associations that focus their activity on advocacy. This is so in the case of the Italian social co-operatives. The shift from advocacy toward direct production has been a consequence of the decreasing role of the public administration in social services provision.[15]

The different roles played by third-sector organisations may explain the co-existence of a variety of organisational and legal forms in the sector. The social, legal and economic context, the evolution of needs, changes in the demand for services, and the development of alternative forms of service provision (public and for-profit) may help in explaining the shift of third-sector organisations from one role to another. Social enterprises are part of this evolution. In particular, they represent an entrepreneurial evolution of third-sector organisations. Understanding this evolution requires that one must first specify the distinctive features and the market failures of the industries in which they operate. One must then determine how the institutional characteristics of social enterprises can exert a relative advantage over other organisational forms in those industries.

3   The peculiarities of personal and collective services

A striking characteristic of the evolution of the personal and collective services sectors over the last twenty years is that supply has not been able to match, either in quantitative or qualitative terms, the rapidly growing potential demand for what are commonly considered to be merit goods.[16] In other words, the traditional producers of these services have grown increasingly unable to satisfy new and recognised needs arising from society. There are two reasons for this trend. Firstly, the socially efficient level of production may not be achieved because, at that level, consumers' capacity to pay is below the price charged by traditional suppliers. In this case, the efficient level can be achieved if the provider is able to mobilise private or public resources so that a reduced fee can be charged to consumers. In other words, the organisation must be capable of mobilising and redistributing resources in favour of the beneficiaries of its services, thus shifting their demand to the efficient level. Secondly, the socially efficient level of production may not be achieved because it is impossible or excessively costly to organise a stable supply to serve an existing and willing-to-pay demand. This may be the consequence of market or organisational failures, whereby traditional providers cannot satisfy the needs arising from society. If a new organisational arrangement is able to overcome the causes of the failure, it will yield an efficiency gain in providing the service. Both elements seem relevant in explaining the provision of social and collective services by social enterprises, in which both income redistribution and innovative production organisation play an important role.

Regarding redistribution, the need arises when initial endowments of income and abilities are perceived to be unjust. Even when this need is recognised by substantial groups in society, government policies may be unable or unwilling to guarantee the desired redistribution of the resources. Private individuals, or groups of people, may then take action to alleviate this failure through organisations based at least partly on donations and volunteer work. The activity of these organisations may take different forms, such as: advocacy for more effective government policies, the direct redistribution of wealth, or the production of specific social services to meet the needs of disadvantaged groups. While third-sector organisations are active in all these areas, social enterprises operate in the latter category, providing services to groups unable to pay a price that fully covers the costs and for which public authorities are unable or unwilling to intervene. This is the case for many new social services, for which a private organisation is able to operate only if its stakeholders accept price discrimination (if they are consumers), or if they agree to provide the necessary financial resources (if they are donors) or production factors (if they are workers or volunteers) free of charge or at a price below market levels.

The market and organisational failures that affect social services often depend on the multi-dimensional nature of either the service or its provision. Typically, social services comprise qualitative dimensions that can be evaluated differently by different users. The multi-dimensionality of a service does not per se constitute a source of market failure, nor is it incompatible with provision by traditional entrepreneurial forms. It may indeed be possible to devise contractual forms, which specify the desired level of each dimension of the service as constraints in the maximisation problem, then leave the organisation free to maximise profits. A mechanism of this kind, however, is not available if some of the objectives are non-identifiable or non-measurable. In this case, the dimensions that cannot be clearly inserted as constraints in the maximisation problem will inevitably be ignored or overlooked by the agents who possess effective control over the organisation (Holmström and Milgrom 1991).

The problem of non-verifiability is particularly relevant to services with a high relational component,[17] for which some dimensions are easily verifiable (for example, unit cost or number of clients served) but others less so (for example, the quality of the service, the degree of client satisfaction, or the relational effort made by the workers). In this case the dimensions which cannot easily be monitored and verified by the parties directly involved (producers and consumers), as well as by third parties, are crucial for the assessment of the service's quality. Indeed, the quality of the service depends on the (informal) relationship between provider and consumer, and it is therefore particularly hard to measure. This may lead to relations characterised by asymmetric information of various types, which we shall now discuss.

The first type of information failure, and the one most frequently mentioned in the non-profit literature, is the informational advantage of producers over consumers concerning the service provided. If consumers are able to pay, but unable to control the behaviour of producers efficiently without incurring substantial costs, they tend to be exploited by profit-maximising producers who enjoy an informational advantage. Third-sector organisations, on the other hand, may be less willing to exploit consumers because they cannot distribute profits or, as in the case of many social enterprises, because they involve consumers or volunteers in management and control of the organisations. These institutional characteristics reduce consumer exploitation, so that third-sector organisations may thus help to reduce the costs of contracting when consumers are weak. This view was considered in section 2 and will not be discussed further.

A second type of information failure characteristic of the social services sector is the informational advantage possessed by consumers with regard to their willingness to pay for the services that they desire. This gives rise to the well-known 'free-rider' problem. Third-sector organisations and social enterprises may attenuate this problem insofar as they induce consumers to reveal their true preferences and allow for price discrimination. Some authors show that co-operatives and other third-sector organisations may help overcome the free-rider problem (Grillo 1989; Bilodeau and Slivinski 1994). Ben-Ner (1986) considers the case in which consumers take control of the organisation, thereby at least partly eliminating the incentive for free-riding. In this case the high costs of contracting (due to producer–consumer and consumer–producer asymmetric information) induce substitution of the market institution with an organisation controlled fully or partially by consumers.

A third type of information failure arising in the production of social services stems from the incompleteness of labour contracts and relates to the costs of ownership. Managers and workers have better information than their principals do on the effort that they put into their work. This applies to any type of production, and generates the much-studied agency relationships within organisations. In the case of personal and community services, however, the problem of effort monitoring is particularly intractable, given the difficulties in organising well-functioning labour relations.[18] It follows that an organisation able to cope efficiently with this problem may be more successful in delivering such services.

However, the latter issue has not received a great deal of attention in the economic literature on non-profit third-sector organisations, with the exception of the relation between the organisation and its managers.[19] The experience of social enterprises shows the importance of the relationship between workers and organisation, as a determinant of the cost and quality of the services produced. For this reason, the remainder of this chapter is devoted to this point in particular, analysing how the institutional features of social enterprises are able to alleviate the effort-monitoring problem.

4   The institutional specificity of third-sector organisations and social enterprises

In most European countries, in the last twenty years, third-sector organisations and social enterprises have been the protagonists of a shift toward a more productive and entrepreneurial stance. Indeed, they offer a stable, continuous, and to some extent autonomous production of a fairly well-defined and limited range of services, characterised by one or more of the following dimensions: labour intensive technology, difficult effort monitoring, and the inability of customers to pay the full cost of production. These services, or the method of their delivery, are often innovative, especially when compared with existing private and public production. The relative importance of some dimensions of the services compared with others translates into the different organisational and legal forms (co-operatives, associations) that social enterprises may assume.

Given the complexity of services, and the variety of social enterprises that have evolved to deliver them, analysis of the phenomenon requires full deployment of the tools offered by institutional theory, paying special attention to the allocation of control rights within organisations. In social enterprises, the allocation of control rights is no less important than the destination of residual income. This is because one of the control rights assigned to the agents entitled to exercise them is the crucial right to determine the objectives of the organisation. This right is exercised through the ultimate control over all contractual relationships, which influences the incentive system within organisations and thus their internal structure.

Like many third-sector organisations, social enterprises do not possess clear-cut mechanisms with which to define those entitled to control rights, and consequently to determine the objectives of organisations (as opposed to for-profit organisations, where it is the contribution of risk capital that matters).[20] However, in the absence of predetermined control, right assignment does not imply the absence of a control structure (Alchian and Demsetz 1972; Hansmann 1996). The control structure has a different, and potentially more variable, characterisation. The variety of systems for the allocation of control rights reflects the differentiation of the third sector and of social enterprises. The literature has already recognised this feature. For example, some stress the role of donors as the providers of the financial resources in donative non-profit organisations, and thus justify their entitlement to exercise the residual rights of control (Fama and Jensen 1983); others argue that there is no clear-cut way to identify who is entitled to control rights, and the allocation follows informal patterns (Ben-Ner, Montias and Neuberger 1993); while Ben-Ner and van Hoomissen (1991) in discussing mainly consumer co-operatives and associations, simply entrust consumers with ultimate control rights. Often, as many of the studies in this book show, control rights are entrusted to more than one category of stakeholders (Borzaga and Mittone 1997). Control over the organisation and over the definition of its objectives gives these stakeholders an incentive to establish and efficiently manage the organisation in the pursuit of its chosen objectives.

In social enterprises, the identification of the controlling stakeholders is a consequence of the type of redistributional needs and market failures that characterise the production of a specific good or service. However, one cannot expect social enterprises to have the same type of control that is observed when the residual income claimants are fully and formally identified. This is due not only to the different institutional mechanisms possessed by the organisation; it is also related to the fact that the objectives of the organisation are not as clear and well established as they are in its for-profit counterpart. On the one hand, the separation of rights of control from rights over residual income strongly suggests that the for-profit motive does not figure importantly among the organisation's formal objectives.[21] On the other hand, the alternative formal objectives cannot be

286 A. Bacchiega and C. Borzaga

stated independently of the conditions that characterise the market in which the organisation operates.

If a line of reasoning applied to government institutions (Tirole 1994) is extended to social enterprises, it is likely that the profit maximisation objective will be substituted, not by a single, alternative goal for the organisation but by a plurality of potentially conflicting objectives. The presence of multiple objectives is clearly more likely when control rights are shared among different categories of stakeholders. These objectives are often intrinsically very difficult to quantify and codify because they concern qualitative dimensions of the activity or general principles (e.g. democracy in the organisation, customer well-being, a certain degree of resource redistribution, and so forth), the translation of which in precise guidelines is extremely difficult. A related problem is that, even when the objectives can be identified, it is difficult to weigh them in order to obtain a stable and well-defined objective function to maximise.[22]

Social enterprises are thus highly complex and diverse organisations, and the national chapters in this book give a broad picture of this complexity and diversity. Consequently, it is difficult, and sometimes simplistic, to apply a single organisational model when seeking to explain them. The degree of effective control and the category of patrons controlling the organisation may vary according to the type of organisation. Goals and objectives are not always clearly codified even within organisations, and stem instead from the history of the organisation and the shared values of its stakeholders. However, this is very different from assuming that their characterising elements can be identified with the non-distribution constraint alone. The patterns of allocation of control rights, together with a consistent governance structure, are of particular importance in productive and entrepreneurial third-sector organisations like social enterprises, given the amount of potential conflict that may arise between the objectives related to the production process and those related to the distribution of the benefits that it generates. At the same time, the allocation of control rights is the main institutional instrument with which a social enterprise can build an incentive structure within the organisation, which is consistent with its objectives.

5   Social enterprises as incentive structures

The actual allocation of control rights in social enterprises can be explained in the light of the two main difficulties that arise in the production of social and collective services, viz. the need to mobilise resources for redistribution and the presence of market and organisational failures. When the redistributive component is very substantial, and social enterprises need a high level of support in the form of donations and volunteer labour, control rights are allocated mainly to volunteers, trustees and local community representatives. When, on the other hand, the redistributive component of the organisation's activity is less pressing, for example when the public authority recognises it by subsidising productive social enterprises, control rights are allocated principally in order to cope with market and organisational failures. In the latter case, control of the organisation is assigned to clients, workers and managers. Moreover, workers and managers often accept monetary compensations which are lower than those that they would receive for comparable tasks in other organisations, thereby accepting a partial redistribution of resources from labour suppliers to consumers.

The picture arising from these considerations is quite complex and dynamic, as the history and the experiences of social enterprises testify. However, since the problems related to the redistributional aspects have been widely analysed by the literature on non-profit organisations, this section is devoted in particular to the ability of social enterprises to mitigate the negative consequences of failures in workers' contractual relations.

The non-standardised nature of social and collective services gives rise to difficulties in effort monitoring and in the use of traditional contractual instruments. Agency problems within the organisation cannot be solved by linking workers' remuneration to the dimensions of their performance that can be monitored. In other words, incentives in the organisations that produce these services tend to be low-powered. This engenders incentive structures in which relatively little weight is given to the more easily measurable and verifiable dimensions of production in order not to jeopardise the pursuit of less verifiable objectives.

One consequence of low-powered incentives is that agents have limited motivation to behave efficiently. Since their remuneration is only loosely related to performance, low commitment on the part of workers with no monetary motivations is to be expected. At the same time, opportunistic behaviour may affect output in such a way that production is not viable. This is especially the case when the price determined by public or private demand for the services only partially pays for their cost, leaving the organisation with a redistributive commitment in favour of its clients. In this case, the organisation must mobilise human and financial resources and select workers willing to exert effort not only in exchange for monetary compensation.

The organisational structure of social enterprises seems better able to avert the danger of opportunistic behaviour, when compared not only with for-profit enterprises and public agencies but also with traditional third-sector organisations (e.g. foundations). This is so because the organisational structure can give rise to incentive systems, which are consistent with organisational objectives. In particular, the nature of the organisation influences the type of incentive system offered to workers and managers. The choice of a particular institutional form thus signals to stakeholders the kind of objectives that the organisation will pursue, and consequently the incentives that it will offer.

The characteristics of social enterprises that seem crucial for definition of their incentive structure are closely related to their social dimension. Particularly relevant are: the existence of an explicit social aim to serve the community or part of it; the direct involvement of a group of people belonging to the community or sharing common needs; limited profit distribution; and democratic and open management. These characteristics are closely related. We will consider them in turn, highlighting their common features.

The existence of an explicit social aim in social enterprises is an important signal of the organisation's nature to both workers and other stakeholders, and also to the outside world. As a consequence, both existing and potential workers and volunteers are able to measure their abilities and expectations against the organisational goals that they will be asked to pursue. This can be seen, for example, in work-integration services, where actual and prospective workers are made aware of the fact that part of the added value they contribute will be used to reward and improve the human capital of disadvantaged workers. It is also evident in social services production, where the organisations commit the realised profits to favour the development of new activities or to broaden the number of beneficiaries. Moreover, explicit social goals and monetary objectives are to a large extent mutually exclusive. A clear signal that no monetary objectives are pursued seems to be consistent with the production of services with non-measurable or non-verifiable dimensions. As noted above, contracts for the production of such services tend to be low-powered, and remuneration unrelated to observable performance.

In fact, social enterprises tend to use a mix of monetary and non-monetary components in a remuneration package in which the wage component is less substantial than in for-profit organisations operating in the same industries.[23] The monetary dimension is not the only, or even the main, dimension of the exchange as much for the agents as the principal. In other words, social enterprises seem able to motivate workers by using non-wage incentives. Of course, the demand for labour expressed by social enterprises can find a matching offer only if there are workers willing to exchange extrinsic (wage-related) rewards for intrinsic motivations. Both experimental (Frey 1997) and empirical evidence suggests that this is the case. A recent empirical study on employment conditions in the Italian social services sector shows that for the large majority of workers in social enterprises the choice of organisation and sector of activity was a consequence of a specific interest in the content of the job, and not dictated by lack of alternatives or attractive monetary rewards (Borzaga 2000). At the same time, work satisfaction was higher for the workers who have joined the organisation in the pursuit of intrinsic motivations.

Indeed, a constant characteristic of social enterprises is more wage moderation and lower wage differentiation within the organisation than in for-profit and public organisations. Moreover, their workers seem to be satisfied with their jobs and less prone to leave the organisation.[24] As a consequence, the worker satisfaction and on-the-job effort crucial for the production of relational services can be achieved in conjunction with cost containment. This point is an important one because wage moderation in social enterprises is sometimes mistakenly taken as an indicator of work exploitation, rather than as an aspect of a peculiar remuneration package. The requirement that the agents who establish and run social enterprises should have a stake in their activities creates trust relations, and strengthens and gives credibility to the goals of the enterprise. Indeed, the opportunistic risk related to low-powered incentives can be at least partially averted if the objectives of the organisation and those possessing control rights coincide to some extent.

In general, the higher degree of freedom for workers to determine the content of the work awarded through low-powered incentives can be used to achieve personal objectives different from monetary profit (although not necessarily coincident with the institutional objectives of the organisation).[25] However, the direct involvement of stakeholders most interested in achieving the social goals of the organisation greatly reduces this risk. Cohesiveness within the group carrying out the activity also increases the degree of awareness of, and control over, the effort exerted by fellow workers. This is especially important when goals have multiple dimensions.

Not much needs to be said about limited profit distribution, which is to be interpreted in relation to the elements discussed above. We have already noted that the existence of social goals is hardly compatible with profit maximisation. The role of a constraint on profit distribution should therefore be only marginal.[26] In social enterprises, the limit on the distribution of profits originates as an institutional choice taken within the organisation, rather than as a characteristic imposed exogenously (by law or by the policy-maker). Obviously, monetary variables are still important when running the organisation, for example in guaranteeing its financial strength and its survival in the market (since these organisations face a significant level of economic risk). However, in this case the monetary dimension acts as a constraint (e.g. a certain return must be achieved in order to reward the capital invested) to the pursuit of the chosen objectives, instead of being a maxim in itself. Nevertheless, the limited profit distribution criterion is important for social enterprises, for two main reasons. Firstly, it is a powerful, although partial, signal for the stakeholders and the outside world, of the real objectives of the organisation. Secondly, it limits the possibility that other, profit-maximising organisations will label themselves social enterprises in order to obtain unwarranted fiscal and reputational advantages. Clearly, this also applies to social enterprises that initially pursue non-monetary goals but then shift towards more traditional profit-oriented behaviour.[27]

Finally, democratic and open management is another major characteristic of social enterprises, and it is consistent with the features discussed above. It is consistent in particular with the need for the constant involvement of workers in affirming and defining the goals of the organisation, and also with the representation and participation of other stakeholders, such as clients and customers. Moreover, democratic management is often correlated with a wage schedule that is relatively flatter than in for-profit organisations. A democratic structure does not sharply differentiate between hierarchical levels when it comes to deciding monetary remuneration. This also seems to correspond with the lower importance of monetary dimensions in social enterprises, and is consistent with the use of low-powered contracts. If contractual relations are necessarily loosely defined, democratic and open management has the important role of redirecting strategies so that they are consistent with organisational goals.

The foregoing analysis supports our initial claim that there is a link between the characteristics of social enterprises and the goods that they produce. Social enterprises emerge as institutional arrangements, which seek to reduce the difference between the goals of the organisation as such, and those of the agents that take part in production. Insofar as they limit opportunistic behaviour, they are successful in reducing the costs of ownership *vis-à-vis* other organisational forms.

Clearly, even if agency problems and opportunistic behaviour may be reduced in social enterprises, they do not disappear completely. Moreover, social enterprises offer an organisational model that is at once very fragile and very unstable. One of the main difficulties faced by social enterprises is achieving a constant balance among organisational goals, the allocation of control rights, the incentive structure, and the characteristics of the markets in which they operate. This is a daunting task for these organisations, especially because there seems to be a lack of points of reference in managerial theory and experience, and because existing incorporation forms significantly limit the stabilisation of their governance structure.

Moreover, social enterprises are extremely sensitive to changes in public policy, especially regarding the types of services eligible for public subsidies. Understandably, social enterprises can be negatively affected by a decrease in public support for the production of social services. But this is not the only example of fragility. Even the decision of public authorities to finance the production of a service previously provided using private resources could require delicate institutional changes, and thus constitute a risk. If the public authority decides to take up the redistributional aspect of a given service, this implies not only contractual change for social enterprises, but also radical change in organisational arrangements, the allocation of control rights, and the incentive structure.

Although these weaknesses are a major obstacle to the development of a social enterprise production model, the studies in this book show that social enterprises may be better able to organise the efficient production of particular goods than are for-profit enterprises, public agencies, and traditional non-profit organisations.

Conclusions

In this chapter we proposed an institutional interpretation of social enterprises as a peculiar incentive system. Social enterprises constitute an organisational form that is able to perform well in the production of personal and collective services that cannot be efficiently produced by for-profit or public organisations for two main reasons. Firstly, these services may involve market and contractual failures (often related to the relational component of the service). Secondly, a certain degree of redistribution from financiers or producers to consumers may be required for production to take place.

The institutional characteristics of social enterprises form an original incentive system that helps to overcome the problems associated with production of personal and collective services. Particularly relevant, from this point of view, are the explicit social aim, the proximity between producers on the one hand and consumers and the local community on the other, and an internal organisation that values open and democratic management over monetary remuneration for workers' effort.

Social enterprises strike a difficult balance between organisational goals, allocation of control rights, incentive structure and characteristics of the markets in which they operate. While these elements allow social enterprises to adapt their internal organisation to the specific problems posed by the production of personal and collective services, they also make the social enterprise a fragile organisational model, extremely sensitive to changes in market conditions and public policies.

Notes

1 As a result, the relative weight of the third sector has grown steadily over the past two decades in most Western economies. According to Salamon and Anheier (1994), the third sector accounted for 12.8 per cent of the new jobs created in the United States between 1980 and 1990 (its relative weight in the economy being 6.8 per cent in 1990), 11 per cent in Germany (3.7 per cent) and 15.8 per cent in France (4.2 per cent). Borzaga (1991) estimates the growth of employment in the non-profit sector in Italy at 39 per cent during the 1980s, while total employment grew by 7.4 per cent only. Employment growth continued at a sustained rate in the period 1990–1995 (Salamon and Anheier 1997). The national chapters in this books testify to the development of numerous traditional and new third-sector organisations.

2 As the chapters of this book show, third-sector organisations are virtually non-existent in most industries. They are concentrated in the production of what could, broadly speaking, be called 'collective services' (the term used by Ben-Ner and van Hoomissen 1991) or 'communal services' (OECD definition). In this chapter, we will sometimes use the term 'social services'. When third-sector organisations operate in the agricultural and manufacturing sectors, the core activity is almost invariably service provision, i.e. the creation of employment opportunities for disadvantaged workers.

3 For example, some social enterprises are incorporated as co-operatives, and are therefore allowed to distribute some of their profits.

4 Starting with Coase (1937).

5 Furthermore, the nature of market contracting implies the replication of these costs for repeated transactions.

6 Each of them, in turn, enables further organisational options.

7 The seminal studies are those by Grossman and Hart (1986) and Hart and Moore (1990).

8 Whether bounded rationality is necessary for a theory of incomplete contracts is a matter of debate. It is sometimes argued that there may be a limited degree of bounded rationality embedded in the fact that third parties are unable to verify some clauses of written contracts (Hart 1990). However, the incomplete contracting approach does not generally assume bounded rationality on the part of the contracting agents. The interpretation of unbounded rationality in incomplete contracting has been recently criticised, most notably by Maskin and Tirole (1999).

9 For a more comprehensive survey of the literature, see Anheier and Ben-Ner (1997).

10 See also Ben-Ner and van Hoomissen (1991).

11 Similar concepts can be found in, e.g. Alchian and Demsetz (1972), Fama and Jensen (1983) and Ben-Ner and Jones (1995).

12 The terms 'control rights' and 'effective control' are taken from Burkart, Gromb and Panunzi (1997). A similar idea is put forward by Aghion and Tirole (1997), who distinguish between 'formal' and 'real' authority.

13 This is the case, for example, in most organisations which issue equity, where the control exercised by owners over managers is limited to a formal assessment, carried out at set dates, of the overall performance of the management activity. Owners do not, as a rule, take day-to-day decisions.

14 This is the approach, for example, taken by the influential empirical study carried out by Salamon and Anheier (1994), in which the definition of 'non-profit' is almost exclusively based on the non-profit distribution constraint.

15 On the different trend toward commercialisation that the US non-profit sector is witnessing, see Weisbrod (1998).

16 All country studies stress the gap between the emerging needs for personal and collective services and the capacity of existing supply to meet them. For a review of research that has tried to measure unsatisfied demand, see Laville and Gardin (1997). Low employment rates in the personal and collective services sector across Europe stand as an indirect proof of the insufficiency of current production (see European Commission 1999).

17 Services have a relational component if the direct relation between producers and consumers influences the quality of the service provided. On this point see Gui (1994, 1996), Uhlaner (1989), and Zamagni (1997).

18 See, for example, Young (1999).

19 See for example Handy and Katz (1998) and Preston (1989).

20 In investor-owned organisations, the subjects entitled to control rights according to their monetary contribution to the venture – i.e. the owners – define the objectives of the organisation (the maximisation of the expected value of the enterprise), thereby determining the incentives structure – usually based on monetary variables – best able to achieve this objective.

21 Note, however, that as a consequence of agency problems, profit distribution may occur even if it is not a formal objective. From this point of view, the distribution of profits within non-profit organisations, when it occurs, will reflect a failure in the *internal* control activity. The traditional literature, on the contrary, considers the distribution of profits rather as the realisation of the covert objectives of the organisation, stemming from inefficient *external* controls.

22 To continue with the previous example, what is the right balance between the level of the democracy within an organisation, the level of consumer well-being, and the degree of redistribution to adopt in favour of beneficiaries?

23 Handy and Katz (1998) explain the lower wage of managers in non-profit organisations as resulting from a signalling game in which individuals committed to the goals of the organisation self-select to the non-profit job.

24 See for example Borzaga (2000). Similar results are found by Mirvis (1992) and Preston (1990).

25 Strangely enough, most criticisms of third-sector organisations have focused on the first aspect (maximisation of monetary return) when modelling the conflict of interests between principal and agents. However, there is no reason to conclude that agents in third-sector organisations do actually pursue non-monetary objectives, such as the maximisation of the size of the organisation, the number of people they have authority over, the quantitative or qualitative level of production.

26 Strictly speaking, social enterprises should be subject to the opposite limitation; that is, they should be prevented from maximising monetary losses in order to finance their non-monetary objectives. In reality, no such limit is needed as the credit market already imposes a strict limit on the borrowing capacity of these organisations.

27 However, it is worth noting that the incorporation forms social enterprises assume do not often allow for change to outright for-profit status (this is the case for example of the Italian social co-operatives).

Bibliography

AGHION, P. and TIROLE, J. (1997) 'Formal and Real Authority in Organizations', *Journal of Political Economy*, vol. 105, 11: 1–29.

ALCHIAN, A. and DEMSETZ, M. (1972) 'Production, Information Costs and Organisation', *American Economic Review*, vol. 72, 5: 777–95.

ANHEIER, A.K. and BEN-NER, A. (1997) 'Economic Theories of Non-profit Organisations: A *Voluntas* Symposium', *Voluntas*, vol. 8, 2: 93–6.

ARROW, K.J. (1963) 'Uncertainty and the Welfare Economics of Medical Care', *American Economic Review*, vol. 53, 5: 941–73.

BEN-NER, A. (1986) 'Non-profit Organisations: Why Do They Exist in Market Economies?', in ROSE-ACKERMAN, S. (ed.) *The Economics of Non-profit Institutions*, Oxford University Press, New York, 94–113.

BEN-NER, A. and JONES, D. (1995) 'Employee Participation, Ownership and Productivity: a Theoretical Framework', *Industrial Relations*, vol. 34, 4: 532–54.

BEN-NER, A. and VAN HOOMISSEN, T. (1991) 'Non-profit Organisations in the Mixed Economy', *Annals of Public and Co-operative Economics*, vol. 62, 4: 519–50.

BEN-NER, A., MONTIAS, J.M. and NEUBERGER, E. (1993) 'Basic Issues in Organisations: a Comparative Perspective', *Journal of Comparative Economics*, vol. 17: 207–42.

BILODEAU, M. and SLIVINSKI, A. (1994) 'Rational Non-profit Entrepreneurship', EconWPA Working Paper IO 9405001.

BORZAGA, C. (ed.) (2000) *Capitale umano e qualità del lavoro nei servizi sociali. Un'analisi comparata tra modelli di gestione*, FIVOL, Roma.

—— (1991) 'The Italian Non-profit Sector. An Overview of an Undervalued Reality', *Annals of Public and Co-operative Economies*, vol. 62, 4: 695–710.

BORZAGA, C. and MITTONE, L. (1997) 'The Multi-Stakeholders versus the Non-Profit Organization', Università degli Studi di Trento, Dipartimento di Economia, Discussion Paper no. 7.

BURKART, M., GROMB, D. and PANUNZI, F. (1997) 'Large Shareholders, Monitoring and the Value of the Firm', *Quarterly Journal of Economics*, vol. 112, 3: 693–728.

CLOTFELDER, C.T. (1992) *Who Benefits from the Non-Profit Sector?*, University of Chicago Press, Chicago.

COASE, R. (1937) 'The Nature of the Firm', *Economica*, vol. 4, 16: 386–405.

DEMSETZ, H. (1997) 'The Firm in Economic Theory: A Quiet Revolution', *American Economic Review*, vol. 87, 2: 426–9.

European Commission (1999) *Employment Performance in the Member States*, Employment Rates Report, Luxembourg.

FAMA, E.F. and JENSEN, M.C. (1983) 'Separation of Ownership and Control', *Journal of Law and Economics*, vol. 26: 301–25.

FREY, B.S. (1997) *Not Just for the Money. An Economic Theory of Personal Motivation*, Edward Elgar, Cheltenham.

GLAESER, E.L. and SHLEIFER, A. (1998) 'Not-for-Profit Enterpreneurs', NBER Working Paper 8610, November.

GRILLO, M. (1989) 'Cooperative di consumatori e produzione di beni sociali', Working Paper POLITEIA no. 39.

GROSSMAN, S.J. and HART, O.D. (1986) 'The Costs and Benefits of Ownership: A Theory of Vertical and Lateral Integration', *Journal of Political Economy*, vol. 94, 4: 691–719.

GUI, B. (1996) 'On Relational Goods: Strategic Implications of Investment in Relationship', *International Journal of Social Economics*, 10–11: 260–78.

—— (1994) 'Interpersonal Relations: A Disregarded Theme in the Debate on Ethics and Economics', in LEWIS, A. and WARNERYD, K.E. (eds) *Ethics and Economic Affairs*, Routledge, London, 251–63.

HANDY, F. and KATZ, E. (1998) 'The Wage Differential between Non-profit Institutions and Corporations: Getting More by Paying Less?', *Journal of Comparative Economics*, vol. 26, 2: 246–61.

HANSMANN, H.B. (1996) *The Ownership of Enterprise*, The Belknap Press of Harvard University Press, Cambridge, MA.

—— (1980) 'The Role of Non-Profit Enterprise', *The Yale Law Journal*, vol. 89, 5: 835–901.

HART, O. (1990) 'Is "Bounded Rationality" an Important Element of a Theory of Institutions?', *Journal for Institutional and Theoretical Economics*, vol. 146: 696–702.

HART, O. and MOORE, J. (1990) 'Property Rights and the Nature of the Firm', *Journal of Political Economy*, vol. 98, 6: 1,119–58.

HOLMSTRÖM, B. and MILGROM, P. (1991) 'Multitask Principal–Agent Analyses: Incentive Contracts, Asset Ownership, and Job Design', *Journal of Law, Economics and Organisation*, vol.7: 26–52.

JAMES, E. (1989) *The Nonprofit Sector in International Perspective*, Oxford University Press, New York.

KRASHINSKY, M. (1997) 'Stakeholder Theories of the Non-profit Sector: One Cut at the Economic Literature', *Voluntas*, vol. 8, 2: 149–61.

LAVILLE, J.-L. and GARDIN, L. (1997) *Local Initiatives in Europe*, CRIDA, Paris.

MASKIN, E. and TIROLE, J. (1999) 'Unforeseen Contingencies and Incomplete Contracts', *Review of Economic Studies*, vol. 66,1: 83–114.

MIRVIS, P.H. (1992) 'The Quality of Employment in the Non-profit Sector: an Update on Employee Attitudes in Non-profits versus Business and Government', *Non-profit Management and Leadership*, vol. 3, 1: 23–41.

ORTMANN, A. (1996) 'Modern Economic Theory and the Study of Non-profit Organizations: Why the Twain Shall Meet', *Non-profit and Voluntary Sector Quarterly*, vol. 25, 4: 470–84.

PRESTON, A.E. (1990) 'Changing Labour Market Patterns in the Non-Profit and For-Profit Sectors: Implications for Non-Profit Management', *Non-Profit Management and Leadership*, vol. 1, 1: 15–28.

—— (1989) 'The Non-Profit Worker in a For-Profit World', *Journal of Labour Economics*, vol. 7, 1: 438–63.

ROSE-ACKERMAN, S. (1987) 'Ideals Versus Dollars: Donors, Charity Managers, and Government Grants', *Journal of Political Economy*, vol. 95, 4: 810–23.

SALAMON, L.M. and ANHEIER, H.K. (1997) *Defining the Nonprofit Sector: A Cross-National Analysis*, Johns Hopkins Nonprofit Sector Series, vol. 4, Manchester University Press, Manchester.

—— (1994) *The Emerging Sector: An Overview*, The Johns Hopkins University Institute for Policy Studies, Baltimore.

SIMON, H.A. (1993) 'The Role of Organizations in an Economy', Lezioni Raffaele Mattioli, 15 February, mimeo.

—— (1991) 'Organizations and Markets', *Journal of Economic Perspectives*, vol. 5, 2: 25–44.

TIROLE, J. (1994) 'The Internal Organisation of Governments', *Oxford Economic Papers*, vol. 46: 1–29.

UHLANER, C.J. (1989) 'Relational Goods and Participation: Incorporating Sociability into a Theory of Radical Action', *Public Choice*, vol. 62: 253–85.

WEISBROD, B.A. (1998) *To Profit or Not to Profit. The Commercial Transformation of the Non-profit Sector*, Cambridge University Press, Cambridge.

—— (1988) *The Non-profit Economy*, Harvard University Press, Cambridge.

—— (1977) *The Voluntary Non-profit Sector*, Lexington Books, Lexington, MA.

YOUNG, D. (1997) 'Non-Profit Enterpreneurship', to be published in *International Encyclopedia of Public Administration*.

—— (1986) 'Entrepreneurship and the Behavior of Non-Profit Organizations: Elements of a Theory', in ROSE-ACKERMAN, S. (ed.) *The Economics of Non-Profit Institutions*, Oxford University Press, New York, 161–84.

—— (1983) *If Not for Profit, for What?*, Lexington Books, Lexington, MA.

YOUNG, R. (1999) 'Prospecting for New Jobs to Combat Social Exclusion: The Example of Home-Care Services', *European Urban and Regional Studies*, vol.6, 2: 99–113.

ZAMAGNI, S. (1997) 'Social Paradoxes of Growth and Civil Society', University of Bologna, Department of Economics, mimeo.

17 The significance of social capital in the multiple goal and resource structure of social enterprises

Adalbert Evers

Introduction

Quite often, new forms of social and economic action have to be conceptualised and the groups concerned seek their own vocabulary. This is also the case with regard to the development of organisational forms of action which have been labelled as 'social purpose businesses', 'civic enterprises', 'community businesses', 'community wealth enterprises'[1] and 'social enterprises'. The challenge for analytical debates is that the term 'social enterprise' seems to blur exactly those frontiers which have been deliberately constructed – between action for the public good and private action, between social action as non-profit and enterprises as private market organisations.

The theoretical and conceptual sketch that we want to put forward suggests that to understand social enterprises we need to see them as organisations that intertwine a multiplicity of goals and resources. Such a theoretical orientation is to a large extent shared with others in the field that point to the role of non-market and non-state resources like donations and volunteering. It also underlines the fact that third-sector organisations can integrate various social goals, ranging from serving the poor to the delivery of public goods.

The argument proposed here is that studying specific resource and goal structures of social enterprises is particularly interesting when we take into account the mobilisation of social capital. Such an approach, by bringing into view the key role of socio-political components, such as the various dimensions of civic commitment which constitute social capital, helps to overcome the risks of a selective, restricted and merely socio-economic conceptualisation of both the mixed resources and the multiple goals of social enterprises.

In the first part of this chapter, we will try to clarify our notion of social capital, stressing that it is not a pre-condition for, but rather something co-produced by public policies (section 1). We then argue that by referring to the concept of social capital, non-market and non-state resources – which are very important for social enterprises – can be captured more widely, and include non-material resources like the readiness for civic commitment and partnership building (section 2). As far as the multiple goals and intended effects of social enterprises are concerned, we will show that many of them can be better understood by using the concept of social capital. This makes it possible to take into account issues of power and civic commitment and thus to show that 'social utility' means more than merely rendering better services (section 3). Finally, we debate how the special link between the development of social enterprises and the use and cultivation of social capital might be better preserved and appreciated by public policies (section 4). But before unfolding these arguments, three preliminary remarks must be made.

First of all, although examples will be taken from one special field of action of third-sector initiatives (the area of social and occupational integration and job creation),[2] it is our opinion that, in principle, social enterprises as a specific entrepreneurial form of third-sector organisations can take shape in many fields and forms. They are not linked exclusively to matters of occupational integration, as is, for example, suggested in the study put forward by the OECD.[3]

Secondly, while these reflections on social enterprises will hopefully contribute to a better understanding of their role as part of an 'intermediate' *social* area, little will be said about the implications of the word *enterprise*.[4] Perhaps this term mainly reflects a general trend in the last decade to take 'entrepreneurial' as a synonym for creative and innovative action as well as for the readiness to take responsibilities and risks in terms of 'social entrepreneurship'. A degree of entrepreneurial orientation would then be imperative for each and every organisation today, irrespective of its location in one or other sector, whether it is a charity or a social assistance bureau, a cultural association or a new computer shop. Only those third-sector organisations that are pursuing social goals and purposes and do so in an entrepreneurial way, would then qualify to be recognised as social enterprises. Obviously, there may often be a link between entrepreneurial and commercial orientation, and the subject of 'enterprising non-profits' (Dees 1998) gives rise to a broad number of critical issues, but these will not be studied here.[5]

Thirdly, it should be noted that this contribution concentrates on analytically defining the specificity of social enterprises as third-sector organisations. It does not provide a historical argument concerning the 'why' and 'when' of such institutional forms. However, by highlighting the impact of social capital and civic commitment, it is possible to make clear implicitly that the development of social enterprises is a much more political and contingent matter than economic analyses of institutional choice might suggest.

1   Social capital

The term 'social capital' refers to elements like trust, civic spirit, solidarity, and the readiness to associate and to build and maintain communities (Coleman 1988; Putnam 1993, 1995). According to Putnam, these elements represent the historical product of an overall well-functioning society, both on the local and the national level, and a degree of positive and 'civilised' interplay of economic, social and political institutions in a defined territorial and local context. As has been made clear in Putnam's study of social capital as a key element for societal development in the Italian regions, the forms of trust and association which are decisive are those directed to the public sphere and which represent the 'weak ties' of secondary associations, cutting across social cleavages and helping thereby to strengthen what he calls 'civic commitment' (Putnam 1993: 175). Putnam's concept[6] does not include every form of trust and association – associations without any link to the public sphere of civil society, like for example, clan building, individual networking or closed family networks are excluded.[7] About the North–South division in Italy, which he studied, Putnam remarks at the end of his book that 'those concerned with democracy and development in the South should be building a more civic community. ... Building social capital will not be easy, but it is the key to making democracy work' (Putnam 1993: 185).

It is not difficult to imagine the close relationships between the development of social capital and that of third-sector organisations. Indeed, third-sector organisations are sometimes labelled as 'civil society organisations' (Salamon and Anheier 1997). Civic associations can rightly be seen as typical and central forms of associating, creating trust and strengthening attitudes which are helpful for civic communities. This is especially clear in that part of the third sector where organisations raise their voice for broad social and public concerns and where their services clearly go to groups in special need. However, it is not always so clear in those parts of the third sector where fairly strong groups voice their partial concerns and organise group-related goods and services in order to dissociate from the surrounding political community.[8]

Putnam's portrait of the relationships between 'good government' and social capital-building involves some points that are unclear. On the one hand, he seems to acknowledge that state policies and forms of governance do in fact play a role in building social capital. On the other hand, his discourse suggests that social capital can be seen as a kind of precondition for economic development and good governance, created in society and by society. In reality, as some critics with an eye on history have noticed, 'the causal relationships between good government and civil society were anything but unidirectional' (Tendler 1997: 156). Politics and the action of governments do in fact influence the ways organisations in civil society act and the degree to which they use and cultivate social capital. Whenever governments by their style of action promote deliberative politics, they support types of trust-building which cut across closely knit but segregated networks in society. State policy can greatly influence the degree to which social organisations are oriented to the public good instead of being mere lobbyists. It can also encourage the dynamics which make neighbourhood organisations sensitive to politics and to the needs of other groups instead of merely defending a narrow conception of their own interest.

Social capital, therefore, by contributing to a more civic society, might be better understood as a co-product than a precondition of state policies.[9] Given the strong mutual links between the development of democracy, the interventions of state policies and the development of civic communities and social capital, it might be more accurate to speak of 'civic capital' (Evers 1998). This would, additionally, make clear that not every form of trust and association is to be covered here insofar as one can also conceive of historical developments where the interplay of authoritarian politics and the mere self-defence of social groups creates trust within social, cultural and ethnic communities in a fragmented society. But the general trust needed for bridging social cleavages will hardly come about without corresponding developments in overall policy. We will stick, however, to the label of social capital because it has been so widely popularised.

According to Putnam, wherever 'civic communities' have developed, private economic action as well as public government can gain efficiency by 'capitalising' on them. But to what degree and in what ways do market actors contribute as well to the *reproduction of social capital?* While there is no doubt that they 'consume' such capital, whether their way of using also contributes to reproducing it is more questionable. Companies can use the broad commitment of their workers but at the same time instrumentalise them in such a way that often too little time and energy is left for them to act as citizens. Yet, good and reliable administration as well as private enterprises guaranteeing a decent job and income to citizens can be seen as indispensable (even though this may not be sufficient) for promoting a more 'civil' society and the reproduction of social capital.

In summary, we have presented some reasons to justify our understanding of the term 'social capital' in the sense of 'civic capital'. Used in this way, the concept of social capital highlights the role of broader political factors, both in terms of their general role in creating trust and associability as well as in terms of their role in shaping the orientation and behaviour of groups and associations in society. Social capital is then to be understood both as an indicator of the degree of development of a civic society (constituted both by social and political action) and as a way to debate civic commitment with an eye on economic development and governance.

2 The key role of social capital in the mixed resource structure of social enterprises

In the debate on third-sector organisations, the notion of a resource mix has little by little won acceptance. The concept of an 'independent sector' where neither any element of the world of markets nor any resource flow from state institutions plays a role has proven inadequate.

In reality, offering a service for social purposes and getting a fee are two options that need not be mutually exclusive. A vast majority of third-sector organisations producing goods and/or services partly rely on *incomes from sales to customers.* These incomes can be derived from private or public organisations, individual users and consumers, but also from state institutions that refund them (at least partly) for the services provided. Among social enterprises offering services for social and occupational integration or concerned with job creation, a certain degree of income by sales often constitutes one of the reasons for calling them 'enterprises'.

Another part of the resources of social enterprises are those granted by state institutions and municipalities in *acknowledgement of third-sector organisations' contribution to the public good*. These resources usually take the form of grants and/or special tax concessions. This source of income should be separated (even though this might often be difficult) from what is earned through contracts for the provision of specified and limited services. Through grants, subsidies for start-up investments, tax exemptions and other similar types of public resources, political authorities acknowledge the organisation's social purpose and orientation. Hence the provision of special procedures for reaching the status of a charity or an organisation for the public good. Social enterprises which offer services for occupational integration or try to create jobs often receive such types of state support because it is felt that they are doing more than, or acting differently from, a private agency which might perhaps restrict itself to picking out the easiest tasks and persons. One must, however, keep in mind that the acknowledgement of the special status of 'public utility' implies a certain ambivalence. In fact, the special purpose of a singular association is not necessarily in line with the notion that the broader public or the policy-makers have of the public good. Therefore, the accommodation between the views of the association and the public authorities 'on the contested nature of the public good' (Mansbridge 1998) is of crucial importance.

The two aforementioned types of resources are well known as constituent elements of the mixed resource structure of third-sector organisations. What is unusual is the demarcation line that we have drawn. We do not distinguish between state and market resources, but between resources which are a remuneration for specific sales of services on the one hand (a kind of market income which can come from both public and private partners) and resources which are obtained within the framework of a state-channelled reciprocal support, in exchange for the contribution to common good issues by third-sector organisations, on the other hand.

The third element in the resource mix of social enterprises – what we have called *social capital* – is very often underestimated. If civic support is mentioned at all among the resources of third-sector organisations, it usually only gets noted in very technical and organisational terms, such as income from donations and support by volunteers – often counted as an equivalent to hours of paid work.[10] In reality, the level of donations and voluntary engagement may be an important indicator for – but should not be confused with – the broader set of social and political resources that are mobilised. The success of a social enterprise for social and occupational integration and job creation, for example, depends on many non-governmental and non-market resources, including the following: it needs good informal contacts with the political and the business community; it builds on a unique level of trust achieved over time; it will have the best chance of success if it is solidly rooted and embedded in the local community; in order to be able to reinsert people, building up partnerships and projects with various economic and social partners will be a key issue. This list of forms and aspects of social capital resources is far from exhaustive.

Conceptualising these resources as social capital has two advantages. Firstly, this concept provides an effective means of taking into account a broad array of resources, in addition to income from sales and state support, giving them that impact and significance which is missing when only enumerating singular items like donations, volunteers etc. Secondly, it indicates the key role of a number of non-material social and political factors, which nevertheless can materialise as an economic and financial advantage to social enterprises. Thus the notion of social capital can bridge socio-political and socio-economic perspectives on the third sector and on social enterprises.

What is important to note is the fact that, while third-sector organisations may survive with minimal public support and without income from sales, a certain level of social capital resources is absolutely critical for their survival as social and civic organisations. A foundation can go on as long as there is a fund, but the social echo and support is finally decisive for its real status, i.e. being a social enterprise or not. Similar arguments can be made for the social welfare organisations in Germany. Even though they are still classified as third-sector organisations, they have turned into para-statal organisations insofar as they have lost all kinds of civic support (although, obviously, this does not mean that such resources are gone forever).

It can be argued that features like state grants and social capital taking the form of trust and support by local social partnerships can also be found in the resource basket of private businesses. Consequently, neither the resource mix nor its social capital elements could thus be considered as characteristics of third-sector organisations in general and social enterprises in particular. In the framework of this article we will restrict ourselves to three remarks on this.

First of all, as far as public resources are concerned, we have highlighted those that acknowledge the broader social utility (verified in a formalised process) of an organisation. These kinds of grants, which differ from subsidies, are not to be found in the resource structure of private enterprises. Giving subsidies to private capital in order to boost employment or to help stabilise a regional context is a different thing; the social effects of the for-profit enterprise that are acknowledged through this kind of public support are merely implicit and unde-clared side-effects.

Secondly, even though private business can, in general, profit from social capital, some forms of social capital (such as volunteer support or donations) are not available to the private sector.

Finally, it has to be acknowledged that there is some truth in the argument that mobilising social capital is not an exclusively third-sector phenomenon. We have already underlined the fact that one cannot easily draw sharp demarcation lines between the private sector, the state/public sector and the third sector. There are highly locally embedded (Granovetter 1985) types of business, trade and commerce, and forms of local and ethnic economy, where the for-profit orientation is remarkably limited by the implicit indebtedness to local social and cultural norms and ties, which express purposes and concerns of the local community (Barber 1995). Local people may voluntarily support small private businesses as a part of their local economy. In fact, many small and medium enterprises in the traditional private sector will share this feature of local embed-dedness with many third-sector organisations, a feature that can be seen at the same time as a special constraint for choice and mobility (Weisbrod 1998b) and as a special (social capital) resource. Whether an enterprise is private or third sector does not matter that much here.[11]

In summary, third-sector organisations build on a particular mix of multiple resources that entails a good deal of non-market income and support in addition to public grants. While many contributors to the debate do acknowledge this, they usually narrow down the non-state and non-market components to some selected material features like donations and volunteering. Introducing the concept of social capital makes it possible to better take into account that part of the resource structure of third-sector organisations/social enterprises which comprises both monetary and non-monetary elements, such as trust, sociability, the readiness for dialogue and co-operation.

3   Social capital as a part and product of the multiple goals and commitments of social enterprises

The specificity of third-sector organisations is classically reduced to their being not for-profit. When an organisation does not work for profit this means, first of all, that a clear and dominating point of reference is not available. When there is such a point of reference, it can help in adjudicating the usefulness of an action. In a for-profit enterprise, it will be easier to delimit the realm of action, e.g. whether one should offer a free service to a community will be discussed in the light of one clear dominating purpose. The dominance of a for-profit-orientation is thus likely to lead to a much more instrumental type of action and orientation. Not-for-profit orientations are comparatively less targeted and more 'expressive'. This creates a more open and diversified structure of effects and a rhetoric that is different from that for organisations centred on share-holder values. Such purposes and effects are, largely, parts of the declared goals, but even if not officially declared as goals and purposes, they may give more room for community-related effects. The opportunities and difficulties encountered by organisations with a social purpose are based on the fact that there are many potential sub-purposes and that there is no simple criterion for arranging them in a hierarchical order. This can possibly result in community-oriented goals being more easily integrated into the package of a social enterprise's declared goals.

Weisbrod has found, as an economist, an expressive way to mark the differ-ence between for-profit and not-for-profit organisations, stating that there are 'two models of organisational behaviour'. He introduces the distinction between 'profit maximisers' and 'bonoficers', the latter term being used as another name for third-sector organisations. In contrast to the former, the latter 'might seek to generate less than maximum profit, while engaging in activities that are socially desirable but unprofitable' (Weisbrod 1998b). Third-sector organisations are a way to address the need for public goods of communities which are smaller than a governmental/administrative unit, or which are delineated differently, such as special cultural or ethnic groups which are not represented by the 'median voter'.[12] In both cases the aim of making a surplus need not be excluded, but it is counterbalanced by the commitment to other, social goals.

By now it should be clear what a multiple structure of goals as a hallmark of third-sector organisations and social enterprises might mean, even though the issue of social capital has not yet been mentioned. What might then be the analytical benefit of introducing the notion of social capital? In order to answer this question, it is useful to remember the limitations of an economic approach, no matter how sophisticated it might be. Even Weisbrod's approach has short-comings insofar as he introduces the broad concepts of 'activities with social utility' or of a 'public good', but these get mostly translated into issues of good and service provision. This leads to neglecting other activities which might serve the public good as well, although in a less material way – activities with social, political and democratic concerns. The struggle for a more democratic decision-making process is very often one of the (explicit) goals of many third-sector organisations. The way third-sector organisations structure themselves and the ways in which they search for co-operation with others may make them work as kinds of 'schools of democracy' (Cohen and Rogers 1994). The action carried out by a third-sector organisation is often more than the sum of single services provided for individual clients, in that it is focused on groups, communities and social problem areas. Including active citizens and volunteers as participants and co-producers does not only represent comparative cost advantages for the organ-isation, but also strengthens trust and civic commitment.

Obviously, these types of goals and these ways of operating an organisation are very important for social capital-building. Social capital, like other capital, is reproduced, maintained and even extended when working with it. Consequently, there is no clear separation between using and creating social capital when, for example, addressing the local public's willingness to make donations or to support in any other way a specific project. Local initiatives usually have a complex mixture of goals. In some cases the moral and democratic aims of these organisations may be silent and implicit ones. In other cases the building of part-nerships and local networks and alliances may also be seen as a purpose in its own right and not merely as an instrument in the pursuit of the social and economic goals of the organisations.

Taking social capital-building as a term of reference offers the advantage of making it possible to take into account not only the social and economic goals of the organisation, but also the other dimensions and effects of its activities, which are specific to social enterprises.

This may also help to sensitise us to the organisational challenges linked with the aim of balancing multiple goals and commitments that have an economic, a social and a civic dimension. This is somehow different from and goes beyond the seemingly clear and single 'non-distribution constraint'. One of the ways that the commitment to various goals of different kinds can be safeguarded is by an organisational structure that involves various stakeholders, including: social groups, public authorities, and groups with a particular ideological background or linked with a social movement. This multi-stakeholder construction is one of the frequent features of social enterprises (Pestoff 1996; Krashinsky 1997; Borzaga and Mittone 1997), and it helps in creating and maintaining the commitment of various organisations and institutions within a civic community. The board of representatives can, for example, include members from trade unions, chambers of commerce, churches, voluntary organisations, the municipality, etc. Social audits and similar institutional features of democratic control can also help to prevent third-sector organisations and social enterprises from becoming 'single-mission organisations', or from being reduced to their economic and social dimensions (Pestoff 1998).

The example of social enterprises for job creation and for social and occupational integration[13] provides a good illustration of the argument developed here. Obviously, a major goal of the organisation will usually be to enable people to find a way back into the ordinary labour market – by means of advice, training etc. However, there may be other complementary goals, such as creating new and additional working places in fields of activity that address particular local needs, and this creation of additional working places is often put into the perspective of promoting a more socially inclusive and labour-intensive type of socio-economic development. This is also often associated with attempts to upgrade the territorial environment or the local social infrastructure, which presupposes that the actors are in touch with the individual and social needs in a given community. Finally, the organisation will seek to achieve a certain level of self-financing and independence through income from sales.

The social and economic activities and services just mentioned might have by-products influencing the stock of social capital, but beyond this, there may be other civic and democratic issues directly linked with social capital-building. For example, the working conditions within the initiative may seek to encourage personal development; the initiative can participate in local democracy, strengthening debates and co-operation on the social, the cultural and the political levels; or the social enterprise may take part in creating a local pact for work and integration among different social partners and the public authorities, which improves their common working conditions. What is important here is the fact that within social enterprises, all these concerns are usually not just by-products of a type of action centred on profit-making, nor are they the mere outcome of constraints laid on the organisation from outside, by state rules and regulations. On the contrary, such aspects are among the aims set by social enterprises in the interaction with their environment.

However, one should not forget that the number and relative impact of the various activities and goals can result in conflicts and can change over time. Taking for example the economic and social goals, the purpose of setting up better community services can be prior to, and in conflict with, the goal of occupational integration. Painful conflicts often arise between the goals of surviving and strengthening an initiative's own economic potential, on the one hand, and the responsibilities taken for the weak members of a community, on the other. For some initiatives, questions concerning the civic culture and their commitment to it may be secondary, while others will try to broaden their legitimacy and trustworthiness by declaring openly their commitment to more democracy in (local) decision-making and criticising politicians or representatives of the business community who deny their responsibility towards the public good.

The differences between social enterprises and commercial organisations (characterised by limited and clearly delineated products) have been made clear in the beginning of this chapter; but it could be argued that the strong social capital-building effect of social enterprises also holds true for state/public organisations and action. Basically, this should not be denied. Once again it shows the existence of a gliding zone between what is usually called the 'public sector' and the 'third sector'. However, differences between the two sectors exist. As far as the structure of goals and the impact of social capital are concerned, these differences may be influenced by various factors.

Firstly, the more an organisation, or the service it provides, represents general nationwide norms and values and the more a society is differentiated or fragmented, the more the public service offered to citizens may represent a central government's aspirations against local needs, preferences and opinions. It may then build on social capital as it is embodied in the general trust of people as citizens, but it will encounter difficulties in winning local trust and support. Decentralising and increasing local autonomy may be a way to deal with this problem. This solution is most prominent in the Scandinavian countries, where decentralisation acts to some degree as a functional substitute for coping with diversity by leaning on third-sector organisations. Likewise, public schools can be oriented towards the community, and local urban planning offices can take an enabling approach. Yet they do so only to the extent to which they learn to resocialise, or to get locally rooted, and thereby lower the differences and the obstacles to organisations based in the third sector, operating in and by the community.

Secondly, public services, in contrast to those which are based in the third sector, can try to become more efficient by limiting their goals and resources and likewise the accompanying constraints. The exclusion of volunteering, full reliance on one type of resource – public money – and focusing on a small number of clearly delineated goals can be considered as positive criteria, which distinguish between a public social service sector and 'voluntary amateurism'. The advantages of such an orientation cannot be easily denied; such one-dimensional and standardised structures are often especially robust. But serving the public good in this way also induces costs and losses, especially when compared with what third-sector organisations, sticking to their multiple goals and commitments, may achieve when it comes to pursuing a broader set of goals, mobilising more of the available social resources and being more in touch with local needs and preferences.

In summary, third-sector initiatives in general, and social enterprises in particular are characterised by a fairly open structure of multiple goals and commitments. The usual way of discussing them is, however, to highlight only some of their dimensions – usually the tension between the more narrow economic and social goals and the broader ones of social utility and the consequent activities for the public good. Taking into account social capital-building as one of the goals of third-sector organisations, helps to give more visibility to a number of their civic concerns and effects which correspond to a broad notion of the public good, including the democratic dimensions. Social capital-building may be an aspect of the social embeddedness and of the manifold and diffuse (side-) effects of such types of action and/or it can become an explicit goal and purpose of the organisation.

4   The influence of public policies on the third-sector's mobilisation of social capital

In the first section we have already argued that the third sector's capacity to create social capital is very much dependent on the framework set by political institutions and on their interventions. The degree to which an environment is positively oriented to the development of third-sector organisations/social enterprises strongly depends on the prevailing types of public policies and of governance. Given this importance of politics and governance, one can say that in a particular sense social capital is constructable. We thus think that recent approaches, which discuss social capital as an asset of societies and local communities, which can be developed intentionally, are right. As a consequence, the preservation and the building of social capital may be considered as a key issue for social and community development strategies (Gittell and Vidal 1998).

In this perspective, the potential for the creation and maintenance of social enterprises depends very much on the surrounding local environment and on the attitudes of the groups and citizens concerned, including civic organisations, the business sector and political and administrative organisations. One can admit that a social enterprise can be a singular phenomenon in an uncaring environment, kept alive only by its direct members and some few channels of support from an administration and a grant. But it can obviously operate far better in an environment with rich and manifold responses and a variety of interrelations. What then should be avoided and what can be done by governments? Two general imperatives follow immediately from the arguments developed above.

First of all, public partners, beyond laying the basis for generalised trust, should develop types of policy-making and programmes which clearly acknowledge and reward the mobilisation of social capital by social enterprises and organisations, instead of taking it for granted. Even if the public authorities may only be interested in a particular service provided by a social enterprise (for example training measures for the long-term unemployed), they should also be sensitive to the conditions needed to preserve such organisations and to facilitate their operations. From such a perspective, special attention has to be given to types of participation in social enterprises that rely on voluntary work rather than on paid jobs. Voluntary work implies participation out of commitment rather than a need for income. It is likewise important to focus on networking and building partnerships instead of seeking best offers on competitive social markets. Furthermore, public authorities should consider what tasks social enterprises can do better than commercial organisations because of the social capital resources at their disposal. For example, if social enterprises can achieve particularly good results in creating and making use of the commitment and trust of other social and economic partners (e.g. making use of voluntary work, activating churches, trade unions and chambers of commerce), maybe they are also more credible when it comes to contacting and to resocialising or reactivating a clientele – discriminated groups, ethnic or local communities, marginalised people – which is at first suspicious and distrustful. Thus, in the area of policies for social and occupational integration, for example, the key role of formalised partnerships for local development and employment (Midgley 1995) – as suggested and illustrated in various EU documents[14] and also recently in OECD studies[15] – should be acknowledged. The same holds true for partnerships with ordinary enterprises and for the creation of informal networks of committed local key persons.

Secondly, public authorities should evaluate what they want to get from social enterprises and whether easy-to-measure short-term effects should be the only criteria when it comes to selecting partners and designing contracts. There is currently a dominant tendency throughout Europe towards creating 'social markets', where public authorities as purchasers and regulators co-opt private services, be they commercial or not-for-profit, and where the provider organisations are seen as competitors which may have completely different histories but which share the same mission. Under these conditions, it seems legitimate to treat all organisations alike, so that grants for not-for-profits are then clearly an element of unfair competition. Within such a quasi-market framework,[16] a multiplicity of goals and the tendency of third-sector organisations not to concentrate exclusively on the marketing of some clearly delineated products will be seen as a genuine weakness. Hence, the general trend towards strengthening partnerships and contracts with organisations that concentrate on few and delimited goals and working tasks as well as measurable short-term results. (For example, in the field of social enterprises for social and occupational integration and job creation, this would be a focus on the number of individuals taken out of social assistance and brought back into the job-market.) In fact, for this type of social problem-solving strategy, highly professional and commercial organisations may be more suitable. Social enterprises are a better alternative when the products requested by the public authorities are more complex and entail civic and political dimensions. Tasks related to urban renewal, revitalising the local economy and community building are examples. A key issue here is the need to rebuild a degree of trust and openness between different scenes, actors and groups in the respective city-quarter. This is something that private, for-profit, organisation can hardly bring about by their operations; it must already be in place or otherwise they will have difficulties in taking effective action. In contrast, third-sector organisations and social enterprises can integrate such tasks into their agenda.

The pursuance of complex aims and activities must however not prevent an organisation and its political and administrative partners from setting precise goals and being accountable for them. It is important to define clearly and even to quantify (wherever possible) the by-products for the public good, the community and social capital-building which are brought about by third-sector organisations and which work as a kind of 'competitive advantage' for them. These can include e.g. social integration in a neighbourhood, stimulation of local action groups, and participation in boards and planning forums etc. Often, such activities which accompany the development of social services and facilities have been taken for granted or assumed as immeasurable. If they are to be acknowledged and remunerated, they must however be defined as clearly as possible, and sometimes even 'prized', Social enterprises could then earn incomes from different partners for achieving different goals. Some resources could come from private organisations, public authorities and consumers for specified services rendered, while others could come from public authorities or the public itself for performing well with respect to social and democratic goals and needs. Obviously, there is a limit to such a strategy of singling out, measuring and pricing broader concerns, especially when they have a heavy political-democratic component. Social enterprises can contribute to making democracy work, but this should not be confused with a measurable working task to be priced like others. Perhaps it is the awareness of this fact that is mirrored in the long-standing practices of rewarding third-sector organisations with an unspecified grant for contributions to the public good which cannot be singled out and priced in a contract.

In summary, one can say that the future of social enterprises (and of third-sector organisations in general) largely depends on the evolution of public policies. In this respect, two issues will be of particular importance. The first one is the ongoing trend towards underrating or even giving up the goal of building a civic society which can be a partner in developing public policies. Consequently, public policy-makers often forget association-building, civic commitment and co-operation in partnerships – the very basis and strength of social enterprises. Social organisations and enterprises may be considered as additional service providers with social goal constraints laid on them by contracts and regulations, but they will then not be appreciated as organisations which, through their link with social capital-building, have particular strengths and weaknesses.

The second crucial point for the future of social enterprises is the degree to which public policy defines itself in terms merely of the management of singularised and tightly delimited goals, rather than in terms of agenda-building which entails long-term commitments, which are difficult to measure. This factor will be decisive for the political acceptance of third-sector organisations that pursue a rich set of multiple goals (economic, social, civic and democratic), which have been articulated here under the label of social capital.

Such critical questions must, however, be addressed also to third-sector organisations themselves. For many of them, assimilating the priorities and style of action of public administrations or commercialising seem to be the only conceivable choices. There are, however, opportunities to develop in a different way. By mobilising and highlighting exactly those resources on which their commercial competitors cannot rely – e.g. voluntary commitment and various forms of community support – they can not only stand competition but also better their status as partners in public policy.

Notes

1 For an overview of labels see BAG Arbeit e.V. (1997).
2 The main reason for this choice was that we had the opportunity to carry out in-depth research about that field as part of an international project and related studies. See Evers *et al.* (2000).
3 OECD (1999: 57).
4 See the introduction to this book by Defourny, as well as Badelt (1997).
5 For an analysis of these trends and problems, see Dees (1998) and Weisbrod (1998a).
6 In contrast e.g. to Coleman (1988).
7 For a similar orientation within the German discourse see Offe (1998); for international differences with respect to trust, see Fukuyama (1995).
8 See the illustrative examples given with respect to wealthy US neighbourhoods in Reich (1991).
9 For a further debate, see Levi (1996), Skocpol (1996), Haug (1997) and Harriss and de Renzio (1997).
10 See e.g. the OECD report on social enterprises (1999).
11 Kramer (1998); see also the contribution by Laville and Nyssens in this book (Chapter 18).
12 Weisbrod (1974); for an overview of the debate, see Hansmann (1987).
13 For a more extended debate and further illustration see Evers and Schulze-Böing (1999) and their contribution in this book (Chapter 16).
14 European Commission (1996); O'Conghaile (1997).
15 OECD (1998; 1999).
16 For a critical review, see Evers (2000).

Bibliography

BADELT, C. (1997) 'Entrepreneurship Theories of the Non-profit Sector', *Voluntas*, vol. 8, 2: 162–78.

BAG Arbeit e. V. (1997) *Soziale Unternehmen in Europa. Projekt zur Schaffung eines europäischen Netzwerks von Beschäftigungsgesellschaften*, Bundesarbeits-gemeinschaft Arbeit e.V., Berlin.

BARBER, B. (1995) 'All Economics are Embedded: The Career of a Concept and Beyond', *Social Research*, vol. 62, 2.

BORZAGA, C. and MITTONE, L. (1997) 'The Multi-Stakeholder versus the Nonprofit Organisation', Università di Trento, Dipartimento di Economia, Discussion Paper no. 7.

BORZAGA, C. and SANTUARI, A. (eds) (1998) *Social Enterprises and New Employment in Europe*, Regione Trentino-Alto Adige, Trento.

COHEN, J. and ROGERS, J. (1994) 'Solidarity, Democracy, Association', in STREECK, W. (ed.) *Staat und Verbände. Politische Vierteljahresschrift (PVS)*, Sonderheft 25, 136–60.

COLEMAN, J.S. (1988) 'Social Capital in the Creation of Human Capital', *American Journal of Sociology*, vol. 94 suppl., 95–120.

DEES, J.G. (1998) 'Enterprising Nonprofits', *Harvard Business Review*, vol. 76, 1: 55–68.

DEFOURNY, J. and MONZÓN CAMPOS, J.-L. (eds) (1992) *Économie sociale. The Third Sector*, De Boeck-Wesmael, Brussels.

European Commission (1996) *Erster Bericht über lokale Entwicklungs- und Beschäftigungs-initiativen. Schlußfolgerungen für territoriale und lokale Beschäftigungsbündnisse*, SEK (96) 2061, Brussels.

EVERS, A. (2000) 'Will Sector Matter? Welfare Dynamics, the Third Sector and Social Quality', in BECK, W., VAN DER MAESEN, L., THOMÈSE, F. and WALKER, A. (eds) *Questioning the Social Quality of Europe*, Kluwer, The Hague.

—— (1998) 'Soziales Engagement. Zwischen Selbstverwirklichung und Bürgerpflicht', *TRANSIT*, 15: 186–200.

—— (1994) 'Part of the Welfare Mix. The Third Sector as an Intermediate Area', *Voluntas*, 6, 2: 159–82.

EVERS, A. and SCHULZE-BÖING, M. (1999) 'Öffnung und Eingrenzung. Wandel und Herausforderungen lokaler Beschäftigungspolitik', *Zeitschrift für Sozialreform*, 45. Jahrgang, Heft 11/12, 940–60.

EVERS, A., SCHULZE-BÖING, M., WECK, M. and ZÜHLKE, W. (2000) *Soziales Kapital mobilisieren. Gemeinwesenorientierung als Defizit und Chance lokaler Beschäftigungspolitik*, Schriftenreihe des Instituts für Landes- und Stadtentwicklungsforschung des Landes Nordrhein-Westfalen, Dortmund.

FUKUYAMA, F. (1995) *Trust: The Social Virtues and the Creation of Prosperity*, The Free Press, New York.

GITTELL, R. and VIDAL, A. (1998) *Community Organizing. Building Social Capital as a Developmental Strategy*, Sage, London.

GRANOVETTER, M. (1985) 'Economic Action and Social Structure. The Problem of Embeddedness', *American Journal of Sociology*, vol. 91, 3: 481–510.

HANSMANN, H. (1987) 'Economic Theories of Nonprofit Organization', in POWELL, W.W. (ed.) *The Nonprofit Sector. A Research Handbook*, Yale University Press, New Haven, 27–42.

HARRISS, J. and DE RENZIO, P. (1997) 'Missing Link or Analytically Missing? The Concept of Social Capital. An Introductory Bibliographic Essay', *Journal of International Development*, vol. 9, 7: 919–37.

HAUG, J. (1997) 'Soziales Kapital. Ein kritischer Überblick über den aktuellen Forschungsstand', Mannheimer Zentrum für Europäische Sozialforschung AB II / no. 15.

KRAMER, R.W. (1998) 'Nonprofit Organizations in the 21st Century: Will Sector Matter?', Nonprofit Sector Research Fund, Working Paper Series, The Aspen Institute, Washington.

KRASHINSKY, M. (1997) 'Stakeholder Theories of the Non-profit Sector: One Cut at the Economic Literature', *Voluntas*, vol. 8: 149–61.

LAVILLE, J.-L. and SAINSAULIEU, R. (1997) *Sociologie de l'association*, Desclée de Brouwer, Paris.

LEVI, M. (1996) 'Social and Unsocial Capital: A Review Essay of Robert Putnam's "Making Democracy Work" ', *Politics and Society*, vol. 24, 1: 45–55.

MANSBRIDGE, J. (1998) 'On the Contested Nature of the Public Good', in POWELL, W. and CLEMENS, E.S. (eds) *Private Action and the Public Good*, Yale University Press, New Haven / London, 3–19.

MIDGLEY, J. (1995) *Social Development. The Developmental Perspective in Social Welfare*, Sage, London.

NOVY, K. (1985) ' "Vorwärts immer – rückwärts nimmer". Historische Anmerkungen zu einem aktuellen Problem', in BIERBAUM, H. and RIEGE, M. (eds) *Die neue Genossenschaftsbewegung. Initiativen in der BRD und in Westeuropa*, VSA-Verlag, Hamburg, 124–41.

O'CONGHAILE, W. (1997) 'Die Rolle von Partnerschaften zur Förderung des sozialen Zusammenhalts', paper presented at the International Conference on Partnerships for Social Cohesion, Institut für Gesundheitswesen, Wien, October 1997.

OECD (1999) *Social Enterprises*, OECD, Paris.

——— (1998) *Local Management for More Effective Employment Policies*, OECD, Paris.

OFFE, C. (1998) ' "Sozialkapital". Begriffliche Probleme und Wirkungsweise', in KISTLER, E., NOLL, H.H. and PRILLER, E. (eds) *Perspektiven gesellschaftlichen Zusammenhalts*, Sigma, Berlin.

PESTOFF, V.A. (1998) *Beyond the Market and State. Social Enterprises and Civil Democracy in a Welfare Society*, Ashgate, Aldershot.

——— (1996) 'Renewing Public Services and Developing the Welfare Society Through Multi-stakeholder Cooperatives', *Journal of Rural Cooperation*, vol. 23, 2: 151–67.

POWELL, W.W. (ed.) (1987) *The Nonprofit Sector: A Research Handbook*, Yale University Press, New Haven.

PUTNAM, R.D. (1995) 'Bowling Alone: America's Declining Social Capital', *Journal of Democracy*, no. 1: 65–78.

——— (1993) *Making Democracy Work. Civic Traditions in Modern Italy*, Princeton University Press, Princeton.

REICH, R. (1991) *The Work of Nations*, A. Knopf, New York.

SALAMON, L.M. and ANHEIER, H.K. (1997) 'The Civil Society Sector', *Society*, vol. 34, 2: 60–5.

SKOCPOL, T. (1996) 'Unravelling From Above', *The American Prospect*, 25, 20–5.

TENDLER, J. (1997) *Good Government in the Tropics*, The Johns Hopkins University Press, Baltimore.

WEISBROD, B.A. (ed.) (1998a) *To Profit or Not to Profit: The Commercial Transformation of the Nonprofit Sector*, Cambridge University Press, Cambridge.

——— (1998b) 'Institutional Form and Organizational Behavior', in POWELL, W. and CLEMENS, E.S. (eds) *Private Action and the Public Good*, Yale University Press, New Haven, 69–84.

——— (1974) 'Toward a Theory of the Voluntary Non-Profit Sector in a Three-Sector-Economy', in PHELPS, E.S. (ed.) *Altruism, Morality, and Economic Theory*, Russell Sage, New York, 23–41.

18 The social enterprise

Towards a theoretical socio-economic approach

Jean-Louis Laville and Marthe Nyssens

Introduction

The phenomenon of social enterprises is the latest development in the evolution of the social economy which began in the nineteenth century and incorporated organisations such as co-operatives, mutual benefit societies and associations. In Europe, the term 'social economy' is identified with the so-called third sector, the latter being the term also most frequently employed at international level. In other words, the third sector does not comprise non-profit organisations alone; it also includes all organisations in which the material interest of capital investors is subject to limits, and in which creating a common patrimony is given priority over a return on individual investment. But comparing social enterprises to traditional third-sector organisations also reveals some differences. In contrast to traditional co-operatives, for example, social enterprises are initiated by groups of citizens who seek to provide an expanded range of services and more openness toward the local community. Compared to mutual benefit societies or traditional associations, social enterprises place a higher value on their independence and on economic risk-taking related to an ongoing activity.

Consequently, it can be said that the generic term 'social enterprise' does not represent a conceptual break with institutions of the social economy but, rather, a new dynamic within the third sector[1] as well as a reorientation and broadening of its possible forms. Moreover, the emergence of social enterprises suggests questions about the socio-economic development of our societies, and sheds light on the possibility of establishing economic solidarity within modern democracies.[2] The social enterprise appears to be at a crossroads; it is a form of enterprise which is different from private for-profit and public enterprises. While its logic is different from that of the traditional private enterprise – to the extent that its power is not based on the ownership of capital – the social enterprise nevertheless develops market activities. Due to its independence, the social enterprise is also different from the public corporation, in spite of the fact that it frequently benefits from public subsidies.

Numerous authors have drawn attention to the fact that there is *de facto* a number of socio-economic principles and types of organisational logic. Some analysts approach economic organisation using a tripolar model.[3] In this essay, we too will use a tripolar analytical grid of socio-economic activities in order to clarify the dynamics of the social enterprise. But while there is nowadays widespread reference in the literature to these three poles, their characteristics remain loosely defined and vary from author to author. In order to define them more precisely, we will analyse, in turn, three aspects of socio-economic organisation.

First, we will analyse the structure of ownership, which determines the objectives of the enterprise. For social enterprises which are not in the sole hands of investors, various forms of ownership are possible (section 1). Second, following Evers in the preceding chapter, we identify the forms of social capital associated with social enterprises. If social capital is present in every type of enterprise, the kind and form of mobilisation of social capital appear, however, as specific in social enterprises (section 2). Following these two parts, which are focused on internal relations, we examine the types of economic relations between social enterprises and their environment (section 3). We describe the various ways of distribution of economic goods and services – exchange, redistribution and reciprocity relations – in order to analyse how social enterprises combine them. As we will see, a characteristic of social enterprises is that part of their resources come from a social capital based on *reciprocal relations* developed in the *public sphere*. The analysis shows a wide spectrum of social enterprises. However, this chapter does not analyse each possible configuration with its benefits and its failures; it rather tries to explore some key dimensions in order to understand the rationale of social enterprises. Methodologically, it uses a comprehensive approach, starting from the national case studies gathered in this book and building on the two former theoretical contributions to propose an 'ideal type' of the social enterprise having a multiple stakeholder ownership and multiple goal structure, combining various types of economic relations. As expressed by Weber who introduced this concept, 'an ideal type is obtained by emphasising uniliterally one or more standpoints and by linking together numerous isolated phenomena ... arranged according to the previous, unilaterally chosen viewpoints in order to form a homogeneous framework of thought' (Weber 1918: 719). This framework of thought is not an exact representation of reality, but emphasises certain features for the purposes of research. The ideal type is not the same as reality; it is a means of gaining knowledge by defining hypotheses more accurately and by characterising phenomena.

1 Social enterprises: ownership, factors of production and objectives

In this section, we analyse how the structure of the ownership of an enterprise influences its objectives. The group of persons holding the right of ownership determines the objectives of the enterprise. Indeed, as Razeto (1988) notes, those who hold the propriety have the power to align the objectives of the enterprise with their own interests. He suggests employing the expression 'dominant factor' to designate this group who, he emphasises, subjects all factors of production to its own objectives. In short, the ultimate aims of an enterprise depend on the type of ownership at hand.

Third-sector organisations belong to stakeholders other than investors

In neo-classical theory, the standard model of the enterprise is one in which ownership rights are held by investors. In such a model, the objective of the enterprise amounts to profit maximisation, i.e. to the accumulation of finance capital. The labour factor is subordinate to this logic of accumulation. Analyses of third-sector enterprises – which differ both from private firms and public corporations – question the rather monolithic vision of ownership and entrepreneurial logic typifying the standard model, which none the less retains its pervasive influence in economic theory.

Indeed, such analyses demonstrate *the diversity of ownership forms*, i.e. the diversity of persons who can hold property rights and determine the objectives of the enterprise. For example, the literature on self-management has examined enterprises organised by workers, and analysis of the co-operative firm has shown the existence of enterprises owned by consumers or suppliers. The aims of an enterprise depend on the structure of its ownership, i.e. on the stakeholders[4] with ownership rights. In contrast to the situation in capitalist enterprises, third-sector owners are not the investors and therefore their objectives are different from the accumulation of capital. In a third-sector organisation, if investors are owners, they are not the only ones. There are potentially as many forms of property rights as there are stakeholder categories: workers, consumers, benefactors, investors, and others (Hansmann 1996; Gui 1991).

One of the goals of social enterprises is to serve the community[5]

Unlike capitalist enterprises, third-sector organisations are not motivated primarily by financial interests that subordinate the act of entrepreneurship to the probability of a rapid return on investment. Unlike public sector corporations, third-sector organisations are not dependent on the type of collective interest whose standards must be established by the mechanisms of representative democracy. And unlike some third-sector organisations which limit their activities to pursuing members' private interests alone – as in the case of many workers or agricultural co-operatives – social enterprises incorporate a goal of service to the community.

Serving the community may be defined as explicitly enhancing collective externalities and equity issues. Externalities arise when the actions of certain agents have an impact – be it positive or negative – on the well-being of other agents not regulated by the price system. Externalities are collective in nature when they concern the community as a whole, for example when they involve social cohesion, public health or local development. Here, collective benefits are not simply induced by economic activity but are, rather, a dimension claimed by those who promote and actually undertake the activity. The pursuit of collective benefits associated with the goods or services produced constitutes one of the incentives and explains the commitment of the individuals who create the social enterprise. If in private for-profit enterprises, as Callon (1999) says, 'the positive externalities discourage the private investments by socialising the benefits', in social enterprises the positive externalities are among the reasons why stake-holders join a collective action to create economic activity.

If we take the example of social enterprises that help previously excluded workers enter the labour force, one notices that their primary aim is not to accu-mulate or to distribute profits. The stakeholders are motivated by a shared opposition to pervasive long-term unemployment combined with a determina-tion to act locally for a common objective, namely social integration. Taking the example of social enterprises in the personal service sector, we observe a concern about social justice in relation to access to the services provided and a desire to promote benefits for the community as a whole, particularly when it comes to social cohesion and education.

Does the goal of community service require a particular form of ownership?

Clearly, analysis of social enterprises does not reveal a single model of owner-ship. Nevertheless, some of their structural characteristics reflect the element of community service.

Firstly, as we have already stated, third-sector enterprises – and therefore social enterprises – tend to promote collective benefits as they are managed by stakeholders who are not only investors. While investors focus on the return on capital, owners of third-sector enterprises promote other types of goals such as the return on work accomplished, the quality of goods produced or the accessi-bility of the services provided. This does not mean that third-sector enterprises always incorporate the goal of service to the community, but we may assume that they place greater emphasis on such a dimension than traditional enter-prises. Some authors note that this goal of service to the community is a characteristic of non-profit organisations. For example, Preston (1993) points out that it is non-profit organisations' concern for social externalities which makes them distinguishable from for-profit organisations.

Secondly – and this is the characteristic most frequently raised in the litera-ture – the non-profit nature of such organisations, i.e. the fact that 'residual control rights' and 'residual income rights' are held by different groups, is pointed out. Indeed, micro-economic analyses, in particular those relating to new institutional economics (Milgrom and Roberts 1992), distinguish between two forms of ownership rights: firstly, 'rights of residual control', meaning ulti-mate decision-making power,[6] and secondly, 'rights of residual income', which refers to the income obtained by a 'residual claimant', i.e. obtained by virtue of the right to appropriate the net income of an enterprise once all expenses have been paid. Most often these rights are tied up. Analysis of third-sector organisations, particularly associations, demonstrates that these property rights are indeed divisible. On the basis of the distinction between these two kinds of property rights, Gui (1991) puts forward the concepts of 'dominant category', i.e. the category made up of individuals who maintain ultimate control, and of 'beneficiary category' i.e. the category formed by those who obtain the residual benefits. When the two categories merge, the organisation involved is said to be one of 'mutual interest'. If these rights are held by different groups, the organisation is said to be one of 'general interest'. The new institutional economics shows how linking residual control and income rights is an extremely powerful incentive. Nonetheless, analyses of associations demonstrate that such rights may also be held by two different groups. In the case of social enterprises, the separation of rights is a recognition of the primacy of community service over members' financial interests. Fixing limits to profit distribution constitutes an attenuated form of this recognition.

Thirdly, certain recent analyses that rely on the concept of 'multiple stakeholder enterprises' have suggested that it might be possible for the very group that owns the enterprise to be heterogeneous.[7] For example, the owners of Italian social co-operatives may be users, volunteers or salaried workers. The creation of multi-stakeholder enterprises provides a way of giving appropriate recognition to collective benefits. By mobilising many different types of agents – workers, users and volunteers – they reveal the actual collective aspect of the benefits, an aspect that too often remains concealed. When volunteers join an enterprise of this type, their objectives exclude personal financial gain and may be associated with the pursuit of collective benefits.[8] This specificity of social enterprises doesn't mean that investor-managed enterprises never take collective externalities into account. Indeed, investor-managed enterprises do recognise collective externalities. But it is also clear that the objective of obtaining a return on capital does not constitute an incentive to recognising these externalities, even if other factors (such as general awareness and pressure from consumers and government) may promote such recognition.

According to Sabel (1996), many local partnerships provoke tensions because there is a contradiction between the general mobilisation of the resources required to ensure the success of each project and the distribution of the fruits of this mobilisation among the few individuals who own the enterprise or will have the opportunity to be employed by it. Social enterprises have a distinctive ability to reduce such tensions: the shared ownership by the various categories of stakeholders in the social enterprise, the limits imposed by statutes that regulate the distribution of surpluses and the creation of a common patrimony constitute possible ways to guarantee, at least partially, that the achievements of the enterprise will not be reduced to private interests alone. This, therefore, enhances trust when building up a social enterprise. By contrast, because ownership is heterogeneous in multiple stakeholder enterprises, the question of governance arises in the context of heterogeneous viewpoints and interests. The converse of the innovative behaviour of social enterprises is an unsteadiness generated by the diversity of stakeholders. This sometimes facilitates the development of a charismatic leadership and the progressive establishment of a single stakeholder ownership that eliminates the original heterogeneity.

2   Social enterprises and social capital

Coleman and Putnam were among the first to use the term 'social capital' in the sociological literature. Coleman defines it as 'the set resources that inhere in family relations and in community social organisation and that are useful for the cognitive or social development of a child or young person' (Coleman 1990: 300), thereby situating it within the realm of personal development. According to Putnam (1993a), who associates social capital with organisational operations, it includes features of social organisations, such as networks, norms and trust, that facilitate co-ordination and co-operation with mutual benefit.

The concept of social capital is now widespread in the literature. Although it remains somewhat vague, it nevertheless allows us to demonstrate the economic role of resources that can not be reduced to financial, physical or human capital. Razeto's distinction between an economic resource and a factor of production is illuminating in this context. Economic resources are all resources that potentially contribute to economic activity. A resource turns into a factor of production when it becomes a concrete part of a production process. For example, individuals seeking work constitute, among other things, an economic resource. When they are engaged by an enterprise, they acquire the status of factor of production. Social capital also constitutes a resource that may be mobilised to a greater or lesser degree within a production process so as to improve its performance. But it is also an end in itself because, as Evers labelled it in his text, it is a 'civic' capital contributing to a democratisation process. Social capital is present in groups, networks and the local social fabric. Inasmuch as it is – at least partly – indivisible and thus cannot be appropriated by any single individual, social capital constitutes a local (quasi) public good.

Social capital reduces transaction costs

Putnam's definition of social capital may be linked with the concept of transaction costs, which plays a key role in the new institutional economics concerned with modes of organisation that minimise transaction costs (co-ordination and motivation costs) among stakeholders. Motivation costs vary with the incentives introduced, within a context of imperfect information, to facilitate co-operation among stakeholders and encourage them to avoid opportunistic behaviour. Indeed, socio-economic organisations face numerous uncertainties and therefore motivation costs. How can users ensure quality service from providers they do not know? How can donors put trust in the way their contributions are used? How can the state maintain control over services when subsidising and delegating them? How can managers of personal service enterprises guard against opportunistic behaviour on the part of their employees?[9]

When faced with these types of uncertainties, mobilised social capital diminishes the transaction costs between external stakeholders (consumers, donors, public authorities) and the enterprise. Social capital can also contribute to improving the productivity of the labour factor through the development of co-operative behaviour. Razeto even ponders the existence of a new factor of production that co-exists with capital and labour, the 'C' factor, which he defines as 'the formation of a group facilitating co-ordination and co-operation so as to improve the efficiency of an economic organisation' (Razeto 1988: 46). His formulation suggests that, to different degrees, social capital is present and reduces transaction costs in every type of enterprise.

By mobilising social capital, the social enterprise is very likely to reduce its transaction costs, especially those that are associated with the lack of trust. As a matter of fact, even though outside parties may view the non-profit status itself as a sign of trust (Hansmann 1996), it is becoming increasingly clear that this status alone is insufficient in building relationships of trust (Ortmann and Schlesinger 1997). The absence of the profit motive does not prevent managers of associations from pursuing objectives – other than explicit profit – that do not necessarily coincide with the interests of the beneficiaries. For example, some associations have tolerated excessive remuneration of managers or the commandeering of the collective objectives by small groups who have the power to make the association stray from its original objectives. But sustainable forms of social capital – often present in social enterprises – can thwart the emergence of such phenomena by establishing trust, thereby lessening the incentive to behave opportunistically.

Social capital reduces production costs

The integration of users and volunteers into the social enterprise and the recourse to gifts and donations are all practices associated with the mobilisation and the development of social capital. Serving the community facilitates the integration of volunteers and users, and access to various gifts. When the dimension of serving the community is present, it becomes possible to create a social support network whose composition may vary but whose members share a sensitivity to a problem considered pressing and requiring action. The incentive to give an impulse to an economic activity comes from a shared perception by various stakeholders that an appropriate response to a problem they have identified is lacking. Thus, the entrepreneur taking the risk in the project does not act alone but, rather, as a catalyst relying on a group of individuals, each of whom is making a voluntary commitment (Laville and Gardin 1996).

Even the salaried workers may contribute to the creation of voluntary work, to the extent that they can opt for less remuneration than they would have received in other organisations, obtaining instead certain non-monetary benefits from their productive contribution.[10] Mobilisation of such resources would not be possible without social capital. Nonetheless, the benefits should not mask the risks involved: volunteer work may end up as endured volunteer work if, due to a lack of funds, the salaried workers do not obtain the common law status and collective rights (in terms of social protection for example) to which they feel they are entitled.

Social capital is an end in itself

While the mobilisation of social capital is important in every production process, the underlying objectives may vary considerably from one situation to another. In enterprises controlled by shareholders, social capital improves the productivity of the production factors and hence the return on financial capital. Here, owners employ social capital to further their financial interests. In social enterprises, social capital crystallises around projects that incorporate a dimension of community service.

In this context, the distinction made by Gui (1995) between the intrinsic and instrumental benefits of social capital is relevant. He links the concept of social capital to that of relational goods, defined as 'intangible capital assets that inhere in enduring interpersonal relationships'. He stresses that relational goods may be valued either as an instrument or as an end in itself. He shows how the development of social capital depends, positively, on the degree to which people value its *intrinsic* benefits. In social enterprises, we can hypothesise that the accumulation of social capital, being part of the collective project, is valued as an end in itself. As Evers points out in his contribution, this is why the social enterprise not only mobilises social capital but also reproduces it.

Indeed, the development of a collective project is closely tied to the mobilisation of social capital. Through their voluntary involvement, participants cultivate a sense of belonging to a community, either by reinforcing an inherited kinship (such as family or ethnicity) or by developing with other individuals a project in which 'their civic identity motivates them to act' (Evers 1997: 54). The interpersonal encounter goes beyond instrumentality or strategy and creates opportunities for greater mutual understanding through 'belonging to a group in which the members are aware that they share a common destiny' (Defourny, Favreau and Laville 1998: 31), as de Tocqueville and Touraine have observed.[11] Such an approach places the emphasis on the associative forces within the social enterprise. Research conducted on organisations in the social economy has shown that they often emerge through a process that transcends private interests while drawing strength from a mutual understanding that has a positive influence on economic performance.

Historically, the mobilisation of social capital in the third sector or in the social economy has occurred when there were social linkages uniting the members of a homogeneous category. This historical constant has not been confirmed, however, by every type of contemporary social enterprise, with recent research demonstrating 'a very low degree of homogeneity among founding groups' (Defourny, Favreau and Laville 1998: 330), in multiple stakeholder enterprises, for example. In such cases, the project is based less on a common identity than on a shared belief that certain issues cannot be resolved through existing institutions.

Social enterprises promote social capital as a factor of democratisation

Clarification of the process through which individuals, brought together by a particular problem, succeed in designing an economic activity, implies linking the economic and political dimensions of the social enterprise. Economic analysis and political sociology represent different disciplines of research but they have to be combined in order to capture the specificity of social capital in social enterprises. Social enterprises promote a special kind of social capital because they allow citizens to intervene in everyday life problems. So, to understand the existence of social enterprises, it is necessary to introduce the political concept of 'public space' or 'public sphere', defined by authors like Habermas and Giddens.

Social enterprises demonstrate their ability to be economically innovative when they constitute 'intermediary areas' (Evers 1995), mobilising social capital by transferring it from the private to the public sphere. The public sphere can be defined according to Habermas as:

> a realm of our social life in which something approaching public opinion can be formed. Access is guaranteed to all citizens. … Citizens behave as a public body when they confer in an unrestricted fashion – that is, with the guarantee of freedom of assembly and association and the freedom to express and publish their opinions – about matters of general interest.
>
> (Habermas 1974: 49)

Consequently, the public sphere differs from the private sphere. In the public sphere, members of the same political community employ rational arguments in order to collaborate in opinion-making. This normative dimension of the public sphere refers to an empirical reality particularly regarding autonomous public spheres that serve as forums for free debate and the airing of controversy (Habermas 1992). These public spheres, open for local discussions between different stakeholders, act as autonomous public spaces (Calhoun 1992) and allow for direct expression by people to develop a shared understanding of the common public good. They can be regarded as developing reflexivity in civil society by problematising aspects of social relations that were previously undiscussed except by a few experts (Giddens 1994). As they emerge, social enterprises, like other forms of association are 'a dimension of the public space in civil societies' (Evers 1995: 159), and they create, on the basis of proximity, autonomous public spheres in civil society. By placing citizens in a situation different from the one conferred upon them as consumers or as recipients of assistance, these spheres allow them to organise activities that they judge relevant to the problem they are facing. Such spheres are organised on the basis of interpersonal relations and from the very start form part of the 'concrete sphere of inter-subjectivity'[12] characterised by certain cultural codes, and they invent productions of goods and services by collective action. The differences with household, informal and underground economies comes primarily from the opening up of these 'public proximity spheres'. They question the role of the private sphere, 'open up spaces for public dialogue and force into the discursive domain aspects of social conduct that previously went undiscussed, or were "settled" by traditional practices' (Giddens 1994: 120).

Social enterprises in the area of personal services illustrate this particularly well. Social enterprises in the service sector facilitate equity of access and are responsive to user demands. For example, the first task of organisations providing home-care services is to maintain family equilibrium. Here, professional intervention alleviates certain tensions by getting the elderly and their families involved in defining the contours of the home assistance. The three-pronged relationship that brings together the association, its users and its salaried workers not only gives families an active role but also enables them to step back and evaluate the situation collectively. It is the role played by users – or by other stakeholders acting in their name – which proves decisive in putting together a proposal to establish a social enterprise, whether on their own initiative, by associating with entrepreneurs, or through the intervention of professionals who, due to their constant involvement in the delivery of services, know about unsatisfied demand (Ben-Ner and Van Hoomissen 1991). Beyond institutional affiliation, personal involvement is critical, for it is the connections made between usually separate systems and types of logic that shifts the focus of problems, allowing them to be approached differently and revealing their hidden potential.

The autonomous nature of the public proximity sphere is decisive, and is even more important than the inter-institutional partnership. The essential goal is to transcend functional logic and to approach services from the standpoint of users' 'actual experience' – to use again Habermas' term – aided by the mobilisation of social capital. Social enterprises have a triple foundation: people's daily practices, the symbolic exchanges and relations which provide the everyday framework of community life and the aspirations, values and desires of the people who use them. It is by taking into account this multi-faceted reality in the public sphere that supply and demand can adjust. The distinctiveness of these services from a user's perspective is that they tend to be actively involved in service design. Services, therefore, do not merely reflect either the use of 'top-down' market research or public planning technologies. That is why projects can overcome a major obstacle to growth in relational services which involve entering into a user's private life. The obstacle is the incompleteness of the information provided – not merely the fact that the information available is asymmetric – which causes users to feel insecure. By creating local public spheres they help make a relationship of trust possible. By paying attention to the way they convey information, projects can help users overcome their fear of seeing caregivers intrude into their private lives. They can then formalise very heterogeneous demands while developing the supply of services (Laville and Nyssens 2000).

Society is affected in that the mobilisation of social capital by social enterprises in their emergent phase has external as well as internal consequences. This has been demonstrated in the area of personal services and in other areas. As mentioned in the first section, the pursuit of collective benefits by social enterprises is part of the entrepreneurial initiative. A sociological perspective helps to explain by which process it becomes possible: these collective benefits are socially constructed in public proximity spheres, which consist of 'spheres of socialisation and individuation allowing individuals to integrate into society' (Eme 1994: 217). Through their actions, social enterprises promote social bonds of a democratic nature. By expanding social networks based on the principles of voluntary involvement, legal autonomy and the equality of members, they attract groups who might otherwise be deprived of such bonds.

Social enterprises mobilise and reproduce a specific form of social capital

One of the difficulties raised by the notion of social capital is its polysemy. As noted above, Coleman's definition refers to the social skills practised by families and to the social networks to which individuals belong, while Putnam's definition refers to the functioning of organisations and networks. These two generic definitions differ stylistically but involve identical limitations through idealising communities by masking the relationships of domination and dependency sometimes present there. They also have another point in common insofar as they identify the development of social capital with collective interests, without noting that social capital may also be used to benefit private interests (Paci 1999; Bianco and Eve 1999).

The characteristics described above allow us to define the specificity of the social capital associated with social enterprises. To show that social enterprises mobilise social capital concretely by creating public proximity spheres means clarifying what type of social capital is involved. We are not dealing here with social capital that is family-centred, or with social capital based on interpersonal relations in the private sphere. Social capital, as we are treating it here, is located in the public domain. It is also different from the use of social capital in the reinforcement of local particularism, clientelist power, secrecy or opacity. The social capital we are dealing with in social enterprises can be identified with civic capital.

If these enterprises have the capacity to generate such social capital, it is because they are based on formal rules involving free commitment and equality among members. As a result, and as distinguished from capital-reliant corporations, they do not accept unequal relations in which the power held is proportional to the investment made or in which the labour contribution is subordinate to the financial contribution.

Another of the ambiguities associated with the concept of social capital stems from its origin. Most analyses take the existence of social capital as a given and proceed to focus on its mobilisation. This explains their deterministic vision of development in which areas endowed with social capital automatically build up their socio-economic capacities, while areas lacking it are locked into a state of underdevelopment and social anomie. There is a circularity in this argument because the social capital increase would only be possible where it already exists. However, we can go beyond this simplified schema and show how civic capital is mobilised and structured in practice.

In areas where social capital is densest and already affects the structure of public life, the social enterprise is in a position to convert part of it into a factor of production. In this way, the social enterprise facilitates the proliferation of civic capital. But even in areas where social capital is underdeveloped, the possibility of the creation of social enterprises should not be precluded. While the obstacles encountered may be numerous, the social enterprise's vision of serving the community can generate initiatives. The improvement of community daily life becomes the common reference determining the economic collective action and the transfer to the public sphere of the social capital previously confined to the private sphere. By such a process, they can contribute to 'the construction of social capital in circumstances – like those of the Italian south – where it has been missing historically' (Harris and De Renzio 1997: 923). A transposition of this sort, though difficult to achieve in an unpropitious environment, may none the less play a role in endogenous development – so long as it is reinforced by appropriate public intervention that carefully monitors local forces and provides them with long-term support. A policy of supporting social enterprises may in this way provide an alternative strategy to investing in major infrastructure projects and, in spite of obstacles, help areas previously seen as deprived of social capital take a more democratic path to development.

In short, the economic and political aspects of social enterprises are inseparable. Stated in economic terms, one of the driving force behind collective involvement in social enterprises is the pursuit of collective benefits associated with the goods or services produced. Clearly, analysis of social enterprises does not give rise to a single model of ownership; the only characteristic they all share, as far as ownership is concerned, is that they are managed by stakeholders other than investors. Nevertheless, some structural characteristics could reflect their dimension of community service. These characteristics include, among others, the non-profit constraint or the limits to surplus distribution and the development of multiple stakeholder forms of ownership. The pursuit of collective benefits allows specific forms of mobilisation of social capital such as involvement of volunteers, donations and development of local partnerships. Stated in political terms, the common affiliation spurring people on to collective action is connecting with a sense of common belonging to the political community that explains the involvement in autonomous public spheres emerging around a common good.

3   Social enterprises and economic relations

Just as enterprises are able to mobilise various economic resources and forms of ownership, so too are they able to activate the various means for distributing goods and services. At least this is the hypothesis formulated by theorists who defend the substantive approach to economics. They propose an extensive concept of economics in which all actions derive from people's dependence on fellow humans and nature. This contrasts with the formal, more restrictive approach which views economics in terms of rational choices of maximisation applied under conditions of scarcity. By following Polanyi's formulation of the substantive approach, the economy may be conceived as a plural economy[13] mixing in different socio-political contexts the economic principles of reciprocity, market and redistribution (Polanyi 1997).

The market principle refers to the matching of supply and demand for goods and services with a view to exchange, facilitated by a price-setting mechanism. The relationship between buyer and seller is established on a contractual basis. The market principle does not assume that agents will immerse themselves in social relationships, since these are 'viewed nowadays by western culture as being separate from institutions with a conventional or strictly economic vocation' (Maucourant, Servet and Tiran 1998: 15). Thus, in contrast to the two economic principles noted below, the market principle is not necessarily embedded in the social system.

Redistribution is the principle by which production is handed over to a central authority whose responsibility it is to divide it up. This presupposes establishing rules for taxation and redistribution. A *de facto* relationship is thereby established over time between a tax-setting central authority and other agents who are subject to it. Redistribution may take the form of benefits in cash or in kind. Redistribution is private when it originates with a private institution, that is, with a corporate entity whose managers have the authority to use a percentage of freed-up surpluses for the purposes of donations or sponsorships. One of the ways to channel this surplus is through private foundations. However, redistribution is primarily public. The modern form of public redistribution, which is sustained by compulsory deductions and is the source of allowances attesting to social rights, was organised around the welfare state.

The principle of reciprocity describes a specific type of circulation of goods and services among groups or individuals. It has meaning only when used to express a particular social linkage among stakeholders. Reciprocity is an authentic principle of economic activity based on the idea that the gift or donation is a basic social fact. But reciprocity has a paradoxical dimension, since groups or individuals receiving gifts are expected to exercise their 'free will' by giving counter-gifts. In practice, while those receiving gifts are encouraged to reciprocate, they are not subject to any external pressures to do so, the decision being theirs alone. Consequently, gift-giving is not synonymous with altruism or giving something away for nothing but is, rather, a complex mix of selflessness and self-interest. The cycle of reciprocity differs from market exchange since it involves human relationships which involve a desire for recognition and power, and from redistributive exchange because it is not imposed by a central authority. One form of reciprocity is that which is exercised within the basic family unit, which Polanyi called the household administration.

Throughout history, various combinations of these three basic principles have arisen. The specific combination reflected by the contemporary economy may be divided into three poles:

- *The market economy.* Here, the market has the prime responsibility for the circulation of goods and services. This should not be taken to mean that the market economy is the product of the market alone but it gives priority to the market and a subordinate role to non-market and non-monetary relations.

- *The non-market economy.* This is an economy in which the prime responsibility for the circulation of goods and services falls within the jurisdiction of the welfare state. Here, the public sector, which is subject to rules enacted by a public authority which, in its turn, is subject to democratic control, redistributes resources.

- *The non-monetary economy.* This is an economy in which the circulation of goods and services depends primarily on reciprocity. Although it is true that a certain number of reciprocal relationships adopt monetised forms (such as donations), it is really within the non-monetary economy that one observes the main effects of reciprocity – in the form of self-production and in the household economy.

The social enterprise and the three economic poles

As it was mentioned above, a social enterprise crystallises around a project providing services to the community, thanks to its ability to mobilise social capital. The mobilisation of social capital is based on reciprocal relations developed in the public sphere. Therefore, the origins of social enterprises are supported by 'norms of reciprocity and networks of civic engagement' (Putnam 1993b: 171). After its starting phase, the social enterprise is strengthened by its long-term capacity to link in various ways, depending on each organisation, the three poles of the economy. According to a plural conceptualisation of the economy and to an ideal type methodology, it is possible to argue that the capacity to sustain a social enterprise in accordance with its initial logic presupposes its ability *to continuously hybridise the three poles of the economy so as to serve the project*. Social enterprises combine the various resources coming from these three poles. Though social enterprises specialise in mobilising donations and volunteers, they can make use of market relations by selling their services and/or use redistributive relations by applying to governments to finance their services. This does not mean that social enterprises mix an equal amount of market, non-market and non-monetary resources; it only means that hybridisation provides a consolidation strategy for social enterprises whose identity has already been formed. A complementarity between a social enterprise's monetary and non-monetary relations guarantees the autonomy of its services – an autonomy based on multiple linkages – and its economic viability. Hybridisation not only means relying on three types of economic relations mobilised over a long period, it also means balancing these economic relations through negotiations among the partners in a manner consistent with the goals of the project. As such, it contrasts with the approach taken in previous periods, when it was possible to finance the goal of social utility primarily through redistribution.

326 J.-L. Laville and M. Nyssens

Hybridisation also means that the three economies are working together rather than in isolation from each other. This helps explain the creation of collective benefits. For example, the role played by redistributive and reciprocal relations may be explained by the dimension of community service. In other words, the presence of collective benefits renders market-based financing inefficient. Market mechanisms can never internalise collective externalities or issues of equity; state intervention is then justifiable. But the intrinsically standardised nature of government action and its dependence on the politically instituted process mean that it is limited in its ability to identify evolving demands and respond to them in new ways. Theorists of non-profit organisations point out that since such organisations are in closer touch with new social demands and are more autonomous, they play a special role in social innovation by responding quickly to such demands (Salamon 1987). The social enterprise's volunteers and donations are thus in a position to introduce innovations. Nonetheless, associations have intrinsic limitations, such as having to mobilise resources on a volunteer basis, something state funding can help overcome. Salamon calls this limitation 'the philanthropic shortfall'. Other limitations include the trend to support specific groups or causes ('philanthropic particularism') and the fact that certain individuals are in a position to determine which services will be provided since they are the source of the funds ('philanthropic paternalism'). The sustainability and future growth of social enterprises are linked to recognition by government-funding sources that social enterprises make a distinctive contribution to the community in terms of services that other forms of enterprise fail to provide.

At issue here is the manner in which the social enterprise is distinguished from other enterprises. It is not simply the development of new combinations of private and public funding which characterises it. It is the mobilisation of social capital, through reciprocal relationships, around a project whose aim integrates a dimension of service to the community, which is the hallmark of the social enterprise at its inception. This dimension of service to the community enables the social enterprise to create an environment supportive of reciprocal relations (in the form of voluntary involvement) and to control certain costs. With a view to hybridising, in various ways, the three economic poles, social enterprises seek to use each of these types of relations consistent with the logic of their projects. Moreover, this hybridisation is developed in the public sphere, which is of primary importance when it comes to mobilising or generating social capital.

Hybridisation as a resistance to institutional isomorphism

Finally, the credibility and the durability of social enterprises derive from their ability to be constantly rooted in the context of a civil and solidarity-based economy; in other words, to be relevant, their economic activity has to remain embedded in solidarity and in the principles of justice and equality. Initiative and solidarity are reconciled since individuals are uniting voluntarily to undertake joint action that creates economic activity and jobs, while simultaneously forging a new social solidarity and reinforcing social cohesion.

Experience with initiatives in the social economy has shown that if, over time, the distinctive features which characterise this 'third force' are downplayed, the initiatives tend to drift toward institutional isomorphism.[14] Some co-operatives have gradually come to resemble other forms of enterprise in the market economy.[15] Similarly, certain mutual benefit societies, through their integration into the social welfare system, have turned into virtual copies of organisations in the public administration. To a significant degree, this trajectory has reflected a reorientation of their initial mission.

While the role of social enterprises in discovering social demands and in introducing innovative practices must be acknowledged, government take-over of funding might suggest that the reciprocal relations stemming from the mobilisation of social capital can disappear with time. To avoid such an evolution, the production of collective externalities associated with the delivery of certain services can be taken into account by the introduction of new forms of redistributive policies from which all enterprises can benefit in the more competitive context. Through active policies, all enterprises can be encouraged to reintegrate workers casualised by the labour market.

Nevertheless, even when governments provide funding for the production of collective benefits, experience shows that civic engagement and mobilisation of reciprocal resources remain central to the creation of certain collective benefits. Social enterprises, by mobilising volunteers and social networks, have a specific ability to strengthen social capital. In the same way, if stakeholders (volunteers, users and workers) get involved, this can create a capital of solid trust, so important to certain services. It is a way to contain the opportunistic behaviours that are likely to arise because the manner in which social enterprises are managed makes them vulnerable to the uncertainties of the market economy, and because their interaction with public policy may make them dependent on funding from redistribution.

Conclusions

The theoretical approach we have proposed here, like that advanced by neo-institutional economics,[16] takes analysis of existing economic institutions as a starting point. At the same time, it goes beyond functionalism which, based on criteria of efficiency related to the reduction of transaction costs, views existing institutions as the only possible ones. So as to avoid naturalising or 'absolutising' existing institutions[17] in such analyses, one must understand their origin, which in turn calls for sociological, historical and legal analysis.[18]

Clearly, analysis of social enterprises does not give rise to a single model of ownership but it highlights the fact that they are managed by stakeholders other than investors. Social enterprises take as their starting point the mobilisation of social capital around a project whose objectives include a dimension of community service. Some structural characteristics could reflect this dimension of community service as the non-profit constraint or the limits to surplus distribution and the development of multiple stakeholder forms of ownership. The pursuit of collective benefits also allows specific forms of mobilisation of social capital such as involvement of volunteers, donations and development of local partnership. In other words, economic projects emerge from relations of reciprocity in the public sphere. Project stakeholders get involved because they believe that by creating collective benefits for other actors or for society as a whole they help democratise economic relations. One of the driving forces behind their common commitment derives from their desire for collective benefits. The social or civic entrepreneurship intrinsic to social enterprises is characterised as much by this trait as by a claim for managerial independence which might keep them away from government or shareholder property.

Beyond the consumer subsidies and quasi-markets through which a part of them and other types of enterprises could obtain funds, the fate of social enterprises depends on their capacity to secure their financing from redistribution to assure the production of collective benefits. Their trajectory is interdependent with public policies. For this reason, the question of the future of social enterprises remains wide open. The process by which they are institutionalised seeks to make them increasingly autonomous by avoiding dependence on one source alone and by enabling them to comply with the objectives of the initial projects. But in order to do this they must confront the issue of sustaining social capital, and reconcile this with the mobilisation of funds obtained via the revenues coming from the redistribution and the acquisition of consistent market financing. In short, the tension between institutional isomorphism and autonomy based on tripolar economic hybridisation is a characteristic of social enterprises.

Notes

1 See the introduction to this book.
2 On such a perspective of solidarity-based economy, see Laville (1994).
3 For example, Mauss, Perroux and Polanyi, to cite only a few. This kind of tripolar analysis has in recent years been taken up again in works on the civil and solidarity-based economy, and attests to the existence of a variety of possible socio-economic principles (see Laville 1994). For a 'welfare pluralism' and a 'plural economy' analysis, see Laville *et al.* (2000); Pestoff (1998) also discusses tripolar analysis in reference to social security; even the World Bank, in its 1997 Annual Report, takes note of tripolar organisational forms (World Bank 1997: 116, French version).
4 By stakeholder, we mean 'any individual or group who has a direct interest in ensuring that the enterprise conducts profitable and sustainable activities' (Milgrom and Roberts 1992: 790).
5 See the contribution of Evers in this volume about the multiple goals of social enterprises (Chapter 17).
6 This may come down to electing individuals to manage the enterprise.
7 Borzaga and Mittone (1997); Pestoff (1998). It should be noted that, to be more precise, we should speak of multiple stakeholder ownership enterprises.
8 This argument is close to the one put forward by Ben-Ner and Van Hoomissen (1991). This article emphasises the importance of representation by stakeholder beneficiaries in organisations producing non-rival goods and hence also in those concerned with collective benefits.

9 This is a central idea of the contribution by Bacchiega and Borzaga in this volume (Chapter 16).
10 On this point, see Bacchiega and Borzaga in this volume (Chapter 16).
11 De Tocqueville (1991); Touraine (1973).
12 As expressed by Godbout and Caillé (1992).
13 OECD 1996.
14 On the notion of institutional isomorphism, see Di Maggio and Powell (1993); Enjolras (1996); Kramer (2000).
15 That said, it should be noted that they generated discussion within the producer co-operative movement, leading to the adoption of the following text at its Lille Congress of October 1997: 'The co-operative movement will work toward a specific status along the lines of Italian social co-operatives, reflecting a new spirit of partnership among users, volunteers and waged workers' [Translation].
16 As typified by Williamson (1975). For a review on these theories in the field of NPO, see Bacchiega and Borzaga in this volume.
17 According to the term employed by Barber (1995).
18 For a critical view of neo-institutional economics developing this argument, see Granovetter (1985).

Bibliography

AGLIETTA, M. (1976) *Régulation et crises du capitalisme. L'expérience des États-Unis*, Calmann-Lévy, Paris.

BARBER, B. (1995) 'All Economies Are Embedded: The Career of a Concept, and Beyond', *Social Research*, vol. 62, 2: 387–413.

BEN-NER, A. and VAN HOOMISSEN, T. (1991) 'Non Profit Organisations in the Mixed Economy', *Annals of Public and Co-operative Economics*, vol. 4, 519–50.

BIANCO, M.L. and EVE, M. (1999) 'I due volti del capitale sociale. Il capitale sociale individuale nello studio delle diseguaglianze', in LAVILLE, J.-L. and MINGIONE, E. (eds) 'Nuova sociologica-economica. Prospettiva europea', *Sociologia del Lavoro*, 73.

BORZAGA, C. and MITTONE, L. (1997) 'The Multistakeholder versus the Nonprofit Organisation', Università degli Studi di Trento, Draft Paper no. 7.

BOYER, R. (1995) 'Vers une théorie originale des institutions économiques', in BOYER, R. and SAILLARD, Y. (eds) *Théorie de la régulation, l'état des savoirs*, La Découverte, Paris.

CAILLÉ, A. (1993) *La démission des clercs*, La Découverte, Paris.

CALHOUN, C. (ed.) (1992) *Habermas and the Public Sphere*, MIT Press.

CALLON, M. (1999) 'La sociologie peut-elle enrichir l'analyse économique des externalités? Essai sur la notion de débordement', in FORAY, D. and MAIRESSE, J. (eds) *Innovations et performances. Approches interdisciplinaires*, Editions de l'Ecole des hautes Etudes en Sciences sociales, Paris.

COLEMAN, J.S. (1990) *Foundations of Social Theory*, Harvard University Press, Cambridge, MA.

Co-operative Union of Canada (1985) *Social Auditing: A Manual for Co-operative Organisations*, CUC, Social Audit Task Force, Toronto.

DEFOURNY, J., FAVREAU, L. and LAVILLE, J.-L. (eds) (1998) *Insertion et nouvelle économie sociale. Un bilan international*, Desclée de Brouwer, Paris.

DE TOCQUEVILLE, A. (1991) *De la démocratie en Amérique*, Gallimard, Paris.

DI MAGGIO, P. and POWELL, W.W. (1993) 'The Iron Cage Revisited: Institutional Isomorphism and Collective Rationality in Organizational Fields', *American Sociological Review*, vol. 48, 147–60.

EME, B. (1994) 'Insertion et économie solidaire', in EME, B. and LAVILLE, J.-L. (eds) *Cohésion sociale et emploi*, Desclée de Brouwer, Paris.

—— (1993) 'Lecture d'Habermas et éléments provisoires d'une problématique du social solidariste d'intervention', miméograph, CRIDA-LSCI, IRESCO-CNRS, Paris.

ENJOLRAS, B. (1996) 'Associations et isomorphisme institutionnel', *Revue des études coopératives, mutualistes et associatives*, vol. 75, 261: 68–76.

EVERS, A. (1997) 'Le tiers-secteur au regard d'une conception pluraliste de la protection sociale', in *Produire les solidarités. La part des associations*, MIRE – Rencontres et Recherches, Paris.

——(1995) 'Part of the Welfare Mix: The Third Sector as an Intermediate Area', *Voluntas*, vol. 6, 2: 159–82.

EVERS, A. and SCHULZE-BÖING, M. (1998) 'Mobilising Social Capital – The Contribution of Social Enterprises to Strategies against Unemployment and Social Exclusion', paper for an EMES Seminar, Brussels.

FOURASTIÉ, J., Préface à GASPARD, M. (1998) *Les services contre le chômage*, Syros, Paris.

GIDDENS, A. (1994) *Beyond Left and Right, The Future of Radical Politics*, Polity Press, Cambridge.

GODBOUT, J. and CAILLÉ, A. (1992) *L'esprit du don*, La Découverte, Paris.

GRANOVETTER, M. (1992) 'Economic Institutions as Social Constructions: a Framework for Analysis', *Acta Sociologica*, 35.

——(1985) 'Economic Action and Social Structure: The Problem of Embeddedness', *American Journal of Sociology*, vol. 91, 3: 481–510.

GUI, B. (1995) 'On 'Relational Goods': Strategic Implications of Investment in Relationships', Dipartimento di Scienze Economiche, Universitá di Venezia.

—— (1991) 'The Economic Rationale for the Third Sector', *Annals of Public and Co-operative Economics*, vol. 62, 4: 551–72.

HABERMAS, J. (1992) *L'espace public, 30 ans après* (French translation), *Quaderni*, no. 18, autumn, 161–88.

——(1988) 'Vingt ans après: la culture politique et les institutions en RFA', *Le Débat*, September-October, Gallimard, Paris.

——(1986) *L'espace public*, Payot, Paris.

—— (1974) 'The Public Sphere', in *New German Critique*, no. 3.

HANSMANN, H. (1996) *The Ownership of Enterprise*, Harvard University Press, Cambridge.

—— (1987) 'Economic Theories of Nonprofit Organisations', in POWELL, W. (ed.) *The Nonprofit Sector, A Research Handbook*, Yale University Press, New Haven, 27–42.

HARRIS, J. and DE RENZIO, P. (1997) 'Missing Link or Analytically Missing?: The Concept of Social Capital', *Journal of International Developement*, vol. 9, 7: 919–37.

JAMES, E. and ROSE-ACKERMAN, S. (1986) *The Non-profit Enterprise in Market Economies: Fondamentals of Pure and Applied Economics*, Harwood Academic Publishers, London.

KRAMER, R.-M. (2000) 'A Third Sector in the Third Millennium?', *Voluntas*, vol. 11, 1: 1–24.

LAVILLE, J.-L.(1992) *Les services de proximité en Europe*, Syros Alternatives, Paris.

LAVILLE, J.-L. (ed.) (1994) *L'économie solidaire*, Desclée de Brouwer, Paris.

LAVILLE, J.-L. and GARDIN, L. (eds) (1996) *Les initiatives locales en Europe. Bilan économique et social*, Commission européenne, CRIDA-LSCI, CNRS, Paris.

LAVILLE, J.-L. and NYSSENS, M. (2000) 'Solidarity-Based Third Sector Organizations in the 'Proximity Services' Field: A European Francophone Perspective', *Voluntas*, vol. 11, 1: 67–84.

LAVILLE, J.-L. and SAINSAULIEU, R. (eds) (1998) *Sociologie de l'association*, Desclée de Brouwer, Paris.

LAVILLE, J.-L., BORZAGA, C., DEFOURNY, J., EVERS, A., LEWIS, J., NYSSENS, M. and PESTOFF, V. (2000) 'Tiers système: une définition européenne', in *Les entreprises et organisations du troisième système. Un enjeu stratégique pour l'emploi*, Action pilote 'Troisième système et emploi' de la Commission européenne, CIRIEC, Liège, 107–30.

LEVESQUE, B. (1997) 'Démocratisation de l'économie et économie sociale', in LAFLAMME, G., LAPOINTE, P. A. *et al.* (eds) *La crise de l'emploi. De nouveaux partages s'imposent !*, Presses de l'Université Laval, Québec.

LEVESQUE, B. and VAILLANCOURT, Y. (1998) 'L'institutionnalisation de la nouvelle économie sociale au Québec: une diversité de scénarios dans un contexte institutionnel relativement favorable', Université du Québec à Montréal.

LIPIETZ, A. (1996) *La société en sablier*, La Découverte, Paris.

MAHEU, L. (1991) 'Identité et enjeux du politique', in MAHEU, L. and SALES, A. (eds) *La recomposition du politique*, L'Harmattan, Paris; Les Presses universitaires de Montréal, Montréal.

MAPPA, S. (ed.) (1995) *Développer par la démocratie?*, Karthala, Paris.

MAUCOURANT, J., SERVET, J.-M. and TIRAN, A. (1998) *La modernité de Karl Polanyi, introduction générale*, L'Harmattan, Paris.

MAURICE, M., SELLIER, F. and SILVESTRE, J.-J. (1982) *Politique d'éducation et organisation industrielle en France et en Allemagne*, PUF, Paris.

MAUSS, M. (1923) 'Essai sur le don. Forme et raison de l'échange dans les sociétés archaïques', *L'Année sociologique*, Paris.

MERRIEN, F.- X. (1990) 'État et politiques sociales: contribution à une théorie néo-institutionnaliste', *Sociologie du travail*, vol. 32: 3.

MILGROM, P. and ROBERTS, J. (1992) *Economics, Organisation and Management*, Prentice Hall International, Englewood Cliffs.

MINGIONE, E. (1991) *Fragmented Societies, a Sociology of Economic Life Beyond the Market Paradigm*, Basil Blackwell, Oxford.

OECD (1996) *Reconciling Economy and Society. Towards a Plural Economy*, OECD, Paris.

ORTMANN, A. and SCHLESINGER, A.M. (1997) 'Trust, Repute and the Role of Non-Profit Enterprise', *Voluntas*, vol. 8, 97–119.

PACI, M. (1999) 'Alle origini della imprenditorialita e della fiducia interpersonale nelle aree ad economia diffusa', in LAVILLE, J.-L. and MINGIONE, E. (eds) 'Nuova sociologica-economica. Prospettiva europea', *Sociologia del Lavoro*, 73.

PERROUX, F. (1960) *Économie et société, contrainte-échange-don*, PUF, Paris.

PESTOFF, V.A. (1998) *Beyond Market and State, Social Enterprises and Civil Democracy in a Welfare Society*, Ashgate, Aldershot.

POLANYI, K. (1997) *The Livelihood of Man*, Academic Press, New York.

—— (1983) *La grande transformation. Aux origines politiques et économiques de notre temps* (French translation), Gallimard, Paris.

PRESTON, A. (1993) 'Efficiency, Quality and Social Externalities in the Provision of Day Care: Comparisons of Nonprofit and and For-Profit Firms', *The Journal of Productivity Analysis*, 4: 164–82.

PUTNAM, R.D. (1993a) 'The Prosperous Community: Social Capital and Public Life', *The American Prospect*, vol. 13: 35–42.

—— (1993b) *Making Democracy Work. Civic Traditions in Modern Italy*, Princeton University Press, New Jersey.

RAZETO, L. (1988) *Economía de solidaridad y mercado democrático*, Libro tercero, Fundamentos de una teoría económica comprensiva, PET, Santiago de Chile.

ROSE-ACKERMAN, S. (ed.) (1986) *The Economics of Non-profit Institutions. Structure and Policy*, Oxford University Press, New York.

SABEL, C. and the LEED Programme, Ireland (1996) 'Partenariats locaux et innovation sociale', OECD, Paris.

SALAMON, L. (1987) 'Of Market Failure, Voluntary Failure, and Third Party of Government Relations in the Modern Welfare State', *Journal of Voluntary Action Research*, vol. 16, 2: 29–49.

STROBEL, P. (1995) 'Service public, fin de siècle', in GREMION, C. (ed.) *Modernisation des services publics*, Commissariat général du plan, Ministère de la recherche, La Documentation Française, Paris.

TOURAINE, A. (1973) *Production de la société*, Le Seuil, Paris.

VIVIANI, M. (1995) 'Tools of Co-operative Identity – Fixing Values in Turbulent Conditions: the Case of Lega della Co-operative', ICA Conference paper, Manchester.

WEBER, M. (1991) *Histoire économique. Esquisse d'une histoire universelle de l'économie et de la société* (French translation), Gallimard.

—— (1918) *Essai sur la théorie de la science* (French translation 1959), Plon, Paris.

WILLIAMSON, O.E. (1975) *Markets and Hierarchies*, Free Press, New York.

World Bank (1997) *Annual Report*, Oxford University Press, Oxford.

ZUKIN, S. and DI MAGGIO, P. (1990) *Structures of Capital: The Social Organisation of the Economy*, Cambridge University Press, Cambridge.

19 Management challenges for social enterprises

Carlo Borzaga and Luca Solari

Introduction

As the number of social enterprises in Europe grows, the managers who run them are faced with an increasingly difficult task. Not only must they establish their organisations and legitimate them, but they must also find suitable ways to manage their key assets including their social mission and efficiency constraints, committed volunteers and employees, and enlarged governance structures. As shown in previous chapters, social enterprises are different not only from for-profit and public-sector organisations, but also from traditional non-profit ones (Steinberg 1997). While traditional non-profit organisations still struggle with problems related to their multi-faceted identities (Young 2000), social enterprises are faced by tougher challenges. They embody a new form emerging in an institutional and competitive arena which appears to be rapidly changing, and in which they must frequently compete with public sector, for-profit and traditional non-profit organisations. They share with traditional non-profit organisations the problem of defining a perceived and recognised external and internal identity (Young 2000) which is harder to bring into focus because of the hybrid and poorly defined nature of the social enterprise form. This hybrid nature is re-inforced by various factors among which the following are prominent:

- A social enterprise is 'essentially a (private) organisation devoted to achieving some social good' (Young 2000: 18) and which must furthermore incorporate, besides the traditional resources of non-profit organisations (donations and voluntary participation), commercial revenue (originating both from public and private customers and founders) and business activity. As Preston (1989a) shows, when modelling the behaviour of for-profit and non-profit organisations, non-profit organisations end up specialising in the production of goods with some positive externalities. This is consistent with the view set out in the theoretical chapters of this book insofar as social enterprises provide private goods with positive externalities or with a redistributive component, and therefore increasingly allow 'for private sector firms to compete by selling a similar good in the market' (Kingma 1997: 140). For-profit organisations may in fact provide the same good by internalising positive externalities without undertaking any social role. For example, a for-profit organisation can compete with social enterprises in the provision of home-care services financed by a local authority, fulfilling the contractual agreement but without caring for the well-being of customers should they need an enriched service, such as more hours of care or a different interpersonal approach. It is for this reason that several authors argue that social enterprises should receive at least partial support from the public sector in dealing with these externalities which in themselves could be valued as positive outcomes of the actions of social enterprises.

- The problem is exacerbated if we consider that the notion of social good is in itself inherently ambiguous. Social enterprises are different from most traditional non-profit organisations because they do not usually produce public goods (non-excludable and non-rival in consumption), nor rarely collective goods (excludable, but non-rival in consumption), but mainly goods characterised by an individual demand associated with a perceived social utility. It should be noted, from this specific point of view, that the nature of this positive externality on the one hand gives rise to increased production costs, while on the other it depends on the preferences of external actors such as public authorities or local communities, and may change in time. This implies that a universal definition of social good cannot be provided unless it is restricted to specific institutional contexts, in both time and space.

- Their multi-faceted mission obliges social enterprises to consider how they can manage commercial activities, which by their very nature require adequate management practices which are typically oriented toward effectiveness and efficiency (Herman and Renz 1998), alongside free resources such as donations and volunteers' efforts and time. As social enterprises move from reliance on donations and funding (a characteristic of most traditional non-profit organisations, at least in the form which emerged in the US) to the delivery of goods and services, the balance shifts from advocacy and fund-raising activities to management of quality and customer satisfaction, which in turn require an increase in operational efficiency.

- Finally, most social enterprises are multi-stakeholder in nature and rely heavily on extended participation by workers, volunteers and/or customers. For this reason, their embedded goals may become even further confused by the need to combine different interests and balance them in the ongoing management of activities.

The hybrid nature of social enterprises resulting from these various factors raises an obstacle against the legitimation of both social enterprises and their managers. Not yet fully legitimated, the identity of social enterprises is confronted by a scenario which is in itself challenging. The external economic, social, and political environment, more or less passively accepts the emergence of social enterprises, while those that have emerged must focus their strategies and management clearly. However, neither the public-sector, the for-profit nor the non-profit literature on management provides models and approaches which can account for the specific nature of social enterprises. Public-sector models rely too closely on bureaucracy and simplification; for-profit models do not account for social mission and values; and traditional non-profit models often fail to deal with the efficiency constraints imposed on social enterprises, focusing on fund raising and social networking.

The key challenges to be addressed in establishing a new, more specific model of management for social enterprises are reviewed in this chapter in order to provide normative guidance for managers of social enterprises. First the external and internal challenges are identified, and analysis is conducted of the ways in which social enterprise managers can deal with them. After a review of the traditional non-profit management literature, the conclusion is reached that this provides inadequate models for the challenges faced by social enterprises. As the key areas demanding action by managers are explored, it is argued that social enterprise managers have been actively involved in issues which require external confrontation and lobbying. Nevertheless, it is the internal challenges that demand more attention because it is they that constitute the key competitive advantages of social enterprises.

1 Challenges to the evolution of social enterprises in Europe

The identity of European social enterprises overlaps with that of many of the existing providers of social services. Social enterprises are an emerging form, and they have been, and continue to be, subject to all the constraints consequent on their lack of legitimation in the institutional environment (Scott 1995; Suchman 1995), and sometimes to attempts to prevent their legitimation by established and pre-existent competitors. The previous chapters of this book, as well as other recent studies (European Commission 1999), reveal that social enterprises, in their collective effort to gain recognition, and thereby ensure the resources for their growth and diffusion, must confront several challenges, most notably:

Challenges re shaping a supportive legislative and regulatory environment

The social nature of social enterprises is not yet taken for granted. Although in some countries, social enterprises have been able to gain tax exemptions or priorities in bidding for services on the basis of their status as non-profit organisations, current legislation is still far from defining a clear support framework for social enterprises. The experience of recent years demonstrates that when recognition (be it complete or partial) has been accorded to the specific nature of social enterprises, the contribution to their evolution and growth has been significant. By contrast, the results have been disappointing when account has not been taken of these specificities. There is, therefore, still a long way to go.

Challenges re ensuring the quality of products and services

The particular nature of social services requires social enterprises to invest constantly in the quality of the service delivered to customers. A high and stable level of quality is a crucial requirement for social enterprises to be able to compete effectively with public-sector, for-profit and traditional non-profit organisations. Social enterprises can profit from their closeness to customers and local communities, but they should be aware that the constant delivery of high-quality services requires appropriate investment.

Challenges re upgrading skills and jobs

One of the major areas of investment to ensure quality is skills and human resources (particularly in a context of growth). Service organisations rely heavily on the expertise, skill and motivation of employees. Social enterprises must better organise the training of their workers and volunteers, devising programmes for the improvement of workforce skills. On the one hand, they must devote a larger share of resources to development; on the other, they might sponsor the development of specific graduate and post-graduate programmes.

Challenges re securing management expertise and support

In their early stages, all organisations strive to attract people with the competencies and skills that they require. Social enterprises are a new form of organisation and for this reason they require professional expertise and support to enhance their viability. A key aspect is the role of leaders and founders of social enterprises, who must improve their managerial competence or delegate control to more professional and skilled individuals.

Challenges re financing

Though some studies appear to demonstrate that the capital requirements of social enterprises are limited, and that they are easily fulfilled once the start-up phase has been completed, financing may be important; especially when, as in traditional co-operatives, self-financing is difficult and the financial structure tends to be undercapitalised. Because social enterprises are a new form, traditional bankers and funding institutions find them difficult to analyse and interpret. Developing a collective structure to finance start-ups and growth processes would greatly foster the sector's development.

Challenges re developing networks and co-operations

A condition for the creation of joint structures of financing is the development of network-based relations of support among social enterprises, both locally and globally. Whilst limited size facilitates keeping customers closer to social enterprises, it constrains the ability to exploit economies of scale and to undertake new ventures, and it may prevent a more proactive approach being taken to strategy-making. Creating second- and third-level organisations is a way to obtain the advantages of size, including economies of scale, slack resources, and knowledge sharing, and to ensure the availability of additional resources to sustain innovation and development, without losing the advantage of small size.

Challenges re establishing adequate governance structures

Social enterprises must devise an architecture which reflects the existence of different stakeholders, with different interests, while preserving their democratic and locally bounded organisational structures. This is sometimes obstructed by the local institutional environment, which may at times impose constraints on the availability of legal forms.

On closer inspection, the challenges confronting social enterprises can be divided into exogenous and endogenous. Exogenous challenges, such as financing and legislative actions, cannot be fully controlled or managed by social enterprises, but at most can be influenced and lobbied for. Endogenous challenges, by contrast, can be affected by the actions of social enterprises, and especially by their leaders and managers. Endogenous challenges depend on the ability of social enterprises and their managers and leaders to enhance the legitimation and operational effectiveness of these forms. To this end, however, managers of social enterprises[1] must identify the key areas of intervention and acknowledge the highly specific nature of the organisations that they manage. Any failure to do so may give rise to painful mistakes,[2] which may undermine the more widespread legitimation of social enterprises, which is after all, the main challenge that confronts them. There is, therefore, a daunting array of issues to deal with. Social enterprises managers seeking answers to how they can cope with these challenges might look at the existing literature on the management of non-profit organisations. However, as the following sections will show, this is not a satisfactory solution.

2   What can we learn from traditional non-profit management practices?

The current literature on the management of non-profit organisations addresses the main challenges to social enterprises only marginally. The principal reason is that this literature is largely concerned with the problems of traditional non-profit organisations, and is mainly concerned with North America. These organisations are, on average, larger, and they rely more heavily on traditional management techniques, supplemented by fund-raising and volunteer management. The predominant view of the non-profit organisation is that it is a donative form, and when it evolves into an entrepreneurial form the common view is that the risks outnumber the advantages (Hansmann 1980). For example, Pappas (1996) describes the problems of organisational change in non-profits as a consequence of greater demands for reliability and accountability. After detailed analysis of these changes, she describes non-profit organisations as hierarchically driven and too internally focused, and argues that they should shift to a service-oriented model more consciously driven by the market (Pappas 1996: 50).

Allison and Kaye (1997) deal with the issue of strategic planning for non-profit organisations. Their study concentrates on larger organisations which are involved in cost-benefit analyses and develop formal strategic plans. Jeavons (1994) emphasises 'charity' among the values pursued by the ethical management of non-profit organisations.[3] He writes: 'many of these organisations depend on the generosity of their supporters for their existence, and ought to display such generosity themselves' (Jeavons 1994: 199), and 'the basis of much of these organisations' support is the expectations that they will be vehicles for building a more caring, more just society' (Jeavons 1994: 200). Moreover, traditional non-profit management approaches view non-profit organisations 'as necessarily hierarchical, with the board of directors in the superior position' (Herman and Heimovics 1994: 138) and managed by chief executives hired by the board. Boards are usually composed of volunteer leaders responsible for ensuring that the organisation fulfils its mission. As a consequence, these approaches to management are extremely difficult to adapt to the management of social enterprises, since the governance structures, mission, goals, roles and organisation models are different.

3   Looking within for competitive advantage: managing human resources

Although it is evident that a clearly-defined identity is important when social enterprises interact with the public-welfare system, and with their customers, we contend that it may prove equally important when social enterprises interact with potential paid and volunteer workers. The kind of customer legitimation required for social enterprises to evolve depends on their ability to deliver services more effective than, and at least as efficient as, those provided by traditional non-profit, for-profit and public-sector organisations. At the same time, social enterprises must preserve their social nature, embedded in positive externalities and in the distribution of the additional value thus created to their customers. The values of social enterprises, their operating size, their relationships with communities, customers and employees, and their history, all impose strict limits on the extent to which they can imitate the leadership and management styles prevalent in traditional non-profit, for-profit and public-sector organisations.

On the one hand, the predominance of the New Public Management view of administration causes problems. Like it or not,[4] efficiency is an undisputed criterion in choices affecting the distribution of public resources. The privatisation of key welfare system activities will attract for-profit organisations (a clear example being the evolution of the healthcare system in the US – see Scott *et al.* 2000); and competition from alternative providers will force social enterprises to improve their internal efficiency. The same kind of pressure is already being applied to social enterprises which rely heavily on revenues from customers. On the other hand, social enterprises must enhance their competitive advantage in managing human resources. Different management styles are required to maintain a competitive advantage based on workers' commitment and involvement, as public-sector and for-profit organisations shift to a leadership style which emphasises participation and identification with a mission. The feature common to all social enterprises is the necessity to maintain a close relationship among values, mission, and organisation. The value-driven employee of a social enterprise wants it to manifest a consistent set of values, norms, and organisational practices. A new governance and organisational form is needed, in which the workforce find:

- greater autonomy;
- a chance to participate in decision-making and ongoing management;
- respect for people and their expectations;
- a balance between efficiency and social mission;
- closer attention to customers and societal issues;
- a feeling that one personally owns the organisation (economically and psychologically);
- emotional and technical leadership; and
- the fulfilment of a broad array of personal needs and desires.

4 Management of social enterprises: how to face the main external and internal challenges

In the light of the foregoing discussion, it appears that the role of managers in social enterprises at their present stage of development is to establish legitimacy externally and internally. Whilst external legitimation has been partially acquired and may benefit from the profound changes taking place in European welfare systems, internal legitimation requires an endeavour to identify the key characteristics of a new organisational form. Sole reliance on the spontaneous nature of the values embedded in the mission of social enterprises when managing their key assets may prove to be a risky strategy. However, it should be pointed out that our research shows that social enterprises are adapting to the institutional framework in which they operate. Consequently, the core characteristics of the social enterprise organisational form have become embedded in a variety of specific, local organisational forms. These differences entail a variety in management styles and behaviours.

In the next three sections we will examine the main challenges faced by social enterprise managers, and the strategies with which they can respond at three levels: 'at the gate', 'at home' and 'from within'.

At the gate: challenging the external role of managers

Since their inception, the managers of social enterprises have had to cope with a largely unenthusiastic external environment. In several European countries, the rise of social enterprises has been perceived as eroding the traditional public-sector role in welfare, and as a threat to long-established non-profit organisations. Social forces like the trade unions have repeatedly accused social enterprises of taking work and activities away from the public sector and, if not actively at least passively, they have opposed their growth. For this reason, the managements of social enterprises have concentrated on the external arena, in order to lobby politicians and regulators and in order to create a shared, positive perception of their identity in society. Many managers have been actively involved in this debate, because they not only run social enterprises but also were their founders and volunteers, and therefore have a marked sensitivity to social issues.

Although social enterprises have increased in importance throughout Europe, the external role of their managers is still crucial, given that the legitimation process is far from complete. The lack of clear policies to sustain social enterprises, and the need for resources and financing which are sometimes provided through parallel and not completely appropriate channels (for example, the use of employment subsidies to organise the provision of social services), continue to be the key factors in the evolution of social enterprises. One of the major obstacles lies at the European level, where social enterprises are still too different to establish themselves as a new, legitimated form with a single identity. They must create and enforce a common identity by adopting common governance structures and working for a shared definition of the distinctive features of a social enterprise. Networking was one of the first answers to these common problems, and it proved to be effective, but more effort is required in this direction.

The European context is now completely different from what it was ten to fifteen years ago. From a social movement, social enterprises have grown into (even in the opinion of most policy-makers) a socio-economic reality which can leverage the resources that it creates such as employment and social benefits, to increase its power and legitimacy. This requires a shift from a claimant stance to negotiation, partnership and consensus, and a different attitude towards key social actors including citizens, the public sector, social forces and movements. As regards the role of social enterprise managers, three levels of intervention can be identified, viz. society at large, the public sector and social forces and movements. The key actions with respect to these three levels vary, and they are now explored in greater detail.

Managers to society at large

Social enterprise managers must continue to devote their time and energies to establishing cognitive legitimation for their organisations, so that social enterprises become a widely recognised organisational form. This requires effort at external communication at both the local and European levels. Important results could be achieved by organising research and events intended to communicate the identity and goal of social enterprises. At the local level, social enterprises should invest in the innovation of service delivery and monitor the evolution of social needs. Moreover, these characteristics should be reinforced by means of service agreements or social reports. The accountability of social enterprise managers is usually enforced in order to counteract the risk of opportunism, although this requirement changes when we move from social enterprises which rely mainly on donations or public funds to social enterprises which operate by selling services directly to final customers, through vouchers or direct payments. Whatever the case may be, closer links with local communities would undoubtedly be to the advantage of social enterprises in their quest for a widely recognised identity.

Managers to the public sector

Social enterprise managers must uncouple their practices and attitudes from those of public-sector managers. They run private organisations with a social mission, and although the public sector will remain a major actor in the provision, or at least the financing, of social services, it cannot be considered to be the only, or even the major, stakeholder. Social enterprise managers must continue to provide the public sector with innovative projects and a broader view of the evolution of social needs. Autonomy and an ability to devise new markets and new strategies are crucial for the legitimation of social enterprises with respect to public-sector organisations. Social enterprises are at risk of a reaction by the public sector, which may seek to gain direct control over them. The consequences would be the hampering of innovation and the confinement of social enterprises to the organisation of a secondary labour market.

Managers to social forces and movements

Social enterprise managers should not forget that the social mission of their organisations is a key characteristic of their identity creation process. If this is removed, social enterprises could be left with an identity that wholly overlaps with that of traditional worker or consumer co-operatives or for-profit organisations, and that would obviously mean the destruction of the social enterprise's identity. In some countries of Europe, this process is particularly difficult because social enterprises are rooted in cultural movements which share contempt for management and economics. The very idea of using revenues and business as a way to achieve social goals is considered at best a heresy. None the less, social enterprise managers need to keep social forces and movements within their scope and reinforce their social mission.

At home: challenging the internal role of managers

Moving to the internal challenges for social enterprises managers, two issues appear critical, given the present state of such organisations. These are governance structures and human resources management. Besides improvement of the internal effectiveness of these forms, we argue that even a share of external legitimation will be determined by the ability to define governance structures and human resources models specific to social enterprises and different from those of other organisational forms. The issue of governance structures intertwines with the heterogeneous nature of stakeholders and their different goals. Governance structures should bear in mind that the relevant stakeholders, such as employees, customers, and the public sector, are diverse, and that their expectations with respect to social enterprises should be incorporated into management goals and balanced.[5] For example, it is evident that voluntary workers are needed to counterbalance the increasingly productive nature of social enterprises, to foster innovation (by providing slack resources), and to prevent the dismissal of the social mission and values.

Managers must recognise the specific nature of social enterprises if they are to deal satisfactorily with the issue of governance. The naive idea that enforcing a non-profit distribution constraint can solve the issues of control is at odds with an institutional environment in which control over organisations follows a radically different logic from that predominant in the USA.[6] In Europe, the variety of governance forms in social enterprises testifies to the search for an original model which can gain local legitimation. This variety is evidenced in the different forms assumed by social enterprises in the European countries, as described by the national chapters in this book. This variety notwithstanding, social enterprises have one distinctive feature in common, insofar as they do not have shareholders rewarded with profits. Hence a straightforward approach to governance within an agency framework lacks the key component of the shareholder as a principal. This is not to imply that social enterprises are left without a principal. If correct governance structures are defined, in fact, the principal role can be performed by customers, funding members, and employees.

This issue has been raised by several researchers (Hansmann 1996; Ben-Ner 1986), who have suggested alternative solutions. Moving from the theoretical point of view to a more practical one leaves us with a key question: who owns social enterprises? The clearest answer is forthcoming from the experiences of social enterprises described in the chapters of this book. Social enterprises are by their nature multi-stakeholder. If only one stakeholder predominates, the differences with respect to traditional co-operative forms or for-profit organisations fade, and the social function of social enterprises is blurred.

The multi-stakeholder approach to social enterprises (Borzaga and Mittone 1997) has a number of consequences for governance structures. From this perspective, a heterogeneous base of representatives within institutional bodies is able to exert control among different stakeholder groups and over managers of social enterprises (when these are appointed from outside the stakeholder base), preventing a betrayal of the mission and reducing asymmetries. The problem is that European social enterprises are at present a collection of slightly different specific national forms, adapted to local institutional and economic environments.

A solution to the issue of governance would be to establish structures which vary according to the prevalent nature of specific social enterprises. When the production of goods/services prevails, control over performance should be ensured by greater customer power in both buying services and participating in governance bodies, this latter solution being adopted when the quality of services/goods is difficult to determine *ex-post*. If donations and public funding are more important, an enlarged governance structure should be favoured, enabling all relevant stakeholders to participate in decision-making processes. When local regulations do not allow for a mixed governance structure and formal participation, as in Sweden, social enterprises must find a way to incorporate this heterogeneous base into their decision-making processes. Yet the role of volunteers and/or representatives of local communities should not be dismissed, since it may provide the impetus towards preservation of a social role for social enterprises, which otherwise would risk becoming less differentiated from traditional worker and consumer co-operatives or for-profit organisations (Alexander *et al.* 1999). Volunteers provide free resources which can be used to produce externalities or to ensure redistributive functions. The presence of volunteers in governance structures is absolutely strategic for those services in which these two components (externality and the redistributive function) are important.

A second challenge for managers is how they should deal with the highly distinctive nature of the relationship between employees and social enterprises. Social enterprises are in most cases labour-intensive organisations. Given their nature as service organisations, this feature raises a number of challenges as regards human resources management. Since employee morale impacts on the quality of the service as perceived by customers, the well-being of employees should be an important concern for social enterprise managers, who should realise that the advantage of a well-educated, motivated workforce may be eroded if it is not adequately maintained and reinforced.

The nature of the exchange between employees and organisations in social enterprises is enriched by the intrinsic value of socially oriented work. Theoretical analyses of employee attitudes and satisfaction in the third sector (Akerlof 1982; Preston 1989b; Handy and Katz 1998) provide strong evidence that the psychological contract between employees and organisations in social enterprises is of a different type.

Social enterprise workers have a mix of motives which differs from those of employees in for-profit and public-sector organisations. Intrinsic rewards play a major motivating role, while extrinsic rewards (namely pay) are apparently less important. Several empirical studies report that social enterprise workers appear to be more satisfied with their work than public-sector and for-profit workers, even when they earn less on average (Mirvis and Hackett 1983; Mirvis 1992; Preston 1990, 1994, 1996; Onyx and Maclean 1996; Borzaga 2000). Their commitment and satisfaction apparently derive from the ability of social enterprises to provide them with a more consistent incentive mix and with an organisational context which is itself part of that mix. Employees are attracted by a mix in which some of the intrinsic rewards studied with regard to voluntary workers acquire greater value, and they prefer one which balances extrinsic incentives, like working hours flexibility or pay, with intrinsic incentives, such as autonomy, higher degree of participation, attainment of moral goals, and training and development.

The ability of social enterprises to deliver an incentive mix of this kind is the reason for their generally marked identification with distributive justice, or the individual perception of the existence of an adequate balance between effort and incentives (Greenberg 1990, 1993; Solari 2000). Besides distributive justice, social enterprises also appear to be characterised by a perception of a procedural justice indicative of an open and transparent organisation, one in which workers are informed about choices and the reasons for them. Thus, social enterprise workers perceive a higher degree of distributive and procedural justice compared to their counterparts in traditional non-profit, for-profit and public-sector organisations. An enriched incentive mix, participation, flatter hierarchical structures, and flexibility encourage this widespread perception. Distributive and procedural justice has been shown to have important consequences on employee satisfaction and commitment (Alexander and Ruderman 1987; Li-Ping and Sarsfield-Baldwin 1996). Managers must grasp the implications of these differences in their entirety, and adapt their style in order to foster workforce identification with the mission and value of the organisation, and they must also adjust their styles and organisational models to those preferred by employees, such as more autonomy, less hierarchy and more flexibility.

Despite the specific characteristics of the mix of motives of workers in social enterprises, two issues should not be overlooked. First, although pay does not appear to be a predominant motive, it still plays a role, which can be interpreted consistently with the hypotheses of Herzberg (1966) as a hygienic[7] factor. Second, the more egalitarian wage structure in social enterprises is at present a source of perceived distributive justice, but it may prove risky as these forms evolve and with the natural change that takes place in motives as people grow older. As time passes, better-performing workers may be lured away by better-paid jobs in for-profit or public-sector organisations.

In many European social enterprises, worker participation seems to be a key characteristic and offers a potential competitive advantage over other forms with tighter governance structures. The literature on worker participation has highlighted the potential benefits of ownership (Defourny and Spear 1995; Kandel and Lazear 1992; Defourny 1990; Katz et al. 1985). Nevertheless, it should be borne in mind that researchers have shown that these advantages are not stable over time. Mirvis (1992) found that differences between non-profit and for-profit firms disappeared as a consequence of improved management in for-profit and a more competitive environment for non-profit organisations.

The action to be taken should involve investment in human resources management, including the following:

- *Reward mix*: managers should reinforce the incentive mix of social enterprises. This requires investment in the training and development of workers, reinforcement of the social mission, more frequent opportunities for workers to interact with customers and their needs, as well as acceptance of a more decentralised structure, with greater autonomy for individual workers and more delegation.

- *Career planning and evolution of the psychological contract*: managers should identify career paths and the typical evolution of employee skills. Pearce (1993) considers the dynamics over time of the different types of motivation to be one reason for the high turnover among voluntary workers. Ageing plays a role, due to changing needs and desires of people. A key issue for managers in social enterprises is whether and how they can keep abreast of these changes by adapting their organisations over time. Given the recent history of the organisational form, the moment may not be far off when employees change at least some of their expectations toward social enterprises and ask for more attention to be paid to extrinsic rewards. A more mature workforce has needs different from those of the past, and it evaluates the mix of intrinsic and extrinsic rewards differently.

- *Communication and reinforcement of the vision and mission*: managers must constantly communicate and share the vision, or long-term view, and the mission, or shorter-term goals, of their social enterprises. This requires devising a communication policy (plan) which covers routine communication, inducement training courses, events and conventions. Internal news should be enriched so that information is shared on broader issues which affect the social enterprise as a whole.

- *Hiring and recruitment*: managers must take care to identify the characteristics of potential employees and devise hiring procedures consistent with internal requirements. The issue is a difficult one because it entails that attention must be paid both to knowledge, skills and abilities and to cultural/group compatibility. In a context of increasing demand for labour, the unavailability of skilled workers could seriously threaten the growth of social enterprises, and their ability to attract potential employees could be a key asset.

- *Training and skills development*: managers should acknowledge that social enterprises are ideal terrain for the development of skills both professional and personal. It is not uncommon for successful managers to leave for-profit organisations and work for large non-profit, mainly non-governmental, organisations. The reason for this is that non-profit organisations offer opportunities to enlarge the scope of management. This more challenging context should be valued by social enterprise managers and enriched by carefully designed training programmes which may even become part of the reward mix.

The importance of employees to social enterprises requires the latter to invest in human resource management. Recruitment, hiring, evaluation, development and the rewarding of employees should be designed in accordance with the above-listed principles. Overall, these instruments are still relatively unsophisticated, but social enterprise managers should be mindful that a major contribution to the success of their organisations will be made by the development of human resource management strategies and by devoting time and effort to their development before it is too late.

From within: challenging leadership and management styles

Finally, the managers of social enterprises are caught between the need to decide and organise and the need to be perceived as participative and open to criticism. Although the majority of studies on leadership advocate a more open and direct relationship with 'followers', in reality the impact of authority and hierarchy within organisations is still greater than presumed. Hierarchy, though, is not completely consistent with social enterprises values and norms. How can a manager lead without a hierarchy?

The ideal social enterprise manager is probably a Theory Y type manager, who has a positive attitude towards people, encourages participation and learning, is open to suggestions and criticisms, and allows experimentation by his/her employees. Nevertheless, social enterprises require managers able to manage the slow institutional decision-making process by acting rapidly, which obviously implies ingenuity in the leadership style required to be effective. There are no shortcuts, insofar as social enterprise managers must meet both require-ments, fostering participation and autonomy but aligning behaviours when this is required by the goals of the organisation.

Conclusions

The emergence of a new kind of management is paramount to the success of social enterprises in Europe. The characteristics of the role of social enterprise managers are different from those of their counterparts in traditional non-profit, public, and for-profit organisations. If the managers of social enterprises are to meet the challenges of the future, they must deal with those confronting them now. This will require a more active endeavour to establish social enterprises as a legitimate organisational form, both externally and internally. The latter has been underestimated, but it will require social enterprises managers to invest in the development of their skills. This endeavour should be matched by policies from universities and research centres aimed at developing a full body of theo-retical and practical knowledge on the specifics of social enterprises.

Notes

1   It should be noted that most social enterprises are currently managed by their leaders and founders. Here the term 'manager' is used to emphasise their role in policy-making and decision-making, in short defining the mission and vision.
2   An example is the adoption of a model of relations with employees which is at odds with the mission and values of these social enterprises, such as that employed by some for-profit organisations. It is also a mistake to perceive the role of social enterprises as

simply an extension of the public-welfare system, or as an alternative which can easily be substituted by direct public intervention.

3   The other values are integrity, openness, accountability, and service (Jeavons 1994).

4   For a *caveat* concerning this blind reliance on the exclusive virtue of efficiency and 'the social' (Arendt 1958) see Alexander *et al.* (1999).

5   Note that, although these stakeholders are also present in for-profit organisations, the nature of their relations with social enterprises is specific, i.e. the very existence and development of social enterprises depends on their ability to involve all stakeholders in their mission.

6   It should be pointed out, however, that even in the USA the advocates of control exerted by stakeholders are growing in number (Ben-Ner 1986).

7   Herzberg (1966) identifies two factors which affect workers' satisfaction and dissatisfaction. While hygienic factors determine non-dissatisfaction, motivation factors facilitate increased commitment.

Bibliography

AKERLOF, G.A. (1982) 'Labour Contracts as Partial Gift Exchange', *Quarterly Journal of Economics*, vol. 97, 4: 543–69.

ALEXANDER, J., NANK, R. and STIVERS, C. (1999) 'Implications of Welfare Reform: Do Nonprofit Survival Strategies Threaten Civil Society?', *Nonprofit and Voluntary Sector Quarterly*, vol. 28, 4: 452–75.

ALEXANDER, S. and RUDERMAN, M. (1987) 'The Role of Procedural and Distributive Justice in Organisational Behaviour', *Social Justice Research*, no. 1: 177–98.

ALLISON, M. and KAYE, J. (1997) *Strategic Planning for Nonprofit Organisations*, John Wiley & Sons, New York.

ARENDT, H. (1958) *The Human Condition*, University of Chicago Press, Chicago.

BEN-NER, A. (1986) 'Non-profit Organisations: Why Do They Exist in Market Economies?', in ROSE-ACKERMAN, S., *The Economics of Non-profit Institutions*, Oxford University Press, New York, 94–113.

BORZAGA, C. (ed.) (2000) *Capitale umano e qualità del lavoro nei servizi sociali. Un'analisi comparata tra modelli di gestione*, FIVOL, Roma.

BORZAGA, C. and MITTONE, L. (1997) *The Multi-stakeholders Versus the Non-profit Organisations*, Università degli Studi di Trento, Dipartimento di Economia, Discussion Paper no. 7.

DEFOURNY, J. (1990) *Démocratie économique et efficacité économique*, De Boeck, Brussels.

DEFOURNY, J. and SPEAR, R. (1995) 'Economics of Cooperation', in SPEAR, R. and VOETS, H. (eds) *Success and Enterprise. The Significance of Employee Ownership and Participation*, Avebury, Aldershot, 8–39.

European Commission (1999) *The Third System, Employment and Local Development*, mimeo, Bruxelles.

GREENBERG, J. (1993) 'The Intellectual Adolescence of Organisational Justice: You've Come A Long Way, Maybe', *Social Justice Research*, vol. 1, 135–48.

—— (1990) 'Organisational Justice: Yesterday, Today, and Tomorrow', *Journal of Management*, vol. 16, 2: 399–432.

HANDY, F. and KATZ, E. (1998) 'The Wage Differential between Nonprofit Institutions and Corporations: Getting More by Paying Less?', *Journal of Comparative Economics*, 26: 246–61.

HANNAN, M.T. and CARROLL, G.R. (2000) *The Demography of Corporations and Industries*, Princeton University Press, Princeton, NJ.

HANSMANN, H.B. (1996) *The Ownership of Enterprise*, The Belknap Press of Harvard University Press, Cambridge, MA.

—— (1980) 'The Role of Nonprofit Enterprise', *The Yale Law Journal*, vol. 89, 5: 835–901.

HERMAN, R.D. and RENZ, D.O. (1998) 'Nonprofit Organisational Effectiveness: Contrasts between Especially Effective and Less Effective Organisations', *Nonprofit Management and Leadership*, vol. 9, 1: 23–38.

HERMAN, R.D. and HEIMOVICS, D. (1994) 'Executive Leadership', in HERMAN, R.D. and Associates, *The Jossey-Bass Handbook of Nonprofit Leadership and Management*, Jossey-Bass Publishers, San Francisco, 137–53.

HERZBERG, F. (1966) *Work and The Nature of Man*, The World Publishing Company.

JEAVONS, T.H. (1994) 'Ethics in Nonprofit Management: Creating a Culture of Integrity', in HERMAN, R.D. and Associates, *The Jossey-Bass Handbook of Nonprofit Leadership and Management*, Jossey-Bass Publishers, San Francisco, 184–207.

KANDEL, E. and LAZEAR, E. (1992) 'Peer Pressure and Partnerships', *Journal of Political Economy*, vol. 100, 4: 801–17.

KATZ, H., KOCHAN, T. and WEBER, M. (1985) 'Assessing the Effects of Industrial Relations Systems and Efforts to Improve the Quality of Working Life on Organisational Effectiveness', *Academy of Management Journal*, vol. 28.

KINGMA, B.R. (1997) 'Public Good Theories of the Non-profit Sector: Weisbrod Revisited', *Voluntas*, vol. 8, 2: 135–48.

LI-PING TANG, T. and SARSFIELD-BALDWIN, L.J. (1996) 'Distributive and Procedural Justice as Related to Satisfaction and Commitment, SAM', *Advanced Management Journal*, summer, 25–31.

MIRVIS, P.H. (1992) 'The Quality of Employment in the Nonprofit Sector: An Update on Employee Attitudes in Nonprofit Versus Business and Government', *Nonprofit Management and Leadership*, vol. 3, 1: 23–41.

MIRVIS, P.H. and HACKETT, E.J. (1983) 'Work and Workforce Characteristics in the Nonprofit Sector', *Monthly Labour Review*, vol. 106, 4.

ONYX, J. and MACLEAN, M. (1996) 'Careers in the Third Sector', *Nonprofit Management and Leadership*, vol. 6, 4.

PAPPAS, A.T. (1996) *Reengineering Your Nonprofit Organisation*, John Wiley & Sons, New York.

PEARCE, J.L. (1993) *Volunteers. The Organisational Behaviour of Unpaid Workers*, Routledge, London.

PRESTON, A.E. (1996) 'Women in the White-Collar Nonprofit Sector: the Best Option or the Only Option?', in *The Review of Economics and Statistics*, vol. 72, 4.

—— (1994) 'Women in the Nonprofit Labour Market', in ODENDAHL, T. and O'NEIL, M. *Women and Power in the Nonprofit Sector*, Jossey-Bass Publisher, San Francisco.

—— (1990) 'Changing Labour Market Patterns in the Nonprofit and For-profit Sectors: Implications for Nonprofit Management', in *Nonprofit Management and Leadership*, 1, vol. 1.

—— (1989a) 'The Nonprofit Firm: A Potential Solution to Inherent Market Failures', *Economic Inquiry*, vol. 26, 3: 493–506.

—— (1989b) 'The Nonprofit Worker in a For-profit World', *Journal of Labour Economics*, vol. 7, 4: 438–63.

SCOTT, W.R. (1995) *Institutions and Organisations*, Sage, New York.

SCOTT, W.R., RUEF, M., MENDEL, P.J. and CARONNA, C.R. (2000) *Institutional Change and Healthcare Organisations. From Professional Dominance to Managed Care*, The University of Chicago Press, Chicago, IL.

SOLARI, L. (2000) 'I lavoratori: l'equità percepita nella relazione con l'organizzazione', in BORZAGA, C. *Capitale umano e qualità del lavoro nei servizi sociali. Un'analisi comparata tra modelli di gestione*, Fondazione Italiana per il Volontariato, 179–208.

STEINBERG, R. (1997) 'Overall Evaluation of Economic Theories', *Voluntas*, vol. 8, 2: 179–204.

STINCHCOMBE, A.L. (1965) 'Social Structure and Organisations', in MARCH, J.G. *Handbook of Organisations*, Rand McNally, Chicago, 153–93.

SUCHMAN, M.C. (1995) 'Managing Legitimacy: Strategic and Institutional Approaches', *Academy of Management Review*, vol. 20, 3: 571–610.

WEISBROD, B.A. (1977) *The Voluntary Nonprofit Sector*, Lexington Books, Lexington, MA.

YOUNG, D. R. (2000) 'Organisational Identity in Nonprofit Organisations: Strategic and Structural Implications', working paper presented at the biennial conference of the International Association for Third Sector Research, Dublin.

Conclusions

Social enterprises in Europe: a diversity of initiatives and prospects

Carlo Borzaga and Jacques Defourny

When the EMES Network was established, the concept of 'social enterprise' was already used by some third-sector organisations and a few researchers. The adjective 'social' or the qualifying phrase 'with social aims', together with the term 'enterprise', or with a specific legal form as the co-operative, were also envisaged in some national legislation. However, whether the so-called social enterprises were a generalised and well-defined phenomenon, with some common characteristics, was an open question.[1]

Against this background, the EMES Network set out four main goals as follows: to provide a definition of social enterprises capable of encompassing different national experiences; to verify the existence of this new entrepreneurial form in European states; to provide a first, albeit provisional, explanation for their development; and, to discuss their contribution to European societies and economies.

The common definition proposed by the Network can be found in the introduction to this book. The national chapters presented in this volume demonstrate that in all the European member states there are organisations fitting the definition, and support the claim that social enterprises represent a common feature of the European social and economic environment. Although not yet in use in legal texts or other official documents in most countries, the expression 'social enterprise' is a useful synthesis for several terms in use at national level, such as 'social economic enterprises' in Austria, 'companies with a social purpose' in Belgium, 'co-operatives with social aims' in Spain, 'social co-operatives' in Italy and Portugal. The theoretical chapters present and discuss some explanations for the emergence of social enterprises, by taking into account and adapting the more widespread theoretical explanations for the existence of non-profit organisations.

In this concluding chapter, we summarise the main results of the research, and focus on: the fields of activities in which social enterprises are engaged (section 1); the explanation for their emergence (section 2); the main differences among countries (section 3); the main contributions of social enterprises to European economies and societies (section 4); their weaknesses and the barriers to their development (section 5). We conclude by reviewing the development prospects and policy implications for social enterprises (section 6). These are also issues that seem to rank high on the political agenda of the European Commission.

1 The main fields of activity

When the different national cases are considered together, social enterprises appear to be engaged in very different activities. However, it is possible to break down these activities into two main fields: work integration and social and community care services provision.

Work-integration social enterprises are basically present in all the European countries. They have evolved from earlier experiences of sheltered employment workshops, but with at least two important differences: firstly, social enterprises generally are, or try to be, less dependent on public funds and pay more attention to market dynamics; secondly, they pursue the objective of ensuring that employed disadvantaged people earn income comparable with that of other workers. Moreover, several social enterprises have the explicit aim of providing disadvantaged workers with job training, and they increasingly organise their activity with the ultimate aim of helping workers to integrate into the open labour market. In some countries, work-integration social enterprises employ very specific groups of workers, mainly those not supported by existing public employment policies (as in Spain). In other countries, social enterprises encompass a broader range of people and employ thousands of workers (as in Italy).[2] Whereas the traditional sheltered workshops occur in the context of passive labour-market policies, the new work-integration social enterprises are innovative tools of active labour-market policies for the same groups of workers.

The second field of activity of social enterprises is represented by social and community care services provision. These social enterprises are to be found in almost all European countries, but have major differences from those involved in work integration, both as to the number of enterprises and the types of service supplied. A significant number of social enterprises have been established to provide new services or to respond to groups of people with needs not recognised by public authorities or excluded from public benefits. Many of the activities were independently started by groups of citizens, with little or no public support. However, since the services provided were acknowledged to be of public interest, after some years the state or the local authorities decided to finance, totally or in part, the activity of several of these social enterprises. Nevertheless, the resulting dependence on public funds does not seem to have completely eliminated their autonomy. Indeed, there are many social enterprises funded both by public authorities and by fees directly paid by the users or combining public funds with resources coming from donations and volunteers. Moreover, a growing number of services provided by social enterprises secure the necessary public resources by participating in calls for tenders, thus competing with other social enterprises, third-sector organisations and for-profits enterprises.

Yet the distinction between different fields of activity is somehow artificial. In fact, many social enterprises combine production of social services and work-integration activities. This overlap has different explanations. It can be due to the fact that some social services are suitable for work integration of disadvantaged workers, as they are labour intensive and appropriate for skills acquisition. It can also be a way to provide for the full social and economic integration of some disadvantaged groups, like drug addicts, for which service provision and work-integration activities cannot be separated. However, in some cases this overlap has been caused by the fact that, lacking clear public funding policies for new social and community care services, social enterprises have been forced to recruit unemployed persons, who are benefiting from employment subsidies, in order to develop these services. Social enterprises have accordingly been able, especially in France, to create innovative social and community care services, by integrating public social and labour policies. Yet they do not have adequate guarantees of survival in the medium term, since the employment subsidies are bound to be of limited duration. On the contrary, Italian law makes it statutorily compulsory for social co-operatives to opt either for the production of social services or for work integration, thus forbidding the overlap of activities.

Beyond the direct beneficiaries of their activities oriented towards work integration or social and community care services, social enterprises also significantly contribute to the development of local economic systems. In some cases, as for example the Finnish village co-operatives, and the UK business communities, such contribution to local development is among the explicit objectives of social enterprises.

Finally, the analysis of the different national experiences indicates that social enterprises are dynamic entities. In most countries, they are already extending their activities to other services, such as environmental and cultural services, less linked to social policies and more generally of interest to the local communities.

2   Some explanations for the emergence of social enterprises

The emergence and subsequent development of social enterprises is due to a mix of factors, some being common to almost all countries, though with varying relevance, while others are more specific to one or some of them.

There is a clear and generalised coincidence between the emergence of the first experiences of social enterprises, at the end of the 1970s, on the one hand, and the decline in the rates of economic growth and the rise of unemployment that occurred in the same decade, on the other. These changes in economic performances were at the origins of the crisis in European welfare systems. In the beginning, this crisis was mainly of a fiscal nature and led to growing public deficits. While public revenues grew at a slower rate than in the past, public expenditures increased faster, especially in countries with generous subsidies for the unemployed and for the retired and pre-retired. In the first stage, most European countries reacted against the fiscal crisis both by reforming employment subsidies and by blocking or slowing down the growth in the supply of social services. The increasing inability of traditional macro-economic and employment policies to reduce unemployment, especially long-term unemployment among the disadvantaged and the low skilled, and to respond to an ever-swelling demand for social services, which proved to be increasingly differentiated and attentive to quality, gave birth also to a legitimacy crisis in European welfare regimes.

When European policy-makers realised that the decline in economic growth was a lasting phenomenon, they tried to reform welfare systems with particular attention to services provision. Action was undertaken in order to steadily reduce the impact of the provision of some services on the public budget, and to tailor the supply of services to users needs. This was done by decentralising some power to local authorities to decide and implement social polices, by introducing prices and tariffs, by privatising some services, and by shifting from passive to active labour and employment policies. However, prices and tariffs often affected the more needy, as in the case of sheltered workshops in Finland and social housing services in Belgium.

Policies for privatisation of social services provision have been implemented both by separating financing responsibility, which was kept by public authorities, from services provision, which was contracted out to private enterprises, and by ceasing the production of some services. This set of changes has allowed for both a growth in the demand for private providers of social services by local public authorities, and for a wider range of unmet needs, which third-sector organisations, and especially social enterprises, have sought to satisfy. Moreover, the supply of services has been made more dynamic by de-centralisation and policies aimed at separating purchasers from providers. De-centralisation and the consequent shift of responsibility to local authorities, closer to citizens' needs, has allowed for a better acceptance of civil society's initiatives and has made their public funding more viable. The separation of purchasers and providers has stimulated supply and especially boosted the establishment of new initiatives in a sector that for-profit enterprises regarded as of little interest to them.

Another explanation for the development of social enterprises derives from the failures of traditional labour policies and from the difficulties in shifting from regulatory, and mainly passive, policies to active ones. These difficulties are associated with workers who find it hard to enter or re-enter the labour market, and whose number and duration of unemployment have progressively increased over the years, especially in France, Germany and Italy. This helps to explain the development of work-integration social enterprises.

3 The national diversities

Although European social enterprises have much in common, the national chapters highlight wide differences among countries regarding numbers, fields of activity and forms of organisation. While for some member states, the organisations analysed match the working definition adopted by the EMES Network, in many other countries the existing organisations do not meet all the criteria. Many social enterprises, especially those providing social services, are heavily dependent on public funds and have a low level of autonomy and economic risk. At the same time, social enterprises often pay more attention to the interests of their employees than to the benefits to the community and/or to the participation by the beneficiaries.

Moreover, the economic weight of social enterprises is unevenly distributed throughout Europe. In some countries (for example, in Italy), there are thousands of organisations which are quite consistent with the working definition. These have developed both in the provision of a range of social services and in the work integration of disadvantaged people, and involve several thousand members and employees. In other countries (Sweden and Finland, for example), the number of social enterprises is significant, but they mainly operate in very specific fields, such as kindergartens and employment services. Conversely, there are countries with a very small number of social enterprises (such as Greece and Denmark) or in which the existing ones are not all clearly different from public or traditional third-sector organisations (Germany and the Netherlands). Nevertheless, social enterprises present innovative characteristics either in the services provided or in the organisation of the production factors, or in both. Furthermore, in some countries, social enterprises have undergone high growth rates (see Italy and the UK) and, above all, high levels of success in the pursuit of their aims (as with labour pool co-operatives in Finland and work-integration enterprises in several countries). Other elements of differentiation include the degree of recognition within the legal system, the type of reputation achieved with respect to the local community and public authorities, and the degree of partnership with public authorities and for-profit enterprises.

These country variations can be explained by referring to a number of factors. The most common are: the level of development of the economic and social systems; the characteristics of the welfare systems and of the traditional third sector; and the development of the legal systems. We will consider these factors in turn.

Differences in economic and social development

The level of economic development influences demand for social services. In countries with a comparatively low level of development (e.g. Greece and Portugal, but also Ireland until the beginning of the 1990s), the perceived need for social services is modest and to a large extent fulfilled by informal, mainly family provision. Demand for more structured social services is confined to situations in which both the family and the community fail. In these cases, supply is often guaranteed by traditional charitable organisations. Accordingly, in less developed countries, social enterprises providing social services are not widespread. Where they do exist, it is to face one of the main problems of these countries, viz. the creation of jobs for groups of people excluded from the labour market (e.g. women in rural areas or the disabled). They are mainly work-integration social enterprises and sometimes take the traditional form of worker or producer co-operatives.

On the contrary, in those countries where the level of development is higher and there is an increasing and larger demand for social and community care services, the spread of social enterprises is greater and their evolution is more lively. The differences found among these countries depend on other factors.

Differences in welfare state and traditional third sector

Although they are often innovative in terms of the type and quality of services provided, social enterprises operate in the same broadly defined fields as public authorities and other third-sector organisations. Since they are the 'late comers' it is quite obvious that their expansion depends heavily on the strength of the other providers, on the resources and the characteristics of the welfare state, and on the state of development of the traditional third sector. With regard to these aspects, European Union member states can be classified into three sub-groups. Although not all countries fit neatly into one of these groups, the classification helps to explain the differences in the spread of social enterprises.

The first group consists of countries with a well-developed, universal welfare state (identified by high public expenditure against GDP and high employment rates in social, and community care services), engaging both in public services provision and in cash benefits (pensions, unemployment benefits, and so forth). Sweden, Denmark and, to a lesser extent, Finland fall within this group. Until the reform that led to quasi-markets, the UK too belonged to this group. In these countries, social enterprises are active only in specific sectors, namely, those in which the government or local authorities voluntarily reduced their own presence as providers, but maintained the role of financiers (as in the case of kindergartens in Sweden), or those in which there was not an organised public supply (as in the case of labour co-operatives formed by the unemployed in Finland). In these countries, the development of social enterprises has not been hampered by the traditional third-sector organisations. The latter, being mainly engaged in advocacy activities, have not felt threatened by the newer organisations.

The second group consists of countries also having a developed and universal welfare state, although largely based on cash benefits, with a limited commitment on the part of government to the direct supply of social services. Here, both the family and the traditional third sector, heavily funded by public authorities, play an important role in social and community care services provision. Germany, Austria, France, Belgium, Luxembourg, the Netherlands and Ireland are the countries that fall within this group. The development of social enterprises in these countries has been more complex and uneven. First of all, the widescale involvement of the traditional third sector in the provision of social services and the well-established financing rules have made the need to change the structures of private supply units to a more entrepreneurial approach, less pressing. Moreover, in some countries, like Germany, traditional third-sector organisations have more or less resisted the emergence of social enterprises. As a consequence, the latter have been developing in niches, mainly in new activities (like in work integration), where traditional non-profit organisations were not active, and by exploiting resources that are not specifically geared to the production of social services (e.g. using employment benefits for the development of social enterprises, as in France and Belgium).

The third group includes countries with a less developed welfare state – especially until the early 1980s – largely based on cash benefits, with public provision of social and community care services confined to a few sectors, such as education and health. As the provision of social and community care services was mainly entrusted to the family and informal networks, the third sector did not develop either. Italy and Spain as well as Greece and Portugal belong to this group. In these countries, the fiscal crisis in the welfare systems prevented the development of a public supply of services exactly in the years in which demand was increasing. Social enterprises were set up to bridge the increasing gap between needs and supply, with little competition either from the government or local authorities, on the one hand, or from the traditional non-profit sector, on the other. In some countries, social enterprises were even supported by the existing third sector and co-operative movement. The development of social enterprises was also supported by public authorities, which progressively realised that services provided by these new organisations would actually meet a new demand for services and accordingly increased their funding role, instead of developing a public supply.

Differences in legal systems

Turning our attention to the national differences in incorporation forms, it is possible to note that the main differences lie in the level of autonomy and capacity to carry out productive activity that different legal systems confer on the two legal forms (the co-operative and the association) which social enterprises tend to use. Where, as in France and Belgium, associations are comparable with a quasi-enterprise or at least are allowed to produce and sell goods and services on the market as a means of achieving their social goal, social enterprises are set up mainly as associations. On the contrary, in countries where associations have mainly been characterised by ideal purposes (Sweden, Finland, Italy and Spain) and co-operatives are easy to establish, social enterprises have mainly chosen this legal form, though changing some of its characteristics. Although the emergence of social enterprises has followed different paths in the two groups of countries, it is possible to envisage a convergence in the organisational forms insofar as associations, by adopting a more entrepreneurial character have come nearer to the co-operative form, which, in its turn, by unfolding its social dimension and by extending benefits in favour of non-members, has come close to the associative form.[3]

The legislative changes, which have been introduced in some countries and are under discussion in others, seem to follow this convergence pattern. Since they tend to stress the entrepreneurial behaviour of the new organisations they have been favouring the co-operative form more than the associative one. This is also true of the Italian and Portuguese law on social co-operatives and of the proposal to establish a 'co-operative of general interest' in France.[4]

4 Main contributions of social enterprises

Having established that social enterprises are present, albeit in various forms, in all European countries, we will now turn our attention to their economic and social role, and to the contribution they may make to the ongoing transformation of welfare systems, to employment creation, to social cohesion, to local development, and to the evolution of the third sector as a whole. Before analysing each of these subjects, it is important to note that social enterprises, although dynamic, still represent a small part of the supply of social and community care services and employ only a small proportion of disadvantaged workers. As a consequence, not all the contributions analysed have always a visible quantitative impact. They indicate possible trends rather than changes that have actually occurred.

Transformation of the welfare systems

The outcomes of the policies implemented to tackle the difficulties of European welfare systems, and especially of the attempts to privatise social and community care services provision, are still uncertain. Indeed, transaction and contract costs have increased more than expected, thwarting cost containment efforts. Furthermore, at least in some cases, the quality of services and jobs has deteriorated. These negative outcomes have emerged mainly in those countries in which governments have particularly relied upon market simulation and for-profit enterprises.[5] As the chapter on the United Kingdom underlines, the nature of quasi-markets, by tending to use prices as a major criterion to discriminate among providers, often favours hard contracting. At the same time, existing regulations are often not sufficiently well defined to guarantee the desired level of quality, especially when for-profit enterprises are involved.

In this context, social enterprises could contribute to the reform of European welfare systems in several ways, such as: by making the income distribution closer to the one desired by the community; by helping cost containment; by providing a greater volume of supply and, in many cases, by helping to maintain or to improve the quality of services and jobs.

The national chapters show that social enterprises, though privately owned and managed, can pursue a redistributive function, thus contributing to modifying the resources and income distribution provided by the joint action of the market and the state. Social enterprises are often created to serve groups of people with needs not recognised by the public policies and base their redistributive action on a mix of free (donations, volunteers) and low-cost (motivated workers) resources, some of which are not available to either for-profit or public providers. When a community in which social enterprises operate clearly benefits from this redistributive action, the enterprises improve their reputation and engender relations of trust.

The book presents several examples of this redistributive function. In some cases, social enterprises have replaced public authorities in their redistributive role. In Belgium, for example, social enterprises provide housing services for marginalised people who are unable to pay the growing rents and to satisfy the conditions required for social public housing. In other countries, social enterprises have autonomously taken up a redistributive action in favour of groups of people with needs not recognised by public authorities, as in the case of socially excluded persons in Spain. In countries where the supply of services organised through public policies is insufficient to satisfy demand, social enterprises contribute to the creation of an additional supply. This is the case for social services that governments are willing to fund only in part. In this context, social enterprises can increase supply through a variable mix of public, market and voluntary resources. This phenomenon can be seen in the experience of work-integration social enterprises and services (like kindergartens in Sweden) for which users are willing and able to contribute.

However, social enterprises, like other third-sector organisations, also influence redistributive public policies. By providing services to new groups of people with needs not fully recognised by public policies, they can move public resources toward these services.[6] Moreover, social enterprises often mix their productive role with more traditional advocacy activities in favour of the same or other groups of users.

In creating new services, not only do social enterprises develop a redistributive function; they can also innovate with regard to services provided. They can make completely new services available, but they can also use new ways of producing traditional services, mainly through innovative forms of involvement of consumers (as co-producers), of local community (volunteers) and of workers themselves. The new organisations created throughout Europe by social enterprises and the changes of both the associative and the co-operative forms are good examples of this innovative behaviour.

A third important possible contribution of social enterprises to the improvement of European welfare systems occurs in the context of the privatisation of service provision. The effectiveness of privatisation policies depends on a competitive supply of social services, and there are several difficulties in establishing contractual relations between public authorities and service providers. Because of their specific nature, social enterprises can contribute to the establishment of a competitive environment and to contractual relations based on trust, and are therefore less inclined to be opportunistically exploited. Since the aims of social enterprises often converge to some extent with the aims of public authorities, this makes negotiations easier for the provision of the services for which effective quasi-market cannot be established. They can also contribute to the reduction of production costs since they do not strive for profits and can mediate between non-convergent interests of public authorities, consumers and workers, thus singling out, better than other organisational forms, the right mix of customer satisfaction and worker guarantees.[7]

Employment creation

Social enterprises can also contribute to the creation of additional jobs. This is clear for the work-integration social enterprises that normally employ workers with minimal possibilities of finding a job in traditional enterprises. However, social enterprises providing social and community care services can also create new employment since they make a sector with a high employment potential more dynamic, especially in countries in which the level of employment in the sector is still low.

The interpretations of slow employment growth and of high unemployment rates in most European countries have recently shifted their emphasis from the rigidity of labour markets to the rigidities of the product markets. These latter are seen as responsible for the slow growth of employment, especially in the service sector, mainly (by assuming the USA as a benchmark) in commercial and tourist services, in business services and in 'communal' or social and community care services.[8] The level of employment in communal services is particularly low in the European countries with a welfare state mainly based on cash benefit (like Italy, France and Germany) and a low public provision or public financing of social services. Moreover, this public expenditure composition is a possible cause of the insufficient employment growth in the sector, especially if combined with the constraints in public expenditure that occurred after the 1980s. Public expenditure composition is also at the origin of the increasing gap between demand and supply of services to people and communities which is now experienced in several European countries.

However, currently the potential increase in employment in social and community care services cannot be achieved simply by increasing public expenditure. The pursuit of such a policy is impeded both by the constraint of reducing the public deficit and by the necessity to use savings on public expenditure to reduce fiscal pressure and indirect labour costs, in order to face the increasing international competition. An alternative policy can be pursued by changing the composition of public expenditure from cash benefits to services provision or services founding and by encouraging the growth of private demand. However, this is unlikely to be fully accomplished either by traditional third-sector organisations or by for-profit organisations. On the one hand, most traditional third-sector organisations are by now too heavily dependent, in defining their strategies and in finding resources, upon the public sector. On the other hand, for-profit enterprises have several shortcomings. They have, at least for the time being, little interest in producing these services, due to low profitability and to information asymmetries that affect market relations both with consumers and local authorities.

Social enterprises, on the contrary, may help in developing both demand and supply, as well as in reconfiguring public expenditure composition. They present several advantages. Since they do not aim at profit maximisation, they can easily be involved in productions entailing low profitability and, if they rely on resources deriving from donations and on volunteers, they can reduce the production costs especially in the start-up phase.[9] Cost reduction is also possible when social enterprises attract workers and managers interested in working in the sector for wages that are lower than in comparable activities.[10] Moreover, by involving consumers and by being rooted in the local community, they can quickly adapt supply to demand and can rely on fiduciary relations to overcome the difficulty for consumers of monitoring the quality of services. This means that social enterprises can produce services for local authorities and for private users at the same time.

Social enterprises can contribute to job growth also if they are fully or partially financed by public funds. When social enterprises are financed with public money, it is because the services supplied are considered to be for the common good. Normally, the higher the redistributive effect, the greater the public funding. However, social enterprises should not be considered a mere substitute for public authorities. Many of them started their activity without, or with negligible, public subsidies and only after some time was their activity recognised by public authorities. As a consequence, they have contributed to increasing the public expenditure directed to services provision and along with it the related employment. Moreover, several social enterprises providing services with a predominantly private component (as in the case of kindergartens and many cultural services), also produce directly for private users, thus clearly contributing to net job creation. By taking into account data referred to in some country chapters (Italy and the UK), it is already possible to assess that a significant share of income of social enterprises derives from the provision of services to private households. This share could be much higher if the tax/income ratio were lower as it is in the United States. Evidently, social enterprises alone cannot either solve the problem of low employment growth in Europe or be a major response to such a global challenge. Yet they have shown the ability to contribute to solving it significantly.

Social cohesion and the creation of social capital

By contributing to solving or to alleviating the problems of specific groups, and by favouring the integration of disadvantaged people into the labour market, with higher wages than those paid by sheltered employment workshops and sometimes for-profit companies, social enterprises also contribute to improving life conditions, the well-being of communities and the level of social integration. Furthermore, social enterprises enhance user protection, especially of the most seriously disadvantaged, thus improving service supply and promoting, in some cases, the involvement of users in the organisation.

In societies that are getting ever more complex, the causes of social exclusion are increasing and becoming more differentiated. It is no longer valid to assume simple correlations between unemployment, poverty and social exclusion. It is therefore more difficult to combat social exclusion by using cash benefits and standardised services. Rather, it is necessary to provide a capacity to address the needs of specific and relatively small groups of people within each community. Such an evolution of the causes of social exclusion has largely contributed to putting European welfare systems to the test, especially those with a high level of centralisation. Decentralising policies, which have been implemented since the 1980s in many countries, have reduced the socio-economic problems, but they have not solved all of them. Social enterprises can give significant support to identifying and to addressing the different and new needs of communities and of the groups of people more at risk. More generally, social enterprises make a contribution to the creation of social capital, by developing solidarity and mutual help, by expanding trust and facilitating citizens' involvement in the solution of social problems, through the promotion of volunteering and the involvement of users.

Local development

Social enterprises are mainly locally based organisations. Accordingly, they tend to be small sized but, at the same time, they are among the actors involved in local development. Close links with the local community in which they operate are, for social enterprises, a condition for development and efficiency, because they facilitate the understanding of local needs, the creation and exploitation of social capital, and the working out of the optimal mix of resources (from public authorities, donations, users and volunteers).

The globalisation process and the diffusion of new technologies have spearheaded productivity growth in manufacturing sectors, but also the increasing instability of employment. They have also weakened the linkage between enterprises and territory. An increase in demand for goods no longer produces increases in production and employment everywhere. The new jobs are generally created in areas different from those where demand arises in the first place. These processes mainly discriminate against the less developed or declining areas, thus creating vicious circles. To tackle the problems of these areas, traditional incentives to localisation are often ineffective. Conversely, new social and community care services, requiring proximity between supply and demand and organised by small local social enterprises can help to create a more stable local source of labour demand. This contribution of social enterprises to local development through the creation of new jobs for people within local communities could increase in the future, if social enterprises expand their action from social services to other services, such as environmental improvement, cultural services, transportation, etc. This process is already underway in some countries, especially where work-integration social enterprises are more active.

Dynamics of the third sector

Social enterprises cannot be simply identified with the social economy, the non-profit sector or with the third sector. In fact, although they are part of it, social enterprises differ both from the traditional non-profit organisations and from the more established organisations of the social economy (such as co-operatives) in many respects. These can be summed up as follows: their innovative behaviour in creating new organisational forms and new services or in addressing new needs; their ability to rely on a more varied mix of resources; and their stronger inclination towards risk-taking especially when they start up new activities.

Moreover, social enterprises can be seen as a breakthrough in the European traditional third sector because they stress the productive and the 'entrepreneurial' dimension of not-for-profit organisations and underline the economic, together with the redistributive, function of the welfare services. This helps to explain the search for new legal and organisational forms by social enterprises. It also sometimes explains the resistance to their development on the part of traditional non-profit and social economy organisations, along with for-profit enterprises and some branches of trade unions. However, this resistance is not found in all European countries. In many of them, the development of social enterprises has been, and is part of, a strategy of the traditional third-sector organisations, as in the case of the co-operative movement in Italy. In other countries, for-profit enterprises do not seem interested in entering the activities in which social enterprises operate. Furthermore, social enterprises are contributing to the renewal of both the third sector and the welfare services industry and this explains the increasing interest in them.

The main innovation introduced by social enterprises in the economic and social arena is that they are neither outside of the market, as are most public and traditional non-profit organisations, nor outside of the public system of resource allocation, as are for-profit enterprises. Rather, they use the reasons and the rules of both the market and the state, though not identifying them-selves with either of them. Such a peculiarity makes social enterprises different from traditional non-profit organisations, which tend to be either 'third parties' with respect to the market and the government (this is the case when they are funded either through donations or volunteers), or depend exclusively upon the allocative action of the public sector. Indeed, social enterprises represent a concrete and successful example of how civil society and private organisations can directly and autonomously deal with some of the problems shared by the community, without necessarily relying upon public funds. The development of forms of social entrepreneurship, which the EMES research identified, are in most cases the result of a spontaneous dynamic of civil society at the local level rather than the outcome of the planned action of public policies or social movements.

Finally, the development of social enterprises is, in some countries, contributing to reducing the gaps between the different, and often separated, families of the third sector. Associations and foundations are moving towards more productive and entrepreneurial behaviour; foundations are somehow shifting to a more democratic governance; and co-operatives are rediscovering, in several countries, the primacy of social objectives. All of these changes contribute to explaining the growing interest in the third sector and the social economy.

5 Internal weaknesses and external barriers

The emergence of a great number and variety of social enterprises has occurred spontaneously, often despite the lack of an adequate legal framework and in the absence of clearly defined managerial and organisational models. As a consequence, social entrepreneurs, who, at the beginning, were often themselves volunteers, had to invent ways of organising the resource mix, to make volunteers work together with paid workers, to mediate between the differing interests of volunteers, workers and users and to establish a reputation with respect to the local communities and public authorities.

Despite its success, the organisational model of most social enterprises remains fragile, based on few well-defined rules and on a high degree of trust among members, sharing common social and redistributive aims. Consequently, this model is difficult to maintain and reproduce. However, this intrinsic fragility is not the only problem social enterprises have to face. Several other external factors have counteracted or at least slowed down the development of these new organisations. It is therefore useful to present and discuss the most common and important weaknesses and barriers. The main weaknesses may be summarised in four points as follows.

The first is the scant awareness that social enterprises, their managers and the movement as a whole have of their role in European society and economic systems and of their own specificity with respect to public, for-profit and non-profit organisational forms. In particular, there is a well-established capability of managing the plurality of objectives that define social enterprises and that bring together social aims with economic constraints. However, the lack of awareness sometimes prevents social enterprises from adopting adequate management and development strategies and contributes to their fragility.

A second weakness is the tendency towards isomorphism, that is to evolve into organisational forms that are better defined, legally stronger and socially more acceptable while being unable to keep and develop the most innovative characteristics in the new organisational forms. Nowadays, the most widespread risk is that social enterprises convert into associated workers' companies, consequently pursuing the exclusive interests of those employed, and losing the linkage with the community and the capacity of fully using social capital. This risk appears to be related to the increase in the availability of public subsidies and the consequent decrease of the autonomous redistributive role played by social enterprises.

A third weakness is the high governance costs of social enterprises, which derive from their character as organisations without well-defined owners. Their apparent advantage, i.e. the involvement of various categories of stakeholders (clients, volunteers, representatives of the local community) in the production and in the decision-making processes, turns out to be an element of inefficiency when conflicting interests limit the capacity of reacting quickly to a changing environment.

Finally, social enterprises are often of a limited size. Partly due to the strong ties with the local community, partly because of high governance costs, social enterprises are unlikely to be able to grow in size beyond a given threshold. This may hinder their capacity to respond successfully to bigger challenges posed by the surrounding environment and may also hinder their reputation-building outside the local community. Moreover, if social enterprises manage to achieve significant growth, they could accelerate the processes of isomorphism outlined above. However, small size does not seem to represent a generalised handicap; in countries where social enterprises are more developed, they have demonstrated a specific ability of grouping together and of setting up groups of enterprises able to exchange information and innovations and to exploit the economies of scale in specific sectors.

In addition to these internal weaknesses, it is possible to identify at least four main external barriers to the development of social enterprises. The most general barrier is the belief prevailing in most European countries that for-profit organisations together with active public policies can efficiently solve all social problems and satisfy overall demand for social and community care services. This belief has led to an underestimation of the potential role of the third sector and probably even more so of social enterprises. Both are often thought to be unnecessary or, at most, transitional solutions, useful as entities dependent on public policies or as organisations that should be active only for the problems that public policies cannot solve.[11]

Such a negative attitude towards social enterprises is stronger in some countries, like Germany, where a very traditional view of the enterprise is still the norm. According to this view, only those initiatives that derive their income from commercial activities and pursue the sole interest of their owners can be defined as enterprises. Accordingly, the concept of enterprise does not include those organisations capable of innovating and organising the production processes in a new way, if they do not base their income on market exchanges and do not pursue the interests of their owners. In this context, social enterprises are looked at with mistrust and suspicion, up to the point of regarding workers involved in social enterprises as not fully employed. This attitude is common also in those countries where the competitive process is more emphasised, thus marginalising activities, such as social and community care services, for which competition is limited by necessity. The argument of the economic importance of a competitive environment is increasingly used by for-profit enterprises, and their representative organisations, in seeking a revision of the fiscal and competitive advantages allegedly conferred on non-profit organisations and social enterprises, even though these advantages are justified by the public interest nature of the services provided.

A second important barrier can be found in the confused and often incoherent relationship between social enterprises, on the one hand, and social and labour public policies, on the other. The shift from direct public provision of social and community care services to the separation of financing responsibility from services provision, together with the autonomous development of private non-profit initiatives, has not been accompanied by a general and coherent change in contractual relationships and funding rules. Old ways of financing non-profit organisations have generally been maintained, while other new contracting-out rules have been established, especially for new services. More competitive practices were given an impetus by the introduction of quasi-markets in the United Kingdom and by the new European rules on contracting-out and public tenders. The result is an unclear mix of direct subsidies and contracting, more or less depending on the countries and the services. When contracting-out practices are applied, the specific characteristics of social enterprises are very often not taken into account. Contracting-out practices tend to favour large companies (for-profits or traditional workers' co-operatives) that have no links with the territory or the community. These companies sometimes take advantage of the difficulties in writing, enforcing and monitoring contracts in order to cut wages, worsen labour conditions, reduce the quality of the services provided or simply try not to respect some parts of their agreements. As a consequence, social enterprises often have to operate in a precarious environment, relying on short-term contracts and without the possibility of planning their development.

Some rigidities of labour policies have accentuated this barrier for work-integration social enterprises. Examples of these rigidities include the difficulties in transforming subsidies granted to the disabled into employment subsidies for the benefit of social enterprises that employ them; or the difficulties in making employment subsidies, granted to unemployed persons engaged in on-the-job training activities in social enterprises, flexible enough to benefit them until they can find a job in the open labour market.

A third important barrier common to most European countries is the lack or inadequacy of legal forms suitable for social enterprises. Some countries have been adapting, or plan to adapt, the co-operative form, by making it assume the characteristics of the social enterprise, but running the risk of preventing the latter from taking on different legal forms. Other countries have allowed social enterprises to use the association form, but without giving it full entrepreneurial status. Only Belgium has specific legislation (yet to be completed) which allows social enterprises to choose among different company legal forms. The lack of adequate legislation limits the workability and the possibility of reproducing social enterprises. At the same time, a legal framework that does not take into account all the characteristics of these new kinds of enterprises can foster the tendency towards isomorphism. Furthermore, legislative deficiencies hinder their activities as well as the possibility of taking part in tenders, of entering contractual and partnership relations and of developing human and financial resources.

Finally, the development of social enterprises is also hampered by a lack of access to industrial policies,[12] which are intended to promote new enterprises, and to public funding for innovative social services, in the provision of which social enterprises already play a significant part in many countries.

6 Development prospects

By taking all the results of the EMES Network into account, it is possible to conclude that social enterprises can be considered as new organisational forms, diffused to a varying extent, throughout the European Union. Although still in an experimental phase, and far from being a well-established reality, the development of social enterprises constitutes a dynamic and innovative trend in the European economic and social arena. The theoretical contributions and country analyses suggest that social enterprises have the potential to develop further and become an additional force for good in the fight against unemployment and social exclusion and for an increase and differentiation in the supply of social and community care services.

However, present circumstances do not allow us to affirm that this potential will be fully realised. The development and strengthening of social enterprises depend on several conditions. Among them, and of crucial importance, are better awareness and knowledge of their functioning and of their specific role in fighting social exclusion, and better defined links with public social policies. As already mentioned, European social policies are going through a serious transformation, but up to now, the reforms undertaken have not fully appreciated the potential of social enterprises. Only recently, have some aspects of social enterprises been taken into account.

To date, public policies designed to support social enterprises have been based on a minimalist approach, which results in interventions mainly aimed at overcoming specific problems. On the contrary, there is the need for a more general approach, which takes into account the role played by social enterprises, thus paving the way for their more autonomous development. This approach would require implementation of a strategy allowing social enterprises to operate jointly with public institutions and private enterprises, as fully entrepreneurial actors. This means that public policies should change from providing specific and often marginal supports for social enterprises to become more broadly based; moreover, new policies are required.

The first policy that would facilitate the development of social enterprises is their full legal recognition and regulation. Both are important for several reasons: (1) to consolidate the most innovative organisational solutions; (2) to foster the replication process and the spread of social enterprises; (3) to protect consumers' rights; and (4) to avoid isomorphism. The fragility of social enterprises could be reduced through proper governance models that clearly set-out legislation could help to define.

A second important aid to the development of social enterprises would be a shift from today's predominantly fiscal policy, based on tax relief for organisations fulfilling certain organisational requirements (usually the non-profit distribution constraint), to policies seeking to foster the emergence and development of new demand for services (both public and, in the medium term, private). Various means could be used to implement this policy. As regards public demand, financial constraints are presently the main problem. However, it is possible to transform part of the public expenditure from cash benefits into service provision in favour of the same groups of people. The emergence of private paying demand (by individuals and families) for social and community care services, and a change from the present informal provision, would be helped by reducing the costs of services through tax allowances in favour of consumers and through the provision of vouchers covering only part of the costs. The amount of the vouchers could be related to the redistributive component of the services and to the real needs of the beneficiaries.

Another important policy would consist of better defined contracting-out and quasi-market strategies. These could be more effective if they recognised the specificity of social enterprises, and the redistributive component of the services produced. This entails acknowledging that social enterprises are based on a peculiar mix of resources and have a local dimension. Both of these require the preservation of strong trust and community relationships, where they exist, or an effort to create them where they do not. Competition is important to achieve efficiency, but it should be balanced with the need to guarantee the continuity and development of already existing network relations that produce trust and social capital and allow the creation of the mix of human resources that help to maintain flexibility and low production costs. A local dimension could be applied to contracting-out procedures, so as to reduce the extent of competition for social and community care service provision. Specific credits could be granted to social enterprises able to attract donations and volunteers and to involve users in their organisations. These proposed changes to the competition rules are warranted both by market failures in the production of social and community care services, although the demand is fully managed by public authorities, and the capability of social enterprises and third-sector organisations to directly and autonomously contribute to community welfare.

Some specific changes in social policies would be important in assisting the development of work-integration social enterprises. A clear distinction between employment policies for long-term and disadvantaged unemployed, and policies designed to increase the supply of social and community care services, is the first of these changes. Employment subsidies for long-term unemployed could work better if designed to reduce labour costs in order to compensate for lower productivity, irrespective of the goods or services produced. Also some flexibility in the duration of the subsidies, if applied to the more disadvantaged, could help in facilitating more complete integration of these unemployed.

Work-integration social enterprises could make a more significant contribution in favour of the unemployed if there was a sufficient and stable demand for the goods or the services they provide. At least part of this demand could be guaranteed by local authorities, through the so-called 'social clause'.[13] The employment of long-term unemployed by social enterprises could be stimulated also through specific contractual agreements. Criticism of the possibility of restricting participation in some public tenders to work-integration social enterprises (social clause), since this would reduce competition or generate unfair competition, is not relevant. The share of demand reserved for work-integration social enterprises tends to be a small part of public demand, and is mostly in activities that are of little interest to traditional enterprises. At the same time, contractual agreements are not sufficiently developed to avoid opportunistic behaviour on the part of for-profit enterprises.[14] Indeed, these may formally abide by the social clause but they can also discharge disadvantaged workers after winning the bid.

Finally, the development of social enterprises could be helped by a set of supply-side policies with the aim of: reinforcing their entrepreneurial behaviour; enhancing the managerial skills of their personnel; favouring the creation of second/third level organisations and increasing their natural propensity to spin off and create new and autonomous organisations. Support for start-ups should take the form of financing the development of new social enterprises (according to models that have been already successfully tested as for-profits) aimed at integrating private and community resources.

In the future, the development of a large sector of social, personal, cultural, environmental and community care services will depend less than in the past on public expenditure and more on the interaction between private demand and supply. Nevertheless, for most of the activities included in the social and community care sector, transactions cannot be based only on market rules. The creation of quasi-markets, where implemented, has often caused a decline in the quality of the services without a significant reduction of public expenditure. The other way to enhance the development of the sector is through the strengthening of new organisations, which are able to combine private action with production of collective goods and to mix the productive with the redistributive function. Therefore, European economies need new organisational forms, similar to those that compose the third sector, but more entrepreneurial. Social enterprises are an example of these forms. The research summarised in this book demonstrates that they can exist and develop. Whether they will be able to develop further depends to a large extent on the decisions of European governments which may choose to rely more or less exclusively on quasi-market policy or decide to combine the latter with a strategy to foster the expansion of new forms of organisation.[15] This book shows that the latter orientation is possible, and is probably more promising.

Notes

1 During this research the term 'social enterprise' was used also by other groups. See OECD (1999).
2 For a wider presentation and a theoretical analysis of the work-integration initiatives, see Defourny, Favreau and Laville (1998).
3 This point has been already stressed at the end of the introduction to this volume (see Figure 1).
4 There are also attempts to provide other forms of social enterprises such as joint-stock companies with several constraints (in profit distribution, in the rules of management, etc.).The most prominent are the law on the 'company with a social purpose' in Belgium and the draft under discussion in Italy on 'social enterprises'. However, to date the result of these attempts is unclear.
5 This seems to be the case of some social services, like home-care services in the UK. See Young (1999).
6 This is the case in countries with a limited public provision of social services like Italy where several services (day centres for handicapped or teenagers, services for drug addict rehabilitation, etc.) were initially created by social enterprises without structural public supports. Only after several years did national and local authorities

decide to fully support the financing of these services and of the organisations providing them.

7 The few comparative studies on employment relations in social service provision (for Italy see Borzaga (2000); for the United Kingdom see the national chapter – Chapter 15 – in this book) indicate that social enterprises tend to pay wages lower than public service providers and higher than for-profit enterprises.

8 As demonstrated in several documents of the European Commission. See, among them, European Commission (1998).

9 A specific category of start-up costs faced by organisations willing to provide new social services are the entrepreneurial costs (Hansmann 1996), i.e. the costs related to assembling sufficient volume of demand to sustain a stable and efficient production. By involving users or their representatives, in many cases, social enterprises can evaluate the potential demand at low costs.

10 This specific advantage can be misused and can create perverse effects on the wage level of the employees. However, when correctly used, it represents an important advantage.

11 As suggested by the explanation of the non-profit organisations as 'problem non solvers' (Seibel 1990).

12 Since in many countries social enterprises are not regarded as enterprises in every respect, they cannot benefit from the subsidies granted to all other enterprises.

13 The social clause is a specific contractual requirement by which local authorities request enterprises participating in bidding to employ a percentage of disadvantaged workers.

14 Social enterprises are often regarded as less costly contractors for government. As Steinberg states: 'non-profit organisations deserve some preference in bidding because they provide benefits to the government (reduced opportunistic behaviour and reduced transaction costs of negotiating, monitoring and enforcing a contract) that cannot be enforceably written into a contract with for-profits' (Steinberg 1997:176).

15 For an analysis of this pluralistic context see OECD (1996).

Bibliography

BORZAGA, C. (ed.) (2000) *Capitale umano e qualità del lavoro nei servizi sociali. Un'analisi comparata tra modelli di gestione*, Fondazione Italiana per il Volontariato, Roma.

DEFOURNY, J., FAVREAU, L. and LAVILLE, J.-L. (eds) (1998) *Insertion et nouvelle économie sociale. Un bilan international*, Desclée de Brouwer, Paris.

European Commission (1998) *Employment Performance in the Member States*, Employment Rates Report 1998, Office for Official Publications of the European Communities, Luxembourg.

HANSMANN, H.B. (1996) *The Ownership of Enterprise*, The Belknap Press of Harvard University Press, Cambridge, MA.

OECD (1999) *Social Enterprises*, OECD, Paris.

—— (1996) *Reconciling Economy and Society: Toward a Plural Economy*, OECD, Paris.

SEIBEL, W. (1990) 'Organizational Behavior and Organizational Function: Toward a Micro-Macro Theory of the Third Sector', in ANHEIER, H.K. and SEIBEL, W. (eds) *The Third Sector: Comparative Studies of Nonprofit Organizations*, de Gruyter, Berlin, 107–21.

STEINBERG, R. (1997) 'Competition in Contracted Markets', in PERRI, 6 and KENDALL, J. (eds) *The Contract Culture in Public Services*, Ashgate, London, 161–80.

YOUNG, R. (1999) 'Prospecting for New Jobs to Combat Social Exclusion: the Example of Home-Care Services', *European Urban and Regional Studies*, 6, 2: 99–113.

Index

Aarhus 74–5, 77, 78–9
Abrahamsson, B. 221
ABS (employment creation and structural development associations) 126–7
Act of 1991 (Italy) 170–1, 172
action and pilot programmes 70–1
active labour-market policy 163, 239–41
Activity Pool 72, 73
Adept Press 256
additional work 245
advocacy 281
Agency for the Development of Proximity Services (ADSP) 105, 109
agricultural co-operatives: Greece 141–2, 142–5 *passim*; UK 253
agriculture 183
agritourism co-operatives 138, 141, 142–5 *passim*
Aktion 8,000 31–2, 36
Alchian, A. 276
Alexander, J. 343
Alix, N. 100
Allison, M. 338
allocation of control rights 285–7
allowance for childcare at home 110, 112
Als, G. 185
AMS (Austrian Employment Service) 39–40, 42
Andersson, C. 84
Anheier, H.K. 47, 298
area-based partnership companies 157, 158
Area Development Management (ADM) 156, 157, 158
ARGE Nichtseßhaftenhilfe 35
Arrow, K.J. 276
Asociación AMICA 207
Asociación Atzegui – Grupo Gureak 207

Asociación Española de Recuperadores de la Economía Social y Solidaria (AERESS) 207
assigned work income 245–7
Association Act (*Vereinsgesetz*) 36
Association of Collectives of Children and Parents (ACEP) 106
Association of Collectives of Children, Parents and Professionals (ACEPP) 105, 107, 111–12
Association of Non-Residential Folk High Schools in Denmark 76–7
associations 5, 356–7; Belgium 47, 55–8; France 100, 104, 110, 113; Greece 138; intermediate 110; mandatory 110, 113; Spain 208; Sweden 222–4
associations for employment creation 126–7
'Atlas of Local Initiatives' 242
Austria 19, 31–46; childcare 37–44; day-mothers and children's groups 41–3; definition of social enterprises 36–7; key challenges 44; personal and proximity services 36; self-governed local employment initiatives 32–3; sheltered workshops 35; social-economic projects 33–5; social inclusion and support to employment 35–6; welfare mix in childcare 38–41
autonomy 17

Bäck, H. 221, 223
Badelt, C. 11, 31
Bager, T. 68
BAN 35
Barber, B. 301
BBB Schilderswijk 244, 245
BBBs (BuurtBeheer Bedrijven) see neighbourhood development schemes
Belgium 14, 47–64, 365; associations 47,